# Introducing
# human
# resource
# management
• • • • • • • • • • • • • • • •

# Longman modular texts in business and economics
•••••••••••••••••

*Series Editors*
Geoff Black and Stuart Wall

# Introducing
# human
# resource
# management
·····················

*Margaret Foot*
*Caroline Hook*

LONGMAN

**Addison Wesley Longman Limited,**
Edinburgh Gate,
Harlow, Essex CM20 2JE, England
*and Associated Companies throughout the world*

*Visit Addison Wesley Longman on the world wide web at:*
*http://www.awl-he.com*

First edition published 1996
Reprinted 1997
This second edition published 1999

ISBN 0 582 36892 8

**British Library Cataloguing-in-Publication Data**
A catalogue record for this book is available from the British Library

**Library of Congress Cataloging-in-Publication Data**
Foot, Margaret, 1946–
 Introducing human resource management / Margaret Foot, Caroline
Hook. – 2nd edn.
  p.  cm. – (Longman modular texts in business and economics)
  Includes bibliographical references and index.
  ISBN 0–582–36892–8 (pbk.)
  1. Personnel management. 2. Employee rights. I. Hook, Caroline,
1949–  . II. Title. III. Series.
HF5549.F5875 1999
 658.3–dc21
                                                                98–47542
                                                                    CIP

Set by 30 Stone Serif 9/12 pt
Printed in Malaysia, PP

# Contents

# Quick guide to employment legislation and related documents

# Preface

We have written this book primarily as an introductory text for students of human resource management as a subject option forming part of a modular degree course or a Higher National Diploma in Business Studies. It will also prove very useful to students who are studying for the Institute of Personnel and Development's professional course, especially for the Core Personnel and Development Module. The content represents an introduction to the basic functions of human resource management and examines the following processes:

- ➤ acquiring employees
- ➤ establishing good relationships with them
- ➤ training and developing them
- ➤ retaining them.

We also consider how to deal with situations if problems develop in the employer–employee relationship.

The book is divided into 16 chapters with the intention of providing a topic each week for a modular course, although if your tutor wishes to involve you in more skills-development work or to go into these areas in more detail, the subject matter in the chapters may be spread over two semesters. Each chapter starts with a list of objectives. These are important as they are things that you should know or be able to do by the time you have finished the chapter. When you have finished the chapter, look back at the objectives and ensure that you have achieved them.

We intend that you should become involved actively in your own learning as you progress through the book, and to this end, as well as the list of learning objectives, there are activities for you to undertake, and opportunities to pause and think about issues raised in each chapter. We recommend that you have a paper and pen beside you as you read the book, so that you can complete the activities. This is important, so resist any temptation to skip them.

Discussion about specific points raised in the activities is often an integral part of the text. There are questions at the end of each chapter so that you can check your own understanding of the chapter and go back, if necessary, to points that you may not be clear about. There are also review questions and activities or sometimes longer questions designed to help you examine key learning points in more depth. Your tutor should have a further set of activities and case studies to help with the main learning points in each chapter.

The activities and case studies in this text are based on real-life situations, but none of the people or organisations named in them actually exists. Details have been drawn together from a number of events to create totally fictional, although realistic, situations. Real organisations are, however, mentioned in the text, particularly where they serve as examples of good practice.

# CHAPTER 1

# Introducing human resource management

## Objectives:

*By the end of this chapter you will be able to:*

➤ define what is meant by the terms 'personnel management' and 'human resource management'
➤ outline the historical development of human resource management
➤ describe the roles of human resource specialists
➤ distinguish between the roles of line managers and human resource managers
➤ outline the range of activities with which practitioners of human resource management are likely to be involved
➤ describe how to market the HRM function.

This book is designed as an introductory text for students studying human resource management (HRM). As stated in the preface we intend that you should become actively involved in your own learning as you progress through the book. Even though you are just beginning this subject, you may already have ideas about some of the topics that you are about to study, and you may even have a general idea of the role and functions of the human resource management or personnel department in an organisation. Your ideas may not all be right, but after all that is why you are studying the subject. Many students talk of studying personnel management because they would 'like to work with people', and they seem to think of personnel/human resource management as a cosy job which involves being nice to people at all times. We shall show in this book that the job is much more complex than first impressions would lead one to believe. Let us start with an exercise to help you focus on your ideas of human resource management. You can compare your answers with the answer that we give at the end of the chapter.

ACTIVITY **1.1**

What do you think are the main areas in which a personnel/human resource manager is likely to be involved? Make a list of these areas. For each of the areas on the list, indicate the type of involvement of the human resource manager and whether other managers are also likely to have a role in handling this activity (use Table 1.1). We have completed the first row of Table 1.1 to start you off.

Our suggestions for this Activity are given at the end of the chapter in Table 1.2.

*table 1.1*
**Main activities of human resource/ personnel specialists: Activity 1.1**

| Main areas of activity of human resource/ personnel specialists | Type of involvement of the human resource/personnel specialist | Type of involvement of line manager |
|---|---|---|
| Recruitment and selection | Design of policies and procedure for fair recruitment and selection in order to contribute to the fulfilment of the organisation's corporate strategy. Carry out interviews or monitor and give advice on interview technique or on terms and conditions of employment. | Carry out interviews |
| Training and development | | |

## The main activities of personnel/human resource management
....................................................................................

The ones that we would list are as follows:

- ➤ recruitment and selection
- ➤ training and development
- ➤ human resource planning
- ➤ provision of contracts
- ➤ provision of fair treatment
- ➤ provision of equal opportunities
- ➤ assessing performance of employees
- ➤ employee counselling
- ➤ employee welfare
- ➤ payment and reward of employees
- ➤ health and safety
- ➤ disciplining individuals
- ➤ dealing with grievances
- ➤ dismissal
- ➤ redundancy
- ➤ negotiation
- ➤ encouraging involvement.

You may have included some slightly different activities as human resource/personnel managers become involved in a wide range of issues and it is difficult to predict the exact nature of the job in any particular enterprise. We have selected the main topics with which we feel most human resource/personnel managers are likely to be involved.

As you can see, for each function we have chosen it is likely that other managers will also be involved to some extent in that function. The fact that aspects of managing the human resource are an element of every manager's or supervisor's job is an important point for you to keep in mind. Some of you may be hoping to pursue a career as personnel specialists, while others may intend to obtain other posts in management and are aware that knowing how to deal with people is important to any manager's career. Many of you will find that your career may take you from line management to personnel/human resource management and then back to line management, or vice versa. The Institute of Personnel and Development defines personnel management both as being a function pursued by personnel/human resource managers and also as a part of every manager's job.

**PAUSE FOR THOUGHT 1.1** *A line manager is a person who has direct responsibility for employees and their work. Since line managers seem to have such a large part to play in human resource/personnel management, to what extent do you think they need personnel or human resource managers at all?*

Obviously, we consider that line managers do need to call on the services and expertise of personnel/human resource managers. If you look at our discussion of Activity 1.1 at the end of this chapter (Table 1.2), you will see that although a great deal of work can be devolved to line managers, there is also a role for a person skilled in human resource management to establish policies, standards and procedures, to integrate these with the organisation's objectives, to provide advice and consistency, and to coordinate and provide training and development. Human resource/personnel practitioners will also often be involved in initiating company-wide programmes such as involvement, communication and consultation. The exact nature of their involvement will vary from one organisation to another, as will the range of activities covered by the human resource/personnel function. The personnel/human resource department may maintain central records on people and may provide advice and expertise for other managers to draw on. In some organisations the human resource/personnel management department may carry out all the activities listed above, while in others many or most of these functions may be devolved to other managers. Increasingly more and more aspects of the personnel function are being devolved to line managers and you will find as you worked through the book that we emphasise the roles of line managers in personnel activities.

### Specialist or generalist?

Even among human resource/personnel managers there will be differences in the scope of their job, with some human resource managers acting as generalists who are involved in most of these activities while others specialise, for example in training and development, reward, resourcing or employee relations. Some specialists work as consultants and are contracted to work for several organisations as and when their services are needed.

## The historical background to human resource management

It may help you to understand the broadness of the roles assumed by personnel and human resource managers if we look briefly at the development of the profession. A variety of names have been used to describe this area of work. It has changed in response to the social and economic conditions of the time and it is still developing dynamically. The relative importance of many of the activities has changed as circumstances have affected the needs of organisations.

### Industrial welfare

The earliest activity with which the HRM/personnel practitioner was involved was welfare work. During the nineteenth century conditions of work for men, women and children in the factories were generally appalling compared to even the worst of today's standards. In 1833 the Factories Act appointed the first (male) factory inspectors, and in 1878 legislation was passed to try to regulate hours of work and conditions at least for women and children, reducing their hours of work to 60 hours per week! The trade union movement was also developing during this period, as individuals realised the strength they could gain by joining together to negotiate with employers. Collective bargaining was developing and in 1868 the first Trades Union Conference was held. In 1885 eleven trade unionists were elected to the House of Commons and demanded improvements in wages and conditions of employment.

**DID YOU KNOW?**

*Mary Wood's first day at work at Rowntree's was rather different from the type of activity you would associate with human resource managers today.*

*Her first morning was spent placing flowers in work-rooms – perhaps not so ineffectual a beginning as might be thought when the drabness of factories and homes at the time was remembered – and in the afternoon she went to visit girls who were sick, ordering groceries for the most necessitous cases and seeing such slums that she had never dreamt existed. Her first opportunity for making headway came during the dinner hours, when the fact that there was no supervision meant that pandemonium broke out. By degrees she brought order and discipline and before long was arranging an occasional concert or talk during the last half hour of the break. She then turned to organising games as an outlet for the high spirits of the younger girls and as a means of strengthening their physique. (Niven 1978, p.22.)*

There were, however, some enlightened employers, who wanted to try to improve working conditions for their employees and adopted schemes to improve the lot of their workforce as part of their company policy. Among these were several Quaker organisations, and it is generally held that the first personnel officer, referred to at that time as an industrial welfare officer, was Miss Mary Wood who was appointed by Rowntree's in York in 1896. She was appointed to be a type of social worker for the factory, with responsibility for ensuring the well-being of women and children in the workforce and to watch over their health and behaviour.

Although the first day at work 100 years ago seems very different from the type of work that we associate with human resource managers of today, welfare and the well-being of the workforce is still an area in which some personnel practitioners will be involved. Many involved in human resource management have sought to distance the profession from its early welfare image, as they feel it is no longer applicable to the modern needs of the business, that it does not portray the right image for the profession and secure for it power and influence. However, we have included sections on welfare as the reality is that it is still of importance in many organisations today, and some organisations employ specialist counsellors or welfare officers to deal with these issues. Health, safety and welfare are also issues affected by legislation that must be complied with, and in many organisations the human resource manager will have a role here.

Rowntree's, as we have seen, approached the issue of welfare by employing a specialist to deal with it. Cadbury's was another pioneering company at this time which developed a totally different approach, believing that the well-being of the workforce was the responsibility of each member of staff. Edward Cadbury spoke in 1900 of the need to 'develop the social and moral character of each worker', stating that 'the supreme principle has been that business efficiency and the welfare of employees are but different sides of the same problem' (Niven, 1978, p. 23).

Although such a paternalistic approach is unlikely to be acceptable today, even in these early approaches you can see the start of the development of involvement in welfare activities for both the early personnel managers and other managers, just as in the Activity that you did earlier there was a role in most activities you listed for both personnel/human resource managers and other managers.

By 1913 the number of industrial welfare workers had grown sufficiently for a conference to be called in York by Seebohm Rowntree, with 60 people attending. At this conference the Welfare Workers Association was formed, which later, after many changes, developed into today's Institute of Personnel and Development, the professional body for those who are active in this area of work.

### Recruitment and selection

The early industrial welfare workers met with great success, and Mary Wood and others were soon asked to start engaging girls, which was the beginning of the development of the role of recruitment and selection. During the First World War there was rapid development in many fields of personnel management, largely as a result of government initiatives to encourage the best possible use of people, and also because of legislation. In 1916 the Ministry of Munitions set up its own Industrial Welfare Department with Seebohm Rowntree in charge, with responsibility for introducing new welfare and personnel policies by persuasion into the factories. It became compulsory to have a welfare worker in all explosives factories, and it was strongly encouraged in munitions factories. There was also a great deal of work done, mainly by the armed forces, during this period on how to test abilities and IQ, and research was undertaken into the human factors at work.

During the inter-war years there was a pool of unemployed labour, and much that had been learnt about the need for efficient selection methods was forgotten, although a few progressive employers maintained their interest in personnel management. In 1921 the National Institute of Industrial Psychologists was established, and its members published results of studies on selection tests, interviewing techniques and training methods.

### Acquisition of other personnel activities

During the Second World War the work spread from welfare to recruitment and selection and then to training; improving morale and motivation; discipline; health and safety; joint consultation and often wages policies. This expansion of duties required the establishment of an adequate personnel department with trained staff.

### Industrial relations

Joint consultation between management and workforce spread during the war, and personnel departments became responsible for its organisation and administration. There was an increased emphasis on health and safety and a need for specialists to deal with industrial relations, so that gradually the personnel manager became the usual spokesman for the organisation in discussion with trade unions and shop stewards.

The institute that represented early personnel officers had changed its name several times since its formation in 1913, to reflect the changed emphasis of the work, and in 1946 it changed its name yet again, this time to the Institute of Personnel Management. It retained this name until the beginning of 1995, when it merged with the Institute of Training and Development and became the Institute of Personnel and Development.

**DID YOU KNOW?**

*The Institute of Personnel and Development is the professional body for all those concerned with people management and development. It has over 85,000 members in the UK and Ireland. (IPD Mission Statement, 1997.)*

Industrial relations was also of great importance in the late 1970s, and the heated climate during that period re-inforced the importance of this aspect of personnel management and saw the development of a specialist role in industrial relations negotiation. In many organisations the personnel manager had executive authority to negotiate deals about pay or other collective issues.

### Legislation

During the 1970s there was a growth in the amount of employment legislation and the personnel function often took on the role of specialist adviser, ensuring that managers did not fall foul of the law and that cases did not end up at industrial tribunals. This can still be an important role for personnel managers, and we have included some chapters in which we discuss their role in relation to particular aspects of law such as contracts, dismissal, and health and safety.

### Flexibility and diversity

In the 1990s the trend has been for employers to seek increasingly flexible arrangements in the hours worked by employees, with a growth in the number of employees who work part-time or on temporary contracts, and an increase in distance working and working from home. The workforce and patterns of work are becoming increasingly diverse: this will provide challenges to employers who cannot rely on their traditional recruitment practices and who will also need to develop policies in relation to managing diversity and the equal opportunities issues that managing an increasingly diverse work force raises. Between 1994 and 2001 male employment is likely to see only a 3% increase while female employment is likely to rise by 11%, so that by 2001 women are expected to make up 45% of the labour force compared to 41% in 1985 (Skills and Enterprise Network, 1996). Although there was falling unemployment during 1996, long-term unemployment was still high in the 1990s among those under 26 and those over 50. If true increased flexibility is to be achieved, employers will also have to address issues related to non-legislated unfair discrimination such as age discrimination. This is discussed more fully in Chapter 3. The Advisory Conciliation and Arbitration Service has also identified a trend towards increasing levels of flexibility, because many jobs are only offered on a part-time basis, resulting in nearly 5% of the workforce holding more than one job (ACAS, 1997). This could have implications for employee loyalty towards their employ-

**DID YOU KNOW?**

*Between 1994 and 2001 part-time employment was projected to increase by 22% at the same time as full-time employment was supposed to decrease by 1%. Among employers who had already adopted flexible work practices by 1995, 25% of employers said that this was in response to employee demands. (Skills and Enterprise Network, 1996.)*

ers; for instance increasing their willingness to leave their employment. Employers, therefore, need to ensure that they provide rewarding and satisfying jobs, and show by the policies and procedures they adopt and the way in which they treat people, that they value them. Organisations need to think strategically about the issues raised, and both personnel/HRM practitioners and line managers alike will have important roles to play if business opportunities are not to be wasted.

## Human resource management
..........................................

The concept of human resource management first appeared in the 80s and the use of the term grew in the 1990s. Its meaning and the range of activities it encompasses have been examined and described by a large number of business writers and researchers (Legge, 1995, summarises much of the debate). The concept has proven to be somewhat elusive, and it is not possible to find a definitive description of HRM in the literature about it. On the contrary the achievement of a definition seems to be problematic. One approach has been to try to contrast HRM with traditional personnel management, a number of researchers providing descriptions of the differences in tabular form, but the boundaries between the two prove to be fluid for a number of reasons (see Storey's much cited table in Storey and Sisson, 1993; Guest, 1987). Rather than embarking on a complex, academic, albeit fascinating, exercise of this nature, we have culled from the literature what are presented as the key characteristics of HRM. We present them here for you, followed by a brief exposition of the major difficulties that have been encountered in trying to encapsulate the essence of HRM. Our references to a number of the recognised experts in the field should provide you with a good foundation to develop a more detailed academic study of the topic should you wish to do so.

### Major characteristics of HRM

The major characteristics of human resource management have been identified as follows.

➤ The importance of adopting a strategic approach is emphasised.
➤ Line managers play a predominant role.
➤ Organisational policies must be integrated and cohesive in order to better project and support the central organisational values and objectives. Along with this, communication plays a vital role.
➤ An underlying philosophy is adopted that emphasises the achievement of competitive advantage through the efforts of people. This can variously be interpreted into actions that are known as hard HRM or those that are known as soft HRM.
➤ A unitarist rather than a pluralist approach prevails in the relationship between managers and employees.

#### Focus on strategy
Throughout the 1980s and 1990s business leaders have come to accept more and more that competitive advantage can be achieved only through the efforts and creativity of the people employed by them. In companies that follow

through with the logical conclusions to this statement, rather than simply paying lip service to the rhetoric, developing strategies for the human resource will inevitably play a prominent role when they are formulating the corporate strategy, and senior managers will want to call on the expertise of a specialist to get the best input possible. Thus strategic activity becomes a major focus for specialists in HRM, but probably only those acting at the higher levels will be involved in board level meetings where strategic alternatives are discussed. It should also be noted that in order to have effective input into the corporate strategy, the HRM specialist will require a high level of business acumen in addition to knowledge of personnel strategies and programmes. It is this recognition that people are a resource to be managed as efficiently and effectively as any other resource that has led to the term human resource management.

### Role of the line manager

We have defined strategic involvement as being a key characteristic of HRM and noted that this means a focus on strategic activity for high-level HRM practitioners. However, the HRM approach recognises the centrality of the human resource for all business activities, and therefore consideration of the people management aspects would be expected in the strategic planning input from managers in all business functions (e.g. production, marketing, etc). Likewise, the importance of active management of people matters becomes more clearly an integral part of every line manager's job. Line managers must combine their commitment to the technical aspects of task completion with attention to people aspects and recognise the symbiotic nature of these two elements of the managerial role.

This means that some activities that might traditionally have been undertaken by specialist personnel management staff have now been devolved to line managers. Increased line involvement in training and recruitment could be cited as areas where this has occurred. There is still, however, a substantial role for the human resource specialist, as you discovered when you completed Activity 1.1, in disseminating information about evolving people management programmes to line managers, in ensuring some consistency in the treatment of employees company-wide, and in general in being supportive partners to line managers in their efforts to achieve company goals.

The pivotal role of the line manager is one of the most often cited characteristics of human resource management (see Storey's table of the take-up of HRM techniques in Storey and Sisson, 1993).

### Integrated policies and effective communication

Proponents of HRM emphasise that policies across the whole HR spectrum (recruitment, selection, reward, employee relations) must be fully integrated and consistent with the organisation's culture. This is logically consistent with the strategic, forward planning nature of HRM. Effective communications are a pivotal aspect of this as they constitute a means of conveying senior management's values and commitment to their goals (Legge, 1995, p. 75).

### Hard and soft HRM

The basic requirement of HRM to serve the corporate strategy and achieve corporate aims by means of a high performance workforce can be read in two ways:

➤ The primacy of business needs means that human resources will be acquired, deployed and dispensed with as corporate plans demand. Little regard is paid to the needs of those human resources and the emphasis is on quantitative aspects. This is known as hard HRM.

➤ In order to gain a competitive advantage through the workforce, regardless of whether they are full- or part-time, temporary or contract staff, all potential must be nurtured and developed, and programmes which pay due notice to knowledge about the behavioural aspects of people at work are developed. This is characterised as soft HRM.

The emphasis in our text lies mainly with soft HRM, but as Legge (1995, pp. 66–67) argues, the two are not mutually exclusive, and you will detect elements of hard HRM in the discussion of human resource planning.

### Management–employee relations

Human resource management is identified as being a unitarist rather than a pluralist approach (Legge, 1995, pp. 72–73). Briefly, the unitarist stance is characterised as a senior management assumption that all members of the organisation are dedicated to the achievement of a common goal with no conflict from personal interests. Pluralism, on the other hand, recognises that within a large group of people there are inevitably a variety of interests and that these have to be managed. The adoption of one or other of these two philosophies obviously has a major impact on the way that managers treat the workforce.

We explore the concepts of unitarism and pluralism in greater depth in Chapter 11 where we come to the conclusion from observing current rhetoric that we may now be witnessing a merging of the two stances in the development of the partnership theme. This promotes the idea that managers and employees can pursue common goals while still recognising that diverging interests exist. The common purpose of the unitarists is pursued in a pluralist framework.

We refer throughout the text to the key characteristics described here and their links with specific activities. In particular, we emphasise the role of the line manager in all of the activities we discuss, but in addition we focus on the theme of strategy in Chapter 2 where we examine the human resource planning activity and the topics of unitarism, employee commitment and communication in Chapter 11.

### *Problems with the concept of HRM*

We do not wish to confuse the issue, having presented the key characteristics of HRM, but the debate about HRM is characterised to such an extent by conflicting statements and pieces of evidence, that it seems appropriate to mention some of them briefly.

➤ There is no definitive agreement among researchers about what the concept includes, and at least one recent publication suggests that we now need to move beyond HRM as a concept to seek a new definition of the role of practitioners in this field (Sparrow and Marchington, 1998).

➤ Some researchers attempt to categorise activities as 'hard' HRM or 'soft' HRM, but there is also some debate about whether the two are necessarily mutually exclusive.

➤ Even the specific concepts identified as characteristics of HRM can also be defined with different meanings, e.g. strategy is variously seen as a planned approach or something which evolves.

➤ Academics try to define and build models of HRM, but research on actual practice shows a multiplicity of combinations of techniques being used in some companies at one and the same time, i.e. some techniques that would be seen as part of the new HRM approach, and some that would be seen as traditional personnel management run simultaneously. Hall and Torrington (1998, pp.108ff) comment on an integrated approach to human resource strategy as being an ideal, but sparsely represented in reality.

➤ A contingency approach to management would suggest that different circumstances call for different actions, so a rigid, prescriptive definition of HRM would in fact be counter-productive. Shaun Tyson (1995) comments on the futility of trying to pin down a definition of HRM practices when HRM is required to adapt rapidly to rapidly changing circumstances.

➤ Practitioners and researchers alike often use the terms personnel management and HRM interchangeably (Hall and Torrington, 1998).

### The HRM debate: a concluding statement

Karen Legge (1995) reviews the literature that has attempted to differentiate between HRM and personnel management, and highlights the problematic nature of these attempts. Because our text is an introduction to the practical work involved in HRM/personnel management, we shall not pursue this academic debate any further. What we consider to be important is not managers' titles, but what managers actually do and how they do it.

We focus mainly on applied aspects of HR practices in the workplace, and we have chosen to focus on those elements identified as soft HRM since these represent recognised good practice in employee relations today. It is, however, important to bear in mind that it is difficult, if not impossible, to designate a definitive set of best practices because the 'right' action will always depend on the contingent circumstances in which any organisation is operating.

### Marketing the human resource management function

We wish to devote a final word to the marketing of the human resource management function, as this may have a great impact on the effectiveness of the function although it has only recently attracted attention and probably did not figure in your list of the activities that HRM practitioners should engage in.

Although we have discussed the fact that some personnel management functions may be devolved to line managers, and that this is in fact a growing trend, this section addresses the specialist HRM department and the need for HRM practitioners to advertise their services in order to maximise their contribution to corporate objectives. We have described human resource management as consisting of a complex range of functions, calling on a wide variety of knowledge and expertise. We have also explained that HRM practitioners sometimes adopt a service role in designing new initiatives, and sometimes act as an authority in enforcing obedience to the law. In the service role in particular, there is little point in the knowledge and expertise being resident (and paid for) in an organisation if the clients are unaware of it and do not know it is there to be called on. It is very difficult in highly structured organisations for staff in one area to know, beyond a vague understanding, what staff in another area do. If HRM practitioners feel they have a valuable contribution to make to their organisations, it is incumbent on them to make sure that everyone knows what they can offer.

ACTIVITY **1.2**

Imagine that you have joined the Human Resource Management department in a large company. How would you market the HRM function? List the activities you would undertake.

### *Discussion of Activity 1.2*

Check your list of activities against the following:

➤ Conduct a customer survey. Companies that know what their customers require and respond to their wishes have a competitive edge. The same can be true of a functional department offering a service within a company. A survey can ascertain several things: what you do well, what you could do better, things you are not doing that your clients would like you to do.

➤ Expand your knowledge of the business. HRM is an integral part of the business, not a separate undertaking. The more you know about how your organisation works, the more responsive you can be in supporting it with HRM initiatives.

➤ Be proactive and innovative in developing initiatives that will contribute to the company's success. Don't wait for problems to arise.

➤ Take your service to your market rather than waiting for clients to approach you:
  – design leaflets, booklets, posters that advertise the service you offer
  – emphasise the benefits your clients will gain from using your services
  – be visible and approachable – have an open-door policy; visit line managers and other employees at their work stations; don't sit in your office all day
  – obtain an HRM slot in briefing sessions, the company newsletter and any other information vehicles.

You will note in these suggestions that the terminology used is very much that of a business selling its products. Parts of the personnel management functions in local authorities are in fact now subject to compulsory competitive tendering, which means that outside agencies as well as in-house teams of practitioners can bid for the personnel work at local councils. This development has focused the attention of the staff concerned on the need to market their services, but the HRM function in any company could benefit from taking this approach, both in terms of sharpening their own definition of what they do and in ensuring that everyone in the company is able to gain the maximum benefit from what HRM can offer.

**REVIEW QUESTIONS**

1   We include here a pictorial representation of this chapter in the form of a mind map (Figure 1.1). Use the key words we have included to refresh your memory of what we have covered in this chapter. Add your own key words or drawings to this mind map to reinforce your learning.

2   Go back to the objectives that we listed at the beginning of this chapter and check that you know, or can do, everything stated in the objectives.

3   Examine three advertisements for jobs in personnel management/human resource management. Make a list of the range of activities described in these job advertisements. Compare your list with the lists we have given for Activity 1.1.

Are there any differences in approach and duties shown by those advertising for human resource managers and those advertising for personnel managers? How does this relate to what we said about these job titles in Chapter 1?

4   Interview a personnel manager or human resource manager about his or her job and main duties. How do your findings compare with what we said in this chapter?

5   Interview a manager about his or her job and try to establish the extent to which it also entails personnel activities. How do your findings compare with what we said in this chapter?

6   The chapters of this book will introduce you to aspects of good practice for the various activities involved in HRM. When you have studied each chapter, imagine that you are an HRM practitioner and you wish to market the function to line managers. Draft the contents of a brochure for each activity. You will need to describe the service that you are offering and state how line managers would benefit from using that service.

7   If you have access to the Internet, use the World Wide Web URLs given on pages 21 and 22 to find out more about issues of concern to those involved in human resource management worldwide. Compare the sites listed in Britain, America and Australia. What are the main topics of concern at the moment? Are there any differences in approach shown by the professional bodies in these countries?

*figure 1.1*
**Mind map of**
**Chapter 1**

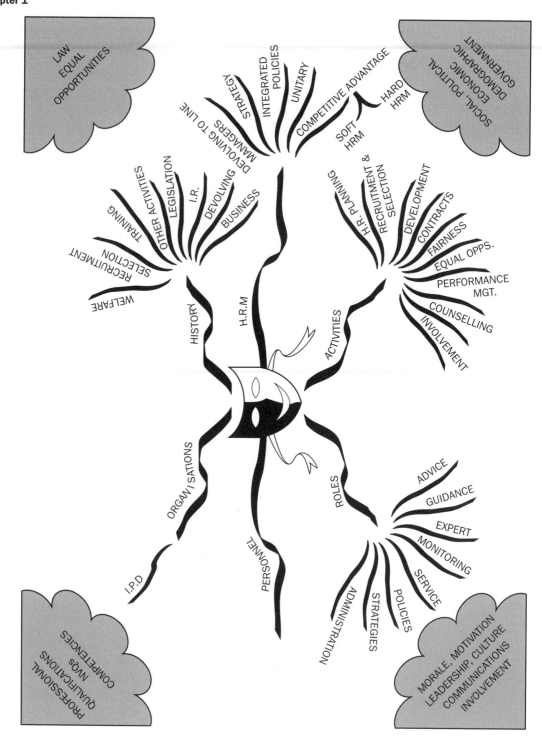

Answer the following multiple choice questions. The correct responses are given on page 420 for you to check your understanding of this chapter.

1   To which of the following do the letters IPD refer?
    (*a*)  The Institute of Professional Development
    (*b*)  The Institution for the Progress of Devolvement.
    (*c*)  The Institute of Personnel and Development.
    (*d*)  The Institute of Personal Development.

2   Which of the following activities are you NOT likely to undertake as part of the process of marketing the human resource management department?
    (*a*)  Conduct a customer survey.
    (*b*)  Be proactive and innovative in developing initiatives that contribute to the organisation's success.
    (*c*)  Be reactive and wait to be approached when problems arise.
    (*d*)  Obtain an HRM slot in briefing sessions.

3   Which of the following statements best sums up the role of the human resource manager in personnel activities?
    (*a*)  The human resource manager is the sole person who should be involved in all personnel activities.
    (*b*)  Both the human resource manager and line manager are likely to be involved in differing ways in a range of personnel activities.
    (*c*)  The line manager always acts alone in all organisations in dealing with human resource management activities.
    (*d*)  The human resource manager is only concerned with personnel activities at the tactical level.

4   Which of the following statements would be true of the human resource management approach to managing people at work?
    (*a*)  It tackles issues in a piecemeal way.
    (*b*)  It relies on traditional forms of communication.
    (*c*)  There is not much involvement of the workforce in decision making.
    (*d*)  It is strategic.

5   Which of the following sums up an underlying theme in the philosophy of HRM?
    (*a*)  People are important whether they are full-time or part-time employees, permanent or temporary, or contract workers who are actually employed by another company.
    (*b*)  People are important only if they are full-time, permanent employees.
    (*c*)  People are important whether they are full-time or part-time employees so long as they are permanent and are employed by your company.
    (*d*)  People are important whether they are full-time or part-time, permanent or temporary so long as they are employed by your company.

*table 1.2*

**Main activities of human resource/ personnel specialists: discussion of Activity 1.1**

| Main areas of activity of human resource/personnel specialists | Type of involvement of the human resource/personnel specialist | Type of involvement of line manager |
|---|---|---|
| Recruitment and selection | Design of policies and procedure for fair recruitment and selection in order to contribute to the fulfilment of the organisation's corporate strategy. Carry out interviews or monitor and give advice on interview technique or on terms and conditions of employment. | Carry out interviews. |
| Training and development | Involved in planning training and development opportunities for the whole organisation, to meet the needs of the organisation as expressed in its strategic plan and to meet the needs of individuals. May design and organise training courses for groups and sometimes run them. May keep training records centrally and request information from line managers as part of planning exercise or to monitor success of training and development. | May also be involved in planning and provision of training and development opportunities to meet the needs of individuals and the needs of the organisation as expressed in its strategic plan, primarily for employees in his or her own department. May provide training and may also keep records of training and provide information to central personnel/HRM department. |
| Human resource planning | Depending on the level of appointment is likely to be involved to various degrees in contributing to the strategic plan. Collection and analysis of data, monitoring targets for the whole organisation. Providing information to managers. Conducting exit interviews and analysing reasons for leaving. | Collect information on leavers and provide information on anticipated requirements for manpower for his or her department. |
| Provision of contracts | Provide written statement of particulars for new employees and issue them to these employees, having checked that the detail is correct. Keep copies of all documentation relating to the employee and advise on any alterations to the contract. | Possibly issue documents and get signature of new employee. |

| | | |
|---|---|---|
| Provision of fair treatment | Involvement in design of policies and procedures for the whole organisation to encourage fair treatment at work. Inform and train people in these policies and procedures. Monitor the success of these policies. | Responsible for fair treatment of people in his or her department to ensure all treat others in a fair way. Listen and respond to grievances as an initial stage in the grievance procedure or informally before someone gets into the grievance procedure. May contribute suggestions about design of policies. |
| Equal opportunities | Involvement in design of policies to encourage equal opportunities. Train and inform managers and all employees throughout the organisation in these. Monitor the effectiveness of the equal opportunities policies by collecting and analysing information. | May also be involved in and contribute to the design of policies. Will be responsible for ensuring that all employees for whom he or she is responsible do not suffer from any form of unfair discrimination while at work. |
| Assessing performance of employees | Involvement in design and implementation of techniques to assess performance of employees effectively in a way that links clearly with the organisation's strategic plan. Train, inform and involve people in performance management techniques. Monitor the effectiveness of the procedures. May maintain central records about performance of individual employees. | Contribute to discussion of performance management techniques. Assess performance of those in own department. Involve teams and individuals in setting and agreeing targets and monitoring performance. Monitor their success and give feedback. |
| Employee counselling | Establish appropriate system, either in-house or by external consultants, for employee counselling. May be involved in counselling employees with problems or may have to refer them to specialised counselling service. | May be involved in the initial counselling of employees in his or her own section, or may need to suggest alternative sources of counselling if he or she does not feel qualified to deal with the situation. |
| Employee welfare | Establish appropriate systems for employee welfare in accordance with the objectives of the organisation. Monitor the cost and effectiveness of this provision. | Ensure the well-being of employees in his or her department and draw their attention to, and encourage use of, any provisions designed by the organisation to improve their welfare. |

| Payment and reward of employees | Establish appropriate payment and reward systems for all employees in order to contribute to the organisation's strategic plan. Monitor the success of these. Collect comparative data for other organisations in area or nationally. Deal with individual problems about pay. May be involved in negotiation about payment or reward systems. Tell individuals of their level of pay when they join the organisation or change jobs. May deal with individual problems or complaints about pay. | May be involved in and contribute views about appropriate systems of payment or reward to be used in the organisation. May be involved in negotiation to some extent over issues relating to own department. May deal with problems concerning pay, raised by employees in his or her department in the first instance. |
| --- | --- | --- |
| Health and safety | Involvement in design and implementation of the organisation's health and safety policy in order to contribute to the organisation's strategic plan. Monitor the effectiveness of this. May sit on safety committee or may have line management responsibilities for safety officer or organisation's nurse. Involvement in promotion of health and safety and encouraging the involvement of others throughout the organisation. | Responsible for health and safety of employees working in his or her department. Encourage the involvement of individuals and teams in health or safety promotion activities. Monitor activities of own staff. Carry out regular safety inspections in own department. May take initial disciplinary action against those who infringe health and safety rules. |
| Disciplining individuals | Design of disciplinary procedure. Monitor the effectiveness of the procedure. Give advice to line managers on disciplinary problems. Organise training for line managers and employees about disciplinary issues. Issue warnings in later stages of disciplinary procedure. Maintain central records of disciplinary action taken. | Conduct informal disciplinary interviews with own staff if necessary. Issue formal warnings as outlined in disciplinary procedure. Maintain records of warnings issued. |

| | | |
|---|---|---|
| Dealing with grievances | Participate in the design of grievance procedure and encourage the involvement of others in this. Inform and train people in grievance handling. Monitor the effectiveness of the grievance procedure. May deal with some stages in the grievance procedure or appeals. | Deal initially with grievances raised by employees in his or her department. This may be handled informally at first or as part of the formal grievance procedure. Deal with grievances within specified time limits. |
| Dismissal | Review procedures for dismissal to ensure that they comply with legislation. Provide advice and guidance on fair dismissal procedure. Provide training for all who may be involved in the dismissal process. May dismiss employee. | In many organisations the actual dismissal will be handled by the personnel/HRM department with the manager being present. Nowadays managers in some organisations will also take full responsibility for dismissing an employee in their section in a fair way. |
| Redundancy | Is likely to be involved in consultation with appropriate people with regard to redundancy. Is likely to be involved in selection of those to be made redundant. May inform employee of redundancy and amount of pay and rights. May organise provision of more generous redundancy payment if this is in line with organisation policy. May organise provision of outplacement facilities either in house or by consultants. | Is likely to be involved in selection of those to be made redundant from his or her department. May be involved in telling them of the decision to make them redundant. |
| Negotiation | Is likely to be involved in negotiation on a wide range of organisation-wide issues. | Is likely to be involved in negotiation on a wide range of issues that affect employees in his or her department. |
| Encouraging involvement | Will have an extremely important role in creating a culture within the organisation in which employees are encouraged to be involved in decision-making. Will be involved in designing policy and procedures to encourage employee involvement in line with strategic plan. Will also provide training to encourage employee involvement. | Will contribute to organisation's policies and will encourage involvement of employees in his or her department. |

## References
•••••••••••••

Advisory, Conciliation and Arbitration Service. ACAS *Annual Report 1996*. ACAS, 1997.

Guest, David. Human resource management and industrial relations. *Journal of Management Studies*, Vol 24, 1987, 503–21.

Hall, Laura and Torrington, Derek. *The Human Resource Function: The Dynamics of Change and Development*. Financial Times Pitman Publishing, 1998.

Institute of Personnel and Development. *IPD Mission Statement*. IPD, 1997.

Legge, Karen. *Human Resource Management: Rhetorics and Realities*. Macmillan Business, 1995.

Niven, Mary. *Personnel Management* 1913–63. IPM, 1991.

Skills and Enterprise Network. *Meeting the National Skills Challenge: A Summary of Labour Market and Skills Trends 1996/7*. Skills and Enterprise Network, 1996.

Sparrow, Paul and Marchington, Mick. *Human Resource Management: The New Agenda*. Financial Times Pitman Publishing, 1998.

Storey, John and Sisson, Keith. *Managing Human Resources and Industrial Relations*. Open University Press, 1993.

Tyson, Shaun (ed). *Strategic Prospects for HRM*. Institute of Personnel and Development, 1995.

## Further study
•••••••••••••

### *Books*

Advisory, Conciliation and Arbitration Service, *Effective Organisations: The People Factor*. ACAS, 1997. (One of a very useful series of ACAS advisory booklets. This one aims to assist anyone involved in improving effectiveness of organisations through the contribution of the people who work in them.)

Hackett, Penny. *The Personnel Department at Work*. IPM,1991. (A useful guide to finding out what the work in a personnel department is really like.)

Hall, Laura and Torrington, Derek. *The Human Resource Function: The Dynamics of Change and Development*. Financial Times Pitman Publishing, 1998. (A research-based book which describes various aspects of human resource management and comments on its status in UK companies in the 1980s and 1990s. The strategic nature of HRM is discussed in Chapter 6, 'Involvement in HR strategy', and the marketing of the function is described in Chapter 8, 'Internal marketing of HR activities and the HR function'.)

Marks, Wilfred. *Politics and Personnel Management – An Outline History 1960–76*. IPM, 1978. (Excellent reading for those interested in the early history of personnel management.)

Niven, Mary. *Personnel Management 1913–63*. IPM, 1967 reissued 1978. (Excellent reading for those interested in the early history of personnel management.)

Storey, John. *Developments in the Management of Human Resources*. Blackwell Publishers, 1992. (Examines the changing nature of people management and the development of a business perspective rather than a personnel-driven picture.)

### Articles

Fowler, Alan. Personnel's model army. *Personnel Management*, September 1994a, 35–37. (A good guide to the history of personnel management and of the various models that have been used to illustrate its development.)

Fowler, Alan. The way we were 1969–1994. Rediscovering humanity in the workplace. *Personnel Management*, mid December 1994b, 23–26. (A clear analysis of trends past and present in personnel management.)

Hodges, Catherine. Stockport sells its HR services. *Personnel Management Plus*, March 1994, 24–25. (A short article that describes how the central personnel unit of Stockport Borough Council designed and marketed its services.)

### Journals

*Human Resource Management Journal* (Quarterly, contains articles on a wide range of HRM issues of interest to practitioners and academics alike.)

*People Management* (Twice-monthly journal produced on behalf of the IPD with topical articles relating to personnel management issues.)

*Personnel Review* (Journal produced six times per year with in depth articles on personnel topics.)

*Personnel Today* (Contains topical articles on personnel management.)

### Audio-visual

Hackett, Penny. *The Personnel Department at Work*. IPM,1991. (There is an audio tape to accompany the book which provides five dramatised scenarios, and selected interviews, to give a flavour of what the work in a personnel department is really like.)

### Internet

Readers who have computers with access to the Internet will find many useful sources of information from around the world relating to human resource management. We have found the following to be particularly useful:

The Advisory, Conciliation and Arbitration Service (Useful articles, news and lists of ACAS publications.) — **http://www.acas.org.uk**

The American Society for Human Resource Management (The web site for a US body that represents HRM managers.) — **http://www.shrm.org**

The Australian Human
Resource Institute
(Many articles relating to human
resource management in Australia.)

**http://www.ahri.com.au**

The Department for Trade
and Industry
(Many useful DTI publications,
discussion documents and booklets
can be found on this site.)

**http://www.dti.gov.uk**

The Government
(Useful information site especially
for the text of legislation.)

**http://www.open.gov.uk**

The TUC
(This gives the TUC's views on
many current HRM issues and
new legislation in Britain.)

**http://www.tuc.org.uk**

The Institute of Personnel
and Development
(The web site for the professional
body that represents personnel and
development professionals in the UK.)

**http://www.ipd.co.uk**

Incomes Data Services Limited
(Some very useful articles on a
range of HRM topics, including
a section on management pay
and remuneration, plus lists of
contents for IDS publications
are published on line.)

**http://www.incomesdata.co.uk/**

*People Management*
(Journal  produced on behalf of
the IPD with topical articles
relating to Personnel
Management issues.)

**http://www.peoplemanagement.co.uk**

*Personnel Review*
(Journal with in depth articles
on personnel topics.)

**http://www.mcb.co.uk**

Workforce online (US)
(Another American site that
provides useful information
about HRM in the USA.)

**http://www.hrhq.com/**

# CHAPTER 2

# Human resource strategy and planning

The chapter introducing human resource management (HRM) established that a key characteristic of the HRM approach is the involvement of the personnel function at a strategic level. We will now look briefly at the different levels at which strategy can be formulated and the generic types of strategy that are encountered, and comment on the links between strategy and consideration of human resource issues. You must remember that we shall be looking at the ideal situation or models of how corporate/business strategy and HR considerations could interact. What we describe as an ideal is not always found in reality, or, indeed, the specific circumstances in which a business is operating might call for a different approach. You will find that occasionally throughout the text we refer to contingency approaches, which means that there is no one right way to manage human resources in an organisation.

Following an overview of corporate/business and human resource strategies, we shall examine the activities that underpin the strategic human resource function, namely the activities involved in human resource planning.

## Strategy

Strategy can be defined as a plan of action for the future, answering the questions, firstly of *what* to do, then of *how* to do it. A strategic plan should have a long-term focus, business plans usually being developed around a five-year perspective. The aim of designing and following a strategic plan is to create a competitive advantage, and all efforts in the formulation and implementation processes will be directed towards this.

As far as work organisations are concerned, strategy can be formulated and implemented at different levels, and there are recognised generic forms of strategy that organisations or sub-divisions of organisations might adopt.

## Levels of strategy

The levels at which strategy is formulated and implemented are most frequently identified as corporate, business and functional (see, for example, Glaister, 1995; Anthony *et al.*, 1996; Marchington and Wilkinson, 1996).

### Corporate and business strategies

Corporate strategy is concerned with the overall direction that an organisation will follow. For large corporations, this is a question of which lines of business they will choose to be engaged in. These organisations would then develop separate business level strategies for their divisions, each of which might be engaged in producing very different products or services. As Anthony *et al.* (1996, p. 84) point out, corporate and business strategy would be one and the same thing for a small organisation dealing only with one line of products or services, and it follows that you will sometimes find writers using the same terminology when they are discussing these two levels of strategy.

### Functional strategy

The functions represented in an organisation depend on the type of business, its size and structure, but may include production, marketing, sales, finance, research and development, and human resources. Each of these functional areas needs to be following strategic plans that are consonant with the corporate and business plans adopted by their organisations. The strategic plans adopted by all these functional departments must be integrated, however, to ensure the success of the organisation; they are interdependent and cannot be formulated in ignorance of each other. Indeed, it can be stated incontrovertibly that the human resource is an integral part of every one of the above-named functions.

## The strategy formulation process

You will find throughout the discussion of the strategic planning process that there is a great deal of emphasis on gathering information as a basis for decision making. There is a need to focus on relevant information, but it is also imperative to be comprehensive so you do not miss something that could have an impact. Since planning implies forecasting future actions, there is always the potential for developments that you may not have foreseen. This means that planning becomes a rolling process, and that a five-year plan developed in 1999 cannot be followed slavishly until the year 2004, but will probably need to be adjusted on an ongoing basis to account for unforeseen developments.

**PAUSE FOR THOUGHT 2.1** *What kinds of information might senior managers in a company manufacturing and distributing consumer goods need to consider in order to formulate strategic plans?*

You may have considered a variety of factors and kept in mind the types of changes that businesses in general are facing. Your list may include some of the following:

- ➤ Product life cycle: Is the product or service a new one with room for development and an expanding potential market? Is the product something that is bought once or do customers replace it? Is the product mature and not likely to attract more customers? Are customers likely to look for an alternative to the product or service?
- ➤ Changing consumer tastes and requirements: How are these likely to affect the demand for the product? Are there changes in customer expectations that organisations need to respond to?
- ➤ Expansion of business into other countries: Are there opportunities to sell your product or service abroad?
- ➤ Competition: What are the threats from competitors and the opportunities to compete? What will be the impact of new issues such as the growth of global competition, for instance from countries like China?
- ➤ Technological developments: Will new technology affect the design of products, work processes and costs?
- ➤ Legislation: What regulations are in the pipe-line and what are the associated implications for costs, work processes and product standards?

These are just some of the factors that affect business planning, and you may be able to identify even more. Information about all of these factors will influence what managers see as threats and opportunities and will therefore affect the strategic choices made and formulation of the strategic plan.

### Generic types of corporate and business strategy

There are a number of recognised generic types of strategies that companies may choose to follow. The over-arching corporate strategies are generally cited as being growth, stability and retrenchment (Glaister, 1995), but there are a number of ways of pursuing each of these. Growth can be achieved, for instance, through the development of new products, by acquiring a larger share of the market for existing products, through mergers and acquisitions. Glaister also lists internationalisation as a possible generic strategy that organisations might wish to follow.

The work of Michael Porter (1980) is frequently cited in discussions of business-level strategies. The generic concepts he developed are cost leadership, differentiation and focus. One or a combination of these can be adopted in order to achieve the chosen corporate strategy. In adopting a strategy based on cost, companies will attempt to improve efficiency by reducing staffing and production costs. A strategy of differentiation means emphasising the distinctiveness of one's products or services, for example by being known for consistent high quality. A market or niche focus approach entails concentrating on a particular segment

**DID YOU KNOW?**

*A number of UK companies in the late 1990s started to notice a side effect of a prolonged period of downsizing (associated with a strategy of retrenchment) in that they were lacking managers with industry know-how based on lengthy experience with the company. German researchers are reporting a similar syndrome, accompanied with severe demands on the younger middle managers now in post. (Süddeutsche Zeitung, 1/2 August 1998.)*

rather than the whole industry. As Glaister comments, this strategy can be pursued in combination with either cost leadership or differentiation. Innovation as a strategic direction has received more attention recently, and Guest *et al.* (1997) make the point that all business strategies need an element of innovation. We shall, therefore, pursue this as an example in our discussion of the linkage between corporate/business strategy and human resource strategy.

### Corporate/business strategy–human resource strategy links

Innovation has been strongly promoted as a necessary part of any effective strategy for the twenty-first century (Guest *et al.*, 1997) and as a requirement to accompany other strategies to guarantee success (Herriot and Pemberton, 1997). Herriot and Pemberton (pp. 47–48) list the human requirements for the successful pursuit of a strategy of innovation as security, a sense of agency, autonomy, access to adequate resources, and 'team working ... especially when the team is composed of individuals with diverse perspectives'. Agency is defined as employees being able to affect what goes on in their workplace, and autonomy is, of course, being able to make decisions about how one's own work gets done.

**PAUSE FOR THOUGHT 2.2**    *What human resource issues do you think would need to be addressed in a human resource strategy that was to support a business strategy of innovation? Looking back at Herriot and Pemberton's list of human requirements might give you some ideas to start with. Take a few minutes to jot down some thoughts before you read on.*

#### Recruitment and selection

The company would obviously need to make sure it had staff of the right calibre, with the right competencies, to be able to achieve the required level of innovation. It might be that these people are already employed by the company, and this fact would be ascertained through the process of assessing the internal supply of human resources which we shall describe in detail later in this chapter. If not, the company would need a recruitment strategy and policies designed to enable them to carry out their recruitment in a purposeful manner. Since the human resource is so crucial to the achievement of the strategic aim, it will also be necessary to adopt a sophisticated approach to the selection of employees. We deal with systematic recruitment and selection in Chapters 3–5.

#### Employee relations

We assume that any right-thinking company will espouse the tenets of equality of opportunity, which we deal with extensively in Chapter 3, but, as we mention there too, some companies recognise the business advantage to be obtained from pursuing a policy of diversity, which is an extension of equal opportunities. Diversity means obtaining innovative ideas by promoting the involvement of employees from a wide variety of backgrounds, working in teams. A strategy of pursuing diversity has implications for the recruitment strategy and policies.

The word 'involvement' was used in the preceding paragraph. You will find in Chapter 13 that we discuss types of involvement and the modern push for partnership between employers and employees. A human resource strategy of involvement and partnership would support a corporate strategy of innovation.

### Training and development

A strategy of innovation implies change which will have to be managed, and requirements for new skills as new products, services or processes are developed. All of these call for skills training, as do some of the other policies outlined in this discussion, such as embarking on a partnership agreement or promoting diversity in the workforce. Training in new skills and multi-skilling can also contribute to the sense of security that Herriot and Pemberton listed as a requirement for innovation. This is because employees develop a higher level of employability through the acquisition of a wider range of skills.

### Reward

After investing so much in obtaining and training employees capable of carrying a strategy of innovation, you will not want to lose them to competitors, so you will need to develop reward strategies that will motivate employees to stay with your company and to reach the highest levels of productivity. We investigate the different ways of paying employees in Chapter 10, but non-monetary rewards can also contribute to the retention of employees, and helping employees to develop skills can play a part in this. We examine relevant aspects of performance management and development in Chapters 7–9.

You will note from the preceding description of human resource strategies that are appropriate to a corporate/business strategy of innovation (a) that a number of facets need to be addressed, and (b) that they affect each other and need to be integrated, e.g. a recruitment policy of promoting diversity engenders training needs for those involved in the recruitment and selection processes.

We have presented these human resource strategies as if they were designed to support a previously established corporate policy of innovation. This places HR strategy 'downstream' from corporate strategy (Marchington and Wilkinson, 1996). Ideally, however, human resource considerations should inform the corporate strategy and affect what is included in it. The costs of pursuing these HR strategies, and the probability of being able to fulfil them in order to achieve the strategic objectives; should have been a factor in the decision to pursue this strategic goal in the first place.

## Human resource planning

Whatever the strategy adopted by an organisation, it is recognised that an unrelenting and increasing rate of change is an unavoidable phenomenon of today's workplace. The implication is that tomorrow's workplace will not be the same as today's. Employment patterns are changing, as we shall discuss in more detail in the chapter on the employment relationship, and changing work methods give rise to requirements for different and new skills and for flexibility from existing employees to acquire new skills or adapt to new methods of working. This highlights the need for human resource planning which responds to this situation by taking a long-term view and works towards preparing an organisation to cope with its future requirements and achieve its strategic objectives. The information acquired through the process of human resource planning provides the foundation for the development of human resource strategies.

The rest of this chapter will examine the stages involved in the human resource planning process, the types of issues and information that need to be considered, and techniques for processing that information.

## Estimating the demand for human resources

Whatever the goals of the corporate/business plan are, they can be achieved only by the application of human skill and effort. One of the primary stages in the human resource planning process is therefore to estimate what will be required in terms of skills and numbers of people to achieve the corporate goals. Let us take some examples of corporate goals so that we can envisage what this exercise might entail.

ACTIVITY **2.1**

Examine the following two scenarios, and evaluate what will be required in terms of human resources in order to achieve the goals stated in each case. What factors would have to be considered in making forecasts of requirements?

1   A distributor of women's clothing wishes to expand its customer base into Germany, France and Spain. It intends to open a warehouse and distribution depot in France.
2   A regional building society and a national bank are set to merge.

### *Discussion of Activity 2.1*

In order to assess the requirements for human resources in the above scenarios, you would have to envisage

➤   what tasks need to be done
➤   the skills required to complete these tasks
➤   how the tasks could be grouped together to form jobs taking the skills requirements into consideration
➤   how many people would be required to complete the volume of work.

Firstly, then, there is a matter of the identification of discrete work tasks, followed by the organisation of those work tasks into jobs (i.e. a collection of tasks that somehow belong together and could reasonably be carried out by one individual), and a qualitative analysis of the skill base required to perform those jobs and achieve the organisation's goals. The records that document tasks and skills in an organisation are the job descriptions (JDs) and person specifications, and the information contained in these documents is collected and organised through the processes of job analysis and job design, which are discussed later. Secondly, there is the task of quantifying the numbers of people required.

In scenario 1 you will have identified the need for the staff to run the ware-housing and distribution processes in the new depot in France. This will include a manager, picking and packing staff, administrative staff and drivers. You may further have considered the need for language skills among some of these staff to cope with communications with the customers in Spain and Germany and with the home base in the UK. The expansion of business into these countries might also mean adding new tasks and skill requirements to existing posts in the home base, or it may mean recruiting a new manager and/or administrative staff who have the requisite language skills and knowledge of marketing and business processes in those countries. At the very least, the expansion of business into new countries implies a need for someone to coordinate the activities with headquarters. You would need additional information about the expected volume of business to be able to calculate how many people will be required in each category of employee.

Scenario 2 requires an examination of where skills and functions overlap within the two types of business, which might imply that some duties can be merged and not all of the existing posts will be needed. Alternatively, because the new, merged organisation will cover a wider range of tasks than either of the separate organisations had, there may be a new requirement for people who can combine and manage skills in both areas.

### Job analysis

Job analysis is an operational function that underpins the strategic level of human resource planning (and other human resource management functions) by providing the database required for analysis and planning. It is a process of gathering together all data about each existing job, which activities are performed and what skills are needed. As far as human resource planning activities are concerned, job analysis and job design (see p. 37) link the tasks of calculating the demand for human resources and calculating the internal supply of human resources, since together they provide the blueprint for what is required but also document the existing complement of employees, what they are doing and what skills they are using.

Job analysis, then, results in documents that pull together information about the tasks, skills and abilities represented in the current array of work performed in the organisation. If tasks and skills needed for the future are incorporated, the process is called job modelling. The products of job analysis are job descriptions and person specifications. Because these documents form the essential basis for recruitment and selection, job analysis is most often dealt with in textbooks in relation to those functions, and we shall remind you of its importance for them in Chapters 3 and 4. We feel, however, that job analysis is an essential part of human resource planning activities which, as you will see, should precede the formulation of recruitment plans.

For the purpose of illustrating how to compose a job description, we shall be using a relatively junior position, which will probably be familiar to you all, but even this example will demonstrate that changes in the workplace can affect positions at all levels and need to be planned for. You will find our sample job description for a receptionist later, in Figure 2.1 (p. 33)

PAUSE FOR THOUGHT **2.3** *Can you list several activities that you might undertake in order to perform a job analysis as defined above?*

## Job descriptions

The first task involved in drawing up a job description is to gather information about the tasks that are performed by the postholder. The following questions need to be considered:

➤ Who can best provide the information?
➤ Who can best gather the information?
➤ What techniques can be used for gathering the information?
➤ Who should write the job description?

*Who can best provide the information?*

Before you read on, stop and ask yourself: 'Who knows most about any particular job?' Most people would probably respond by saying: 'The person who actually does the job.' The postholder is, therefore, a good source of information about any post. But is the postholder the best source, or the only source? The direct line manager will also know the job requirements intimately, and will probably have a better perspective on how the job fits into the wider context of the company. Gathering information from both of these individuals will create a better picture of the post than gathering information from only one of them.

Personnel specialists also develop detailed knowledge of the tasks performed throughout the company, particularly if they are involved in the human resource planning process, so they can bring an even wider perspective to the description of an individual post. To that extent they can also provide input to the job description, but their major role as far as job descriptions are concerned is not about providing information.

Information given by any person will be influenced by his or her perceptions and self-interest. Consider the pros and cons of gathering information from the postholder, and from the line manager. Your list might include the following points:

1 The postholder:
   ➤ knows the job in detail
   ➤ may wish to inflate the importance of certain duties as a matter of status or self-image
   ➤ may represent preferred duties as most important duties
   ➤ may have incorrect perceptions of level of authority
   ➤ may not have the specialised skills needed to gather information and compose job descriptions
   ➤ may be reluctant to spend the time necessary to develop a good job description.

2 The line manager:
   ➤ knows the job well, but not as well as the jobholder
   ➤ can give information about how the job fits in with other functions performed in the company

➤ may sometimes be reluctant to define which tasks his or her subordinates have full authority for

➤ may not have the specialised skills needed to gather information and compose job descriptions

➤ may be reluctant to spend the time necessary to develop a good job description.

*Who can best gather the information?*
This is the role that the human resource specialist can best fulfil. Although line managers may often put job descriptions to good use, most of them would not consider the production of JDs to be part of their duties, and there is no reason to assume that line managers in a wide range of functions would necessarily have the skills needed in order to produce a good job description. The human resource management function would normally provide this as a service to line management, and of course people with the requisite skills would be recruited and selected to perform this duty. Depending on the structure of the HRM division, the task could be allocated to a specialist job analyst, a recruitment specialist or a human resource management generalist.

*What techniques can be used for gathering the information?*
A range of techniques are available for performing job analysis, including observation and critical incident analysis.

Observation involves shadowing employees and observing what they actually do. Obviously this can be very time-consuming and could stretch over a long period if, for instance, some tasks were performed infrequently. This technique is therefore most appropriate in the case of routine jobs with a narrow range of repetitive tasks.

Critical incident analysis involves getting a number of jobholders and their supervisors to describe events that showed successful behaviour on the job and events that showed unsuccessful behaviour. The analyst collects a large number of such anecdotes and condenses out of them a list of dimensions that represent the job. The advantage of this is seen as being that it focuses on behaviours, i.e. what people actually do, but the process is very time-consuming and may miss some of the more routine aspects of the job.

A sound approach for gathering information would involve written questionnaires and interviews. A structured questionnaire can be used to gather initial information from the jobholder, supplemented with details from the line manager. The job analyst can then interview both and obtain clarification on the details outlined in the questionnaire. The draft job description should then be submitted to the jobholder and line manager for further comment. A structured questionnaire will guide people into giving relevant and adequate information.

**PAUSE FOR THOUGHT 2.4**   *If you were asked to design a form in order to conduct a job analysis, what questions would you include?*

The questions on a job analysis form might be dictated to some extent by the type of company you are working in. For instance, if you worked in a bank which is closed in the evening, you would not include questions about night shift work, whereas if you worked in a chemical plant with a 24 hour process, you obviously would ask questions about night shift work. If we ignore such differences between organisations, however, there are some basic data that you would want to include in any job analysis. These would include such details as:

- a description of the duties performed
- the most important or responsible duties
- time spent on each duty
- how often each duty is performed (daily/weekly/monthly/annually)
- levels of supervision/independence
- the skills and skill levels needed to perform each task
- any special conditions related to the performance of these tasks.

The questionnaire and interview should be designed so that information needed for each section of the job description will be obtained. If employees and their managers are asked to describe ways in which they think their jobs will change, this adds information to the job analysis beyond what is already observable about the job. When this information is incorporated into the job profile, the exercise is known as job modelling.

Although many people are happy to talk about their job, some people do not respond well to questioning or lack good powers of expression. The job analyst needs to develop good interviewing techniques to extract all the relevant information. Interviewing skills are an essential part of many jobs in human resources management and you will find more information about techniques and skills development in Chapters 4, 9, 11 and 14.

*Who should write the job description?*
Again the personnel specialist can best perform this task because of the writing skills required and the opportunity to become familiar with jobs throughout the company. This means that all job descriptions will be written in a uniform manner, providing an excellent database of all tasks performed within the company. This will facilitate the analysis of the information contained in job descriptions for human resource planning purposes.

## How to write a job description

*Structure and content*
If a collection of job descriptions is to serve as a database of all tasks performed within an organisation, it makes sense to adopt a standard format for all job descriptions. This will ensure that the same types of information are gathered for each post, and will make the information more accessible to the reader and facilitate coding if the data are to be entered on to a computerised information system. The following elements are commonly found in job descriptions:

- job title
- reporting structure:
  - reports to
  - responsible for
- purpose of job
- major duties.

*figure 2.1*
**Sample job description**

| Job description | |
| --- | --- |
| Job title: | Receptionist |
| Reports to: | Office Services Manager |
| Responsible for: | Junior receptionists (2) |
| Purpose of post: | To ensure that visitors to the company are received in a welcoming fashion, to answer routine queries and to ensure that all other queries are handled expeditiously by the appropriate staff member. To ensure that all telephone queries are handled in the same manner. |
| | As the first point of contact for the company, the receptionist must maintain high standards of customer care. |
| Contacts: | All customers and other visitors to deal with initial and routine queries. All members of staff to pass on queries as appropriate. |
| Major duties: | ➤ Greet walk-in visitors and ascertain purpose of their visit. Handle or redirect queries as appropriate. |
| | ➤ Answer phone queries as above. |
| | ➤ Answer all initial queries about receipt of payments using the on-line payment receipts system. |
| | ➤ Open and sort incoming post by department. Organise delivery of post by assistant receptionists. |
| | ➤ Perform clerical tasks assigned by departments in agreement with the Office Services Manager. |
| | ➤ Supervise assistant receptionists and delegate work as appropriate. |
| | ➤ Perform other duties as assigned by the Office Services Manager or other authorised manager. |

These are the essential elements of a job description, but you will find an assortment of other elements included in some job descriptions, for example: contacts, working conditions, salary grade, performance standards. Each organisation must decide what factors should be included in a job description, and this will depend on the nature of the business. For instance, some local authorities include a description of the contacts their employees are expected to deal with because they have complex internal structures, and contact with the public is an important part of their operation. The four elements listed above, however, are the basic information you would expect to find in any job description.

Most JDs contain a summary description of the post or, as we have called it, an outline of the purpose of the job. This is a brief paragraph encapsulating what the job is all about – what the jobholder contributes to the organisation. The major part of any JD is the list of major duties, itemising in detail the activities the jobholder undertakes and what he or she is meant to achieve.

Torrington and Hall (1998) demonstrate the inclusion of performance standards in job descriptions. This can certainly enhance a job description by giving more information about what is expected from the jobholder. For instance, the second duty in our sample JD might read: 'Answer phone queries within three rings.'

*Writing style*

One important pointer when you are writing a job description is to use verbs to describe what a person is doing. For instance, the phrase 'responsible for letters' does not indicate what this employee would actually be doing. It is much better to employ a verb and say: 'writes letters'; 'sorts and distributes letters'; 'replies to letters'.

You should also where possible avoid the temptation to use the phrase 'assists with', as again this does not give a clear picture of what an individual employee is actually doing. Take, for example, the phrase: 'assists the manager with invoices'. It must be possible to get a clearer idea of which duties have been delegated to the employee and what activities are retained by the manager. 'Sorts the invoices by date'; 'processes invoices and forwards them to appropriate departments'; 'ensures invoices are processed and payment made': each of these indicates a different activity and a different level of responsibility, and certainly is more meaningful than 'assists the manager with invoices'.

**Uses of the job description**

It has been mentioned previously that job descriptions can be used for a number of purposes. These will be dealt with more extensively in other chapters, but it is worth pausing here to reflect briefly on what the other applications of job descriptions are and whether they have any implications for how job descriptions are compiled and written. The major uses of job descriptions are as follows:

➤ human resource planning
➤ recruitment and selection
➤ day-to-day performance management
➤ long-term performance management/performance appraisal
➤ identification of training needs
➤ job evaluation.

Can one description provide all the information needed for the whole range of these activities? Some personnel managers may argue that different input is needed, for example, for the job evaluation process. More detailed information may be needed about the amount of freedom that employees have to make decisions independently, the impact their actions have on other colleagues, or the financial implications of their work. The question arises of whether a different job description is needed for the purposes of job evaluation. You can form a better opinion on this when you read about these other activities and the uses of job descriptions to support them.

ACTIVITY **2.2**
...............

1 Design a generic questionnaire that could be used to solicit adequate information from an employee to draft a job description. (It might help you if you have one or two posts in mind while you design the questionnaire: what sorts of question would you need to ask in order to elicit all the relevant information? You may also wish to work with a group of fellow students to pool your ideas about the questionnaire design.)

2 Test your questionnaire on a friend, relative or other willing volunteer, and follow up with an interview to fill in the gaps.

3 Analyse this process and make recommendations for improvement.

4 Draft the job description from the information you have gathered.

## Person specifications

The person specification is a document that outlines the skills and qualities a person would need to have in order to be able to do the tasks on the job description. Drawing up a person specification requires a fair amount of judgement in assessing what level of skill is necessary. Often there is a tendency to inflate these requirements, especially with regard to academic qualifications, resulting in an unjustified rejection of skills and knowledge acquired through experience. The requirements detailed in a person specification should be the minimum standards required for a person to be able to perform the job. There should be an expectation that any person will improve performance while doing a job, and the fact that training could be provided should also be considered.

### How to write a person specification

Several models of person specifications are available, those designed by Alec Rodger in 1952 and John Munro Fraser in 1978 being the most widely known. We shall briefly describe the criteria set out in these two models, with some indication of how you might interpret the recommended dimensions, and then apply a simplified version to our sample job description.

Rodger developed the seven point plan which described people in terms of:

| | |
|---|---|
| ➤ Physical make-up | ➤ Any particular physical requirements of the job, such as visual acuity |
| ➤ Attainments | ➤ Education and training |
| ➤ General intelligence | ➤ It is difficult to make a meaningful statement about intelligence unless you intend to test for it |
| ➤ Special aptitudes | ➤ Verbal, numerical and diagrammatical abilities related to the job |
| ➤ Interests | ➤ Current wisdom is that private interests are not good indicators of job performance |
| ➤ Disposition | ➤ Job-related behaviours such as persuasiveness |
| ➤ Circumstances | ➤ Only job-related circumstances such as availability for shift work |

The criteria suggested by Fraser are known as the five-fold framework:

- Impact on others
- Similar to Rodger's physical make-up and disposition

- Qualifications and experience
- Education, training and skills developed through work experience

- Innate abilities
- Similar to intelligence in Rodger's plan

- Motivation
- Difficult to apply for human resource planning and selection purposes since differing motivational structures can lead to equally good performance

- Emotional adjustment
- Relevant personality factors such as the ability to cope with stress

In essence, the person specification should cover three areas of requirements:

- knowledge
- skills
- personal qualities.

The person specification can be drawn up by examining each task in the job description and determining:

1   what each task requires in terms of knowledge, skills and personal qualities
2   how these skills, knowledge and personal qualities might be acquired.

As mentioned earlier, a high level of judgement is needed to decide on relevant criteria, and one person's judgement may differ from another's. You must be able to justify any requirement you make and be ready to explain why it is reasonable, particularly when the specification is to be used later in recruitment and selection. You should also take care to avoid meaningless clichés like 'a sense of humour', when what is really required is the ability to deal calmly with stressful situations.

Once you have a list of the criteria you are looking for, they must be arranged in a logical and understandable fashion:

- similar criteria, e.g. all skills and knowledge involving numeracy, should be grouped
- criteria can be designated as essential for the post or merely desirable.

The sample person specification in Table 2.1 relates to the sample job description on page 33.

**PAUSE FOR THOUGHT 2.5**   *One of the major requirements for the job described in Figure 2.1 has been missed out of the model person specification in Table 2.1. Can you identify it? What can you add to the person specification to cover this requirement?*

The job description mentions use of an on-line system to answer queries about receipt of payment, yet there is no requirement for computer skills in the person specification. Obviously a low level of skill is required. It would not, for instance,

*table 2.1*

**Sample person specification**

| Person specification | | |
|---|---|---|
| **Post: Receptionist** | | |
| | **Essential** | **Desirable** |
| Knowledge | Knowledge of clerical systems | Knowledge of the company |
| Skills | Experience of clerical work Experience in handling queries in person and over the telephone | Supervisory experience |
| Personal qualities | Polite manner Ability to work under pressure | |

be appropriate to ask for programming skills, but it would be reasonable to require the 'ability to extract information from a computerised database'.

ACTIVITY **2.3**

Draft a person specification for the job description in Figure 2.1 using the models provided by Alec Rodger and John Munro Fraser. Compare your drafts with those of other students and incorporate the best ideas into a final version.

### The use of competencies

Many companies are now using competencies and developing competency profiles to describe the array of skills, knowledge and qualities required in a post. Competency profiles are often used to define the skills and abilities required from managers and leaders, but they have also been applied to other jobs, including sales and technical positions (Wisher, 1994). If they are used for human resource planning purposes they will also be used consistently to underpin recruitment, selection, job evaluation and performance appraisal.

Wisher (1994, p. 37) describes competencies as 'clusters of behaviour, underpinned by a set of personal characteristics: motives, traits and self-perceptions'. Organisations identify a combination of competencies required to perform well in a particular job, for example, strategic thinking, communications and selling skills, and then describe the behaviours that would be expected in each of these competencies at different levels. W. H. Smith is one company that has developed descriptions of the competencies it looks for in managers (Jacobs, 1989). These include elements such as leadership, planning and organisational skills, and analytical ability. Leadership is further described in terms of ability to direct group activities, skill in building an effective team and involving all team members, and ability to give help and advice when required.

### *Job design*

When new tasks arise and new skills are required to complete them, existing jobs may have to be re-designed to incorporate these additional requirements or new posts may be created. It is important to obey certain principles when designing jobs in order to enhance the motivating potential of the job, and consequently increase the contribution of the employee to the organisation. It is beyond the scope of this text to examine the tenets of motivation theory in detail, but the major thrust of job design is to provide for variety, responsibility and autonomy in a person's work. This can be effected by the mix of tasks that are combined into one job and by setting up work processes so that individuals have responsibility and autonomy. A recognised way of achieving this is to design jobs so they can be done by teams of employees. This incorporates the motivational elements noted above and is recognised as good HR practice (Marchington and Wilkinson, 1996, p. 396). You can find a fuller explanation of motivation and job design in Rollinson *et al.* (1998).

Paper copies of the documents produced from the processes of job analysis and design – JDs, person specs, competency profiles – may be used to support recruitment, selection, job evaluation, training needs analysis and performance appraisal. For human resource planning purposes, however, where an overview of the whole workforce is needed, it is evident that computerisation of these data will be necessary even for medium-sized firms, so that alternative scenarios can be set up and analysed and the impact of change can be assessed by running 'what if' scenarios. Database systems for HRM functions are commonly known as computerised personnel information systems (CPIS) or human resource information systems (HRIS). For the information obtained from job analysis to be computerised, the elements of the job description and person specification would need to be standardised across jobs, and some coding, for example, of categories of employee, would be necessary. We can look further at the sorts of data that are needed for human resource planning when we look at how to estimate the supply of human resources later in this chapter.

It may seem as if job analysis is a major, time-consuming task to carry out for a company of any size and that this might slow down the development of strategic plans. This thought is confounded by two arguments:

➤ the planning process cannot take place without a proper database of information to work on
➤ once the database of job descriptions and competency profiles/person specifications is established, job analysis becomes a matter of reviewing these documents to incorporate new tasks and skill requirements. This is not as onerous as starting from scratch.

The effective application of computerised human resource data to strategic purposes is proving to be a challenge for HR specialists which, according to research reports, is not always met successfully (Kinnie and Arthurs, 1996; Liff, 1997). This is one of the areas in which HR specialists could develop to strengthen their position and enhance their contribution to business success.

### Quantitative aspects of estimating demand

Having worked out what is required in terms of tasks to be done and skills needed to do those tasks, an analysis is required of how many people are needed for the volume of work.

*Imagine you are a manufacturer who is going to export clothes to mainland Europe. You have estimated that you will require sewing machine operators to produce an additional 10,000 blouses in the first year. What methods could you use to estimate how many people you would need for this task?*

If you have no previous measures of how much work is produced by your employees, you can engage in work study techniques. This involves determining how the task can be performed most efficiently and timing the operation. You would then calculate how many blouses can be sewn at this rate in one year by one operator and divide your production target of 10,000 by this number to get the number of employees required.

If prior data do exist, you can use past production figures and calculate the ratio of operatives to the number of blouses produced by taking the total figure of blouses produced divided by the total number of operatives engaged in this or similar work. In this case, you might also be applying managerial judgement to choose a task that would be similar to producing a blouse.

Another historical ratio employers might use is the ratio of various categories of personnel to the volume of sales or the number of customers. For instance, if a distribution company has one invoice clerk for every 10,000 customers, and it intends to increase its customer base by 10,000, the historical ratio indicates a need for one additional invoice clerk.

You would need to take account of the fact that new employees might not work at full capacity until fully trained, or you might envisage savings from economies of scale or from changing work methods or the technology used. In other words, even when statistical methods are used to calculate the demand for human resources, managerial judgement will also be a factor.

## Estimating the internal supply of human resources

As with estimating the demand for human resources, you will need qualitative as well as quantitative data to assess whether the requisite resources will be available. The organisation's collection of job descriptions for existing posts represents a database of tasks that are currently being performed, and the person specifications/competency profiles are a partial database of existing skills.

*Why do you think it was stated above that a company's collection of person specifications/competency profiles is a partial database of the supply of existing skills?*

A fact that employers often forget is that people frequently have skills that their employer may not have required them to use in their current post. These could include facility in foreign languages, computer knowledge, training skills, and interpersonal skills. In order to have a full picture of skills available from the current workforce the company needs to develop a skills inventory in addition to JDs and person specs, and these should be recorded on the personal records of employees, which will form part of the organisation's HRIS. The skills inventory should list skills that are available but not being used in addition to those that are being used.

A properly designed HRIS will also provide data on the numbers of employees in various categories of posts, and personal data that may have an impact on how long they are likely to be with the organisation. There are some simple statistical techniques that enable employers to forecast fluctuations in their workforce numbers. The basic figure that most employers calculate is the labour turnover rate, sometimes referred to as the wastage rate or the separation rate, which represents the proportion of employees who leave in a given period of time, usually a year or a quarter. This figure is calculated as a percentage by dividing the number of leavers by the total complement of staff and multiplying this figure by 100. If the requirements for staff vary during the time period, the total complement can be calculated as an average of the number required at the beginning of the period and the number required at the end. This would give an overall turnover rate for an organisation, but it is usually more useful to calculate the rate for specific categories of staff such as secretarial staff, systems analysts, employees in specified production areas, etc.

For example, if a company requires 50 machinists throughout the year, and 5 of these have left in one year, then the turnover rate is $(5/50) \times 100 = 10\%$. The average turnover rate experienced over a period of time can be used as a trend to forecast requirements for the future. For instance, if the turnover rate for machinists at one company has been fairly stable at about 10% over the past three years, then this employer knows that it is likely to be necessary to recruit five machinists next year to maintain his or her supply. If the demand forecast implies that additional machinists will be needed over the next few years, the 10% turnover rate should be factored into the calculation.

ACTIVITY **2.4**
..............

At the end of 1999, the employer in question decides that she will require 10 additional machinists in each of the next three years. They are to be recruited at the beginning of each year. How many machinists will she have to recruit during each year to maintain the workforce?

### Discussion of Activity 2.4

These figures are best calculated by tracking the base figure required each year, the increase in personnel required, and an adjustment for the expected turnover. As you can see, the manufacturer needs not only to recruit the additional employees, but also to cover the turnover on the new base figure. In 2000, potentially five of the original employees will leave, and perhaps one of the new employees. The figures are presented in Table 2.2.

*table 2.2*
**Estimated recruitment figures adjusted for labour turnover**

| | Number of machinists required | Increase over previous year | Projected turnover during year | Number to recruit |
|---|---|---|---|---|
| End of 1999 | 50 | | | |
| 2000 | 60 | 10 | 6 | 16 |
| 2001 | 70 | 10 | 7 | 17 |
| 2002 | 80 | 10 | 8 | 18 |

Another calculation that can be made is known as the stability index. This also gives an indication of turnover, but provides information additional to the base turnover figure and is calculated as follows: (Number of people currently employed with one year or more of service/number of people employed one year ago) × 100.

ACTIVITY **2.5**

This is a simple activity which will help you to focus on the information that can be gleaned by analysing the same data in different ways.

1   You are asked to perform a simple calculation for each of three situations.
   (a)  Your company has 20 drivers. In one year, 5 of these drivers leave and have to be replaced. Calculate the turnover rate.
   (b)  Your company has 20 drivers. At the end of one year, you still have 19 of those drivers with you, but you have had to recruit 5 times to keep your staff complement up to 20. Calculate the turnover rate and the stability index.
   (c)  Your company has 20 drivers. In one year, 5 drivers leave. Each of them had 2–5 years of service. You have had to replace each of them and your new recruits are still with you. Calculate the turnover rate and the stability index.
2   What do these turnover and stability index figures tell you?

### Discussion of Activity 2.5

You should have calculated a turnover figure of 25% for each of these circumstances. On its own, the turnover figure reveals nothing about the underlying causes of turnover, and this is emphasised by the fact that you have the same figure for two very different circumstances. The turnover rate on its own becomes meaningful only if you can compare it with rates experienced by other companies in your industry for similar categories of staff. Then you can deduce whether you are performing in a competitive way in terms of retaining staff, or whether there are problems you need to investigate.

The stability index figures, 95% in scenario (b) and 75% in scenario (c), are much more revealing. The similarity among all three scenarios in the exercise is that there have been five recruitment actions in each case; the stability index, however, reveals that the situations are different and the reasons for the vacancies differed. The higher figure, which means that the turnover is not occurring among the longer serving employees, indicates that there is a problem with retaining new recruits. The lower figure indicates that the problem lies with the retention of longer serving employees. Each problem requires different action to remedy it, and this will be very important when you arrive at the stage of formulating human resource management action plans.

**PAUSE FOR THOUGHT 2.8**   *In the discussion of Activity 2.5, we mentioned that comparing your turnover to that experienced by your competitors might prompt you to analyse retention problems. If your turnover rate was unfavourable in such a comparison, what might some of the problems and remedies be?*

Some of the problems and remedies associated with excessive turnover are represented in Table 2.3.

*table 2.3*
**Labour turnover:
causes and
remedies**

| Cause | Remedy |
|---|---|
| Poor handling of new recruits | Design and implement induction process |
| Unfavourable salary/terms and conditions of employment | Revise reward strategies |
| Job dissatisfaction | Improved job design |
| Low morale | Organisational culture change<br>Employee involvement<br>Attitude surveys |
| Recruits not equipped for work demands | Improve recruitment practices<br>Improve training |

There are some other factors that have an impact on the turnover rate. These might be reflected in long-term trends or they may cause occasional fluctuations. One such factor is the age of employees. Retirement may account for a certain percentage of leavers on an ongoing basis, but it also sometimes happens that a company has a large number of people due to retire at the same time, which will temporarily increase the turnover rate. These factors need to be taken into consideration in forecasting the supply of human resources and when adjusting the estimates to reflect the effects of labour turnover. The HRIS should be set up so that it can provide this information.

**DID YOU KNOW?**
*The average labour turnover rate for firms employing more than 25 people in Britain was 14% in 1995/96 and 21% in 1996/97. (Employee Development Bulletin, April 1998, p.11.)*

In addition to information about numbers, the analysis of various aspects of the workforce can highlight a range of problems or issues that deserve consideration. Some of the analyses that could be obtained are:

➤ the male/female distribution of personnel across the whole workforce or in each category of employee
➤ the distribution across the workforce or by employee category of members of specified ethnic minority groups
➤ age profiles
➤ length of service for each of the above.

These analyses could help managers to see where new approaches or policies are needed to help the organisation reach its goals.

## Assessing the external supply of human resources

At the same time as analysing their internal supply of human resources, employers need to be aware of the availability of potential employees externally in case the internal supply falls short of what is required. If the internal supply of employees cannot meet the demand, managers must know whether there are problems with the availability of employees from outside the company.

The labour force is defined as the number of people aged 16 and over, and who are either in employment or available for work. As such, those members of the labour force who are not currently employed by a particular employer constitute that employer's external labour market. Sometimes separate figures are given for people of working age, but since some people continue working past the state retirement age, figures for persons in their late sixties and seventies are included in estimates of the total labour force.

**PAUSE FOR THOUGHT 2.9** *There are many factors that have an impact on:*

➤ *the size of the labour force in general*
➤ *the availability of employees from the labour force to any particular employer.*

*Before you go on to read about these factors, make a list of as many of them as you can think of. You may also wish to consider what employers might have to do to counteract any problems you identify.*

### Size of the labour force

British labour force projections for the years 1998–2011, as reported in *Labour Market Trends* (Armitage and Scott, 1998), include the following data:

➤ between 1997 and 2011 the labour force is set to increase by 1.8 million persons from 28.0 to 29.8 million;
➤ 1.3 million of this increase will be women;
➤ in 2011, women will represent 46.1% of the labour force (44.2% in 1997);
➤ the number of people in the labour force aged under 35 will decline by 0.7 million while the group aged 35 and over will increase by 2.4 million.

Changes in the numbers of people in the labour force are caused by a combination of population effects and activity rate effects. The largest population effect is the variation in the number of births. There was a peak birth rate around 1964 which accounts for some of the increase in the 35 and over age group in the projection period, and the birth rate was particularly low in the years 1973–1979. Economic activity rates also affect the size and composition of the labour force. Increasing numbers of young people are choosing to study full time which, together with birth rate effects, accounts for the lower numbers of people in the lower age groups available for work. However, this may be counteracted by an increase in the numbers of students who work on a part-time basis.

The growing proportion of women in the labour force is attributed in part to socio-economic influences such as the greater availability of part-time work and the social acceptability of women in employment. All of the factors discussed in this section have implications particularly for employers who have a traditional view of whom they might employ, for instance in positions thought of as being suitable for school leavers. The changing demographic structure of the external labour market may oblige employers to adopt more open approaches to recruitment and to consider the necessity of providing training.

The figures provided by surveys of the national labour force are important in providing a broad indication of factors to be considered in human resource planning. There are, however, some limitations on their usefulness. The statistics are only estimates, projections of the numbers of people expected to be economically active in the future. As such, they have to be predicated on some basic assumptions linked with patterns of economic activity observed at the time the analysis is performed. Obviously, unexpected events can occur which may have a sizeable impact on the validity of the projected figures. The IDS study, *The Future Workforce* (1996), provides some useful guidelines on how to interpret statistical data culled from workforce surveys.

### Unemployment

Rates of unemployment and the prevalence of redundancies have an obvious impact on the numbers of people looking for work. This does not necessarily mean, however, that meeting one's requirements for human resources is automatically easier in times of high unemployment. One example of this is the numbers of coal miners made redundant by the closures of coal mines in the early 1990s. Coal miners may have a range of skills, but not necessarily in the areas required by other employers. There is also resistance among newly redundant people to accepting a large immediate drop in earnings. The existence of large numbers of unemployed or newly redundant people, therefore, does not equate directly with a ready supply of human resources.

### Skill shortages

Skill shortages are estimated by reviewing the number of posts that employers report having difficulty in filling. Although admittedly some of these difficulties may arise because of poor salaries or terms and conditions, most employers comment that lack of skills in the labour force is one of the main reasons for their difficulty in recruiting. A survey conducted by the Industrial Relations Services (IRS, March 1998) revealed that 74% of the manufacturing companies responding to the survey and 64% of the service companies had experienced recruitment difficulties in 1997. The authors note, however, that an element of self-selection among the respondents (i.e. those experiencing few difficulties are less likely to respond) may account for these high percentages, and figures resulting from a number of other surveys are also quoted in the article.

The occupational groups cited by the IRS as presenting most difficulties included technology, engineering, skilled manual and managerial jobs. Other potential or actual skills shortages that have been reported recently in a number of sources, including news broadcasts on TV and radio, include nurses (due to the increased spending planned for the National Health Service), police officers with the skills to take on senior managerial duties, construction workers (Incomes Data Services, 1998), and a range of jobs in the hospitality industry (Ruth Prickett, 1998; see also the reference to the Barzone web site). The geographical areas most affected included London, Merseyside and Scotland.

**DID YOU KNOW?**
The recruitment consultant Elan Computing reported an increase of 348% in its placement in 1996–98 of IT experts over the age of 45. As contract workers, these people are earning about £50,000 per year compared with the £30,000 paid to permanent employees. (Guardian: Jobs and Money Section, *16 May 1998, p. 24.*)

In recognition of the potential difficulties posed to the economy by skill shortages, the Government has set up a Skills Task Force to investigate the problem and recommend solutions.

### Opportunities for education and training

In connection with the concern over skills shortages, employers will be interested in government plans for youth training, what is taught in schools, and how well people are prepared for employment. Many employers develop links with educational institutions to improve the likelihood of relevant skills being available to them. Asda is one example of a company that has developed a scheme to provide part-time employment to students with the aim of creating a pool of graduate applicants with relevant work experience in the future.

### Competition

The presence of competitors in an employer's locality, who also need people with the same skills, will obviously influence the availability of human resources. This may have a direct impact on recruitment and pay strategies as employers try to attract the best people in direct competition with other companies. For the purposes of human resource planning, it will be important to assess the likelihood of new competitors arriving on the scene.

### Geographical considerations

The distribution of the labour force across the country is affected by the availability of housing and transport and by patterns of migration. Changes in the availability of public transport might mean you can no longer depend on obtaining workers from a particular geographical area, so it is important for employers to be aware of the plans of privatised transport companies and developments in the infrastructure.

The type of job you wish to fill will influence whether you consider availability of resources in your locality (junior, low-paid work) or whether it makes sense to broaden your horizons. There could be a problem if you wish to recruit large numbers of low-paid employees locally and they are not available. This would have a direct impact on your strategic plan and might entail relocation to an area where the resources are available. Alternatively, you might consider turning to the global labour market to have computerised work done. Information technology systems have broken down geographical boundaries for work that can be sent across the world via satellite.

### Summary

All the factors that affect the labour force are important to employers. Up-to-date information is the key to effective human resource planning, and managers need to be aware of local, regional, national and global trends and be able to integrate this knowledge into their strategic plans. Knowledge of the key issues will enable companies to assess the threats and opportunities in their environment, and to evaluate their ability to respond with their existing and available resources.

## Comparing demand and supply forecasts
······················································

A comparison of your expected demand for human resources and your expected supply will identify what you need to accomplish in your human resource plans in order to achieve your corporate goals, or, as already mentioned, there may be an indication that the corporate/business plan needs some adjustment. Basically you can be faced with three situations:

➤ supply = demand
➤ supply > demand
➤ supply < demand.

Since there are so many changes affecting organisations in the 1990s, as we have already discussed, and since this is likely to continue for the foreseeable future, supply is not likely to equal demand. This is more likely to occur in very stable conditions. If supply is greater than demand, human resource plans will need to focus on eliminating the surplus through either redeployment or redundancy. When supply is less than demand, a company will be involved in recruitment or other methods of acquiring the necessary skills.

## Developing and implementing human resource strategies
···························································································

In Chapter 1 we described the major personnel management functions as resourcing, development, reward and relations. It is useful to refer to these categories to identify the areas in which it is necessary to develop human resource strategies and action plans.

### *Resourcing*

If demand exceeds supply, the organisation will have to develop plans to acquire the additional skills it needs. This may involve recruitment activities, but there may also be a need for career and succession planning for existing employees, and the company may consider subcontracting work. If supply exceeds demand the company may have to release staff, but consideration should first be given to redeployment and to providing the training that this might entail.

### *Development*

If the skills the company needs are not present in its current workforce, the company should make plans to develop those skills through training, team and individual development, and performance management.

### *Reward*

A review and restructuring of the reward system might enable a company to attract and retain the required complement of human resources. The company should examine its pay levels and the attractiveness of its benefits packages and terms and conditions compared with those of competitors. Action plans should also address the issue of linking rewards properly to the achievement of corporate goals.

### Relations with employees

Improvements in the contribution of employees to their employing organisation can often be achieved through developing better employee relations. Areas to consider include consultation, communications, employee welfare, employee involvement and the development of a partnership approach.

Many of these functional areas are discussed in greater depth in the chapters that follow. Figure 2.2 is a model giving an overview of the human resource planning process, incorporating these functional areas.

A final word should be said about the evaluation of the effectiveness of human resource strategies and the planning process. Organisations should develop systems to review and evaluate their performance in all activities and to ensure that there is feedback from this assessment into the corporate/business strategies. The human resource strategy is interpreted into action plans in a variety of functions, as outlined above, and each of these needs to be monitored and evaluated. You can read more about this in the other chapters of this text.

**REVIEW QUESTIONS**

You will find brief answers to these review questions on pages 420–421.

1  Describe the different levels of strategy found in organisations, and comment on their interconnecting nature.
2  Describe the process of job analysis, and comment on the contribution it can make to an organisation's systems and goals.
3  Outline the major stages of the human resource planning process, and comment on the major considerations at each stage.
4  'Information is crucial as a basis for decision-making in the human resource planning process.' Comment on this statement, and describe the sources of information available to management.

**SELF-CHECK QUESTIONS**

Answer the following multiple choice and short answer questions. The correct responses are given on page 421 for you to check your understanding of this chapter.

1  Name the three major generic strategies available at the corporate level.
2  Name the three business level strategies described by Porter.
3  Which of the following is NOT a factor listed in Rodger's Seven Point Plan?
   (*a*)  Intelligence
   (*b*)  Job-related competencies
   (*c*)  Physical make-up
   (*d*)  Circumstances.
4  List the five elements usually included in a job description.
5  Name five uses of job descriptions other than human resource planning.
6  What phrase is used to describe a job analysis exercise when information about potential developments in the job is incorporated into the resulting job profile?
7  A local supermarket employs 50 sales assistants on a part-time basis. Over the past year the personnel department has had to recruit 25 new employees to keep the establishment full. Of the assistants who were hired over a year ago, 40 are still working with the supermarket in the same positions. Calculate the turnover rate.

*figure 2.2*
**Model of the
human resource
planning
process**

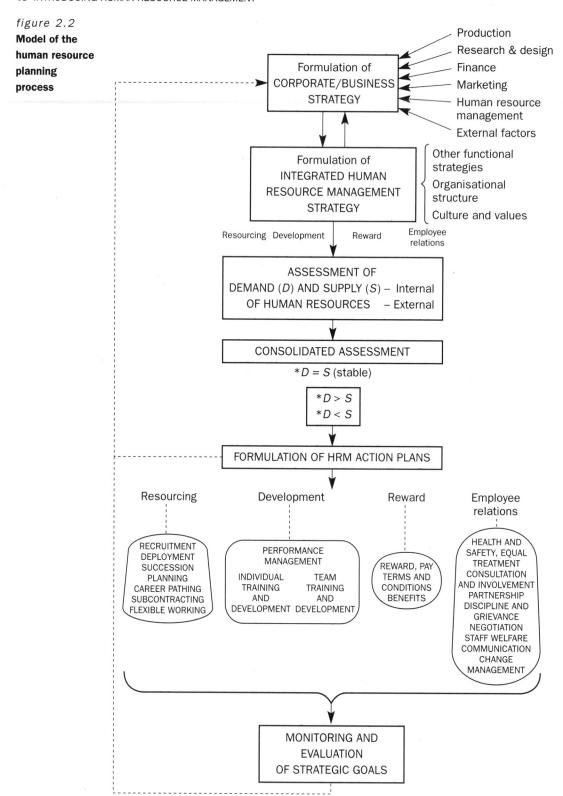

8 **Calculate the stability index for the situation in question 7.**
9 **What does the stability index indicate?**
10 **Which stage has been left out of the following brief description of the human resource planning process?**
   - ➤ **development of corporate strategy**
   - ➤ **estimation of the demand for human resources**
   - ➤ **formulation of human resource management plans**

## References
················

Anthony, William P., Perrewe, Pamela L. and Kacmar, K. Michele. *Strategic Human Resource Management*. 2nd edition, Harcourt Brace, 1996.

Armitage, Bob and Scott, Mark. British labour force projections: 1998–2011. *Labour Market Trends*, June 1998, 281–291.

Fraser, John Munro. *Employment Interviewing*. 5th edition, Macdonald and Evans, 1978.

Glaister, Keith. Introduction to the strategic management process. In: Clarke-Hill, Colin and Glaister, Keith (eds). *Cases in Strategic Management*. 2nd edition, Pitman Publishing, 1995.

Guest, David, Storey, John and Tate, William. *Innovation: Opportunity through People. Consultative Document*. Institute of Personnel and Development, June 1997.

Herriot, Peter and Pemberton, Carole. Facilitating new deals. *Human Resource Management Journal*, Vol. 7, No. 1, 1997, 45–56.

Incomes Data Services. *IDS Focus: The Future Workforce,* No. 80, December 1996.

Incomes Data Services. Viewpoint: scene set for buoyant pay rises in the construction industry. *IDS Report*, No. 757, March 1998, 1–3.

Industrial Relations Services. Solving the skills crisis: an IRS survey of practice. *Employee Development Bulletin,* No. 99, March 1998, 6–20.

Jacobs, Robin. Getting the measure of management competence. *Personnel Management*, June 1989, 32–37.

Kinnie, Nicholas J. and Arthurs, Alan J. Personnel specialists' advanced use of information technology: evidence and explanations. *Personnel Review*, Vol. 25, No. 3, 1996, 3–19.

Liff, Sonia. Constructing HR information systems. *Human Resource Management Journal,* Vol. 7, No. 2, 1997, 18–31.

Marchington, Mick and Wilkinson, Adrian. *Core Personnel and Development*. Institute of Personnel and Development, 1996.

Porter, Michael E. *Competitive Strategy*. Free Press, 1980.

Prickett, Ruth. Campaign set to promote value of a life behind bars. *People Management*, 19 March 1998, 19.

Rodger, Alec. *The Seven Point Plan*. National Institute of Industrial Psychology, 1952.

Rollinson, Derek, Broadfield, Aysen and Edwards, David. *Organisational Behaviour: An Integrated Approach*. Addison Wesley Longman, 1998.

Torrington, Derek and Hall, Laura. *Human Resource Management*. 4th edition, Prentice Hall, 1998.

Wisher, Vicky. Competencies: the precious seeds of growth? *Personnel Management*, July 1994, 36–39.

## Further study
·················

Advisory, Conciliation and Arbitration Service. *Absence and Labour Turnover*. ACAS, 1997.

Advisory, Conciliation and Arbitration Service. *Recruitment Policies for the 1990s*. ACAS, 1997.

Bramham, John. *Human Resource Planning*. 2nd edition, IPD, 1994.

Cascio, Wayne F. *Applied Psychology in Personnel Management*. 4th edition, Prentice Hall, 1991. (A good introduction to the benefits of and techniques used for job analysis and human resource planning is provided in Chapter 10, 'Job analysis', and Chapter 11, 'Human resource planning'.)

Crabb, Steve. Jobs for all in the global market. *People Management*, 26 January 1995, 22–27. (A look at information technology work that is being farmed out on a global basis.)

Hackett, Penny. *Personnel. The Department at Work*. Institute of Personnel Management, 1991. (This book is written as a guide for people considering personnel work. It provides a brief overview of the activities involved in various functions and highlights the skills needed by the personnel management specialist to fulfil these functions effectively. Chapter 3 focuses on planning human resources.)

Industrial Relations Services. *Employee Development Bulletin*. (This periodical frequently contains information useful for human resource planning purposes.)

Industrial Relations Services. Solving the skills crisis: an IRS survey of practice. *Employee Development Bulletin*, No. 99, March 1998, 6–20. (In addition to statistics about skills shortages, this article reports on the strategies that various companies have adopted to counteract this problem.)

Institute of Personnel and Development. *People Make the Difference. An IPD Position Paper*. IPD, 1994. (This paper was presented at the IPD's annual conference in 1994, and included with the first issue of *People Management* in January 1995. The focus of the conference was managing people in a context of change. This brief paper outlines the major sources of change facing companies and the implications for the effective management of people.)

Johnson, Paul. Population ageing and employment policies. In: Bradley, Keith (ed.). *Human Resource Management. People and Performance*. Dartmouth Publishing Co., 1992. (A look at population effects on a global basis and the impact on employment strategies.)

*Labour Market Trends*. (A monthly journal. Contains statistical analyses of various facets of the workforce, and articles and news items about issues of current interest. Essential reading for keeping up-to-date.)

McBeath, Gordon. *The Handbook of Human Resource Planning*. Blackwell, 1992.

Pearn, M and Kandola, R. *Job Analysis: A Manager's Guide*. 2nd edition, IPD, 1993. Chapter 3: 'The ten most useful JTR methods'. (The information in this chapter builds on the simple approaches to job analysis which we have described.)

*People Management.* (Produced for the Institute of Personnel and Development, this magazine is aimed at keeping HR practitioners informed, and frequently contains articles on HR strategy. A good source of case studies.)

Torrington, Derek and Weightman, Jane. *Effective Management: People and Organisation.* 2nd edition, Prentice Hall, 1993. (Chapter 4, 'Strategy and policy-making' and Chapter 5, 'Resource management' provide good background reading.)

Tyson, Shaun (ed.). *The Practice of Human Resource Strategy.* Pitman Publishing, 1997. (Provides case studies of human resource strategies in action in companies in a number of countries.)

Tyson, Shaun. *Human Resource Strategy.* Pitman Publishing, 1995. (A discussion of HRM, and an examination of the links between business and functional HR strategies.)

### Internet

| DATABASE/HOME PAGES | INTERNET ADDRESS |
| --- | --- |
| Barzone<br>(This site has been set up to inform young people about careers in the hospitality industry, and to attract them to it.) | **http://www.barzone.co.uk** |

# CHAPTER 3

# Recruitment

## Objectives:

*When you have read this chapter you will be able to:*

➤ explain the aims of recruitment and describe how specified policies and procedures contribute to these aims
➤ understand the role of human resource managers and line managers in the recruitment process
➤ describe the legislative framework that affects recruitment activities
➤ describe and design support documentation for the recruitment process – job description, person specification, job advertisement, application form, letters to applicants
➤ evaluate and draft recruitment policies and procedures.

The processes of recruitment and selection are closely linked. Both activities are directed towards obtaining suitably qualified employees, and recruitment activities lay the groundwork for the selection process by providing the pool of applicants from whom the selectors may choose. However, although the two functions are so closely connected, each requires a separate range of skills and expertise, and each function may in practice be fulfilled by different staff members, so it makes sense to treat each function separately. This chapter will deal with recruitment actions, policies and procedures which, of course, should be designed to meet the strategic objectives of the organisation. Recruitment can be defined as:

➤ all activities directed towards locating potential employees
➤ the attraction of applications from suitable applicants.

## The aims of recruitment

Organisations do not operate in a vacuum, and recruitment drives are one of the times when an organisation has direct contact with the outside world. Other factors affecting recruitment are the framework imposed by legislation, and the fact that no organisation will want to spend money on unnecessary activities. In keeping with this and the definition of recruitment given above, the aims of recruitment are:

➤ to obtain a pool of suitable candidates for vacant posts
➤ to use and be seen to use a fair process
➤ to ensure that all recruitment activities contribute to company goals and a desirable company image
➤ to conduct recruitment activities in an efficient and cost-effective manner.

These statements intimate that a number of judgements have to be made about how recruitment is carried out. What is meant by a 'suitable candidate', and who decides this? Does the company have a process for evaluating the need to fill a post? What is a fair process and in what terms can fairness be evaluated? What recruitment actions can contribute to or damage a company's good image?

What are the costs involved in recruitment and how can they be managed to maximise the efficiency of the process? An umbrella to all of these considerations is also the need to tailor recruitment action to the corporate strategic plan which itself should have incorporated factors in the environment such as skills shortages, technological advances etc.

Most human resource management issues can be analysed in terms of legal, moral and business considerations. With reference to the stated aims of recruitment, these considerations could be said to be:

➤ *legal* – to comply with anti-discrimination legislation
➤ *moral* – to avoid unfair discrimination for moral reasons as well as obedience to the law
➤ *business* – to ensure that all efforts are directed towards achieving corporate and not personal goals.

If one is to achieve all these aims, and in consideration of the fact that recruitment is likely to involve a wide range of people within an organisation, it is important to have a systematic approach so that all steps of the recruitment and selection process are conducted in line with:

➤ the company's human resource strategy
➤ equal opportunities goals.

The first step towards ensuring that the recruitment process achieves these aims  in a coordinated manner is to develop and implement appropriate policies and procedures.

*Figure 3.1*
**Mind map of recruitment considerations**

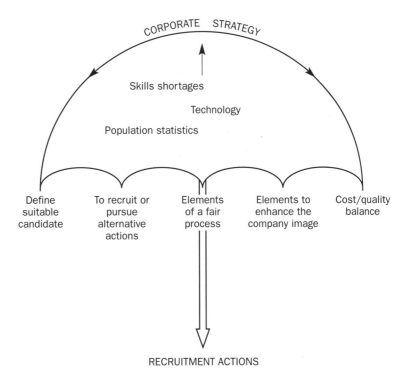

Can you add any features to this mind map?

## Recruitment policies
••••••••••••••••••••••••

A policy is simply a statement of intent on the part of a company; it outlines the approach everyone is expected to adopt and the standards they should achieve. A recruitment policy enables all employees involved in the process to direct their efforts towards achieving the company's goals and to know that they are acting in the spirit intended by the company.

A basic recruitment policy should at the very least include statements about the company's stance on:

> ➤ the overall goal of recruitment
> ➤ equal opportunities.

To show that they value their employees, wish to retain them, and want to provide them with every opportunity to develop, companies may also adopt a policy of giving preference to suitably qualified internal applicants over external applicants, and this too would need to be stated explicitly in the company's recruitment policy. Such a policy would have implications for the way that recruitment procedures are developed.

One argument that is sometimes raised against internal recruitment policies is that they may lead to entrenching any equal opportunities problems that exist. That is, if the company has previously not hired from a particular ethnic group, then it will not improve its record by hiring from within. A counter argument to this is that if current employees are moved to new positions, presumably they eventually leave a vacancy that must be filled by external candidates. Companies following good equal opportunities policies would be able to address any problems at this stage.

Companies that wish to take the human resource management approach to enhancing the contribution and commitment of their employees should certainly consider adopting a policy on internal recruitment.

**PAUSE FOR THOUGHT 3.1**   *Imagine you are in a company which has decided to formulate a recruitment policy that reflects its commitment to equality of opportunity along with an intention to give preference to internal candidates. Before you read on, consider what might be included in a recruitment policy for this company.*

The following is an example of how such a policy might be worded:

This company aims to employ the best suited person for each post without regard to sex, marital status, racial origin, disability, sexual preference, religion, age or any other factor that cannot reasonably be construed as being related to a person's ability to do the job.

The company values the contribution of its employees and so will seek wherever possible to help employees develop new skills so that they may be considered for promotion opportunities. The company will advertise vacancies externally only if there are no suitably qualified internal candidates for transfers or promotions.

Since equal opportunities issues play such an important role in all recruitment activities, we shall now examine the relevant legal framework before returning to the discussion of the processes involved in recruitment.

## Equal opportunities

Legislation exists to protect the interests of groups of people who have historically been discriminated against in terms of employment and services. The legislation provides protection against unfair discrimination on the grounds summarised in Table 3.1.

*table 3.1*
**Anti-discriminatory legislation**

| Act | Areas covered |
| --- | --- |
| Sex Discrimination Act 1975 | Sex and marital status |
| Race Relations Act 1976 | Race, colour, nationality, national or ethnic origins |
| Equal Pay Act 1970 | Male and female pay for like work, work rated as equivalent, and work of equal value |
| Disability Discrimination Act 1995 | Disabled persons |
| Rehabilitation of Offenders Act 1974 | Persons with spent convictions |

### The Sex Discrimination Act (1975) and the Race Relations Act (1976)

The Sex Discrimination Act (SDA) and the Race Relations Act (RRA) address unfair discrimination in similar ways. Both refer to three kinds of discrimination:

➤ direct discrimination
➤ indirect discrimination
➤ victimisation.

*Direct discrimination* occurs when someone is treated less favourably for a reason directly to do with his or her sex, marital status, race or racial origin. Examples of this would be to refuse a woman a job as a truck driver simply because she is a woman, or to refuse a Chinese person a job in a school kitchen simply because all the other employees are white European, and the employer fears that a person of a different racial background will not 'fit in'.

*Indirect discrimination* occurs when someone is treated unfairly because of some requirement that would disproportionately exclude the particular group that person belongs to, and when the requirement cannot be objectively justified. For instance, if you wished to hire someone to clean the windows in your building, and you stipulated that applicants must be 6 feet tall, could this requirement be justified in terms of the skills and abilities required to do the job? Which groups might such a requirement discriminate against? Fewer women than men, for instance, are 6 feet tall. This requirement therefore discriminates indirectly against female applicants.

ACTIVITY **3.1**

Can you think of any other instances of indirect discrimination and identify which groups might be affected by them?

Look through the records of cases heard by Employment Tribunals and you will find some examples. To find reports of such cases you can use several sources.

> ➤ A number of human resource management journals have a section that gives updates on the law and describes recent cases. Look for instance in *People Management* and *Personnel Today*.
> ➤ You can look in the subject index of the *Legal Journals Index*, for instance under the heading 'sex discrimination'. This will give a brief summary of the major points of the case, and refer to a journal in which you can read more about the case.
> ➤ You may find some publications that include descriptions of a number of employment law cases, such as the one by Gwyneth Pitt listed in the suggestions for further reading.

You may wish to compare the instances you find with those found by others in your class.

*Victimisation* occurs when someone is treated less favourably because that person has made a complaint or indicated an intention to make a complaint about sex or race discrimination. An example of this might be a woman who has complained to the Equal Opportunities Commission about lack of promotion in comparison to similarly qualified men and who is subsequently dismissed unfairly.

The legislation also stipulates that this unfair treatment must be to the disadvantage of the person so treated. In the case of employment this means that the person is refused employment, promotion or training opportunities or is dismissed.

**DID YOU KNOW?**

*In most cases an employee needs to have completed a two year qualifying period of employment to take a complaint of unfair dismissal to an employment tribunal. This qualifying period does not apply if the complainant feels that the reasons for the unfair dismissal were connected to sex or race discrimination. You can read more about this in Chapter 15.*

### Good practice in equal opportunities

The Sex Discrimination Act established the Equal Opportunities Commission (EOC) and the Race Relations Act established the Commission for Racial Equality (CRE) to promote and monitor equality of opportunity. As part of that duty, the EOC produced a code of practice in 1985 and the RRA produced a code of practice in 1984.

The codes provide guidelines to employers and employees on the meaning of the relevant legislation, on practical measures that can be taken to eliminate discrimination, and on techniques that can be used to promote equality of opportunity. These guidelines refer to all phases of employment, including the recruitment and selection stages. The commissions also give advice to employers as well as dealing with complaints from those who feel they have encountered discrimination. The commissions may decide to take a complaint to an Employment Tribunal.

The EOC and CRE can also issue a non-discrimination notice against employers if they investigate a complaint and find that there is evidence of discrimination in an employer's actions, whether intentional or unintentional. A non-discrimination notice may oblige an employer to inform the EOC and CRE about changes it has initiated to bring its employment practices more in line with the codes of practice.

Essentially, to operate within the spirit of the SDA and RRA, all actions and documents involved in the recruitment process must be free of any criteria that could be interpreted as being discriminatory within the terms of the legislation. Advertisements, job descriptions and person specifications must not include anything that could be construed as an intention to discriminate on an unlawful basis.

Advertisements should not include words that might indicate a preference for hiring females rather than males or vice versa. For instance, it is not lawful for a restaurant to advertise for waitresses as this would imply that men could not apply for these posts. This would be direct discrimination on the basis of sex.

> **DID YOU KNOW?**
>
> *It is interesting to note that it is generally regarded as unacceptable to request an applicant to attach a photograph to a job application in the UK, whereas this is still common practice in France and Germany. Such a requirement would conflict with the spirit of the UK legislation, as a photograph can only provide information about sex and racial background and not about skills and knowledge. The use of such input can only be seen as unfair discrimination.*

In exceptional circumstances there may be a requirement for an employee of a particular sex or racial background. These are known as genuine occupational qualifications (GOQ). Such requirements are acceptable in instances where authenticity is required, say in entertainment, modelling (for instance male or female fashion clothes) or providing food in ethnic restaurants, and where privacy and decency in the provision of personal services are concerned. An example of a genuine occupational qualification would be to advertise for a female care attendant to provide personal services to a female stroke victim.

Note that the word 'genuine' is used. It is a term that is meant to be narrowly defined and not regarded as a loophole to avoid compliance with the legislation.

Employers are not the only participants in the recruitment process who are bound by the terms of the SDA and the RRA. Publishers of advertisements also have a duty to ensure there is no unlawful discrimination in the advertisements they print. If a particular sex or a member of a particular racial group is required, the publisher must also ensure that a reference to the relevant section of the legislation is included. For instance, an advertisement for a female project leader to provide personal support to young homeless women might carry the statement 'section 7(2)(E) of the Sex Discrimination Act applies'.

Note that the presence of a genuine occupational qualification means not only that persons from the specified group are being invited to apply, but also that such a person will be selected. This is often confused by less informed job-seekers with encouragement for members of under-represented groups to apply for vacancies so they can be considered along with all other qualified applicants in the selection process. You can read more about the recruitment of under-represented groups later in this chapter, under the heading 'targeted recruitment'.

The existence of a good person specification can help an employer to avoid inadvertent sex or race discrimination. The design and use of person specifications was discussed more fully in Chapter 2 and will be addressed again with specific reference to recruitment in the section on procedures. Sex and race discrimination are rarely overtly expressed ('We really don't think a woman can do this job'). The intention to discriminate can be inferred from various events, and introducing new criteria after the person specification has been agreed is one such event.

Companies that wish to promote equality of opportunity can also introduce complaints procedures, so that applicants who feel they may have been discriminated against can appeal in the first instance to the company concerned. This would normally mean that at least one staff member would be designated as responsible for the promotion of equal opportunities, so that applicants felt they were approaching a disinterested person.

### European legislation relating to transsexuals and sexual orientation

A European Court ruling in 1996 specified that sex discrimination laws also apply to transsexuals. This means that employees are protected if they suffer less favourable treatment than other employees because they have undergone, or are undergoing, a change in gender.

In spite of this judgement, the European Court of Justice ruled on 2 February 1998 that South West Trains did not breach European equality laws when they refused Linda Grant, a railway worker, travel concessions for her partner Jill Perry. The judges at the European Court ruled that the transsexual case only applied when there was a change from one sex to another, but did not apply to questions of sexual orientation. The European Court felt that although Ms Grant did not receive the same perks from the rail company as a heterosexual couple working for the railway, she was nevertheless not being directly discriminated against since a male gay couple would have been treated in exactly the same manner. South West Trains claimed that their policy not to award equal travel concessions was not discrimination on the grounds of sex, but was based on sexual orientation which is not at present covered by European Community laws. There is likely to be continued pressure, however, on governments now to outlaw discrimination against gays. There is also scope under the Treaty of Amsterdam for a new article in the EC treaty allowing action to eliminate discrimination.

### Equal Pay Act 1970

Most problems related to issues covered by the Equal Pay Act and its subsequent amendments tend to arise once people are in employment and can compare their pay with that of other employees in the same organisation. The act provides for members of one sex to claim equal pay with a member of the opposite sex who is doing like work, or work of a different nature which can be shown to be similar in terms of the requirements for skill and effort, i.e. work of equal value. The Equal Pay Act is dealt with in more detail in Chapter 10, which examines payment systems and the evaluation of jobs. The major point here is that it would be unlawful to advertise different pay rates for men and women doing the same work, or to offer employees of one sex disadvantageous terms and conditions.

### The Disability Discrimination Act 1995

The Disability Discrimination Act 1995 (DDA) updated and replaced previous legislation relating to disabled people. Disability is defined under the Act as 'a mental or physical impairment which has a substantial and long-term adverse effect on a person's ability to carry out normal day-to-day activities. People who have a disability, and people who have had a disability, but no longer have one, are covered by the Act' (Minister for Disabled People, 1996).

Under the Act employers no longer have to have 3% of their workforce who are registered as disabled, but instead new rights have been created for those with disabilities. While these rights do not go as far as many would have liked, they nevertheless do provide a basis for improvements in various areas including employment. In relation to employment, job applicants should not be discriminated against because of a disability or be treated in a less favourable way than other applicants unless 'the treatment in question is justified'. While it is disappointing to find that opportunities for less favourable treatment towards disabled people can sometimes be justifiable under the Act , nevertheless this is the first legislation to give disabled people rights not to actually be discriminated against because of their disability. It has also established, for the first time, the right for anyone who feels that they have suffered discrimination because of a disability to take their case to an Employment Tribunal.

The DDA also makes it clear that employers of 20 or more people must 'make reasonable adjustments in any arrangements or to work premises' in order that disabled employees should not be disadvantaged. This could have a substantial impact on opportunities for people with disabilities to gain employment, since no longer can employers justify their failure to employ a disabled person by saying that they cannot modify the premises or work practices. Under the DDA they must consider making these modifications.

**DID YOU KNOW?**
*More people acquire disabilities as they get older than are born with them. (Social Trends, 1996.)*

The DDA not only applies to employment, but also affects any organisation which provides a service to the public. Such organisations must under the Act make reasonable adjustments to their premises or to the way in which they provide services in order to accommodate the needs of disabled people.

The DDA has been criticised for its narrow definition of disability, based as it is on medical rather than social models of disabilities. It has also been criticised for failing to establish any body specifically set up to champion the rights of the disabled in the way that the Equal Opportunities Commission and the Commission for Racial Equality can regarding sex discrimination and racial issues respectively. There have also been criticisms as the DDA only applies to

**DID YOU KNOW?**
*People with disabilities at work have the same productivity levels as the general population, a better than average safety record, and lower rates of absenteeism and sickness. (P. Prescott-Clarke, 1990.)*

organisations which employ more than 20 employees, and merely says that as a question of good practice, small employers should be encouraged to follow the Act's provisions voluntarily. At the time of writing this is subject to a review and consultation process with small employers.

### Rehabilitation of Offenders Act 1974

The Rehabilitation of Offenders Act 1974 stipulates a range of time periods after which convictions for various offences are regarded as being spent. This means that a past offender should not be expected to reveal his or her offence once the conviction is spent, and should not be denied employment because of this previous offence. An offence that attracts a sentence of life imprisonment or a sentence of more than 30 months' imprisonment is never spent. The time periods over which convictions do become spent vary from 10 years for a prison sentence of 6 to 30 months to 1 year for a probation order (longer if the order covers a longer period) to the period of a disqualification for driving. You will find a more detailed table in *Tolley's Employment Handbook* (Slade and Giffin, latest edition). A number of exceptions to these rules about spent convictions apply to people who in the course of their jobs have unsupervised access to minors, meaning that for this category of employee certain convictions can never be regarded as spent. An example of this is explored more fully in Chapter 5.

### Non-legislated unfair discrimination

As well as the groups that are identified and protected by legislation, there are many human characteristics that render people prone to discrimination. Recruiters are no more free from personal biases than other people; the important thing is to be aware of them and recognise that such criteria have nothing to do with selecting a person for a job. Many of these biases will have most impact at the selection stage when the parties first meet face-to-face. In Chapter 4 you will find a list of biases that may amuse you; there is, however, one prejudice against which there is currently no legislation in Britain, and which is seen frequently at the recruitment stage: discrimination on the basis of age.

**DID YOU KNOW?**
*In 1996, the publishers of* People Management *adopted a policy of refusing to publish employment advertisements that stipulate age ranges in order to exclude applications.* (People Management, *11 January 1996, p. 22.)*

Advertisements are still often seen that stipulate an age range for the ideal candidate, usually between the ages of 25 and 35. There is a range of very questionable assumptions behind this about the normal progression one might expect in a person's career and about the abilities and attitudes of persons over the age of 35. The IPM issued a statement on age and employment (1991, p. 6) which condemns age discrimination in the following terms.

> The use of age, age bands, age guides and age related criteria reduces objectivity in employment decision making. It increases the likelihood of poor quality and inappropriate decisions which are harmful to individuals and wasteful of people's skills.

**PAUSE FOR THOUGHT 3.2** *Setting age limits such as 17–28 for applicants could prove to constitute indirect sex discrimination against women. Why is this so?*

Setting upper age limits for applicants can be indirect sex discrimination, as women are more likely to take a career break for reasons of maternity in their twenties and early thirties and are therefore likely to progress through their careers at a different rate. This means that women of this age are less able to apply for such posts than men of this age.

It should also be noted that companies such as B&Q have had success through deliberately hiring older workers and benefiting from their particular expertise.

ACTIVITY **3.2**

Mrs Meninder Patel applied for a post as a careers officer with a local authority. The advertisement and person specification for the post had listed three years' experience in careers advice as one of the criteria being sought, and Mrs Patel had worked as a careers officer in local schools for four years. The careers service received a number of good applications and the selection panel had difficulty in shortlisting a small number of applicants to call for interview. After some deliberation they decided that they would interview those candidates who had experience dealing with adults, because the careers service was going to expand into this area and the panel decided that this specific experience would be valuable. Mrs Patel was not one of the applicants called to interview. She felt that she was well qualified for the post according to the advertisement and the job description and person specification that had been sent to her. Mrs Patel felt that she must have been discriminated against unfairly and decided to pursue the matter.

Comment on the equal opportunities implications of this case. Why might Mrs Patel feel that she has been the victim of unlawful discrimination? What should the local authority do?

### *Discussion of Activity 3.2*

In times of high unemployment it is common to find large numbers of people applying for vacancies. It is difficult to achieve the correct balance between a tight person specification and one that excludes people unnecessarily. But introducing criteria after applications are in could be seen as an attempt to exclude people for covert reasons, e.g. to exclude women or certain racial groups. Depending on who was ultimately hired for this post, Mrs Patel could believe that she had been discriminated against because of her sex, marital status or ethnic origin.

Let us assume that there was no discriminatory intent on the part of the selection panel and that they were merely seeking a device to enable them to carry out the shortlisting exercise. The case points out the importance of developing a good person specification in the first place, and the equal opportunities implications that this can have.

The local authority should ensure that there is an adequate internal mechanism for dealing with Mrs Patel's query. The fact that an employer tries to address any problems of this nature in a sincere fashion would be recognised by the EOC and CRE as part of good equal opportunities practice.

The employer should also ensure that training is provided to all employees involved in recruitment and selection to ensure that they understand the importance of each element of the process.

### Managing diversity in the workplace

Some organisations go much further than mere compliance with legislation as they are keen to promote the concept of diversity in the workplace. According to the IPD (1997) managing diversity means 'that people should be valued as individuals for reasons relating to business interests, as well as for moral and social reasons. It recognises that people can bring fresh ideas and perceptions which can make the way work is done more efficient and products and services better.'

**PAUSE FOR THOUGHT 3.3**  *In what ways is this different to the legislative approach to equal opportunities? How would this approach manifest itself within an organisation?*

### Discussion of Pause for Thought 3.3

There are some quite fundamental differences in this approach. Firstly all differences are recognised, not just differences based on race, sex or age. These include differences such as academic or vocational qualifications, social background, accent and political views. There is also another fundamental difference in approach in that the differences are perceived as positive; there is a recognition that everyone is different and as each person is unique they also bring a unique range of talents to the organisation from which the organisation will benefit. The organisation, therefore, needs to develop a culture that is supportive of individual differences so that creativity and innovation will flourish. Workplace policies and procedures also need to be continuously reviewed to ensure that they are not inadvertently providing barriers to opportunities.

In order for managing diversity to work there must be involvement from a wide range of people from the Chief Executive and the Board through to the human resource manager and the line managers. According to the IPD, 'Managing diversity needs to become a mainstream issue which influences all employment policies and working practices.'

### Recruitment procedures

The description of recruitment procedures has been preceded by the discussion of equal opportunities issues because these issues should guide your actions at every stage of the recruitment process.

The first step in the recruitment process is to decide that you have a vacancy you wish to fill. The vacancy may be a new post that has been identified through the corporate strategic plan, or it may have arisen because an employee has resigned, retired or been dismissed. The latter are sometimes referred to as replacement posts to distinguish them from new posts. You may also decide to recruit a job-share partner for an established employee who no longer wishes to work full time.

The planning process that precedes the creation of new posts was described in Chapter 2. A planning process should also precede recruitment for replacement posts; they should not be filled automatically. When a jobholder leaves, HR and line managers should take the opportunity to examine the work done and consider whether it can be covered in another fashion. Here are some of the factors that could be considered:

➤ Are all the tasks necessary?
➤ Can some tasks be incorporated into another post?
➤ Should the job be redesigned to include more interesting and challenging work?
➤ Can some tasks be completed in other ways, e.g. by machine, by computer?
➤ Can the work be done on a part-time, flexi-time or job-share basis?
➤ Is there a permanent need for the output of the post or should it be filled on a temporary basis or even contracted out?

Recruitment procedures include:

➤ preparation of all supporting documents such as job descriptions and person specifications
➤ guidelines on actions to be taken such as writing and placing advertisements, and administrative procedures related to contacting prospective candidates.

## *Job descriptions and person specifications*

In companies that engage in human resource planning there will be ongoing work dedicated to producing and maintaining job descriptions and person specifications, since these documents contain much of the information required for the planning process. The process of job analysis which is followed to produce these documents was therefore described in Chapter 2. However, even in companies that do not engage fully in human resource planning, it is essential to produce job descriptions and person specifications for all existing posts as a basic framework for recruitment activities. These two documents contain the information around which the job advertisement and the assessment of candidates will be structured. If you have not read the section on job analysis in Chapter 2, you should read it now.

### The job description in the recruitment context

We have seen already (p. 32) that the four basic elements of the job description are: the job title; the reporting structure, i.e. the job title of the person to whom the postholder reports and the number and categories of the people the postholder is responsible for; a statement of the purpose of the post; and a description of the major duties. Taken together, they should provide a job applicant with a good idea of what the job entails.

The job title, such as sales assistant, warehouse supervisor, marketing department manager or nurse, already contains a lot of information about the position. In choosing a job title you should be careful not to inflate the level of the job, for instance by the use of words such as executive or director, and you should avoid any potentially biased language such as waitress and foreman.

The information given in the sections on reporting structure enables applicants to see where the job fits into the organisation's structure and whether the post has any supervisory responsibilities. If there are particularly pertinent details about terms and conditions, such as shift work or a requirement to work on Sundays, they should also be included since this will enable candidates to judge whether they are willing to take on such responsibilities.

**The person specification in the recruitment context**

The very fact that an employer draws up a person specification demonstrates an attempt to introduce some objectivity into what can otherwise be a very subjective process. Rather than relying on instinctive personal judgements about the knowledge, skills and qualities the successful candidate should possess, the employer with a person specification is following a much more methodical and reasoned process. It is also a much more open process, since the specification is a written record of what the employer is basing his/her selection decision on. These written records can be requested by Employment Tribunals should anyone complain of unfair treatment, but many employers now share this information openly with applicants for posts, so applicants also know in detail what the employer is looking for in a candidate.

Care should therefore be taken that no-one is unfairly excluded from being considered for a position because the requirements were set unnecessarily high. This could constitute indirect discrimination, as certain disadvantaged groups may have more difficulty in acquiring some qualifications. Care should also be taken that none of the criteria set are directly unlawfully discriminatory.

The information about skills, knowledge and personal qualities should be summarised and included in advertisements for the post.

As mentioned above, the person specification can be included with the information sent to candidates to give them more details about requirements. It is an excellent practice to design and send to candidates a form showing each requirement and how it will be assessed, e.g. from information included on the application form, at the interview, or from references. Table 3.2 shows an example of this, based on the person specification for a receptionist which is given in Chapter 2 (Table 2.1).

### Job advertisements

Once you know you have a vacancy to fill, you must decide what is the best way to let people know about it. The following are some methods of advertising the existence of vacancies:

- ➤ company noticeboards
- ➤ local/national newspapers
- ➤ professional journals
- ➤ minority group newspapers and magazines
- ➤ recruitment agencies
- ➤ university/college/school careers centres
- ➤ job centres
- ➤ radio/television (including text pages)/cinema
- ➤ Internet sites
- ➤ set up a stall at a recruitment fair or exhibition.

**table 3.2**

**Assessment of person specification criteria**

**Post: Receptionist**

| Attributes | Criteria | How assessed |
|---|---|---|
| Knowledge | Knowledge of clerical systems | Application form<br>Interview<br>Work sample test |
| | Knowledge of the company | Interview |
| Skills | Experience of clerical work | Application form<br>Interview<br>Work sample test |
| | Experience of handling queries in person and on the telephone | Application form<br>Interview |
| | Ability to extract information from a computerised database | Application form<br>Interview |
| | Supervisory experience | Application form<br>Interview |
| Personal Qualities | Polite manner | Interview |
| | Ability to work under pressure | Interview |

## Deciding where to place an advertisement

You will need to assess the available advertising methods in terms of their appropriateness for a particular vacancy. Considerations will include the likelihood of finding people with particular skills in a particular geographical location; the type of qualifications you are seeking and which publications people with those qualifications are likely to read; salary level and whether you are likely to be able to attract someone to move to your area for the salary you are offering. Obviously some judgement is required to make these decisions, but one should always be wary of making assumptions about what people will do given their personal circumstances, and one should strive to keep recruitment open and fair. It may be unfair, for instance, to restrict applications to your geographical area as there may be good candidates who would be willing to move to your area for the sake of the job. That should remain the personal decision of the prospective candidate.

> **DID YOU KNOW?**
> Suffering from a shortage of school teachers, the Department for Education and Employment launched a series of advertisements in cinemas and on television in the late 1990s. Designed to catch the attention of young people making career direction decisions, the advertisement used sound-bites from well-known personalities (e.g. Tony Blair, Stephen Hawking, Joanna Lumley) naming teachers who had had a positive influence on them, and ending with the catchphrase: 'No-one forgets a good teacher'.

The costs of advertising are also a factor. You may be more willing to spend a large portion of your advertising budget on a senior post than on a junior one. However, you may have a relatively junior post that requires skills not readily available in your locality, or you may have a large number of low-paid posts and the need to fill these posts may call for the willingness to spend more on advertising.

Word-of-mouth advertising is often listed in textbooks as a possible method of recruitment, and it is used to varying extents in some companies. It is mentioned here for clarification but excluded from the recommended list because of its potentially discriminatory effects. Companies that recruit heavily by word of mouth run the risk of perpetuating the gender and ethnic make-up of their workforce. In general, employees tend to recommend people like themselves from among their family and friends. For example, in general, if a company's workforce were all white Europeans, word-of-mouth recruitment would tend to bring in more white Europeans. A commitment to equality of opportunity means that this cycle has to be broken, and one way of doing this is to advertise in the ethnic press.

New methods of recruitment can evolve or be designed to meet the requirements of new situations. Many information technology posts, and increasingly a range of other posts too, are now being advertised on the Internet and accessed directly through individuals' personal computers. Vacancies are listed by some companies on their own web site and in other cases by recruitment agencies.

> **DID YOU KNOW?**
>
> *The BBC is maintaining a database of electronically submitted CVs which can be matched with suitable vacancies as they arise. For more information, visit their web site at www.bbc.co.uk/onlinetalent. (People Management, 28 May 1998, p. 11.)*

One advantage of using a web site for recruitment purposes is that companies can provide easy access to a lot of information for prospective candidates. You can easily find some current job advertisements that include an Internet address and visit the site to see for yourself how employers are using the world-wide web for recruitment. Human resource managers need to be aware of innovations such as this to maximise the effectiveness of their recruitment process.

### Designing recruitment advertisements

First consider what the objectives of a job advertisement are, and what techniques might be used to achieve those objectives. The overall aim of the advertisement is to secure sufficient applications from suitably qualified persons with the end result that the employer will find 'the best person for the job'. Note that advertisers wish to obtain a reasonable number of applications, and not an overwhelming number. The first principle of writing job advertisements is therefore to *give sufficient information about the post so that suitable candidates will apply* but also so that *unsuitable candidates will be discouraged from applying*.

What will attract good applicants to a post? Consider these factors and also consider how they should be incorporated into an advertisement to achieve maximum impact. For example, is salary a major selling point for your company? Should salary figures be included or excluded? Should they be displayed at the top of the advertisement, in the body of the text or at the end? A job advertisement is an opportunity to tell people what you can offer as well as what you require. The following are some suggestions of the kind of factors you may wish to include in a job advertisement:

➤ company name and information
➤ job title and major duties
➤ qualifications, skills and experience required

- opportunities and challenges
- salary and benefits
- statement of policy on important issues such as equal opportunities and smoking in the workplace
- how to apply.

*Company name and information*
Obviously people need to know whom they are applying to. Information about the company's prospects and what it can offer as an employer can be a selling point.

**PAUSE FOR THOUGHT 3.4** *Where will you find a record of the information you should include relating to the job title, duties, skills and experience?*

*Job title and major duties*
The job title should be the one used in the job description, and the main duties should be summarised for the advertisement.

*Qualifications, skills and experience required*
The person specification will provide a good basis for summarising the qualifications, skills and experience you are looking for.

*Opportunities and challenges*
The tasks in a job can be described as requirements, but it is much more appealing to most people if you emphasise the opportunities a job will offer them to use their skills and feel a sense of achievement, and the challenges that will provide them with a chance to develop.

**DID YOU KNOW?**
*The Institute of Practitioners in Advertising (IPA) and the Institute of Personnel and Development (IPD) annually offer awards for excellence in recruitment advertisements. Previous winners include: Saatchi and Saatchi Advertising; Park Human Resources; Macmillan Davies Hodes.*

*Salary and benefits*
Every organisation will have records of the salary ranges and benefits that are attached to each job. A company might have a particularly attractive range of benefits that could be the deciding factor for someone deliberating on whether or not to apply for a position. You can read more about salaries and benefits in Chapter 10.

*How to apply*
A range of possibilities exist, and the most appropriate will depend on the particular post being filled, the volume of applications expected or desired, and the systems and capabilities of the department receiving the applications. You may request interested applicants to do any of the following:

- call in person
- attend an open day interview event
- phone/leave a message on a 24 hour answerphone
- write a letter applying for the post

➤ contact a particular person
➤ request and return an application form
➤ request further information
➤ send a curriculum vitae (CV) and covering letter
➤ send a CV or acquire and return an application form by computer
➤ apply by a certain date.

*Information packages*
Information packages are usually prepared for more senior posts, and contain brochures and other documents that give a range of information about the post, the company, and possibly the attractions of moving to the geographical location the company is in.

ACTIVITY **3.3**
················

1  Draft a letter to accompany a requested application form.
2  Design a recruitment package for a real or imaginary company of your choice.

### Discussion of Activity 3.3

You will find a model letter in Appendix 3.1 to compare with your draft. Designing a recruitment package is a major undertaking. You may wish to work with a group of fellow students to pool your resources. You could choose a currently advertised vacancy to base your recruitment package on, and use the resources of your library to find out more about the company.

### Style of writing

The style of writing that is appropriate for a job advertisement depends on the nature of the position. Traditionally, advertisements were written in a very formal style, using phrases like: 'The successful candidate will possess a university degree and two years of directly related work experience.' In recent years most advertisements have been written in a less formal and more direct style, using 'you' as if the recruiter were speaking directly to the prospective applicant.

Other techniques that have been used to attract the reader's attention are the use of questions and bold or controversial statements such as:

Are you looking for your next challenge and an opportunity to develop your project management skills?
or
You'd have to be crazy to take on this job!
or
We can offer you long hours and tiring days ... but plenty of rewards too.

These are acceptable techniques for producing job advertisements, but care should be taken that they are not overused, thereby losing their freshness and impact. A list of questions at the start of an advert can become tedious. Once you've caught your reader's attention, you should proceed swiftly to giving information. You should also avoid using hackneyed phrases, clichés or essentially meaningless phrases. Most employers would like to employ enthusiastic, intelligent, well-motivated and outgoing people. However, since practically no-one is likely to admit to not being any of these, it seems pointless to include them as criteria in a job advertisement, as they help neither qualified persons to identify themselves nor unsuitable persons to screen themselves out.

### Job advertisements: whose responsibility?

Earlier in this chapter we considered who should participate in writing job descriptions. Now consider who should be responsible for producing job advertisements.

Is the post of a routine nature, with simple duties or a job description that has not changed much? Does a previous advert exist that can be used without much change? A junior member of the HRM department could handle this or the administrative staff in any unit where this activity has been devolved to line management.

If the post is new or has changed considerably, the line manager should be more involved in deciding the content, and more expertise in composing advertisements will be needed so someone with more experience in this area and well-developed writing skills should take on the task.

If the post is difficult to recruit for (maybe due to a local skills shortage), you may consider using the specialised skills of a recruitment advertising agency. The additional cost of this would be a factor to weigh against the cost of unsuccessful recruitment attempts.

If you have any doubts about your writing ability, get help! Advertisements are very expensive and very public, and can contribute to the public image of your company. If the requisite skill is not available within your company, you may have to consider using the services of an advertising agency.

ACTIVITY **3.4**
..............

You have retained the services of a recruitment advertising agency and are discussing the content of an advertisement for a senior administrative post with them. They are trying to get a good picture of what you want for this post, and they ask you what age range you have in mind. You tell them that you do not wish to discriminate on the basis of age, but they are pretty insistent that it will help them to picture in their minds what kind of person you are looking for.

1   How will you respond now? Discuss your response and the reasons for it with others in your class.
2   Assuming that you are determined to resist the request of the recruitment agency and wish to convince them that your approach is correct, list the arguments that you could present to them.

### *Discussion of Activity 3.4*

Arguments could include:

➤  an ethical stance that eschews any inappropriate form of discrimination, especially if you are a member of the IPD
➤  specific arguments about age discrimination – age is not related to the skills and qualities desired
➤  a reminder that you are the client and are ultimately in control of and responsible for the outcome of the advertising campaign.

### Targeted recruitment

The Sex Discrimination Act, Race Relations Act and Disability Discrimination Act are designed to protect specified groups against unfair discrimination in employment. What they do not prescribe is affirmative action to redress any imbalance that may have been caused by discriminatory practices prior to the legislation's coming into force. Targeted recruitment is a method of encouraging previously disadvantaged groups to apply for vacancies but, in keeping with the intention of equal opportunities legislation, any subsequent selection must be based on merit only.

Targeted recruitment can take several forms:

➤ A statement that encourages underrepresented groups to apply for a post, for example: 'We welcome applications from people with disabilities, women, and members of black and ethnic minority groups as they are under-represented in the company in positions at this level.'
➤ Photographs and text that show people in non-traditional roles, thus emphasising an employer's desire to receive applications from groups that do not traditionally apply for particular posts.
➤ An assurance that qualified candidates with a disability will be invited to interview.
➤ Photographs showing a mix of men, women and members of various racial groups.

Employers who engage in targeted recruitment have recognised that good, able people have become discouraged from even applying for jobs because of a history of discrimination. A number of such companies were profiled in a *Personnel Management* article (Paddison, 1990). The experience of these companies was that targeted recruitment attracted a much greater pool of suitable candidates, and not only from the specified groups. There was an overall improvement in the quality of applications. Targeted recruitment, then, speaks loudly about a company's level of commitment to equal opportunities, but a side-effect is that it also attracts applications from better candidates in general.

### Application forms

Once you have provided people with information about your vacancy, you must decide on the best way for interested candidates to present information about themselves. The major choices are:

➤ application form
➤ curriculum vitae (CV)    } submitted on paper or electronically
➤ letter of application
➤ handwritten/typed submission
➤ personal call.

Many companies prefer to use their own application form because of the advantages this can offer. Application forms can be designed to elicit information specific to the types of work done in your company. The information can be arranged so that very important information is seen first, for example, academic qualifications or membership of professional bodies without which a person could not be considered for particular posts. One advantage of application forms over CVs is that the company controls the information that is given, not the applicant. In this way the company can ensure that the same types of information are gathered from all applicants, that the information is relevant to the work the company can offer, and that information that could potentially lead to unlawful discrimination is excluded.

The application form is a bridge between the recruitment process and the selection process. Once a completed form has been received, it can be used as a basis for the initial selection exercise, but until this occurs, it is part of the recruitment process and its design should be subject to recruitment considerations. A poorly designed form – one, for instance, that requests inappropriate information – could alienate potential applicants and discourage some from applying.

When deciding which information to obtain from job applicants you can submit your queries to two tests.

1   Will this query result in information that can be construed as discriminatory in a way that is unlawful according to employment legislation?
2   Will this query elicit information that is strictly related to the applicant's ability to do the job as reflected in the skills, qualifications and personal qualities outlined in the person specification?

If your query passes these two tests, you can be assured that you are not infringing the equal opportunities laws and that you are on the way to recruiting in a fair manner. This issue will be of great importance once you are involved in the selection processes, but it needs to be kept in mind at all stages of the recruitment process and may, for instance, influence the way you design your application form.

**PAUSE FOR THOUGHT 3.5**   *Can you think of any kinds of information that some managers might be tempted to find out, but are considered as inappropriate in terms of equal opportunities legislation?*

Many managers feel that they need to know details about a candidate's personal circumstances in order to judge whether or not the candidate will be able to fulfil the requirements of the job. They want to know, for instance, whether a person is married, especially in the case of young women. The implication is that a young woman may become pregnant and either leave or have to be temporarily replaced. They may also wish to know how old a person's children are. Again this information can be interpreted in a fashion that is discriminatory against women, as there is an assumption that they will be responsible for child care, and that any problems such as a child being ill will lead to the woman's taking time off work. Application forms should not request details about dependants or marital status.

You should consider the following criteria when designing an application form:

➤   the layout should be clear and simple, be easy to fill in, provide adequate space for information, make it obvious where details are to be entered
➤   the language used should be clear and unambiguous
➤   the form should be capable of acquiring a range of information about qualifications and skills for a variety of jobs

➤ applicants should not have to repeat details
➤ you should be aware of equal opportunities implications – ask only for relevant information; do not ask for potentially discriminatory information
➤ you should provide applicants with an opportunity to give all relevant information supporting their application
➤ applicants should not feel confused or irritated by questions on the form
➤ you should ensure that the purpose and use of equal opportunities monitoring information is clear.

Although we have presented the advantages of using an application form, there are some advantages to using CVs too. If an advertisement required all applicants to submit a CV, the organisation would have eliminated the step, and therefore the cost, of sending out application forms. It must be remembered, however, that designing a CV requires a fairly good standard of writing skills, so it would not be appropriate to require this for all positions. Many advertisements for managerial posts request interested candidates to apply by sending in a CV.

ACTIVITY **3.5**

1  Choose an employer and design an application form that could be used for all posts with that company. Check that your form elicits all relevant information from applicants. Consider the design and layout of your application form: is it easy to complete; is it easy for selectors to locate relevant information?
2  Compare your application form with the sample form given in Activity 4.3.

**Equal opportunities implications**

In order to promote access to jobs, employers may wish to assist those with poor language skills in completing application forms. There are many posts where the duties to be performed do not require the levels of reading, writing and language ability that are necessary for a person to be able to complete an application form. Positive measures so that such people are not unfairly excluded from such posts would be an example of good practice and could lead to a company's acquiring committed employees.

Many application forms now contain an equal opportunities monitoring section so that employers can evaluate their success in attracting applications from qualified members of designated groups, and also monitor the handling of these applications at all stages of the selection process. The information on this form should be used only to provide feedback to the company that it is operating in a non-discriminatory fashion, and should not be used as part of the selection process. It is best if the monitoring form can be detached from the application form so that it is clear to applicants that the monitoring and selection processes are completely separate. Monitoring forms usually request information about sex, marital status, ethnic origin and disability, since these are directly addressed in the legislation on discrimination. You will find a sample monitoring form on the final page of the application form in Figure 4.2, where you will notice that we have also decided to monitor age as a matter of good practice.

### *Administrative procedures*

The final aspect of the recruitment process we need to consider is how you are going to handle applications. You will need to design administrative procedures that address the following issues:

➤ accepting applications by phone/walk in
➤ sending forms/information
➤ acknowledgement of applications received.

In deciding on the appropriate administrative procedures you will need to address questions about what you want to achieve, but also the question of cost. There is a public relations element in every recruitment exercise, as your company will have contact with many people who will not become employees, but who may be potential customers and who will certainly relate to others how you treated them. You will want to create a good impression with every applicant, but the desire to do this must be tempered by the question of cost. Many companies are now alerting potential applicants that they will not receive an acknowledgement of receipt of their application form due to rising postal costs and the numbers of applications expected. A sample letter can be found in Appendix 3.1, but one alternative is to include a statement on the application form as you can see on the sample form in Activity 4.3.

## Conclusion
..............

This chapter has discussed the aims of recruitment and examined the impact of legal, moral and business issues on decisions made about the recruitment process. The particular importance of equality of opportunity in employment has been explained.

We have reviewed the range of policies and procedures involved in effective recruitment and emphasised the need for a methodical approach, using job descriptions, person specifications and well-designed advertisements and application forms to support the process. The next two chapters will examine the processes and techniques involved in making a selection from the applications you receive.

**REVIEW QUESTIONS**

You will find brief answers to review questions 1, 3 and 5 on pages 421–422.

1   Outline the major legislative factors that affect the recruitment process. What can a company do to ensure it is an equal opportunities employer?
2   Choose five current advertisements for job vacancies from different sources. Comment on the structure, content and placement of the adverts, evaluate their effectiveness, and suggest improvements.
3   Describe the uses of the job description and person specification in the recruitment process.
4   Interview someone about his/her job. Draft a job description, person specification and advertisement for the post.
5   Comment on the approaches to recruitment an employer can adopt in order to create and project a positive public image.

**SELF-CHECK QUESTIONS**

Answer the following multiple choice and short answer questions. The correct responses or page references are given on page 422 for you to check your understanding of this chapter.

1  Which of the following are the laws that protect groups against unfair discrimination in Britain?

  (*a*)  Equal Opportunities Act; Disability Discrimination Act; Race Relations Act.

  (*b*)  Disabilities Act; Race Relations Act; Equal Opportunities Act.

  (*c*)  Sex Discrimination Act; Race Relations Act; Disability Discrimination Act.

  (*d*)  Anti Sex Discrimination Act; Disabilities Act; Racial Discrimination Act.

2  Which of the following is not an example of a GOQ?

  (*a*)  An Indian person to wait on tables in an Indian restaurant.

  (*b*)  A man to cut hair in a men's hair stylist's shop.

  (*c*)  A woman to provide personal care to a woman with multiple sclerosis.

3  Which of the following types of discrimination is NOT unlawful in Britain?

  (*a*)  Discrimination on the basis of age.

  (*b*)  Discrimination against married persons.

  (*c*)  Discrimination on racial grounds.

4  You have interviewed a 25-year-old man called John Brooker for a position as a truck driver delivering goods from a soft drinks manufacturer to major retail outlets in England and Wales. Because you are concerned about the potential for theft, you asked during the interview, 'Do you have any criminal convictions?', to which he replied 'No'. You consider that he is well qualified and able to do the job. On the morning that you are going to phone and offer him the job, a colleague stops by your office and says, 'By the way, did you know that Johnny Brooker was once put on probation for stealing somebody's welfare cheque? I think he was about 19 at the time.'

  (*a*)  Will you still offer the job to John?

  (*b*)  Was John dishonest in denying that he had a criminal conviction?

5  List three things you'd consider when deciding whether or not a vacancy exists.

6  Name three standard methods of advertising vacant posts.

7  List the major components you would include in a job advert.

8  Does targeted recruitment mean that members of under-represented groups will be selected in preference to other candidates (YES or NO)?

9  Everyone involved in selecting candidates should see the equal opportunities monitoring form. TRUE or FALSE?

10  List the major ways in which people can submit their applications for vacant posts.

## References

Central Statistical Office. *Social Trends 26*. HMSO, 1996.

Institute of Personnel and Development. *Managing Diversity: An IPD Position Paper*. IPD, January 1997.

Institute of Personnel Management. *Age and Employment: An IPM Statement*. IPM, 1991.

Minister for Disabled People. *The Disability Discrimination Act, Employment DL70: Disability on the Agenda*. April 1996.

Paddison, Lorraine. The targeted approach to recruitment. *Personnel Management*, November 1990, pp. 54–58.

Prescott-Clarke, P. *Employment and Handicap*. Social and Community Planning Research, 1990.

Slade, Elizabeth A and Giffin, Nigel D. *Tolley's Employment Handbook*. Tolley Publishing Company, latest edition.

## Further study
● ● ● ● ● ● ● ● ● ● ● ● ● ● ● ●

### *Books*

Advisory, Conciliation and Arbitration Service. *Recruitment and Induction*. ACAS, 1997. (One of the advisory booklets, that provide succinct advice on good practice.)

Cascio, Wayne F. Recruitment and initial screening, In: *Applied Psychology in Personnel Management*. 4th edition. Prentice Hall, 1991.

Commission for Racial Equality. *Code of Practice for the Elimination of Racial Discrimination and the Promotion of Equality of Opportunity in Employment*. CRE, 1984.

Courtis, John. *Recruiting for Profit*. Institute of Personnel Management, 1989.

Courtis, John. *Recruitment Advertising. Right First Time*. IPD, 1994. (Courtis writes in a humorous style based on many years of experience as a recruitment and selection consultant. He makes many interesting points worth noting and considering.)

Employment Department. *Equality Pays: How Equal Opportunities Can Benefit Your Business. A Guide for Small Employers*. Employment Department, 1995. (An excellent booklet which crystallises the benefits for small enterprises of good practice in equal opportunities.)

Equal Opportunity Commission. *Code of Practice for the Elimination of Discrimination on the Grounds of Sex and Marriage, and the Promotion of Equality of Opportunity in Employment*. EOC, 1985.

Hackett, Penny. Recruitment and Selection. In: *Personnel. The Department at Work*. Chapter 4. Institute of Personnel Management, 1991. (This book is written as a guide for people considering personnel work. It provides a brief overview of the activities involved in various functions and highlights the skills needed by the personnel management specialist to fulfil these functions effectively.)

Herriot, Peter. *Recruitment in the 90s*. Institute of Personnel Management, 1989.

Institute of Personnel Management. *The IPM Equal Opportunities Code*. IPM, 1991.

Institute of Personnel Management. *The IPM Recruitment Code*. IPM, 1990. (The IPD's codes provide an excellent, concise overview of major issues and good practice.)

Minister for Disabled People. *A Brief Guide to the Disability Discrimination Act, DL40: Disability on the Agenda*. 1996

Pitt, Gwyneth. *Cases and Materials in Employment Law*. Pitman, 1994. (An excellent source of information about the laws of discrimination and recent court cases in this area.)

Plumbley, Philip. *Recruitment and Selection*. 5th edition, Institute of Personnel Management, 1991.

Torrington, Derek and Weightman, Jane. *Effective Management: People and Organisation*. 2nd edition, Prentice Hall, 1993. (Chapter 13, 'Equal Opportunities and the Management of Diversity', gives a brief overview of the major forms of stereotyping.)

Slade, Elizabeth A and Giffin, Nigel D. *Tolley's Employment Handbook*. Tolley Publishing Company, latest edition. (This is an excellent reference book on employment law. The sections on equal opportunities issues are very readable. The book is updated fairly frequently, so you should always make sure you are working with the latest edition.)

*Sources of Information and Advice: Employing People with Disabilities*. The Employment Service, 1995.

### Articles

*People Management,* 11 January 1996, 18–23. (A number of articles about age discrimination.)

Recruiters aiming for a wide audience. *Personnel Management*, January 1990, 79. (A very brief case study, reporting the results of a recruitment campaign geared to specific circumstances.)

### Audio-visual

Hackett, Penny. *Personnel. The Department at Work*. Institute of Personnel Management, 1991. (This audiotape develops issues covered in the book of the same title. One section explores the area of recruitment and selection.)

### Internet

Several recruitment agencies are now using the Internet and many newspapers also have pages on it. If you are able to 'surf the net' you may find others. Be very careful to type the Internet address exactly as given, as a full stop or / in the wrong place can cause problems. Interesting sources of information on the Internet that we have checked include the following:

| DATABASE/HOME PAGES | INTERNET ADDRESS |
| --- | --- |
| BBC World of Opportunity (The BBC is one example of a large corporation that regularly advertises job vacancies on its company web site.) | **http://www.bbc.co.uk/jobs/jobnow.htm** |

Career Mosiac
(An Internet employment service
which provides advice on job resumes,
career trends and salaries. Each
organisation has its own page with
details on employment conditions
and company activities.)

**http://www.careermosaic.com/**

Disability issues

**http://www.open.gov.uk**

Price Jamieson
(An international recruitment
agency – jobs updated weekly.)

**http://www.gold.net/PriceJam/**

Monster Board
(A world wide professional
employment and job search agency.)

**http://www.monster.uk/**

The Commission for
Racial Equality

**http://www.open.gov.uk/cre/crehome.htm**

## Appendix 3.1 Sample letter to accompany application form

# XYZ Company
## 1 Company Lane
## Companytown
## XY1 1YZ

Mr D White
3 Candidate's Close
Everytown
EF3 4GH

March 31, 1999

Dear Mr White

Thank you for your query about the post of Marketing Assistant.
Please complete the enclosed application form and return it to
us by April 21, 1999.

We regret that due to increasing postal costs we are unable to
acknowledge receipt of applications. However, if you wish to
enclose a self-addressed and stamped postcard or envelope, we
would be pleased to return this to you to indicate that your
application has been received.

The selection committee will complete its review of all
applications within three weeks of the closing date, and selected
candidates will then be notified of an interview date. We intend
to hold interviews in the week of May 29, 1999.

If you have not heard from us before May 22, 1999, you should
assume that you have not been successful on this occasion.

Yours sincerely


N Barkley
Human Resource Manager

# CHAPTER 4

# Selection: shortlisting and interviews

## Objectives:

*When you have studied this chapter you will be able to:*

➤ explain the aims of the selection process
➤ name and describe the steps that can be taken in the selection process
➤ identify typical interviewer errors and explain how to avoid them
➤ plan an interview process and formulate appropriate questions
➤ conduct an interview, assess the candidates, and record your evaluation
➤ justify your decision and provide feedback to unsuccessful candidates.

A successful recruitment campaign will have resulted in a good number of applications from people who are suitably qualified for your vacancy, and the next task is to select the most suitable person from this number. Employers must consider who should be involved in this task and provide support in terms of policies, procedures and training. This chapter will examine these factors as well as discussing the expertise needed to participate successfully in the selection process.

## Aims and objectives of the selection process

The ultimate goal of selection is usually expressed as 'to choose the best person for the job'. Selectors attempt to predict performance on the job, but they also need to ensure that the suitability of candidates is such that the job is acceptable to them and they are not likely to leave within a short period of time. The objectives of the selection process, which will lead to the fulfilment of the main goal, are as follows:

➤ gather as much relevant information as possible
➤ organise and evaluate the information
➤ assess each candidate
  in order to
➤ forecast performance on the job
  and
➤ give information to applicants
  so that
➤ they can judge whether or not they wish to accept an offer of employment.

## Collecting information

Gathering and evaluating information in order to make the selection decision can be done in a number of stages. The most common methods used include:

➤ shortlisting from information on application forms and CVs
➤ interview
➤ tests
➤ biographical/extended application form
➤ assessment centre
➤ references.

This chapter will deal with shortlisting and interviewing as these two processes tend to be used in almost all cases. Alternative or supplementary methods of gathering information for the selection decision and methods of providing information will be discussed in Chapter 5.

## Policy and procedures

It is amazing how many managers still claim to be good judges of character and ability based on very short acquaintance. These managers will tell you that within a few minutes they can tell whether they are going to get on with someone, and whether that person will do well in the job. This kind of overconfidence is a major contributing factor to the low validity of interviews as a selection method. The concept of validity will be discussed in more detail later in the chapter, but it can be stated here that the HRM approach would suggest that employees are too valuable a resource to be selected or rejected in such a subjective and uninformed manner.

Every effort should be made to design a methodical and objective system for selecting employees. Personal factors and perceptions cannot be totally eliminated, but having objective policies and procedures in place can help to obviate any potentially harmful effects of individual persuasions. Good selection policies and procedures provide guidance and support to line managers and others involved in the selection process to carry out this duty successfully, confident that they are following the tenets of best practice.

Selection policies, like recruitment policies, are a statement of a company's intentions and should normally address such issues as equality of opportunity, maybe giving information about targeted groups. A selection policy might read as follows:

> The objective of the selection process is to obtain employees who will be productive and committed members of staff, working and developing to their full potential. This company will select employees on the basis of merit only. Internal and disabled applicants who have the required knowledge and skills are guaranteed an interview.

Selection procedures should address the following issues:

> ➤ the stages and techniques that should be used
> ➤ who is to be involved in assessing candidates
> ➤ administrative processes.

Several factors would be decided on for each of these issues, and relevant guide-lines provided. The procedures documentation might, for instance, indicate that a shortlist must be prepared and interviews conducted for each vacancy; guidelines might be given on who is to prepare the shortlist and conduct the interviews, and what methods should be used to accomplish these tasks. Further issues to be addressed in selection procedures include: guidelines on non-discriminatory questioning; the appropriateness of testing; whether references should be called and when. All these issues will be addressed in this and the following chapter.

## Shortlisting
. . . . . . . . . . . . . . .

As mentioned earlier, most employers will wish to interview a number of applicants before offering a position. In most instances, however, a successful recruitment campaign will attract more applicants than it would be possible to interview. The first step is therefore to reduce the applications to a manageable number, and this process is known as shortlisting. The shortlisting of applicants is, then, a selection procedure that is usually performed purely on the basis of the written information that applicants have supplied.

Often candidates for a post give information in their applications which is not required for making a selection decision, and which could lead to accusations of unfair discrimination if it were taken into consideration. For instance, candidates might describe their family situation in order to explain a gap in their employment record. Applicants also, obviously, have to give their name so that the company can communicate with them. A name, however, can reveal information that is not apropos to the selection process, such as gender and racial origin. A useful technique to avoid being influenced by such information is to assess the application and make notes that refer only to relevant selection criteria. Furthermore, if these notes refer to the candidates only by their initials, any information that might indicate gender or racial origin is eliminated. If the persons shortlisting refer to these notes instead of the original applications when drawing up the shortlist, they will be greatly assisted in eliminating any unconscious biases.

As well as avoiding criteria that have been designated as unlawfully dis-criminatory, selectors should take care to avoid considering any other criteria that are not strictly related to the candidate's ability to do the job.

**PAUSE FOR THOUGHT 4.1**    *Before you read on about poor practices in selection, can you suggest a methodical approach to shortlisting that would be fair and effective?*

Selectors have been known to introduce a wide range of criteria that reflect their own preconceived ideas about people's circumstances and how people are likely to act in those circumstances. This is a matter of imposing one's own assumptions on other people. Some examples of this are selectors who exclude applicants who do not live locally, assuming they will frequently be late for work or will not wish to relocate; selectors who exclude applicants who are currently earning more than the vacancy offers; selectors who exclude people who are currently unemployed. You should even think twice before rejecting an application simply because the writing is difficult to read. Medical practitioners notoriously have poor handwriting (although this is a stereotypical image and as such should be questioned), yet they hold responsible, professional jobs.

So what is the right way to shortlist applicants? If you have read the chapter on recruitment (Chapter 3), you will remember that certain documents should be available to support the whole of the recruitment and selection process. The person specification, in particular, plays an important role throughout the selection process. Applications should be assessed certainly against the skills and knowledge requirements listed on the person specification, and where possible against the personal qualities, although it may be more practical to assess the latter at the interview stage. Selectors should note where candidates meet the requirements of the person specification and where they lack the required skills and knowledge. Each application could be scored with a series of + and – signs or with numerical grades if you wish to weight the criteria you have selected. To provide you with an example, the application form that appears later in this chapter, in Activity 4.3, has been assessed in relation to the receptionist person specification in chapter two (see Table 4.1).

*table 4.1*
**Assessment of application form (with reference to person specification)**

| Post: Receptionist | | |
|---|---|---|
| | **Essential** | **Desirable** |
| Knowledge | Knowledge of clerical systems + | Knowledge of the company – |
| Skills | Experience of clerical work + Experience in handling queries in person and over the telephone ? Ability to extract information from a computerised database – | Supervisory experience – |
| Personal qualities | Polite manner ? Ability to work under pressure ? | |

**PAUSE FOR THOUGHT 4.2**  *Why do you think some of the skills and personal qualities listed in the person specification in Table 4.1 have been marked with a question mark?*

A preliminary evaluation of most of the skills of the applicant can be made at the shortlisting stage, but in this particular instance it is not possible to judge the applicant's personal qualities, for instance, based on the information contained in the application form. Assessment of these elements will have to be made later in the selection process, and the question marks merely indicate that no assessment can be made at present.

**DID YOU KNOW?**

*Some organisations are beginning to use the Internet in their shortlisting process for graduates. By getting students to complete on-line career and personality questionnaires which are matched against identified competencies, it is claimed that organisations can filter out as many as 90% of applications at a very early stage in the selection procedure. (Jilly Welch reporting on graduate recruitment,* People Management, *28 May 1998, p.14)*

At least two people should undertake to shortlist from the applications received, and they should do this independently of one another. After the initial selection they can then compare their evaluations of applicants, discuss any discrepancies in their judgements and justify the decisions they have made. If the two shortlisters are following the same objective process, there should be a fair amount of agreement about suitable candidates, but the involvement of two people increases the objectivity of the process and helps to eliminate the effects of individual biases. The shortlisters should end up with a ranked list of candidates using the number of pluses and minuses given to each candidate. Typically they will try to obtain six suitable candidates to be invited for interview for a single vacancy, but this number will vary according to circumstances.

## A shortlisting checklist

- At least two people to shortlist applications independently.
- Note where applications meet and fall short of the person specification.
- Separate all applications according to agreed criteria: suitable/possible/unsuitable.
- Rank the suitable applications.
- Shortlisters to confer on person specification criteria only and select suitable number to call for interview.

## Interviewing

Almost every employer includes a face-to-face interview as part of the selection process. The initial selection interview might even be delegated to a recruitment agency or a local job centre, but most employers would be reluctant to take on new employees without having met them first in person. This continues to be the most popular and frequently used method of selection, even though research studies have found interviews to be poor predictors of future performance in a job (Makin and Robertson, 1986). This is referred to as low validity. The poor validity of interviews means that they do not test what they purport to test, i.e. ability to perform a job well. The reasons for this mainly lie with the interviewer concerned. A number of interviewer errors contribute to the low validity of interviews, and awareness of these is one step towards eliminating them or at least reducing their impact.

## Interviewer errors

Interviewer errors arise because of the perceptual process all of us use to deal with the world around us. From the myriad stimuli that surround us, we select those to which we will pay attention. This process is known as perceptual selection, and what we select is determined by our own experience, personality and motivation. This means that we focus on certain aspects of our environment and ignore others. Our own experience etc. might lead us into focusing on inappropriate stimuli in some circumstances and ignoring information that is in fact apposite. A number of such perceptual errors have been identified, and those most relevant to the selection process are described here.

### The halo effect

Some candidates for interview make a very strong impression on the interviewers as soon as they enter the room. They may be well-dressed and attractive, have a firm handshake and a very confident manner. Research has shown that if interviewers form an initial good impression of a candidate, this has two effects. Firstly, this good impression tends to influence positively their interpretation of everything else that happens in the interview. Secondly, the interviewers will seek more positive information to confirm their initial judgement. This is known as the halo effect, but it can also happen with an initial negative impression. This is sometimes referred to as the horns effect and can be detected when interviewers start to seek negative information to confirm their first impressions.

### Making snap decisions

It is often said of interviewers that they make up their minds about a candidate in the first five minutes and then do not change their assessment of that person's suitability. In terms of the perceptual process this means that interviewers are responding to a limited range of stimuli and not taking the opportunity to elicit a wide range of information.

### Hiring people like oneself

There is an innate human tendency to identify with people who are like us and share several of our characteristics. An outgoing person may feel more comfortable with other extroverts and the opposite is true for a more reserved person. These characteristics do not, however, necessarily equate with the ability to perform a job, and it is probably detrimental to a company to have only like-minded people on its staff. If interviewers fall prey to this tendency, they are said to be hiring in their own image.

### Stereotyping

Allowing one's stereotyped images of people to influence selection decisions is probably the most dangerous of the perceptual errors, and could very often equate to racial or sex discrimination. Stereotyping occurs when a person is identified primarily with some group that he or she belongs to and then is assumed to have a range of characteristics that are thought to be common to all members of that group. Racial stereotypes are particularly harmful. Some examples of stereotypes are that Scots are frugal; that all students are irresponsible and lazy; that Americans are brash and loud. It is not possible for all members of a group to have the same characteristics, and we should all guard against forming biases of this nature.

Stereotyping can lead to the rejection of candidates for some very peculiar reasons, for example:

➤ men who wear suede shoes
➤ fat people
➤ thin people
➤ short men
➤ too much make-up
➤ unfashionable dress
➤ the way a person laughs
➤ people living in certain towns or areas of the country
➤ dislike for a regional accent
➤ people with a public school education
➤ men who wear an earring
➤ young, unmarried men (deemed to be irresponsible).

You can probably add some stereotypes you have encountered to this list.

### Making assumptions

The halo effect, making snap decisions and stereotyping are all specific forms of assumptions based on limited information, but this can also be a more generalised fault. There are many instances where interviewers are willing to impose their own personal view of how they would act in particular circumstances, instead of ascertaining how the interviewee would act. One example of this is assuming that women will bear the major responsibility for child care, or that women are less likely to move their families to take up a new post.

### Gathering insufficient or irrelevant information

Again, all the specific perceptual errors discussed in this section could be attributed to gathering insufficient or irrelevant information. Interviewers obviously need to be aware of this as a general fault and make sure they use proper techniques to counteract it.

### The contrast effect

Imagine yourself in the following scenario. You are a final year student and you have been asked by one of your lecturers to judge presentations being made by students in the first year of your course. You are using a scale of 1–5, with 1 being poor and 5 being excellent. You watch one presentation and the student makes a really poor job of it. The presentation is boring, too long and the student uses no visual aids. You rate this presentation as poor and give it a score of 1. The next student gives a presentation which is somewhat better, and it is a relief to you that this presentation is not as boring. The contrast between the two presentations is likely to have an effect on your judgement, and you will probably rate the second presentation higher than you would have done on some objective measure. If the presentation actually merits a 3, you may rate it as a 4 because of the contrast with the preceding poor presentation. This is known as the contrast effect. It means that candidates at interview may be rated more highly than they merit by interviewers because they were preceded by a poor candidate, and by contrast they appear to be better than they are in reality.

### Interviewer errors: summary

➤ Making snap decisions.
➤ Gathering negative/positive information to support first impressions.
➤ Hiring in one's own image.
➤ Stereotyping.
➤ Making assumptions; imposing one's personal view of how one would act in other people's personal circumstances.
➤ Gathering insufficient/irrelevant information.
➤ Contrast effect.

### Eliminating interviewer errors

As stated earlier, the very fact that you are aware of interviewer errors can help you to eliminate them if you wish to do so and if you make a conscious effort while you are interviewing. There are also some techniques that you can consciously employ to diminish the effects of interviewer errors.

#### Gather sufficient information

This is a general rule that will help to eliminate most interviewer errors. The interviewer should not decide early in the interview that a candidate is unsuitable and then fail to pursue the whole range of information necessary to make a proper decision. Interviewers who persist in gathering information even when a candidate has initially made a poor impression are achieving several goals that may contribute to better decisions:

➤ they are resisting the halo/horns effect
➤ they are making an effort to gather the full range of information
➤ they are giving candidates every opportunity to present themselves.

#### Structured interviews

Conducting interviews in a structured fashion will also contribute to the aim of gathering sufficient information on all candidates. Structured interviews involve the following steps:

➤ design a set of questions to elicit information relevant to the selection decision
➤ provide all candidates with an opportunity to answer this set of questions.

**PAUSE FOR THOUGHT 4.3** *How would you go about designing a relevant set of questions? Why should you ask all of the questions of each candidate?*

The way to design the basic set of questions for a structured interview is of course to refer to the person specification and the job description and create questions related to the tasks, knowledge, skills and personal qualities listed there. The quality of the information gained will be influenced by the types of question asked, and this is dealt with later in this chapter.

Asking all candidates the same questions means that you will have a similar profile for each candidate which you can compare and use to assess each candidate against the others. Notice that the structured interview gives you a basic set of comparable details; you may wish to supplement this with individualised information on each candidate, clarifying particular details of their experience etc. In other words, the structured interview guarantees that you will collect certain information, but it is not a straitjacket that restricts you to that information. As well as preparing and using the questions for the structured interview, the interviewer must be adept at using probing questions described later.

Giving all candidates an opportunity to respond to a set of questions can also help to diminish the halo effect and gives a nervous candidate time to relax and do better as the interview proceeds. Preparing a set of questions in advance also means that interviewers:

➤ can relax during the interview and concentrate on the candidates' responses, rather than be thinking about what to ask next

➤ are less likely to inadvertently ask questions that may be construed as discriminating illegally.

### More than one interviewer

In general, the one-on-one interview is not regarded as best practice for selection purposes. One reason for this is to do with equal opportunities; the interviewer errors that arise because of individual perceptions are less likely to occur if more than one person is involved in interviewing. Since human resource management specialists often hold responsibilities for a company's equal opportunities programmes, they often participate in the interviewing process.

Obviously, line managers know most about the work that needs to be done and can judge whether candidates have the appropriate knowledge, skills and personal qualities. Consideration can also be given to involving others affected by the post, such as co-workers or members of other departments. Acceptance of the new employee can be increased if others are involved in the selection process, but this must be balanced against unwieldiness and, of course, everyone involved in interviewing must be trained.

### Only trained people involved in interviews

Although the people involved in interviews may have different interests, they should all be working towards the same outcome, i.e. to select the best person for the post in a fair and objective manner. Training for interviewers usually includes an awareness of equal opportunity issues and development of questioning skills.

### Allow sufficient time for interviews

Line managers often see interviewing as a disruption to their normal work, and wish to minimise the amount of time devoted to interviews. It is up to the HRM specialist to resist this pressure. Ten minutes is not long enough to find out sufficient detail to base such a decision on. In 1995 the BBC broadcast a series of programmes showing the recruitment processes followed by a number of organisations; one of the managers who took part in these programmes commented on the length of a courtship that precedes the decision to marry compared with the length of a selection interview on which one will base the decision about someone one may be working with on a daily basis for many years. He expressed a great sense of unease about the need to make such an important decision on such short acquaintance.

### *Eliminating interview errors: summary*

➤ Gather sufficient information.
➤ Allow adequate time.
➤ Structured interviews: gather the same information from all candidates.
➤ More than one interviewer.
➤ Only trained people involved in interviews.

ACTIVITY **4.1**
••••••••••••••

George, the personnel manager, and Ruth, one of the personnel assistants, were both conducting preliminary interviews of candidates for the post of PR assistant in the busy public relations department of a large organisation. The PR assistant would have to deal directly with the general public, sometimes with extremely irate people, and would also have to communicate with the press. George and Ruth had decided to interview the candidates separately and then get together to compare their impressions. Ruth was rather inexperienced at interviewing as she was new to the personnel office. She was a quiet person who liked to approach work in a calm, methodical manner.

Ruth particularly liked one of the candidates, Jane Marsden. Jane seemed somewhat tense at the beginning of the interview, and Ruth empathised with this as she had recently gone through a number of interviews herself before she got her current job. Ruth got Jane to relax by talking about her interests, and her feeling that Jane was an interesting person was confirmed by the discovery that they shared interests in learning languages and travelling abroad. Ruth went on to tell Jane a little about the job, and Jane said she thought it sounded very interesting. Ruth also confirmed that Jane had actually dealt with customer complaints in previous positions.

Ruth noted the following points in her assessment of Jane:

➤ turned up for the interview looking well-dressed and professional
➤ showed enthusiasm for the job
➤ has relevant experience.

She also wrote: 'Jane makes a good impression. I'm sure she'll be good at the job.' Ruth reflected that the other two candidates she'd seen that morning hadn't seemed as enthusiastic as Jane, weren't as smart in appearance, and hadn't been very expansive about their experience.

When they got together to discuss the candidates afterwards, Ruth recommended Jane to George, but George responded by saying: 'Well, when I asked her to describe her experience of dealing with an irate customer, she told me that she had always worked in offices dealing only with correspondence. I think some of the other candidates have more suitable experience.'

1  Identify the perceptual errors that may have occurred in this case.
2  Suggest what George might do to help Ruth to avoid such errors in the future.

### *Discussion of Activity 4.1*

The perceptual errors you identified may have included the following:

➤ Identifying with candidate/focusing on irrelevant details: Ruth seems to pay undue attention to similarities between herself and Jane, and much of the interview seems to have focused on matters other that Jane's knowledge, skills and work-related qualities.

➤ *Halo effect*: Jane makes a positive first impression by being well-dressed and looking professional. It may be that Ruth seeks evidence to support this impression.

➤ *Collecting inadequate information*: The fact that Jane had dealt with customer complaints proved to be insufficient to judge her abilities for the current post. Rather than accepting a superficial answer to the question about relevant experience, Ruth should have probed for more detailed information.

➤ *Contrast effect*: Jane seems to be a better candidate than she is because Ruth is comparing her with other candidates she has assessed as being poor.

The techniques for eliminating interviewer errors listed before this Activity could serve as guidelines for George in helping Ruth to develop better interviewing skills. He could discuss with her the need to gather appropriate information, and help her to structure her questions in preparation for interviews. If they interviewed together, Ruth could probably learn about good techniques by observing her more experienced manager: she would witness the use of more expert questioning techniques and also be privy to the information they elicit from candidates. Finally, George could arrange some further off-the-job training for Ruth.

### *Interviewer skills*

In addition to the techniques you may wish to employ to avoid common interviewer errors, there is a range of skills you can develop to ensure your effectiveness as an interviewer. Since we have established that both HRM specialists and line managers should be involved in selection interviews, these skills are important to both. The skills are presented below, followed by a more detailed discussion.

➤ Carry out thorough planning and preparation for the interview.
➤ Put candidates at their ease.
➤ Remain detached: don't send signals to candidates.
➤ Ask a range of relevant questions.
➤ Encourage the candidate to talk.
➤ Record the information.
➤ Respond to candidates' questions.
➤ Close the interview.
➤ Evaluate information and reach a decision.
➤ Record and justify the decisions.

#### Planning and preparation

The list of interview skills could almost double as a list of interview stages, and indeed the planning stage entails thinking through and planning the whole process, especially if you are responsible for coordinating it. This includes:

➤ arranging for the reception of candidates
➤ ensuring you have a private room available where you will not be interrupted
➤ reviewing the application forms so that you are properly informed about candidates

➤ reviewing the job description and person specification so you are properly informed about the requirements of the position

➤ preparing the interview questions

➤ ensuring everyone knows what role he or she is to play in the process.

### Put candidates at ease

It is widely acknowledged that most job applicants feel nervous about interviews, and this anxiety may be increased if the candidate is faced by a panel of interviewers or a series of interviews with different people. In some cases, interviewers deliberately subject candidates to stress, arguing that they wish to test the person's ability to handle stress in the job.

A counter-argument to this is that the interview situation is stressful enough anyway, so there is no need to induce stress artificially. If one of the main objectives is to acquire as much information as possible from candidates, it is probably better on balance to try to get candidates to relax and talk freely. It is also worth remembering that for every candidate who eventually joins your company, there may be five or more for whom the interview is their only contact with you. It is better for a company's public image if these five leave the interview feeling they were treated properly.

**PAUSE FOR THOUGHT 4.4** *Make a list of three things you could do to help put interviewees at ease.*

The techniques you might use to help put candidates at ease include:

➤ making introductions and explaining the interview process so that candidates have a chance to settle in before they have to respond

➤ engaging in small talk about the traffic difficulties, how the candidate travelled to your location, etc.

➤ starting the interview with easy questions that entail straightforward description rather than opinion or interpretation, for instance 'What are your major duties in your current post?' rather than 'How do your current duties make you qualified for this position?'

### Remain detached: don't send signals to candidates

It is important that interviewers do not influence candidates during interviews by indicating whether or not the candidate is doing well. This is especially so if a candidate starts out with weak responses, as any sign of impatience or boredom on the part of the interviewer will no doubt make the candidate more nervous, contributing to the horns effect.

### *Questioning techniques*

Although we shall examine a variety of types of question in this section, there is another component of effective questioning technique that is probably just as important as asking the right questions. That is listening.

It is difficult to concentrate for prolonged periods of time, and often recruiters will find themselves involved in a series of interviews stretching over many hours or even a number of days. Interviewers need to become practised in the techniques of active listening to ensure that they maintain their concen-

*figure 4.1*
**How not to put
candidates at ease**

tration and gather as much information from the interviewee as possible. You will find a fuller discussion of active listening in Chapter 11; it will suffice for now to highlight some of the techniques of active listening:

- ➤ maintain good eye contact with the interviewee
- ➤ look interested; do not yawn or look bored
- ➤ make encouraging remarks such as 'Yes, I see'; 'That's interesting'; 'Do go on'
- ➤ summarise what the interviewee has said to check your understanding: 'So you are saying that you prefer to work in an office on your own?'

Actively practising these techniques will help the interviewer to stay alert and concentrate on what the interviewee is saying. A further effect of active listening is that the interviewee is constantly reassured of your attention, which makes him or her more comfortable with the process.

### Types of question

There are a number of ways of phrasing a question, and each will have an effect on the likely response. In choosing which type of question to ask, you should consider what the purpose of the question is. What type of information do you wish to elicit from the candidate?

The three basic forms of question are the closed question, the leading question and the open question. The closed question invites a response of 'yes' or 'no'; the leading question indicates to the interviewee what kind of response is expected; the open question is phrased in such a way that the interviewee is encouraged to speak freely and give information about himself or herself. Here are some examples of each type of question, together with a comment on what sort of response might be expected.

*Closed questions*
- ➤ Did you work with a computer at XYZ Ltd?
- ➤ Have you had sales experience?

*Comment*

Each of these questions could be answered by a simple response 'yes' or 'no'. If the interviewer is trying to elicit as much information as possible, these questions are not very useful. Closed questions can, however, be useful for checking the correctness of information. An example might be: 'Did you use Windows on the word processor at XYZ Ltd?'

**PAUSE FOR THOUGHT 4.5**  *Before you go on to read about leading questions and open questions, stop to rephrase the two closed questions in the example above as open questions. That is, how would you put these questions so that an interviewee would be encouraged to speak more freely?*

*Leading questions*

➤  You do enjoy working with the computer, don't you?
➤  You have had sales experience, haven't you?

*Comment*

The phrasing of these questions implies that an affirmative response is expected of the candidate. At the very least this will destroy the confidence of a candidate who answers in the negative. It could also induce a nervous candidate to give false information on the spur of the moment. It is so easy just to answer 'yes' to questions like those above.

*Open questions*

➤  What experience have you had of working with a computer?
➤  Tell me about your experience working with a computer.
➤  What did you like about working in sales?
➤  How did you decide to take up a career in personnel management?

*Comment*

None of these questions can be answered with a one word answer, nor do they indicate what the questioner expects to hear. Open questions usually start with words like what, why, or how. Alternatively the interviewee can simply be asked to talk about something: 'Tell me about ...'

It should be obvious that the majority of the questions in an interview should be phrased as open questions, with relatively few closed questions to check facts. Leading questions are not very useful and should be avoided.

*Situational/patterned behaviour description questions*

It is a fairly straightforward task to gather information about qualifications and skills by careful questioning and listening and by using a variety of tests. Assessing attitudes and interpersonal skills is more difficult. Situational and behavioural questions are suitable for this purpose, as well as for assessing skills and how these would be interpreted into behaviour in the workplace. Research also indicates that the use of these two types of question improves both the reliability and the validity of selection interviews (Latham *et al.*, 1980; Weekley and Gier, 1987).

Both types of question require an analysis of critical incidents in the job. Interviewers can ascertain what would be critical incidents in the post using methods like those used to draw up a job description or to develop criteria on which to appraise a person's performance or evaluate a post. You will be able to read about the last two issues in Chapters 9 and 10. For the purposes of selection, you will need to design questions that will get candidates to talk about their performance in these areas and the competencies they would call upon.

**PAUSE FOR THOUGHT 4.6** *Can you list some of the methods used to gather information for writing a job description? Jot down a few ideas and then check them against what was said in Chapter 2, p. 31.*

### Situational interview questions

The interviewee is presented with a situation that represents a typical incident in the job for which he or she is being interviewed, and is then asked to describe what he or she would do in this situation.

The responses to a situational interview question need to be assessed carefully in order to achieve increased reliability between interviewers. There should be prior agreement on what constitutes a poor, an acceptable, and a good answer to the question. A model of each type of answer should be designed, and points can be assigned to each level of response. Each interviewer then grades the actual answers of interviewees accordingly.

Gary Latham and his colleagues (1980) describe a fairly complex manner of designing the graded responses to situational questions, involving knowledge of what was said by previous candidates who turned out to be poor, average or good performers. For most interview situations in practice it is probably adequate for managers to suggest the type of behaviour that they would regard as poor, average and good performance.

An example of a situational question and graded answers for the receptionist post described in Chapter 2 is shown on page 94.

### Patterned behaviour description interview questions

These questions are similar to situational questions in that the interviewee is presented with a situation that represents a typical incident in the job for which he or she is being interviewed. The interviewee is then asked to recount what he or she did in a similar situation in a past position. Although this is a very useful approach, there are disadvantages compared to situational interview questions:

➤ Candidates who do not have any previous experience of the specific incidents will be at a disadvantage. Interviewers will have to decide whether it is the previous experience that is important or the way people would behave in a given situation.

➤ It is not possible to design and rank expected answers, as candidates may respond with reference to a wide range of examples of when they encountered similar situations. It should be possible, however, to identify the range of skills and competencies you would expect candidates to allude to in their answers.

An example of a behavioural question for the receptionist post is: 'Tell us about an incident when you had to deal with several things at the same time.'

*Critical incident*
Dealing with several customer enquiries simultaneously, maintaining a customer-centred approach and a friendly manner.

*Situational question*
One of the junior receptionists has just gone to the cafeteria for his 15 minute coffee break and the other one is working in a nearby office on some invoices that have to be cleared this morning. You have just answered the phone and the caller has a query to which you don't know the answer. Suddenly a number of people come to the reception desk at the same time, so you have a queue of people wanting assistance. How would you handle this situation?

*Ranked answers*
3 (poor performance)
  ➤ Ask the caller to call back in the afternoon.
  ➤ Deal with the people at the reception desk.
  ➤ Find out the answer to the phone query.

4 (average performance)
  ➤ Ask the caller to hold.
  ➤ Deal with the people at the reception desk.
  ➤ Find out the answer to the phone query and deal with the phone caller.

5 (good performance)
  ➤ Explain the need to find out data to the phone caller, and offer to call back.
  ➤ Apologise for the delay to the people at the reception desk, and recall the junior receptionist to the reception area. Deal with the customers together.
  ➤ Find out the answer to the phone query and call the customer back.

ACTIVITY **4.2**

1 Choose a job and design a situational and a behavioural question for it. The job could be one you have experience of or know something about, or one for which you have found an advert in the press.
2 Try out your question on members of your class. Judge the usefulness of the response in terms of making a selection decision.

*Probing questions*
Interviewers need to get over their inhibitions about pursuing information, and practised interviewers often go back to clarify what candidates have said before. The interview is essentially a one-time-only opportunity for both the interviewer and the candidate, and if candidates seem evasive, they may legitimately not realise what you want to know. It is fairer to do all you can to gather relevant information than to superimpose your own assumptions: you should find some polite but insistent way of doing it. It is better to reject

someone for something you know than for an assumption made because information was missing.

Within this context it should be noted that interviewers will have to ask individualised questions to obtain clarification related to individual applicants. The set of questions designed for the structured interview is not meant to inhibit the collection of relevant information.

### Questions to be avoided

In spite of what we have said about relating interview questions to the job description and person specification for the post, you will still no doubt encounter many interviewers who ask questions that do not seem to have been designed in this way. Some very general questions have almost become standard fare in interviews, such as:

➤ What are your strengths and weaknesses?
➤ Where do you see yourself in five years' time?
➤ Tell me about yourself.

Such questions might elicit relevant information, but they are vague, and given the time constraints of the interview process, it is better for the interviewer to focus more narrowly on essential information.

There are other questions that do not overtly contribute much to the selection process, apart perhaps from attempting to relax a nervous candidate by asking easy questions. These include questions like 'What were your favourite subjects at school?' or 'What do you do in your spare time?' In the limited time available for an interview, there are job-related questions that can be answered in a straightforward fashion which can be used to help candidates relax and which will contribute more to the proceedings. Such a question might be: 'Tell me what you do on a typical day at work.'

A third variety of questions of dubious merit consists of those that seem intended to put candidates on the defensive, including statements such as 'You seem to think very highly of your interpersonal skills.'

All these questions should be judged against what they are meant to achieve. Better results are achieved by interviewers who concentrate on formulating questions related to the job and the skills, knowledge and qualities needed to perform well in the post. It bears repeating here that your questions should be linked to the job description and person specification, that you should be able to demonstrate that this is the case, and that you should be able to justify why every question is being asked.

### Questions for candidates with little or no work experience

We have firmly established that it is best practice to acquire work-related and job-specific information from applicants to make good selection decisions. However, we must concede that a modified approach may be necessary when dealing with individuals who have no work experience, little work experience or no recent work experience. Typical examples we can identify include:

➤ school leavers
➤ students graduating from college and university
➤ the long-term unemployed.

**PAUSE FOR THOUGHT 4.7**   *Review what we have said about questioning techniques, and consider how you might have to adapt your approach if you were interviewing an applicant in this category.*

Asking open questions about work experience related to the tasks involved in the vacancy would obviously not be very productive with this group of applicants. However, it should still be possible to ask about relevant transferable skills. The interviewer might need to give fuller explanations about the requirements of the company before asking about the applicant's related knowledge and abilities. You should have identified that situational questions are suitable for people with little experience, so it would make sense to develop such questions in this case rather than patterned behavioural questions. In addition, interviewers faced with people who are not currently accustomed to the working environment might recognise the potential for increased nervousness, and therefore decide to spend more time at the commencement of the interview on putting the applicant at ease.

*Discriminatory questions*

If you conduct structured interviews with a planned set of questions that have been designed on the basis of a properly constructed person specification, you are unlikely to ask any questions that are discriminatory in terms of the SDA or RRA. The implication behind your questions is that if you ask the question, you intend to use the information to make your decision. Avoid any question that would result in your acquiring information on things the legislation or your policies have said would constitute unfair discrimination, for instance marital status, race, age of dependants.

One procedure that is often recommended to avoid accusations of unfair discrimination under the SDA is to ask the same questions of all candidates, both male and female. This will supposedly preclude any suspicion of an intention to discriminate against female applicants. However, in today's society there is still generally an expectation that women bear more of a responsibility for child care than do men. If a young woman said she had two children under the age of five, and a young man said the same thing, most people would draw different conclusions about the relative impact of this.

These assumptions are based on each individual's own experiences and are not necessarily true for other people. It is best practice, therefore, simply to avoid questions about personal circumstances unless there is some specific element of the job, such as the ability to undertake shift work, where personal circumstances are in fact relevant. Even then, candidates can be asked whether something like shift work will cause them any problems, rather than the interviewer's imposing his/her own view of whether or not the applicant should undertake such work.

Before we leave this discussion of the interviewer's questions, we should once again emphasise that it is more important for the candidate to talk than the interviewer. Interview questions are designed as keys to unlock information, and sometimes a pause to allow the candidate time to reflect can be more effective than jumping in with a new question.

**Encourage candidates to talk**

Proper formulation of questions should ensure that the candidate does most of the talking and not the interviewers. However, it is worth repeating that allowing candidates to talk to obtain the information you need is the objective of the interview, and interviewers should practise due restraint.

For all questions, you should decide in advance what it is you are trying to find out with the question; you can then rephrase and probe if the candidate does not respond with the expected information.

### Record the information

You could simply note how each candidate scored on the criteria you are using to assess applicants, but it is much more helpful to have a record of what the candidate actually said. This means that it is necessary for someone to take notes during the interview. It is difficult to take notes, pay attention to what the candidate is saying and keep a normal flow of conversation going, but interviewers develop this skill with experience. It is also best to explain to candidates what you are doing and why.

ACTIVITY **4.3**

As Office Services Manager, you have received the completed application form shown in Figure 4.2 for the position of receptionist described in Chapter 2. The personnel trainee has prepared three sets of questions, and asked you which set you would like to use in the interviews.

1   Review these sets of questions and choose the one that you feel would get the best results. Give reasons for your choice and state why you rejected the other two sets.
2   Develop any further questions you would like to ask.
3   Use the chosen, revised set of questions as a basis for mock interviews with members of your class, using the data on the application form as the interviewee's background. Evaluate whether or not you have obtained sufficient information to make a selection.

### Interview questions

*Set 1*
1   I see you've been with Marvel Appliances for a year. Do you like working there?
2   How do you think your past work experience has prepared you for this job?
3   Can you tell us of a time when you had to deal with several things at the same time?
4   One of our junior receptionists is male and he's older than you. Do you think you'd have any problems being his supervisor?
5   What do you think contributes to good customer care?

*Set 2*
1   I see you've been with Marvel Appliances for a year. Can you tell me a little about what you do there on a typical day?
2   How do you think your past work experience has prepared you for this job?
3   I'd like to describe a typical situation you might encounter in this post, then ask you how you would respond to it.

One of the junior receptionists has just gone to the cafeteria for his 15 minute coffee break and the other one is working in a nearby office on some invoices that have to be cleared this morning. You have just answered the phone

figure 4.2

## XYZ Company

XYZ is striving to become an Equal Opportunities Employer. All appointments are made in keeping with our Equal Opportunities Policy.

### APPLICATION FOR EMPLOYMENT

POST *Receptionist*   LOCATION *Manchester*   REF NO R101/HO

Please type or write clearly in black ink. Give all details in full.

SURNAME *Reives*

FORENAME *Joan*

ADDRESS *23 Barns Street*
*Dorton, Manchester, M16 0BF*

TELEPHONE   HOME: *0161–000–000*   WORK: *0161–000–000*

Do you hold a current driving licence?   (YES) / NO

EMPLOYMENT EXPERIENCE

PRESENT OR MOST RECENT EMPLOYMENT

NAME & ADDRESS   JOB TITLE: *Junior Receptionist*
OF PRESENT EMPLOYER   START DATE: *July 1998*
*Marvel Appliances*   END DATE: *Still there*
*10 Dean Street*   (if applicable)
*Stalybridge*   PRESENT SALARY: *£7,500*
*MN19 2GF.*   PERIOD OF NOTICE
   REQUIRED: *Two Weeks*

DUTIES:
*I welcome visitors to the company and call the person they want to see to the reception desk. I operate the switchboard and I transfer phone calls to other employees.*

---

PREVIOUS EMPLOYMENT (START WITH MOST RECENT POST)

| FROM MONTH/YEAR | TO MONTH/YEAR | EMPLOYER | JOB TITLE AND BRIEF DESCRIPTION OF DUTIES |
|---|---|---|---|
| *July 1997* | *Sept 1997* | *Allgood's Department Store* | *Sales Assistant Assisted customers to choose purchases and completed cash or credit card transactions.* |

EDUCATION AND TRAINING

| SCHOOL/COLLEGE/UNIVERSITY/OTHER | QUALIFICATION | FROM | TO |
|---|---|---|---|
| *Stalybridge High School* | *3 'A'–Levels 6 GCSE's* | *1996* | *1998 1996* |

MEMBERSHIP OF PROFESSIONAL ASSOCIATIONS

## ADDITIONAL INFORMATION

Please state why you are interested in the position you are applying for, and explain how your qualifications and work experience relate to this post. Please supply any additional information you feel may assist the selection panel in evaluating your application for this post. You should include any unpaid or voluntary work experience or any leisure activities where you feel you have developed relevant skills.

*I have lots of experience as a junior receptionist and working with customers. I am ambitious and hardworking and I know I could do a good job as a receptionist. I think I am ready for a promotion.*

## REFERENCES

Please give the names, addresses and telephone numbers of two referees. One of these should be your current or most recent employer. Please indicate if you wish to be consulted before we contact your current employer.

1 Name: *Mr Willis*       2 Name: *Mrs Green*

Address: *Marvel Appliances*       Address: *Allgood's Dept. Store*
*10 Dean Street*              *The Crescent*
*Stalybridge*                *Manchester*
*MN19 2QF*                   *MS3 9MN*

Tel No: *0161—000—000*       Tel No: *0161—000—000*

Position: *Manager*          Position: *Manager*

## DECLARATION

I certify that the information provided in this form is correct and accurate to the best of my knowledge. I understand that any misrepresentation makes me liable to disqualification or dismissal should I be engaged.

Signature *J Reives*       Date *15/9/1999*

Thank you for completing this form. Please return it to:

Director of Human Resource Management
XYZ Company
Ourtown
Ourcountry
PC1 6YZ

We regret that we are unable to acknowledge individual applications. If you wish to have confirmation that your application has been received, please enclose a stamped, addressed envelope. If you have not heard from us within three weeks, you should assume that your application has been unsuccessful on this occasion.

Surname: *Reives*

Forename: *Joan*

Date of Birth: *3.8.80*

Male  [ ]    Female  [✓]

Are you Registered Disabled?  YES  NO⃝

If so, what is the nature of your disability?

How would you describe your ethnic origin?

Afro Caribbean  [ ]    Asian  [ ]

UK Afro Caribbean  [ ]    UK Asian  [ ]

UK European  [✓]    Other European  [ ]

Other ...................

and the caller has a query to which you don't know the answer. Suddenly a number of people come to the reception desk at the same time, so you have a queue of people wanting assistance. How would you handle this situation?

4   Can you describe any supervisory experience you have had?

5   What do you think contributes to good customer care?

*Set 3*

1   I see you've been with Marvel Appliances for a year. Why do you want to leave?

2   How do you think your past work experience has prepared you for this job?

3   Can you tell us of a time when you had to deal with several things at the same time?

4   What kinds of hobbies do you have?

5   If we employed you, how long do you think you would stay with us? What about your personal plans for the future?

## Candidates' questions

It is good practice in an interview, usually at the end, to allow candidates an opportunity to ask questions about the post. Remember that both parties can benefit from the interview being a two-way process; it is important that prospective employees find out about the job and the company so that they can make an informed decision if offered the post. This may help to avoid the situation where someone is hired, only to decide after a short while that he or she is not suited to the job. As well as responding to candidates' questions, companies can employ other techniques to supply information to applicants. Some of these, such as supplying job descriptions and company literature, are relevant to the recruitment process, and others, such as realistic job previews, usually take place during the selection process. Realistic job previews are discussed more fully in the next chapter.

## Closing the interview

To close the interview, the interviewer should thank the interviewee for attending and inform him or her of what to expect next. This may include a second stage of interviews for selected candidates, a variety of tests, the time frame for the decision and details about how candidates will be informed about the outcome.

## Evaluating information

Even if the interview has been carefully structured, with the involvement of several interviewers and the use of a range of well-designed questions, there is still a temptation at this stage to revert to making a decision based on gut feeling or the overall impression that candidates have made. In order to achieve a more objective evaluation of the mass of information that has now been gathered, it is possible to devise a scoring system, either for the answers to interview questions or for the elements of the person specification. Marks can be allocated to each question and questions can be weighted according to their relative importance. It would also be possible to stipulate that a candidate should achieve a passing mark on a question of particular significance in order to be considered further. For instance, candidates for a personnel position might be rejected for giving an unacceptable answer on a sex or race discrimination issue, no matter how well they performed in the rest of the interview.

A numerical score for each candidate will allow the interviewers to create a ranked order of candidates following an agreed method. Another system that could be used is quite simply to mark the person specification for each candidate, + for the criteria that have been met, and – for those that have not. The use of essential and preferred categories implies some weighting of elements.

### Record and justify decision

The methodical approach described in the previous section means that it should be easy for the selection panel to justify why they have selected the chosen candidate and why the others have been rejected. All reasons for the decisions reached should be expressed in terms of where candidates did or did not meet the criteria stipulated in the person specification.

It is important to keep a written record of these factors for several reasons:

➤ To be able to present evidence of a proper and fair procedure should a candidate decide to pursue a case under the Sex Discimination Act, the Race Relations Act or the Disability Discrimination Act.

➤ To be able to provide feedback to candidates who request it. Increasingly, applicants for posts do this in their quest to make a good impression and to improve their chances of finally securing a post. As you will read in the next chapter, there is an obligation to provide information to candidates who have completed psychometric tests, but it is part of a company's good image to be able to respond to requests of this nature from rejected applicants in any case.

➤ To ensure that interviewers follow a rigorous and methodical process.

## Monitoring for equal opportunities purposes

On a longer term basis, it is important for the human resource management department to monitor the selection process in order to ensure that no unlawful or unfair discrimination is taking place, to keep managers informed of the company's performance in terms of equal opportunity, and to initiate appropriate programmes should any issues need to be addressed. Monitoring involves analysis of the information gathered on the equal opportunities monitoring section of the application form, and would normally relate to different stages of the recruitment and selection process:

➤ who applied for the position
➤ who was called for interview
➤ who was selected after the interview, either to be hired or to proceed to further stages.

## Administrative procedures

The interview may represent the end of your recruitment and selection process. If so, you would proceed at this stage to offer the post to the successful candidate and to inform those who had not been successful. However, you may decide to incorporate additional stages in your selection process, such as a number of tests. These are discussed in the next chapter, and you will find more information about closing the selection process at the end of that chapter.

ACTIVITY **4.4**
............

**Recruitment and selection case study: The Fabric Brothers' Recruitment Drive**

Thomas and Edward Fabric founded a small clothing manufacturing company in the early 1960s in the North of England. Over the years the company has grown and recently the Fabric brothers won a new contract to manufacture dresses for a catalogue company. This has necessitated their taking on 10 new sewing machine operators.

Edward's son, John, has taken care of recruitment since he joined the family enterprise in 1978. He let the girls in the sewing room know that he was looking for some additional employees, and he posted a notice on the factory gates, advertising the vacancies as a good opportunity for, as he put it, 'ladies looking to make some extra money while your children are in school'.

John interviewed a few people who dropped in to ask about the job, and he was able to fill his 10 vacancies with no bother. He was very surprised a few weeks later to get a letter from the Commission for Racial Equality stating that two Asian women, who had applied for the post and been interviewed but not selected, felt that they had been discriminated against on the basis of race. Talking it over with his father, John said: 'Well, I did ask them questions about how long they had been in England and whether they felt their English was good enough for the job, but surely that's not racial discrimination?'

John was actually quite upset because he did not think of himself as a racist. Of course, all the girls in the sewing room were white, but that's just the way things had worked out. Imagine his surprise, then, when a few days later he received a similar letter from the Equal Opportunities Commission stating that a man he had rejected had complained that he had been rejected on the basis of sex. This man had once worked as a tailor, so he felt he could not have been rejected on the grounds of competence.

John knows that you have some background in personnel issues, so he has turned to you to explain to him how all this could have happened and to give him some advice about what to do both now in response to these complaints, and in handling recruitment and selection in the future.

**REVIEW QUESTIONS**

You will find brief answers to these review questions on pages 422–423

1   Describe the aims of the selection process and comment on a methodical approach that can be used to achieve these aims.

2   Explain the terms validity and reliability with reference to employment interviews.

3   What factors contribute to the low validity of employment interviews and how can this be overcome?

4   Critically assess the value of different types of questioning in employment interviews.

Answer the following multiple choice and short answer questions. The correct responses are given on page 423 for you to check your understanding of this chapter.

1    Which of the following questions is an open question?
   (*a*)  Did you get here by train?
   (*b*)  Don't you enjoy working with computerised files?
   (*c*)  What experience have you had in dealing with after-sales support services?
   (*d*)  So you worked with your last employer for three years?

2    Is the following statement true or false? Of all the selection methods available to employers, interviews have been found to have the highest validity.

3    Which of the following is the best definition of validity?
   (*a*)  A method of assessment that gives the same results when it is applied by a number of different people.
   (*b*)  A method of assessment that measures what it sets out to measure.
   (*c*)  A method of assessment that uses a wide range of techniques.
   (*d*)  Interviews conducted by more than one person.

4    An interviewer is very impressed by the smart appearance and confident manner of a candidate. The interviewer tends to seek positive information from this candidate and readily overlooks any negative information. This is known as:
   (*a*)  stereotyping
   (*b*)  the contrast effect
   (*c*)  closed questioning
   (*d*)  the halo effect.

5    The validity of an interview can be increased by:
   (*a*)  being aware of potential interviewer errors
   (*b*)  structuring interviews to obtain the same information from all candidates
   (*c*)  having interviews conducted by more than one interviewer
   (*d*)  all the above
   (*e*)  none of the above.

6    Which of the following is the best definition of (i) a situational interview question, (ii) a patterned behaviour description interview question?
   (*a*)  The interviewee is asked to describe a situation in which he or she has performed well.
   (*b*)  The interviewee is presented with a situation that represents a typical incident in the job for which he or she is being interviewed. The inter-viewee is asked to recount what he or she did in a similar situation in a past position.
   (*c*)  The interviewee is presented with a situation that represents a typical incident in the job for which he or she is being interviewed. The interviewee is asked to describe what he or she would do in this situation.
   (*d*)  The interviewee is presented with a situation that represents a typical incident in the job for which he or she is being interviewed. The interviewee is asked to describe what the ideal behaviour would be in this circumstance.

7    Which of the following best defines how to assess the responses to a situational interview to achieve increased reliability?
   (*a*)  Decide in advance what could be regarded as a good, an adequate and a poor response. Assign points to each level of response. Each interviewer grades answers accordingly.

(*b*) **Each interviewer reviews responses from all candidates after the interviews. Each interviewer ranks the responses according to acceptability and compares the results with the other interviewers.**

(*c*) **The interviewers as a group review the responses from all candidates after the interviews. The interviewers as a group rank the responses according to acceptability.**

(*d*) **Decide in advance what could be regarded as a good, an adequate and a poor response. Assign points to each level of response. Interviewers as a group grade responses accordingly.**

8 **Is the following question a situational question or a patterned behaviour description question? 'Can you tell us about a situation where someone approached you with a problem that was affecting his or her work?'**

9 **What is the term that is used for analysing recruitment and selection data to ensure that no unfair or unlawful discrimination is taking place?**

## References

Latham, G. P, Saari, L. M., Pursell, E. D. and Campion, M. A. The situational interview. *Journal of Applied Psychology*, Vol. 65, No. 4, 1980, 422–427.

Makin, Peter and Robertson, Ivan. Selecting the best selection techniques. *Personnel Management*, November 1986, 38–40.

Weekley, Jeff A. and Gier, Joseph A. Reliability and validity of the situational interview for a sales position. *Journal of Applied Psychology*, Vol. 72, 1987, 484–487.

## Further study

### *Books*

Hellriegel, D., Slocum, J. W. and Woodman, R. W. *Organizational Behavior*. 7th edition, West Publishing Company, 1995. (Chapter 3, 'Perception and Attribution', provides an excellent introduction to the perceptual process with many work-related examples.)

Herman, Susan J. *Hiring Right: A Practical Guide*. Sage, 1994.

Smith, Mike and Robertson, Ivan T. *The Theory and Practice of Systematic Personnel Selection*. 2nd edition, Macmillan, 1993. (A thorough discussion of all the stages involved in selection, and of issues such as ethical considerations, discrimination and validity of selection methods.)

Torrington, Derek and Weightman, Jane. *Effective Management: People and Organisation*. 2nd edition, Prentice Hall, 1993. (Chapter 22, 'Selecting team members', provides a concise overview of the selection process.)

### *Articles*

Bayne, Rowan. A new direction for the Myers–Briggs Type Indicator. *Personnel Management*, March 1990, 48–51. (Bayne explores the uses of the Myers–Briggs test in identifying the strengths and development needs of interviewers.)

Jenks, J. M. and Zevnik, L. P. ABCs of job interviewing. *Harvard Business Review*, July–August 1989, 38–42. (This article discusses how to formulate questions and gives practical guidelines.)

Latham, G. P., Saari, L. M., Pursell, E. D. and Campion, M. A. The situational interview. *Journal of Applied Psychology*, Vol. 65, No. 4, 1980, 422–427. (This article describes research into the validity of situational interviewing, and provides an example of a question used for manual employees.)

McDaniel, Michael A.,Whetzel, Deborah A., Schmidt, Frank L. and Maurer, Steven D. The validity of employment interviews: a comprehensive review and meta-analysis. *Journal of Applied Psychology*, Vol. 79, 1994, 599–616. (Provides a good review of the results of a wide range of research into the validity of employment interviews. An excellent starting point, both because of its content and the extensive list of references, for anyone wishing to compile an academic report on this topic.)

Weekley, Jeff A. and Gier, Joseph A. Reliability and validity of the situational interview for a sales position. *Journal of Applied Psychology*, Vol. 72, 1987, 484–487. (This article describes research into the reliability and validity of interviews, particularly interviews using situational questions. A sample question is provided, together with suggestions on how to assess responses.)

### *Audio-visual*

British Broadcasting Corporation. *Situation Vacant*, 1995. (This is a series of programmes about the selection process in a variety of organisations, first broadcast in 1995. The programmes lack detailed background about the job descriptions, person specifications, application forms, etc., but they provide an interesting insight into how managers make selection decisions and portray a range of selection techniques.)

Open College. *Interviewing*. Programme 1. Produced by Yorkshire Television for the Open College with Channel Four, 1988. (This is the first programme in a series of five on interviewing skills in the workplace. The programme covers basic interviewing skills, including questioning techniques.)

# CHAPTER 5

# Selection: supplementing the interview

## Objectives:

*When you have studied this chapter you will be able to:*

➤ name and describe selection methods that can be used to supplement the interview

➤ design work sample exercises

➤ assess the suitability of selection methods designed to supplement the interview

➤ decide how to integrate a range of techniques into the selection process

➤ describe the steps to be taken to complete the selection process.

In Chapter 4, we have discussed interviewing techniques in great depth, and this is justified because of the predominance of interviewing as a method of selection. However, there are some strong arguments for developing a broader perspective on the selection process, and these are mainly to do with the validity of the interview as an assessment tool and with the importance of the selection process to the achievement of the strategic goals of the organisation.

## Selection as a strategic activity

We have established in Chapters 1 and 2 that employee selection contributes to the achievement of strategic goals and so is too important an activity to be conducted on the basis of what is familiar or expedient. Companies may, therefore, depending on the circumstances, need to engage in a broader array of activities rather than simply interviewing alone. Sophisticated selection has been identified as part of the best practice associated with the HRM approach (Marchington and Wilkinson, 1996, pp. 396/397) and thus a necessary part of a strategic approach dedicated to obtaining the competitive edge that comes from having a superior workforce. Supplementary techniques may not be needed for every vacancy, but at least the process should be examined and the appropriate action chosen for each contingency.

### Interview validity

Many questions have been raised about the predictive validity of interviews, i.e. do interviews result in good decisions; do the people who are selected for posts actually perform well on the job? Another question which is rarely addressed but ought to be of concern is whether those who are rejected really are unsuitable for the post; in other words, is the selection process rigorous enough to ensure that good candidates are not inadvertently eliminated?

Most writers on selection methods refer to the fact that research has not been able to show that interviewing has high predictive validity as a selection technique (Smith and Robertson, 1993; Murphy and Davidshofer, 1994). The major reasons for this have to do with interviewer bias and the fallibility of human judgement. The problem of the low validity of interviews is compounded by evidence about poor interviewer reliability, i.e. that two interviewers may form very different opinions about the same candidate. Structured interviews and the use of situational and behavioural questioning go some way to correcting these interview faults, but it is worth considering whether there are some other methods of improving the validity and reliability of the selection process.

**PAUSE FOR THOUGHT 5.1** *If the results of interviews are not always reliable or valid, what can be done to improve the selection process? Write down three things employers could do to supplement the interview process.*

In trying to think of some methods of supplementing the information gained during interviews, you may have focused on improving reliability or validity and decided that it would be a good idea to obtain some objective information, such as test results that can be scored objectively and are not subject to individual interpretation. This would help to counteract any interviewer bias present in the process.

Alternatively you may have focused on simply acquiring additional information from a range of sources including other people's opinion of the candidates, for example by soliciting references, or even by conducting a second stage of interviews. A further issue you may have considered is the timing of these supplementary activities: should they occur before the interviews to facilitate the process of shortlisting or to reduce the number of interviewees, or after the interviews to assess further those who have passed the interview as the first hurdle? There is no hard and fast rule about this; it is a matter of judgement and depends on what you want to achieve in a particular circumstance. As you read this chapter, you will find examples of employers who have used a variety of selection methods at different points in the interview process.

You may also have remembered that the interview is not meant to be a one-way process and that it is important for candidates to be given adequate information so that they too can make an informed decision about the suitability of the post for them. Ways of giving this information may be included in your list. One of these is known as the realistic job preview, which is described later in this chapter.

Your list may include some of the following activities:

➤ psychological tests
  – ability
  – intelligence
  – interests
  – motivation
  – personality

➤ work sample
➤ role play; demonstration
➤ observation at work
➤ assessment centres
➤ references
➤ medical examination
➤ criminal record check
➤ drug use check
➤ lie detector test
➤ graphology
➤ phrenology
➤ astrology
➤ realistic job preview
➤ company tour
➤ opportunity to meet prospective colleagues.

The rest of this chapter will review some of the available selection methods and conclude with an overview of the activities that need to be undertaken to complete the selection process.

## Supplementary selection techniques

Note that we are using the term 'supplementary' and not 'alternative'. In spite of reservations about the effectiveness of interviewing, interviews are not likely to be replaced as a selection method. You will need to choose which methods to use to complement the information gained from interviews, and integrate these additional measures into your selection and decision-making processes. The description of supplementary techniques in this chapter should enable you to do this.

The essential criterion in choosing supplementary methods is that they should provide information that is directly related to performance on the job. This should be the guiding principle both in choosing off-the-shelf tests and in designing exercises tailor-made for a particular workplace. In their review of what they call personnel testing, Murphy and Davidshofer (1994) stress that better results are obtained the closer a test, such as a work sample test, resembles things that are actually done in the job concerned. A related issue is that candidates can easily see the point of a test that requires them to do something they know will be done on the job. This increases the face validity of the test, making it more acceptable to the candidates. This, in turn, may affect the candidates' willingness to take the test seriously and their motivation to perform the task to the best of their ability. Face validity is therefore something that should be taken into consideration when choosing or designing a test.

### *Psychological testing*

Psychological testing is sometimes referred to as psychometric testing, and is a method of acquiring objective information about a range of individual abilities and traits. Psychological tests are defined as having the following characteristics:

> ➤ they are professionally developed and checked for reliability and validity
> ➤ they are administered and scored in a standardised manner
> ➤ they test maximum performance and habitual performance
> ➤ they result in scores that can be compared to norms for relevant populations.

These characteristics will be explained more fully as we examine the various issues surrounding the uses of psychological tests.

The characteristics of psychological tests listed above indicate that their inclusion in the selection process will:

> ➤ add an element of objectivity
> ➤ increase the predictive validity of selection decisions
> ➤ measure some factors that cannot be assessed through the application form and interview.

The standardised administration of tests means that all applicants answer the same test questions in the same conditions, and objective scoring means that the scores are not open to individual interpretation as is the case with interview responses. There is a vast amount of research that underpins the development of commercially produced tests, including proofs of their reliability and validity. If this is properly documented, the user of the tests can rest assured that the tests will improve the validity of the selection process.

Because psychological tests are such complex instruments, they should be used only by people who have had specific training in how to administer them and how to interpret the results, and in fact reputable test providers will only supply commercially developed tests to properly accredited persons with appropriate training. The British Psychological Society (BPS) has approved the standards of training needed to administer and interpret tests at various levels and to give feedback to test takers, and this training is available from various sources, including the suppliers of tests, who also provide additional training in the use of their own products. The basic level of training, which qualifies persons to use ability tests, is the BPS Certificate of Competence in Occupational Testing (Level A). This training takes approximately five days. Further training of approximately five days with a follow-up day some time after the initial training is necessary to be able to use personality questionnaires. There is a cost implication in this for employers, but the cost of training staff and of staff time for administering tests may be offset by the improved validity of selection decisions. An alternative to having a trained member of staff is to use the services of an occupational psychologist on a consultancy basis when the use of psychological testing seems to be appropriate.

The IPD *Guide on Psychological Testing* (1997) outlines what to consider when deciding whether to use a test. Firstly, the test should be directly relevant to requirements specified in the personnel specification. There is a very wide selection of tests to choose from, and test suppliers provide brochures outlining the sort of information each test will provide and what types of job each test might be appropriate for. Tests are designed with different groups of people in mind, and test suppliers offer advice about who the tests are suitable for. Some examples of designated groups for whom tests are available are middle to senior managers, administrative/supervisory employees, skilled operatives and staff who have direct customer contact. Secondly, test suppliers should provide evidence that the test is reliable, valid, and free of racial or sex bias; and, thirdly, ease of administration and interpretation should also be considered. Further indicators of when to use psychometric tests and questionnaires are:

➤ when a wrong hiring decision would be extremely costly, for instance for very senior positions or when employee errors could render employers liable for high financial outlay

➤ when the selection ratio (the ratio of applicants to the number of positions to be filled) is high and additional information is needed so that the number of candidates can be reduced.

Psychological tests cover a range of human characteristics and may assess:

➤ intelligence
➤ ability
➤ interest
➤ motivation
➤ personality.

### Intelligence tests

General intelligence tests assess ability in a range of skills such as verbal, arithmetical and diagrammatical reasoning, producing an overall score.

### Ability tests

Ability tests focus on specific mental abilities and produce separate scores for the different skills. Sometimes a distinction is made between tests of attainment and tests of aptitude, but in fact it is not always easy to distinguish between the two. Attainment tests assess skills and knowledge that have been acquired through experience and learning, and aptitude tests measure individuals' potential to develop ability. The results of an attainment test, say after learning a foreign language, might also be an indicator of aptitude for learning that language. Since both kinds of tests examine verbal, arithmetical and diagrammatical skills, it is probably more helpful to think of them under the general heading of ability tests.

Work sample tests or school exams are examples of attainment tests, and the use of these would not require the special training outlined above. There are aptitude tests for specific occupations such as word processing, and test batteries that produce a profile of the candidate over a range of abilities.

### Tests of interest and motivation

The relationship between interests and motivation and successful performance is not a straightforward one. For this reason these tests are not used for selection (Smith and Robertson, 1993), but interest tests can be used for career guidance and counselling, and motivation tests can be used for decisions about how best to manage people and enhance their performance by responding to what motivates them.

### Personality questionnaires

The expression 'personality questionnaire' has been used in preference to 'personality test', because in terms of measuring personality characteristics there are no right and wrong answers as would be the case in questions of verbal or arithmetical reasoning. Ability tests are examples of tests of maximum performance, meaning that they reflect the best performance an individual is capable of at that point in time in the skill being tested. Personality questionnaires are indicators of habitual performance, meaning that they reflect stable traits that are likely to be revealed in typical behaviour. Of all the assessments that are carried out in the workplace, personality questionnaires are probably the most contentious, especially with regard to acceptance by candidates. For this reason, it is particularly important to explain to applicants how the test is related to performance on the job concerned and to provide feedback on the results. Test users should also monitor results to ensure that tests do not discriminate unfairly.

Personality questionnaires examine aspects of personality that have been shown through research to correlate with performance at work. Murphy and Davidshofer (1994) refer to evidence that some personality characteristics are related to job performance in general, including agreeableness, conscientiousness and openness to experience. Together with extraversion and neuroticism these traits are known as 'the big five', which are the focus of much interest in current psychological research (Fletcher, 1993).

Most personality questionnaires are of the self-report variety, where applicants are asked to record how they see themselves on a range of characteristics or traits. Some items may be open-ended questions asking about preferred activities, and some items may be a choice from a number of statements, asking persons to choose which statement most resembles them or is most unlike them. These measures usually result in a profile of the person on a range of personality dimensions. One of the most well known of these instruments is Cattell's 16 Personality Factor test (16PF), now in its fifth edition. The 16PF is based on Cattell's work in isolating a range of 16 elements which he believed could be used to describe the whole spectrum of an individual's personality. Cattell's personality dimensions include reserved–outgoing, tough-minded–sensitive, conservative–experimenting and relaxed–tense.

Other established tests include the Saville and Holdsworth Occupational Personality Questionnaire and the Myers-Briggs Type Indicator. The Myers-Briggs test is most often used within the framework of training to identify personality types and examine their impact on personal interactions. There are also questionnaires that measures characteristics that predict success in specific occupations. For example, Saville and Holdsworth have a Sales Personality Questionnaire which gives measures of confidence, empathy and persuasiveness among other personality dimensions.

One of the reasons why personality tests are sometimes regarded with some scepticism is that in self-reporting, candidates may try to give the answers they think are expected. It is also recognised that the situation can affect the responses that people make, so personality test results are not always reliable.

This leads to a very important point with regard to the use of psychological tests in general: they should never be the sole means of assessing candidates, but should always be used as part of a wider process. Information about suppliers of psychological tests is available from the IPD to its members. Toplis *et al.* (1997) provide a brief description of the whole range of available tests, and the series of brief articles edited by Fletcher (1994) in *Personnel Management* gives some insight into currently available tests.

### *Work sample tests*

As the term suggests, a work sample test consists of getting a candidate to perform some task or element of a task that forms part of the job. You can gain a better understanding of work sample tests by working through the design process using a familiar example.

#### How to design a work sample test

Let us take an example of a job with which you are all familiar, that of a university or college lecturer. If you were invited to design a work sample test to be used in hiring a new lecturer in human resource management, what preliminary issues would you consider? How would you approach the task?

The first consideration is that a work sample test makes sense only if it demonstrates abilities that are a major and integral part of the job. A critical incident analysis and selection of a critical task are therefore the first step in designing a work sample test. Remember that you can perform a simplified critical incident analysis by interviewing a number of lecturers and heads of department, and asking them what they consider to be the most important activities that contribute to success in the job. Without doubt most lecturers would identify the ability to conduct a seminar as a critical task.

A second consideration ought to be how the performance of the work sample will be assessed, as this will affect the way the exercise is designed, and it may influence the instructions that are given to candidates.

**PAUSE FOR THOUGHT 5.2** *List the criteria on which you would assess a candidate's performance in delivering a seminar.*

In deciding on your assessment criteria, you will no doubt have identified the lecturers you regard as being excellent in their seminar delivery, and then you will have identified the competencies and techniques that are part of that excellence. If you have worked with a group of colleagues you may have discussed what each of you considers to be important and agreed on a list. Your criteria will include some of the following:

- choice and relevance of topic
- knowledge of subject
- style of delivery
- use of materials
  - content
  - variety
  - visual aids

➤ ability to stimulate participation/discussion
➤ adequacy of preparation
➤ ability to handle questions.

For some of these criteria, you may also have outlined how each would be judged. Adequacy of preparation, for instance, might be judged by absence of hesitation, well-ordered notes and materials, observable structure, control of physical equipment.

Some work samples, such as typing tests, can be assessed on an objective basis using a mathematical formula, but assessment of activities like delivering a seminar will still be subjective. It is important to have assessment guidelines to provide some level of standardisation and consequently to improve reliability among the assessors. Assessment criteria should obviously be related to what is regarded as superior performance on the job. This being the case, documentation relating to performance appraisal should be a good source of material to be used when designing work sample tests.

ACTIVITY **5.1**
••••••••••••••

Make a list of the factors on which you would judge the criterion 'style of delivery'. Discuss your list with a group of fellow students and devise a set of assessment criteria for this criterion.

Since acceptability of the test to the candidate is an important factor, it may improve the face validity of the test to inform candidates how they will be assessed. You should consider incorporating this into the instructions to be given to candidates. For example, the instructions on conducting a seminar might be phrased as follows:

As part of the selection process you are requested to conduct a seminar in your subject area. The seminar should last one hour and be appropriate for a foundation level course. Your performance will be judged in terms of the appropriateness of your material, the style of delivery and your ability to stimulate participation.

**Assessing performance in the work sample exercise**
The assessment criteria will already have been established in the process of designing the work sample. What remains is to ensure that all the assessors involved are fully cognisant of the criteria, and that there is some agreement on what represents acceptable standards of performance. This goal can be facilitated in two ways:

➤ the involvement of line managers both in the design of the work sample test and in the selection process
➤ the use of a scoring sheet listing the assessment criteria.

An example of a scoring sheet for the lecturer's work sample test is given in Table 5.1.

*table 5.1*

**Work sample assessment record**

**Post: Lecturer in HRM; delivery of a seminar**

Assess each of the following criteria on a scale of 1–5, where 1 = poor performance, 3 = acceptable performance, 5 = outstanding performance. An indication of factors you might consider is given for some of the criteria.

| | Candidate 1 | Candidate 2 | Candidate 3 | Candidate 4 |
|---|---|---|---|---|
| Choice and relevance of topic | | | | |
| Knowledge of subject: up-to-date issues included | | | | |
| Style of delivery: ability to attract and keep attention; use of humour; movement about room | | | | |
| Use of materials: content; variety; visual aids | | | | |
| Ability to stimulate participation/discussion | | | | |
| Adequacy of preparation: absence of hesitation; well-ordered notes and materials; observable structure; control of physical equipment | | | | |
| Ability to handle questions | | | | |

We can now summarise the steps you have just worked through to design a work sample exercise:

➤ identify key critical factors of performance
➤ choose factors that can be tested appropriately by a work sample
➤ identify assessment criteria
➤ design the work sample exercise
➤ write instructions for the candidate
➤ design the assessment form
➤ train the assessors.

**Integration of work sample tests into the selection process**

Work sample tests can easily be included in a selection process to provide additional information without necessarily developing a fully fledged assessment centre approach as described in the next section. A written work sample can, for example, be requested along with submission of the application form. This is especially useful if you are expecting a large number of applications for a particular post. One example of an organisation that has done this is a local authority in Yorkshire which requested applicants for a personnel manager position to submit a report along with their completed application forms. Applicants were given the following instructions: imagine that you are approached by a departmental manager who asks for advice about making a number of people redundant in readiness for the compulsory competitive tendering of services provided by his department. The manager wishes to make an in-house bid for the contract for these services and feels that the only way to make a competitive bid is to reduce costs by reducing staffing levels. Prepare a report recounting how you would advise this manager.

**PAUSE FOR THOUGHT 5.3** *What factors was the local authority attempting to measure with this work sample test? In what ways could this device supplement the application form to assist it in its selection process?*

By asking applicants to submit a written report along with their application form, the authority was potentially gaining a vast amount of additional evidence about applicants' capabilities beyond what it would be able to glean from the application form alone. This includes evidence of:

➤ knowledge – more so than the assumption of knowledge because of academic qualifications and related experience
➤ report writing skills
➤ ability to deliver work under the pressure of deadlines
➤ attitudes and abilities reflected in the content of the report. Did the candidate assess the whole situation or merely respond with information on how to handle redundancies; how much consideration was given to the consultation and involvement of affected parties?

If these factors were included in the job specification, this information would have greatly assisted the authority in its shortlisting task. The exercise no doubt also brought the additional advantage of discouraging any applicants who were not seriously interested in the post or not willing to make the effort to complete the assignment.

ACTIVITY **5.2**

Think of three occupations and decide on a job sample test that could be used prior to shortlisting or that could be run within the context of an interview day. Describe the test and explain how it would provide information that could be used to assess a person's suitability for the job.

When you have compiled your own list of three jobs, get together with two other students to compare your lists. Select the best three examples and present these to the rest of the class.

### Assessment centres

As Woodruffe (1993) points out, an assessment centre is a method rather than a place, although some employers, particularly large organisations, might have premises dedicated to assessment, especially if they use them for both selection and development purposes. Since an assessment centre is a method, it can be used flexibly by all employers. Each organisation can decide how many or how few of the assessment methods to use, but a range of techniques would have to be used to classify a selection event as an assessment centre and usually the number of methods used would mean that the process would stretch over two or three days.

Basically, an assessment centre approach means that a number of people are assessed together by a number of assessors, using a variety of selection techniques. This enables the collection of a range of information and observation and evaluation of how individuals interact with other people. The basic assumption underlying the validity of assessment centres is that the behaviours displayed will be carried over into the workplace.

The range of activities that can make up an assessment centre include:

➤ work simulations
  – work samples
  – in-tray exercises
  – role plays
➤ group exercises and discussions
➤ psychological tests
➤ interviews
➤ peer assessment and self-assessment.

Makin and Robertson (1986) identified group discussion as the kind of exercise most used in assessment centres.

### Work simulations

As the phrase suggests, work simulations entail engaging candidates in performing tasks that would actually be done on the job. These exercises can be performed by individuals as in the in-tray and role-play exercises described below, or in groups, if for example one of the tasks is to participate in interdepartmental meetings. One issue to keep in mind when deciding what kinds of exercise to use is that individual exercises such as role plays are more demanding in terms of assessor time, since one assessor will have to be assigned to one individual rather than a group.

Work sample tests are an example of simulation, and have already been discussed in detail. In-tray exercises and role plays should be developed in the same way as we outlined for work samples in terms of isolating critical tasks, setting the assessment criteria, designing the exercise and assessing it. A typical in-tray exercise is to present a candidate for a managerial post with a number of different tasks that a manager would encounter at the beginning of the day, with instructions to prioritise the issues, write memos, make phone calls etc. A role play could be used in situations where the employee would have to deal with customer complaints, and it would be usual for one of the assessors to take on the role of the customer.

### Group exercises

A variety of tailor-made tests or exercises have been devised by various employers to assess leadership qualities that cannot easily be judged from application forms or straightforward questioning. These tests may be used in designated assessment centre days, but some of them can also be integrated into interview days if a number of candidates are called together. The following are some examples of the kinds of exercises that are used, together with some examples of employers that are known to have used them.

➤ A group of applicants sit around a table; four or five assessors sit around the room behind the applicants. The lead assessor explains that he or she has four or five topics (depending on the number of candidates), which will be read out one at a time. When a topic has been announced, one candidate must volunteer to take that topic and conduct a discussion on it. Five minutes will be allowed for the discussion, and the discussion leader will be alerted when four minutes have elapsed. No further information is given to the candidates regarding what is expected of them. (A metropolitan police force; civilian post.)

➤ Round table interview. The participants are candidates who have passed a preliminary interview. Candidates introduce themselves, and contribute to a discussion of what a manager's job entails. This is followed by a team exercise with instructions to devise an employment strategy for a new store. (A retail outlet selling toys; trainee manager.)

➤ Candidates engage in teamwork to get equipment across a stream with limited physical resources; sometimes with a designated leader, sometimes as a leaderless group. (The Army; officer.)

As with work sample tests, candidate performance can only be judged fairly if assessors have agreed in advance which competencies and job-related behaviours they are looking for.

**PAUSE FOR THOUGHT 5.4** *Look again at the exercise used by the metropolitan police force. What competencies and qualities do you think they were trying to assess?*

The assessors would be looking for evidence of negative and positive behaviours: domination of the discussion, assertiveness, who has good ideas, ability to get people discussing a range of ideas, sensitivity to conflicting ideas, ability to incorporate conflicting views.

### Issues

Woodruffe (1993) identifies a number of issues that must be considered when deciding to use the assessment centre technique, in designing it, running it, and assessing its effectiveness. Some of the major issues will now be discussed briefly.

As with any other selection technique, all the exercises used in the assessment centre must be designed to identify and measure specific competencies needed in the vacant post. There is a need to involve managers and others such as current postholders in identifying what the critical competencies are. The activities involved in designing assessment centre exercises should be directly linked with the activities performed in the context of job analysis that you read about in Chapter 2.

Since assessment centres are very demanding in terms of time and effort, the need for acceptance of the centre by all parties becomes crucial. Line managers are being asked to give their time to the development and the assessment of exercises and to accept that the use of assessment centres will lead to better selection. Line manager acceptance is increased if they are involved at all stages. There is also a need for candidates to feel that the assessment methods used represent a relevant process, especially as the assessment centre is more demanding in terms of their time and energy than a simple interview would be. This can be achieved partly by proper design of the exercises and partly by providing feedback.

We should also briefly consider the pros and cons of assessment centres. Certainly there are identifiable costs associated with assessment centres. These include the training of a number of assessors; the design of exercises and line manager time devoted to this; arrangements for facilities; the time needed to organise the events and coordinate group activities with individual activities, particularly when one assessor is needed per candidate as in role-play exercises; additional expenses for candidates; time spent giving feedback. The argument for assessment centres is that these costs are balanced by the acquisition of additional information, the opportunity to evaluate several candidates together, and the increased validity of selection decisions.

Whenever a number of assessment techniques are used there is a need to assign a weight to each technique. This is addressed later in this chapter after all assessment methods have been considered.

### Biodata

To a certain extent biographical details (biodata) are available to selectors from application forms, CVs and interviews, and are inevitably incorporated into the decision-making process, even if they are not directly connected with factors specified in the personnel specification. This occurs when, for instance, a selector takes into account factors such as how many posts an applicant has had within the past five years, how long the applicant has stayed with each employer, whether there is an obvious progression in the person's career. More detailed application forms or biographical questionnaires can be developed so that biographical data can be used in a more formalised manner and assessed more methodically. The underlying assumption is that biographical factors give rise to certain personality traits that are interpreted into behaviours that affect work performance.

The use of extended biodata, however, presents something of a conundrum. On the one hand there are claims that decisions based on biodata have a high validity (Gunter *et al.*, 1993), and yet the types of information that are routinely mentioned in descriptions of what biodata to collect are contra-indicated by the tenets of good practice in the area of unfair discrimination. For example, it has been suggested that prospective employers might gather such details as age and marital status (Smith and Robertson, 1993), number of dependants, parents' occupations (Gunter *et al.*, 1993), and family background and upbringing (Graham and Bennett, 1992).

The evaluation of biodata is also a problem. The simplest approach is to identify groups of current employees who perform successfully and groups who perform less successfully. Examination of biographical data from each group leads to identification of factors that are present in the successful group and not in the unsuccessful group and vice versa. These factors could then be compared with biographical details of applicants to determine who is likely to be successful in the job and who is likely to be less successful. This kind of empirical approach could only be used in larger companies with large cohorts of people performing the same job and with the capacity and expertise to perform the requisite statistical analyses. Another problem with this approach is that it does not attempt to explain the causal link between biographical characteristics and work performance. The potentially most serious problem, however, is that if the successful group happens, for instance, to be all male, this could lead to unlawful discrimination against females.

### References

References are another method of gathering information on applicants, and a number of surveys indicate that the popularity of references as part of the selection process comes second only to the interview (Makin and Robertson, 1986; Newell and Shackleton, 1991). This is so in spite of the reference's poor showing in the validity league table. In their analysis of the accuracy of selection methods, Anderson and Shackleton (1994) found that references rated a correlation coefficient of only 0.13 (0 being equivalent to chance and 1.0 being the equivalent of perfect prediction). These facts seem to suggest that you will find the acquisition of references to be a part of most selection processes you will be involved in, but that great care is needed in their interpretation.

**PAUSE FOR THOUGHT 5.5**  *At what stage in the selection process should a reference be solicited? Which candidates would you solicit a reference for?*

There are no hard and fast rules that provide an answer to these questions, except that it is usual to solicit a reference for a selection of applicants only. There are various circumstances to consider, and this is another area where policy should be formulated to provide guidance to managers.

Most employers recognise that there are costs to providing references, so they would not wish to impose an unnecessary burden on other employers. This means restricting requests for references to an essential minimum. This would imply asking for references at a late stage in the process, after candidates have been assessed using a variety of other techniques. A further argument in support of this approach is that candidates on the whole prefer their current employer not to be approached unless there is a serious possibility that the candidate will be offered the post. The disadvantage of this view is, of course, that some time may elapse before a reference is received and the prospective employer will not want to delay in making the decision.

Some organisations use all their other assessment techniques and make a job offer subject to receipt of a supportive reference. It must be remembered, however, that references are given in confidence, and in this instance, if a job offer is retracted, then the applicant will know it is because of his or her reference. This may have an impact on the extent to which referees are prepared to be truthful. Every organisation needs to think through these implications, design a policy, and stick to it.

In addition to the questions of when to secure a reference and for whom, there are considerations about what information to request, how to interpret the information supplied, and indeed what information to supply to those requesting a reference from you.

Part of the reason for the low validity of references lies in the perceptions and skill of the person writing them or in hidden agendas that may influence what is or is not said. The effects of perceptions that may occur here are similar to the interviewer errors that were discussed in Chapter 4 in that our opinions of people, even when we have known them for some time, are influenced by our own perceptual set. Lukewarm descriptions of people's abilities may also be due to inadequate powers of expression or reserve on the part of the writer.

Often references reflect the personal views and the characteristics of the person giving the reference as much as the person being refereed. In one case known to the authors a person was provided with three testimonials relating to her performance in one post, and was therefore able to observe that each had a very definite and a very different emphasis. (Usually references are given in confidence and are not seen by the subject of the reference; testimonials are provided to the subject because of circumstances that may make the provision of references difficult, such as emigration to a distant country.) One testimonial emphasised her ability to bring calm to a hectic workplace involved in a wide range of activities, the second emphasised her achievements in recruitment alone and did not acknowledge her involvement in other activities, and the third dwelled on her development of community programmes for disabled employees. Each of these writers had felt something different was important, so the testimonials provided were as much a reflection of their interests and perceptions as they were of the subject of the testimonials.

Because of the low validity of references, employers are sometimes advised to use them to check factual information only, but references may indicate some serious problem that should be pursued for further clarification or some discrepancy in factual information such as dates of employment which should also be pursued. References should obviously, therefore, be used with caution, and human resource specialists should find ways to improve the quality of the information their companies receive in response to requests for references.

### Requesting a reference

What could you do to improve the quality of references you have solicited?

Referees are able to respond better if you indicate what areas you would like feedback on, such as skills and personal qualities. Since you are seeking information on these as they relate to performance on the job, it would be useful to provide a job description or a brief outline of critical tasks. You might also consider supplying a referee with documents and checklists you will be using to evaluate candidates, such as the person specification or checklists of competencies and behaviours.

Some employers provide a questionnaire to guide the referee and help him or her to save time when composing a reference. This, together with a covering letter explaining your request, shows courtesy to referees and may contribute to the probability of your receiving a useful response.

### Supplying references

Although you are not involved in making the selection decision when you provide a reference, it is worth considering the responsibility of the referee at this stage. In giving a reference to a potential employer, referees owe a duty of care to the receiving company. That is, referees would render themselves culpable if they knowingly deceived another company and misled it into hiring a person whom they knew to be unsuitable. In the case of *Spring* v. *Guardian Royal Exchange* (1994), the House of Lords also ruled that an employer has a duty to the employee to provide a reference composed with due care and may be held liable for losses due to negligent mis-statement.

### Criminal record checks

You may remember that the Rehabilitation of Offenders Act was mentioned in Chapter 3. Essentially this act outlines offences that are spent and protects offenders from having to reveal these spent offences for ever. There are, however, some offences that are never spent, and some positions for which those guilty of particular offences will not be suitable. For example, any person who has been found guilty of assaulting a child would not be considered suitable for a position working in a school where unsupervised contact with children might occur. Such positions are excepted from the Rehabilitation of Offenders Act, and the Home Office has arrangements with organisations such as local authorities to provide a check of criminal records for individuals applying for posts such as these.

### Graphology, phrenology, astrology, lie detector tests

These tests have been grouped together because of their somewhat dubious predictive validity, and none of them is used to any great extent in the UK, if at all. Graphology refers to the analysis of handwriting, phrenology to the examination of bumps on the head, and astrology to the influence of the stars. Lie detector or polygraph tests involve the measurement of physical reactions that supposedly reveal whether a person is lying or telling the truth when answering a set of questions. Polygraph tests are known to identify correctly people who are lying, but they also sometimes identify people, as lying who are telling the truth.

### Health checks

Most positions require only general good health, and the completion of a routine questionnaire should suffice to judge a candidate's suitability. Information about absence records can also be specifically requested as part of the reference from former employers. If medical evidence is required from an applicant's general practitioner, the applicant's consent must be obtained first.

## Making the final selection

In the two chapters on selection we have described a number of techniques for your consideration. An important issue to identify and emphasise at this stage is the need to use *all* the information that has been gathered.

There is a tendency to focus on the last stage of the process one has engaged in and to forget prior information, or at least to attribute undue weight and importance to the last stage. For instance, it will often happen that a person who is well qualified on paper but has poor interview skills is eliminated. Is the possession of polished interview skills really a critical success factor for the post in question? Is it wise to allow the interview to be so influential, given the evidence on the reliability and validity of interviews? If you are using a variety of selection techniques, you must decide in advance what each method is going to contribute to the overall assessment. Some things will carry more weight than others, and this should be decided in advance and each component appropriately weighted. Some things will be designated as essential prerequisites, and the lack of other things may be balanced by the presence of something else. For a post managing an accounting unit, for example, good writing skills may be allowed to balance a lack of polished presentation skills, but mathematical ability will be essential. You must decide what to do if there is conflicting evidence, for instance if someone performs well in the interview but not in the ability tests or vice versa.

### *Scoring and ranking*

It is, then, important to find some methodical approach to evaluating the information you have gathered, enabling you to rank the candidates in order of preference. There are several approaches to this and a variety of issues to consider:

➤ Decide on the cut-off percentage score a candidate must achieve in order to be considered.
➤ Decide which criteria must be met and which can be traded off against each other.
➤ Use ticks and crosses to record the assessment of candidates.
➤ Decide on the relative weight of each assessment criterion and assign points accordingly to each factor, amalgamating scores from the various assessment methods. Calculate a total score for each candidate.

Table 5.2 is a sample form to record and tabulate results.

After all the selection activities have been completed, all the selectors should compare their rankings of the candidates and decide on the best candidate. If there are discrepancies in the ratings, these discrepancies can form the basis of discussion and, if necessary, of further information-seeking.

### *Providing information*

It is often forgotten that applicants for a post also have a decision to make about whether or not they wish to accept the offer of employment. It is risky to assume that merely applying for a job means the applicant will ultimately want the post. If new employees leave shortly after being hired, this can hardly be considered to be successful selection. Just as the selectors gather information on which to base their decision, so the applicants should gather or be given information so that they too will make the right decision.

*table 5.2*

**Sample candidate assessment form**

| | Job knowledge Weight factor: .8 | Organisational ability Weight factor: .6 | Experience Weight factor: .5 | Ability to persuade Weight factor: .6 |
|---|---|---|---|---|
| Key for individual scores: 5 = excellent, 3 = good, 1 = acceptable | | | POST: _____ ASSESSOR: _____ | |
| Minimum acceptable scores Job knowledge: 38.4/64 (60%) Total score: 74.5/149 (50%) | | | | |
| Application form Weight factor: 4 | 3 × 4  12 | | 4 × 4  16 | |
| Interview Weight factor: 6 | 4 × 6  24 | | 3 × 6  18 | 3 × 6  18 |
| Work sample test Weight factor: 6 | 4 × 6  24 | 5 × 6  30 | | |
| Ability test Weight factor: 4 | | 3 × 4  12 | | |
| Personality questionnaire Weight factor: 4 | | | | 4 × 4  16 |
| Weighted criterion totals | 48 | 25.2 | 17 | 20.4 |

Candidate total score: 114.6
Candidate ranked against others: 2nd of 6

**Explanatory notes**

The form indicates weightings that would be agreed on some justifiable basis. In this case, job knowledge is weighted higher than the other criteria, and more weight is given to the interview and work sample test than the other assessment methods.

The line under the scores would appear on the blank form to indicate which factors are to be scored under each assessment method.

Any score that fell below the agreed minimum could be ringed on the form to draw attention to the fact that the candidate is no longer to be considered.

---

One obvious way of giving applicants information is to encourage them to ask questions during the interview. In this way you know that you have clarified any points that are important to individual applicants, and these may of course differ from one person to the next. Also, if your interview questions and work sample tests are properly constructed to obtain job-related information from applicants, these questions and tests will have imparted a wealth of information to the interviewee, albeit obliquely. Applicants may, however, still be unaware of certain aspects of the job, and it is incumbent on the selectors to make sure that applicants know about any factors that might influence their decision, and in particular the likelihood of their remaining with the company for a reasonable length of time if they do accept an offer of employment.

Very often the factors that cause rapid turnover among new employees are to do with unpleasant working conditions. If recruitment and selection were just about getting people to accept employment with your company, it would make sense to hide information about the negative aspects of your workplace. Many companies have realised, however, that there is a greater likelihood of retaining new recruits if they are open and honest about the less pleasant aspects of their work environment. Offering interviewees information of this nature is known as a realistic job preview. Realistic job previews can take the form of oral information given by interviewers either to individual interviewees or in a group session before the interviews, or written documentation provided to candidates, for instance statements about the working conditions included in job descriptions. There are, however, some more innovative ways of providing this kind of information.

In 1995 students in the Transport and Logistics department at the University of Huddersfield created a short video film for a distribution company which wanted to alert applicants to the fact that the jobs in its warehouse involved cold, uncongenial working conditions, as most of the work took place in refrigerated areas. This film was made available in job centres so that people who did not wish to work in such conditions would not even apply in the first instance. Realistic job previews can, then, be provided at any stage in the recruitment and selection process, but they are probably most useful at the interview stage, when there is an opportunity to discuss and clarify details.

Additional activities that could be undertaken with the specific purpose of giving information to candidates include a tour of the company premises which gives applicants a first-hand look at the environment they would be working in, and an opportunity to meet prospective colleagues. Letting applicants chat unattended with prospective colleagues means that managers have no control over the kinds of information that will be exchanged; it is rather akin to using the 'sitting next to Nellie' method of training you will read about in Chapter 7. However, the exercise would make additional information available to potential employees, and it is worth considering the inclusion of such an opportunity in your selection process.

## Administrative procedures

Once you have completed your selection process and made a decision about the successful candidate, there are a number of things you need to do to close the process:

➤ The successful candidate
   – Offer the position to the successful candidate.
   – Secure his or her acceptance of the position.
   – Agree the details of the appointment.
   – Confirm the details in writing.
   – Check essential qualifications.
   – Initiate new employee processes.
➤ The unsuccessful candidates
   – Inform the candidates of the outcome.
   – Provide feedback if appropriate.

➤ Prepare adequate records.

➤ Monitor the process.

### Offer the position and agree details of appointment

Many employers prefer the personal touch of using the telephone to speak directly to the person they hope will be joining their organisation. Some organisations still prefer to make the initial offer in writing. Important details that need to be agreed at this stage include the start date, the starting salary and details about salary progression.

### Confirm details in writing

Although an oral agreement can be regarded as a contract, most employers and employees feel more secure about the arrangement if it is put in writing. Usually the employer will write to the candidate to confirm the appointment and in turn require written confirmation of acceptance from the candidate. There is also a legal obligation to give a statement of terms and conditions to most employees, and this is discussed in more detail in Chapter 6.

### Check essential qualifications

If specific qualifications are required for the post, for example, a degree, a driving licence or professional certification, the selected candidate should be required to present the documentation as proof that he or she does in fact possess the relevant qualifications.

A further, general requirement that applies to all employees is, of course, that they are legally entitled to work in the UK. The Asylum and Immigration Act 1996 reinforced the employer's responsibility for ascertaining that every new employee has the appropriate status. If employers selectively check only those applicants who, because of their appearance or a foreign sounding name, arouse doubts about their citizenship status, such action could be deemed to be unlawful racial discrimination. To avoid this and at the same time fulfil the requirement to check employees' status, employers need to audit the documentation of all new employees at some stage in the selection process. A record of documented evidence of a person's national insurance number, such as a pay slip issued by a former employer, has been deemed to be adequate proof of the fact that an employer has carried out this duty. The Home Office has a web site where employers can get more information on this issue.

### Initiate new employee processes

In addition to the appointment letter and check of credentials, there are a number of administrative details that need to be attended to for each employee. These include such things as acquiring details on pension arrangements, ascertaining preferences with regards to benefits (if a cafeteria system of benefits is in place, and employees can choose some benefits in preference to others), acquiring personal details such as bank account data for payroll purposes, and determining whether the person wishes union dues to be deducted from salary if a check-off system is in place. These administrative details will vary from one workplace to another, and it is sufficient here to note that they need to be planned and administered.

### Inform the unsuccessful candidates of the outcome

Unsuccessful candidates should be treated with courtesy and informed as soon as possible of the outcome of the selection process, usually as soon as the preferred candidate has accepted the post. We have mentioned before that there is a public relations element in the way that recruitment and selection are performed. It is probably one of the few times that outsiders are invited into your company and are able to observe first-hand how you treat people. You will usually reject more people than you hire, and these people could be customers or even still potential employees whom you would not wish to alienate. Most candidates who have made it through the interview stage are serious about wanting the post, and inevitably will be disappointed that they have not succeeded. The rejection message needs, therefore, to be delivered with some sensitivity and, if possible, to avoid implying that these candidates have failed or are of inferior calibre.

ACTIVITY **5.3**
..............

Compose a standard letter that could be used for informing applicants that they have not been selected for a position. A model letter is given in Appendix 5.6 for you to compare with your proposed letter.

### Feedback to candidates

Usually employers do not offer feedback to rejected candidates unless psychological tests have been used, in which case it is considered to be good practice to do so. However, some candidates are aware that asking for feedback can make a good impression with potential employers and that honest feedback might assist them in their further job search. Proper assessment of candidates should enable employers to be ready to give feedback to candidates in a sensitive manner.

### Record keeping

The assessment record can form part of the recorded justification of why candidates were selected or rejected. In addition, preparing a summary statement of the reasons for the decisions, i.e. a statement of why the selected candidate was the preferred candidate and why the unsuccessful candidates were rejected, adds some rigour to the process. It is also necessary to keep such records to be able to provide evidence of good practice in case any applicant feels he or she has been subjected to unlawful discrimination and takes a complaint to an employment tribunal. Since the time limit for presenting a claim of discrimination to an employment tribunal is three months, it would seem sensible to keep detailed records of selection decisions for at least that period of time.

### Monitor the process

The selection process should be monitored for several purposes:

➤ to ensure that selection is being conducted within the framework of the organisation's policies and discrimination legislation
➤ to examine the validity of selection decisions
➤ to ensure there is an acceptable level of reliability among assessors and interviewers.

A statistical analysis of the candidates who proceed through the various stages of selection will identify trends and provide feedback about how various groups fare throughout the selection process. The data could be analysed in terms of groupings of internal vs. external candidates, male vs. female, age profiles, racial groups and the disabled.

Another important consideration is whether the selection process results in the acquisition of high performing employees. Data from performance appraisals and information about promotions could be cross-referenced with the ratings awarded to candidates in the various selection exercises to show whether assessment during the selection process correlates with performance on the job.

The ratings arrived at by individual interviewers and assessors can be compared and the reasons for discrepancies investigated. This information can be used to identify the training needs of those involved in selection.

### Conclusion
••••••••••••••

Now that you have done all you can to find a person who is going to be a productive colleague, you must turn your thoughts to what you can do to help integrate this person into your organisation as quickly and smoothly as possible. You will find a discussion of induction activities in Chapter 8. You should find the case study at the end of this chapter a useful exercise in putting together and applying all you have learned about recruitment and selection in this chapter along with Chapters 2, 3 and 4.

**SELF-CHECK QUESTIONS**

**Answer the following multiple choice questions. The correct responses are given on page 423 for you to check your understanding of this chapter.**

1   **What kind of exercise did Makin and Robertson identify as being used most in assessment centres?**
    (*a*) **handwriting tests**
    (*b*) **group discussion**
    (*c*) **work sample**
    (*d*) **information technology skills**
2   **A good selection technique predicts success on the job. Is this validity or reliability?**
3   **Interviews, according to Makin and Robertson, are used more than psychological tests. Is this because they have a higher validity? YES or NO**
4   **Psychological tests are most useful when the selection ratio is high. TRUE or FALSE?**

5  **Which of the following tests is regarded in the UK as being the least acceptable?**
   (*a*)  **personality questionnaires**
   (*b*)  **leaderless group test**
   (*c*)  **graphology**
   (*d*)  **attainment test**

6  **Applicants for teaching posts are often asked to conduct a seminar in their subject as part of the selection process. This is an example of:**
   (*a*)  **a leaderless group exercise**
   (*b*)  **a job sample test**
   (*c*)  **a personality test**
   (*d*)  **an attainment test**

7  **Is the following statement true or false? The benefit of a realistic job preview is that it persuades people to join the company by presenting positive information about the job.**

8  **Which of the following statements best describes an assessment centre?**
   (*a*)  **An assessment centre is a location where groups of candidates can be assessed by a number of assessors using a range of tests and exercises.**
   (*b*)  **An assessment centre is a method of collecting information where groups of candidates are assessed by a number of assessors using a range of tests and exercises.**

9  **References are one of the most valid techniques of acquiring information about candidates. TRUE or FALSE?**

10 **When an activity has face validity, it means that it**
   (*a*)  **tests what it purports to test**
   (*b*)  **resembles the activity it is testing for**
   (*c*)  **includes a one-on-one interview together with written tests.**

## Major assignment: recruitment and selection

### *Background information*

You are the Head of Personnel Management at the headquarters of the Recovery Insurance Group. The group has 40 branch offices based in the North of England. The Regional Head Office is in Leeds, and this is where you are based. You determine company personnel policy for the region. You normally have three personnel assistants who report to you, but there is a vacancy in one of these posts which you hope to fill soon. Each personnel assistant is responsible for the day-to-day personnel activities in a group of about a dozen branch offices which are generally between 15 and 20 miles apart from each other, but some of these are located 100 miles or so away from Leeds. Because the responsibility for some of the branches requires more travelling than others, the custom has been to rotate the allocation of branches among the personnel assistants on an annual basis.

You have been with the Recovery Group for just over one year. You are professionally qualified yourself. You undertook a BA in Business and Finance before getting your first job as an administrative assistant in a personnel department in a bank. While you worked there, you studied part-time for your IPD qualifications (though it was still the IPM at that time) and progressed to being one of the personnel officers for the bank. Since then you have worked for a further two years for another insurance company in the south of England before taking up your present post as Head of Personnel at Recovery.

The company operates a performance appraisal scheme and at present has a manual system for keeping personnel records. You have been particularly concerned by the fact that the system seems unable to provide information about employee timekeeping and absences. However, the senior managers in the company had decided to introduce a computerised personnel and payroll system in the future, and during your first year with them you have had the responsibility for leading a team which chose and recommended the purchase of a system called PersPay. Now one of your major responsibilities will be to ensure the successful implementation of this system.

You have persuaded the senior managers of Recovery to upgrade the vacant personnel assistant post, as you will need to have someone to help with the development of the computerised operations. This person will have to work closely with members of the payroll office as some parts of the system will be linked, for example, the entry of salary figures, and start and termination dates. Relations between the payroll and personnel offices have been good, but each department is facing increasing workload demands with no possibility of acquiring extra staff, so there may be some difficulty in agreeing the assignment of duties between the two departments.

Incidentally, you have also secured the agreement of the senior managers that you may rename your department and call it the Department of Human Resource Management to reflect the change in approach you wish to bring to the management of employees at Recovery.

### Your tasks

1 One of the first things you want to do is fill the vacancy for the personnel assistant. You find a job description on file (see Appendix 5.1), but you feel it could be better written and it needs to be updated. Produce the new job description.

2 Produce a person specification to accompany the job description.

3 Design an advertisement, and say where you will place it and why.

4 Outline the selection process you intend to follow, including any techniques you will use to supplement the interview.

5 Prepare a set of questions to be asked at interview. Write a brief rationale for these questions.

6 Among the applications you receive are four included here as Appendices 5.2, 5.3, 5.4 and 5.5. Assume for this part of the exercise that you are willing to accept CVs as well as completed application forms. Evaluate these four applications, and explain whom you would invite for interview, giving your rationale for reaching these decisions.

## References
••••••••••••••

Anderson, Neil and Shackleton, Viv. Informed choices. *Personnel Today*, 8 November 1994, 33–34.

Fletcher, Clive. Selection tests and tools. *Personnel Management*, January–November 1994.

Fletcher, Clive. Testing times for the world of psychometrics. *Personnel Management*, December 1993, 46–50.

Graham, H. T. and Bennett, R. *Human Resources Management*. 7th edition, Pitman, 1992.

Gunter, B., Furnham, A. and Drakely, R. *Biodata: Biographical Indicators of Business Performance*. Routledge, 1993.

Institute of Personnel and Development. *IPD Guide on Psychological Testing*. IPD, 1997.

Makin, Peter and Robertson, Ivan. Selecting the best selection techniques. *Personnel Management*, November 1986, 38–40.

Marchington, Mick and Wilkinson, Adrian. *Core Personnel and Development*. Institute of Personnel and Development, 1996.

Murphy, Kevin R. and Davidshofer, Charles O. *Psychological Testing. Principles and Applications*. 3rd edition, Prentice Hall International Editions, 1994.

Newell, Sue and Shackleton, Viv. Management selection: a comparative survey of methods used in top British and French companies. *Journal of Occupational Psychology*, Vol. 94, 1991, 23–36.

Smith, Mike and Robertson, Ivan T. *The Theory and Practice of Systematic Personnel Selection*. 2nd edition, Macmillan, 1993.

Toplis, J., Dulewicz, V. and Fletcher, C. *Psychological Testing: A Manager's Guide*. 3rd edition, Institute of Personnel and Development, 1997.

Woodruffe, Charles. *Assessment Centres: Identifying and Developing Competence*. 2nd edition, IPD, 1993.

## Further study
••••••••••••••••••

### Books

Advisory, Conciliation and Arbitration Service. *Recruitment and Induction*. ACAS, 1997. (A concise overview of good practice in recruitment and selection.)

Bawtree, Susan and Hogg, Clare. *Assessment Centres*. Factsheet 22 issued with *Personnel Management*, October 1989. (A concise overview of the major features of assessment centres.)

Graham, H. T. and Bennett, R. *Human Resources Management*. 7th edition, Pitman, 1992. (One of the M & E Handbook series, this volume provides definitions and concise descriptions of major human resource management concepts.)

Gunter, B., Furnham, A. and Drakely, R. *Biodata: Biographical Indicators of Business Performance*. Routledge, 1993. (An in-depth examination of biodata instruments, their construction and their uses.)

Institute of Personnel and Development. *IPD Guide on Psychological Testing*. IPD, 1997. (A concise guide to the issues involved in choosing to use psychological tests and advice on how to use them in a professional manner.)

Murphy, Kevin R. and Davidshofer, Charles O. *Psychological Testing. Principles and Applications*. 3rd edition, Prentice Hall International Editions, 1994. (Chapter 18, 'Psychological measurement in industry: issues in prediction', presents a good overview and evaluation of the uses of a variety of selection tests, including the interview and the use of biodata.)

Smith, Mike and George, Dave. Selection methods. In: Cooper, Cary L. and Robertson, Ivan T. (eds). *Key Reviews in Managerial Psychology*. Wiley, 1994. (An overview of research conducted on selection techniques, this chapter will be useful to anyone wishing to write an academic report.)

Toplis, J., Dulewicz, V. and Fletcher, C. *Psychological Testing: A Manager's Guide*. 3rd edition, Institute of Personnel and Development, 1997. (Provides an excellent overview of everything managers need to know about psychological testing in the workplace in order to be able to make informed decisions.)

### *Articles*

Anderson, Neil and Shackleton, Viv. Informed choices. *Personnel Today*, 8 November 1994, 33–34. (A brief overview of the popularity and accuracy of various selection methods and a comment on patterned behaviour description and situational interviews.)

Fletcher, Clive. Selection tests and tools. *Personnel Management*, January–November 1994. (Various authors contributed to this series of eleven reviews of psychological tests, commenting on their usefulness in the workplace. The tests reviewed include the 16PF (February); the California Personality Inventory-309 (CPI-309), used to measure integrity, initiative and leadership potential (April); the Discovery of Natural Latent Attributes (DNLA) test (June); and the Organising Skills Battery (July).)

Fowler, Alan. How to create effective job simulations. *People Management*, 11 June 1998, 52–55.

Fowler, Alan. How to monitor equal opportunities. *Personnel Management Plus*, April 1991, 22–23.

Fowler, Alan. How to plan an assessment centre. *Personnel Management Plus*, December 1992, 21–24.

Fowler, Alan. How to select and use psychometric tests. *People Management*, 25 September 1997, 45–46.

Fowler, Alan. How to use games to choose winners. *People Management*, 13 June 1996, 42–43.

Fowler, Alan. How to use references. *Personnel Management Plus*, May 1993, 22–23. (The 'How to ...' series provides very useful summaries of the major considerations in a range of human resource management activities.)

Korn, Anthony. Take care with references. *Personnel Today*, 25 October 1994, 17. (A review of the legal position of referees.)

Lynch, Brian. Graphology: towards a hand-picked workforce. *Personnel Management*, March 1985, 14–17. (A review of some personal responses of various individuals to an analysis of their handwriting.)

North, Sarah-Jane. Firms pry into murky pasts. *Personnel Today*, 26 July 1994, 13. (A brief summary of the state of play with regard to employers' right of access to job applicants' criminal record.)

Sanders, Debora. Improving recruitment and selection at Pearl Assurance. *IRS Employment Trends: Employee Development Bulletin*, Vol. 101, May 1998, 3–5. (An interesting case study touching on issues of human resource planning, recruitment strategies, psychological testing and the use of an assessment centre.)

### *Audio-visual*

British Broadcasting Corporation. *Situation Vacant*. BBC,1995. (A series of programmes about the selection process in a variety of organisations, first broadcast in 1995. The programmes provide an interesting insight into how managers make selection decisions and portray a range of selection techniques.)

Open College. Interviewing. Programme 2. Produced by Yorkshire Television for the Open College with Channel Four, 1988 (video). (The second programme in a series of five on interviewing skills in the workplace. The programme covers the use of testing as part of the selection process.)

### Internet

| DATABASE/HOME PAGES | INTERNET ADDRESS |
| --- | --- |
| Kiersey Temperament Sorter (Gives an on-screen questionnaire to complete and enables you to score the questionnaire.) | **http://www.kiersey.com/cgibin /kiersey/newkts.cgi** |
| (This site explains the four temperaments, types of personality, identified in the test, and gives analyses of some famous people's personalities.) | **http://www.kiersey.com/aboutk ts.html** |
| Immigration and Nationality Directorate (This site will give you very detailed information about employers' responsibilities with regard to the Asylum and Immigration Act 1996.) | **http://www.homeoffice.gov.uk/ ind/emg1.htm** |

# Appendix 5.1
· · · · · · · · · · · · · · · · ·

Recovery
Insurance Group

JOB DESCRIPTION

*Job title:* personnel assistant

*Responsible to:* personnel manager

*Responsible for:* no one reports to this position directly, but can request work from the word-processing pool and personnel records clerks

*Main purpose:* to provide a day to day advisory service to branch managers on personnel policy and procedures

*Duties:* to monitor application for employment forms submitted by branch managers for candidates selected by them
to agree salary details (in accordance with company pay scales) with branch managers
to pass rejected applications to word processing for standard rejection letters and check and sign those letters
to enter agreed salary, contract, job title and joining details on selected applications and pass to word processing for documentation
to sign joining documentation on behalf of company
to advise branch managers on the interpretation and implementation of the company's disciplinary procedure
to advise branch managers on the interpretation and implementation of the company's sick pay scheme
to advise branch managers on the interpretation and implementation of relevant legislation - including Employment Protection, Race Relations, Rehabilitation of Offenders, Disabled Persons, and Health and Safety at Work
to pursue references, by letter and telephone, for selected applicants
to provide references, by letter and telephone, for past employees
to advise branch managers on current employees' salary entitlement, according to company incremental scales
to advise branch managers on the purpose and use of the company's performance appraisal scheme
to visit branches to advise on problems in any of the above areas, as necessary

*General circumstances:* Recovery Insurance Group has divided its business into four areas for administrative purposes, each containing about 12 branches. The branch managers are all experts in insurance, not necessarily in staff matters. As all are at different locations in the North of England, much of the communication with the personnel department is by telephone, although about one day per month is normally spent visiting branch offices.

**Appendix 5.2**

............

---

## RECOVERY INSURANCE GROUP

The Recovery Insurance Group is striving to become an Equal Opportunities Employer. All appointments are made in keeping with our Equal Opportunities Policy.

### APPLICATION FOR EMPLOYMENT

POST *Personnel Assistant*    LOCATION *Leeds*    REF NO HRM 96–001

Please type or write clearly in black ink. Give all details in full.

SURNAME *Paulson*

FORENAME *Jenni*

ADDRESS   *9 Queens's Way*
*Harrogate, HA4 5BC*

TELEPHONE   HOME: *0423–000–000*    WORK: ——

Do you hold a current driving licence?   (YES) / NO

### EMPLOYMENT EXPERIENCE

PRESENT OR MOST RECENT EMPLOYMENT

NAME & ADDRESS OF PRESENT EMPLOYER
*Hartley Building Society*
*Regents Road*
*Cheltenham*
*Wiltshire.*

JOB TITLE: *Personnel Coordinator*
START DATE: *1990*
END DATE: *1994*
(if applicable)
PRESENT SALARY: *Final salary was £22,000*
PERIOD OF NOTICE REQUIRED:

DUTIES:
*I was responsible for overseeing all personnel operations for the SW region of the building society. This included recruitment and selection, advice on policy and procedure to managers, and coordination of training.*

---

### PREVIOUS EMPLOYMENT (START WITH MOST RECENT POST)

| FROM MONTH/YEAR | TO MONTH/YEAR | EMPLOYER | JOB TITLE AND BRIEF DESCRIPTION OF DUTIES | FINAL SALARY |
|---|---|---|---|---|
| *Sept 1987* | *July 1990* | *Hart, Fleet and Barthorne Legal Group* | *Assistant Personnel Manager Recruitment of office staff, induction and training* | *£17,000* |

### EDUCATION AND TRAINING

| SCHOOL/COLLEGE/UNIVERSITY/OTHER | QUALIFICATION | FROM | TO |
|---|---|---|---|
| *Hillingdon Girls School* | *9 GCSEs A Level English German Maths* | *1975* | *1982* |
| *University of London University of Nottingham* | *BA (Hons) 2.1 English MA in Industrial Relations* | *1982* *1985* | *1985* *1987* |

### MEMBERSHIP OF PROFESSIONAL ASSOCIATIONS

*MIPD (1992)*

## ADDITIONAL INFORMATION

Please state why you are interested in the position you are applying for, and explain how your qualifications and work experience relate to this post. Please supply any additional information you feel may assist the selection panel in evaluating your application for this post. You should include any unpaid or voluntary work experience or any leisure activities where you feel you have developed relevant skills.

*I have 7 years experience in responsible personnel management positions and excellent academic qualifications. I have experience in all areas listed in your job description and feel sure I would enjoy the work at Recovery and be a very capable employee.*

*During my career break since 1994 I have organised a mother and toddler group and I have been active at my local church.*

## REFERENCES

Please give the names, addresses and telephone numbers of two referees. One of these should be your current or most recent employer. Please indicate if you wish to be consulted before we contact your current employer.

1 Name: *Mr Peter White*

   Address: *Hartley Building Society*
             *Regents Road*
             *Cheltenham*
             *Gloucestershire*
             *CH4 9TS*

   Tel No: *01242–000–000*

   Position: *Personnel Director*

2 Name: *Reverend Mark Acton*

   Address: *St. Nicholas Church*
             *Parkes Road*
             *Harrogate*

   Tel No: *01423–000–000*

   Position: *Vicar*

## DECLARATION

I certify that the information provided in this form is correct and accurate to the best of my knowledge. I understand that any misrepresentation makes me liable to disqualification or dismissal should I be engaged.

Signature *Jenni Paulson*    Date *10.4.99*

Thank you for completing this form. Please return it to:

Head of Personnel Management
Recovery Insurance Group
Capital Square
LEEDS
LX1 1YZ

We regret that we are unable to acknowledge individual applications. If you wish to have confirmation that your application has been received, please enclose a stamped, addressed envelope. If you have not heard from us within three weeks, you should assume that your application has been unsuccessful on this occasion.

## EQUAL OPPORTUNITIES MONITORING INFORMATION

This information is collected ONLY to assist us in monitoring equal opportunities in our company. We are asking you to provide the information on this tear-off strip so that it can be retained in the Human Resource Management department before your application is circulated to other managers. The details given here will NOT be considered as part of the selection process.

If you choose not to complete this section, this will not affect your application.

Surname: *Paulson*

Forename: *Jenni*

Date of Birth: *14.4.1964*

Male [ ]    Female [✓]

Are you Registered Disabled? YES (NO)

If so, what is the nature of your disability?

How would you describe your ethnic origin?

Afro Caribbean [ ]   Asian [ ]

UK Afro Caribbean [ ]   UK Asian [ ]

UK European [✓]   Other European [ ]

Other ..................

## Appendix 5.3
··················

43 Jackland Road
Newcross
Huddersfield
HD9 5CK

Head of Personnel Management
Recovery Insurance Group
Capital Square
LEEDS
LX1 1YZ

9 April 1999

Dear Ms Jones

Please accept the enclosed CV as my application for the position of Personnel Assistant with the Recovery Insurance Group.

I have had a number of years of experience in personnel jobs, working first as a secretary in a personnel office and then moving into administrative posts. I have attended a few IT courses and used a range of computer packages. I was made redundant when Dywell was taken over by another company in 1998, and I have been working in temporary posts since then.

I am very interested in this post and would appreciate the chance to discuss my application with you at an interview.

Yours sincerely

*A Walters*

Amanda Walters

Amanda Walters
43 Jackland Road
Newcross
Huddersfield
HD9 5CK
Tel: 01484 000 000

**PERSONAL DETAILS**

Date of Birth:     25 August 1953
Marital Status:    Divorced with one adult son

**QUALIFICATIONS**    1974 Secretarial Course. Typing 80 w.p.m
Shorthand 120 w.p.m

Short courses in word processing, data bases and
spreadsheets, including software for Windows.
Short courses in health and safety, supervisory
skills, equal opportunities, and presentation
skills.

**EMPLOYMENT**

1975–1986    Secretary to General Manager, Dyason's
Cleaning Products.
1986–1988    Office Manager, Dywell Clothing Company.
1988–1991    Personal Assistant to the Director of
Personnel, Dywell Clothing Company.
1991–1998    Assistant Personnel Officer, Dywell Clothing
Company.
1999         Temporary jobs for Ace Recruitment Agency.

**REASONS FOR APPLYING FOR THIS POST**

I have worked for ten years in a personnel department and I
have a wide range of experience including recruitment and
selection, administration of personnel records, and running
short courses in health and safety and supervisory skills. I am
a trained secretary and have kept up my typing skills as well
as updating my skills in office software. I feel that with my
experience and background in personnel I have a lot to offer in
a personnel position.

**INTERESTS**

I enjoy travelling abroad in the holidays, walking my two dogs,
and I am also a member of the operatic society. I have taken part
in several productions in recent years.

# Appendix 5.4

## RECOVERY INSURANCE GROUP

The Recovery Insurance Group is striving to become an Equal Opportunities Employer. All appointments are made in keeping with our Equal Opportunities Policy.

### APPLICATION FOR EMPLOYMENT

POST  Personnel Assistant    LOCATION  Leeds    REF NO  HRM 96-001

Please type or write clearly in black ink. Give all details in full.

SURNAME  Hamid

FORENAME  Karim

ADDRESS  5 Merton Road
Coldfield,
Leeds, LS14 3BD

TELEPHONE  HOME: 0113-000-000    WORK: _____

Do you hold a current driving licence?  (YES) / NO

### EMPLOYMENT EXPERIENCE

PRESENT OR MOST RECENT EMPLOYMENT

NAME & ADDRESS    JOB TITLE: Personnel Assistant
OF PRESENT EMPLOYER    START DATE: 1997
Meltham Office Supplies    END DATE: March, 1999
The Causeway    (if applicable)
Bradford    PRESENT SALARY: £12,000
BD1 6XJ    PERIOD OF NOTICE
REQUIRED:

DUTIES:
I created personnel files for all new starters and kept the files up to date. I sent all details to the payroll office. I placed adverts for all positions and organised the applications and interviews for the managers.

### PREVIOUS EMPLOYMENT (START WITH MOST RECENT POST)

| FROM MONTH/YEAR | TO MONTH/YEAR | EMPLOYER | JOB TITLE AND BRIEF DESCRIPTION OF DUTIES |
|---|---|---|---|
| Oct 1995 | Feb 1997 | Meltham Office Supplies | Wages Clerk Recorded hours worked by part-time staff and calculated wages. |

### EDUCATION AND TRAINING

| SCHOOL/COLLEGE/UNIVERSITY/OTHER | QUALIFICATION | FROM | TO |
|---|---|---|---|
| High School | 4 GCSEs A Level History Business studies | 1988 | 1995 |
| Metropolitan University of Leeds | Professional Management Foundation Programme (1st stage of IPD programme) | 1998 | 1999 |

MEMBERSHIP OF PROFESSIONAL ASSOCIATIONS

## ADDITIONAL INFORMATION

Please state why you are interested in the position you are applying for, and explain how your qualifications and work experience relate to this post. Please supply any additional information you feel may assist the selection panel in evaluating your application for this post. You should include any unpaid or voluntary work experience or any leisure activities where you feel you have developed relevant skills.

*I am very interested in continuing my career in personnel. I feel I can use the skills I learned at Meltham Office Supplies. I have successfully completed stage one of the IPD qualification and I hope to continue with this in the near future.*

## REFERENCES

Please give the names, addresses and telephone numbers of two referees. One of these should be your current or most recent employer. Please indicate if you wish to be consulted before we contact your current employer.

1 Name: *Mrs Briggs*  2 Name: *Dr Meyer*

Address: *Meltham Office Supplies*  Address: *Metropolitan*
*The Causeway*  *University of Leeds*
*Bradford*  *Leeds*
*BD1 6X9*  *LS5 7JS*

Tel No: *01274-000-000*  Tel No: *0113-000-000*

Position: *Personnel Manager*  Position: *Lecturer*

## DECLARATION

I certify that the information provided in this form is correct and accurate to the best of my knowledge. I understand that any misrepresentation makes me liable to disqualification or dismissal should I be engaged.

Signature *Karin Hamid*  Date *11th April 1999*

Thank you for completing this form. Please return it to:

Head of Personnel Management
Recovery Insurance Group
Capital Square
LEEDS
LX1 1YZ

We regret that we are unable to acknowledge individual applications. If you wish to have confirmation that your application has been received, please enclose a stamped, addressed envelope. If you have not heard from us within three weeks, you should assume that your application has been unsuccessful on this occasion.

## EQUAL OPPORTUNITIES MONITORING INFORMATION

This information is collected ONLY to assist us in monitoring equal opportunities in our company. We are asking you to provide the information on this tear-off strip so that it can be retained in the Human Resource Management department before your application is circulated to other managers. The details given here will NOT be considered as part of the selection process.

If you choose not to complete this section, this will not affect your application.

Surname: *Hamid*

Forename: *Karin*

Date of Birth: *10 March 1977*

Male  [✓]  Female  [ ]

Are you Registered Disabled?  YES  (NO)

If so, what is the nature of your disability?

How would you describe your ethnic origin?

Afro Caribbean  [ ]  Asian  [ ]

UK Afro Caribbean  [ ]  UK Asian  [✓]

UK European  [ ]  Other European  [ ]

Other ...............

## Appendix 5.5
··················

**CURRICULUM VITAE**

**NAME**　　　　　Arthur Jackson

**ADDRESS**　　　19 Craigley Road
　　　　　　　　Eastleigh
　　　　　　　　Hants.

**TELEPHONE**　Eastleigh 000000

**EDUCATION**

1977–1982　　Eastleigh Comprehensive School, Eastleigh.
　　　　　　　Obtained 4 GCSEs.

**WORK EXPERIENCE**

1982-1988  Office Clerk, Bilton Insurance Company, Eastleigh.
1988-1990  Assistant Supervisor, Bilton Insurance Company.
1990-1991  Assistant Training Officer, Bilton Insurance Company.
1993-1994  Temporary Office Worker, Eastleigh Council.
1994-1996  Insurance Salesman, Staywell Insurance, Portsmouth.
1996-1998  Personnel records clerk, Staywell Insurance.
1998-1999  Personnel Assistant, Stay well Insurance.

I would like this job because all my jobs have been in insurance companies and i have lots of experience in personnel and
training.

# Appendix 5.6
..................

Company name and logo
Company address
Town
PC1 1XX


Ms C Candidate
1 Named Street
Candidtown
PC1 1XX


1 June 1999

Dear Ms Candidate

I regret to inform you that the selection panel has selected another candidate for the position of Human Resource Assistant. I would like to thank you for the time and effort you put into your application for this post and for your participation in our selection process. The panel was impressed with the calibre of the candidates and had a difficult decision to make.

Please do not hesitate to apply again for any suitable position with Company Name.

Yours sincerely


A Barker
Director of Human Resources

# CHAPTER 6

# The employment relationship

## Objectives:

*When you have read this chapter you will be able to:*

➤ understand and describe the rights and obligations of both parties to the employment relationship

➤ understand the basis of the contract of employment and describe the terms that should constitute a basic contract of employment

➤ describe the main areas of protection provided to employees by legal statute

➤ describe a variety of working conditions and assess their usefulness and impact for both employers and employees

➤ describe the issues to be considered when an employee leaves an organisation.

The relationship between employers and their employees can be described in many ways. To get a clear picture of what this might entail, think first of any relationship between people, including personal relationships between friends, life partners, and relatives; that is, think about relationships, but not necessarily in the context of employment. Any relationship is formed within a context of rights, expectations and obligations on the part of each party to the relationship. These rights etc. may be individualised for each pair of individuals as in marital relationships, or it may be that a group of people see themselves as forming one party to a relationship and that they therefore have shared interests which they wish to see represented on a collective basis. Some of these rights, expectations and obligations are unspoken: you assume that your close friends will not purposely do anything to harm you, but you do not feel that this needs to be said explicitly. In other things, you may need to negotiate and reach agreement: in spite of the much heralded concept of the 'new man', the division of labour in the household can still be a contentious area in heterosexual relationships. Beyond what individuals agree among themselves, both implicitly and explicitly, there is a legal framework that imposes obligations and guarantees rights, such as the division of possessions when a marital relationship fails. Relationships are also affected by cultural norms, custom and practice, views on what is and is not acceptable and the balance of power. These influences may be relatively stable for long periods of time, but the twentieth century has been recognised to be a period of great and rapid change, a phenomenon which will no doubt continue in the twenty-first century.

**PAUSE FOR THOUGHT 6.1** *Stop to consider the last two sentences in the preceding paragraph. Can you identify examples of these issues either in your own life or in people that you know? What are the determinants of power in personal relationships? What changes in these areas can you identify? Discuss this with a group of fellow students, and you will probably identify a surprising number of influences and changes.*

If you accept that this complex framework applies to personal relationships, it should not come as any surprise that the employment relationship is governed by a complex mix of individual and collective agreements, implicit and explicit understandings, rights and obligations enshrined in legal statutes, and that other influences such as culture and the balance of power apply to it too. This chapter will attempt to give an overview of the many threads that weave together to create the canvas of the employment relationship, and also look at how trends within it can be monitored. In particular we shall examine the legal aspects of the employment relationship, together with some cultural and psychological factors. We shall also look briefly at what happens on the termination of the employment relationship.

## Rights and obligations of the two parties

### *Balance of power*

The extent to which one party in a relationship has rights and the extent to which that party has obligations depend in some measure on the balance of power between the two parties.

**PAUSE FOR THOUGHT 6.2** *Put aside for the moment the notion that as a proponent of the HRM approach you would be seeking to develop a workforce that shared a common purpose with management and with which there was therefore little conflict. If you regard an individual employee or a group of employees as having some areas of conflict with a manager, who would you judge to have more power than the other? List your reasons. What are the implications of this balance of power for the relationship between workforce and managers?*

In spite of legislation that protects a range of employee rights, the general feeling in the industrial relations arena in the 1990s was that the balance of power lay with the employer. These sentiments had been fuelled by legislation throughout the 1980s and early 1990s which progressively curtailed the powers of the trade unions, and by high levels of unemployment and frequent redundancies which undermined many employees' sense of job security.

The implications of this for the relationship between employees and their managers lie in the areas of trust, openness, willingness to cooperate, and amenability to different points of view. Where there is an imbalance of power, these areas of a relationship can suffer or at least they can be difficult to maintain. In the workplace this means that managers will have to find ways of reassuring employees that they will be treated as equal partners in the relationship. Managers will attempt to do this if they believe that an employee relationship based on partnership is in fact a contributory factor in the success of their organisation. We shall explore this belief more fully in our examination of employee involvement in Chapter 13.

The Labour Government elected in 1997 is producing a programme of employment measures that emphasise the development of fairness at work and a partnership approach to the relationship between employer and employee. As these measures are implemented, there may be an observable shift in the general tenor of employee relations. We shall return to this theme also in Chapter 13 where we provide a more detailed discussion of the employee relations scene.

## Expectations of the two parties: the psychological contract

The concept of the psychological contract aroused much interest amongst observers of HRM in the late 1990s, even to the extent that the IPD National Conference adopted it as its major theme in 1996. Attributed initially to Argyris (1960), the concept was further developed by Schein (1978) among others. It concerns the expectations that each party holds with regard to the other, and although the term itself may not be part of current parlance among non-HRM specialists (Dyer *et al.*, 1998), it is nonetheless a phenomenon which has an impact on the way people behave in the workplace. The psychological contract is akin to the implied terms in a legal contract, i.e. much of it will be assumed and unspoken. It includes factors that result in feelings such as loyalty and perceptions of fair treatment, and any factors that affect motivation. Much of the debate in the 1990s has been about feelings of job security as an element of the psychological contract and the extent to which such feelings can be maintained.

The nature of the psychological contract and the motivation of the individual can be influenced by the culture of an organisation and its predominant management style, and can be seen as coercive, calculative or cooperative (Charles Handy, 1985). Coercion, where people are motivated to expend effort in order to avoid punishment, is generally regarded as unproductive and inappropriate for today's work organisations. A calculative contract will come into being where the connection between effort and reward is explicit, and each employee can calculate the value to him or herself of expending extra energy on the company's behalf. The cooperative contract arises when individuals identify with the goals of their organisation. The latter is the kind of psychological contract one would expect to find in an organisation that espouses the human resource management approach of maximising the contribution of its employees.

The cooperative contract implies a more participative style of management and greater employee involvement in decisions in the workplace. Individuals differ, however, in what they perceive as motivating, as Handy points out, and he goes on to say that managers may sometimes be disappointed at a lack of response when they try to change from, say, a calculative contract to a cooperative contract. However, if an organisation is run on participative lines, it is likely to engender positive attitudes in new employees, and perseverance with new techniques may help to alter attitudes among existing staff. The renewed emphasis of the late 1990s on fairness at work and partnership between employers and employees ties in well with this concept of a cooperative contract, and more recent work by David Guest and Neil Conway (1997) also highlights the link between a climate of employee involvement and a positive psychological contract. You will read more about partnership and the techniques that can lead to a cooperative psychological contract in Chapter 13.

## The legal framework

### Contract and common law

Contract and common law, the latter being law established by judges' decisions rather than by statute, are important components of the legal framework that delineates the employment relationship. The first question that arises is whether or not a person is regarded in the eyes of the law as being an employee in the first place, and this has implications for a person's ability to claim the right to the protections provided by statutory employment law.

As with many legal questions, there are instances where there is no straightforward answer to the question of whether two parties have the relationship of employer and employee, and it is up to the courts to interpret the law and come to a decision. There is also no single definitive test that will give a conclusive answer, but some combination of the following factors can be considered in order to conclude whether a person is rendering services as an employee or on a self-employed basis. A person is an employee if:

➤ the employer is entitled to exercise control over what the employee does and how he or she does it
➤ the employee is integrated into the structure of the organisation
➤ there is a mutual obligation to supply and accept work.

A person who is performing work for someone on a self-employed basis is not entitled to the rights enshrined in statutes such as the Employment Rights Act 1996 since such a person is not an employee in the eyes of the law.

### The contract of employment

It is a common misapprehension that the letter offering employment or the written documentation supplied by an employer to an employee constitutes the contract of employment. A contract is basically an agreement, and despite the saying that 'an oral contract is as good as the paper it is written on', if a person offers you employment over a cup of coffee in a restaurant and you accept the offer, you have a contract with each other. The written statement is evidence or proof that a contract exists, but it is not a contract per se; it is a statement of what has been agreed.

#### Implied and express terms

Contracts are made up of express terms and implied terms. As the phrases indicate, an express term is something that is regarded as important enough to be dealt with specifically and agreed on. Some terms may be assumed and not stated explicitly. For instance, it may be stated how much notice an employee is to give if he or she wishes to terminate the contract of employment, but if it is not explicitly stated, the implied term would be whatever is customary in that particular industry or line of work. There is a statutory minimum as far as the amount of notice that an employer should give is concerned, so if there is no explicit mention of this in the contract, the statutory minimum will be the implied term.

On the whole it is best for employers to be explicit about any terms they require, for instance with regard to mobility. If you are likely to require an employee to work at various locations, particularly if you already have establishments in various locations, it is advisable to include this requirement as an express term in the contract. Even then, the enforcement of such contract terms is not without difficulties; you have to be able to show that the term is justified. In a case involving a British Council requirement of its employees to work anywhere in the UK on promotion to a certain grade, *Meade–Hill* v. *British Council*, it was held that this could amount to indirect sex discrimination unless the broadly stated requirement could be justified. Such a clause could be seen as indirect discrimination because fewer women would be able to comply with it than men.

Implied terms include:

> - on the part of the employer
>   - the duty to maintain mutual trust and confidence
> - on the part of the employee
>   - the duty to obey lawful and reasonable orders
>   - the duty of fidelity
>   - the duty to work with due diligence and care.

The duty of fidelity can be explained as the obligation to act in good faith in dealings with an employer or on behalf of an employer. For instance, submitting a tender for a contract that your employer is pursuing could be construed as breaching the implied duty to give faithful service. The employee also has an implied duty not to disclose confidential information, and a duty to cooperate with the employer, i.e. not to deliberately cause disruptions.

**Variation of the terms of a contract**

An employer must give written notice to an employee of any intended changes in the terms of the contract. The employer does not, however, have the right to vary unilaterally the terms of the contract, but must consult with employees and if possible obtain their agreement to the changes. If an employer tries to enforce a change without the agreement of an employee, this can be taken as a fundamental breach of contract which has the effect of repudiating the contract. In these circumstances, the employee can resign, claiming constructive dismissal, and pursue compensation at an Employment Tribunal. An example of a variation of terms would be, for example, insisting that a person who had been contracted to work an evening shift should start working the day shift.

*Employment law*

A variety of employee rights are protected by legal statute, but it is beyond the scope of this text to provide a comprehensive description of employment law. We shall give a brief explanation of how European Union law affects UK legislation, and then focus on some of the issues that have been of recent interest and that you are likely to be asked about as either a line manager or a human resource practitioner. Remember that the law can be very complex and its interpretation most difficult. A number of professional journals, for instance, publish regular briefings which help employers to interpret the law, especially in the light of new decisions on tribunal or court cases. We shall be looking at some aspects of employment law in greater detail, but remember that if you are in any doubt about an employee's rights, it is best to consult a solicitor. You should also keep in mind the fact that the law usually states the minimum entitlement of an employee, and in most circumstances employers can decide to enhance the legal provision with more generous contractual provision. Enhancing entitlements may be a way of attracting and retaining employees with superior abilities, and so may be a consideration in pursuing the corporate strategy, particularly one of growth or innovation. All employees should ensure that they are aware of their employer's contractual provisions, but as a line manager or personnel practitioner, you are likely to be asked for explanations.

We have dealt with certain employee rights in other chapters, so we shall not repeat that information here. You will find a discussion of the legal protection against unfair sex, race or disability discrimination in Chapter 3, certain aspects of the right to consultation and information in Chapter 13, dismissal and redundancy rights in Chapter 15, and health and safety regulations in Chapter 12. Our discussion here will focus on:

- ➤ the statement of particulars of employment
- ➤ notice of termination of employment
- ➤ employee rights to time off work
- ➤ rights relating to maternity
- ➤ the rights of part-time staff
- ➤ transfer of undertakings
- ➤ guarantee payments
- ➤ the written statement of reasons for dismissal
- ➤ parental leave
- ➤ working hours
- ➤ protection of employee data.

**The European Union (EU) and UK employment law**

EU law takes effect in a number of ways, the most important being regulations which have direct effect in member states (i.e. they override domestic law) and directives which have to be implemented through national legislation. Some directives, for instance those that encourage improvements related to health and safety, can be adopted by qualified majority voting, which means that they must be enacted by all member states, including the minority that voted against them. An example of this is the European Working Time Directive which was adopted in 1993 with dissension from the then Conservative Government of the UK. As the directive was considered to be a health and safety measure, the UK was obliged to accept and implement it. This contrasts with directives concerning the social rights and interests of employees, which require unanimity and from which individual member states can opt out. For example, the Conservative Government in the UK opted out of several social measures that were adopted by the rest of the EC at the time of the Treaty on European Union 1992 (the Maastricht Treaty). Since then, however, the Labour Government has signed up to the Social Chapter which is now integrated into agreements made in the Treaty of Amsterdam (1997).

Employees in the public service sector can rely upon the direct effect of directives, i.e. if the directive has not been implemented, this group of employees can take their case to the European Court. National courts also take account of the purpose of directives when interpreting national legislation. This gave rise, for instance, to the House of Lords finding in 1994 that the two-year threshold to be able to claim a range of employment protection rights should apply to all employees irrespective of the number of hours worked, in spite of the fact that this was not stated explicitly in UK law at the time of the finding. (See the later section in this chapter on part-time employees for more detail.)

### Written statement of particulars of employment

Although the documentation referred to in this section does not constitute a contract as such, an employer is bound by law to issue a statement of terms and conditions to most employees, and the content of these documents serves as proof of the existence of a contract and evidence of the terms that were agreed. The legislation covering this statement is to be found in part I of the Employment Rights Act 1996 (ERA). This Act consolidates various individual employment rights which had previously been enshrined in a number of pieces of legislation including the Employment Protection Consolidation Act 1978, the Employment Protection (Part-Time Employees) Regulations 1995 (both of these now completely replaced by the ERA 1996), and parts of the Trade Union Reform and Employment Rights Act 1993 (TURERA).

The ERA sets out what kinds of information employees are entitled to receive about their contract with their employer, and the time frame within which this should be issued, i.e. within two months of the commencement of employment. This entitlement includes all employees contracted to work for one month or more irrespective of the number of hours worked. Parts of the documentation may be given in instalments within that two-month period.

**PAUSE FOR THOUGHT 6.3** *The information to be included in a statement of particulars of employment is indicated in the ERA 1996. What would you expect to be included in this list?*

The statement should contain certain details and at least refer to other documents so that employees are aware of their existence and know where they may examine them. The details to be made explicit in the statement are:

> the names of the parties to the contract
> date of commencement of employment
> date of commencement of period of continuous employment
> hours of work
> location of the workplace and an indication if there could be a requirement to work elsewhere
> details about pay – rate of pay or how it is calculated; frequency of payments (weekly, monthly, etc.)
> job title or a brief description of the duties
> holiday entitlements
> arrangements about sick pay and sick leave
> details about any company pension plan

➤ · entitlement to receive notice of termination of employment and obligation to give notice

➤ date employment ends if the contract is for a fixed term

➤ any terms of a collective agreement that affect working conditions.

Employees are entitled to be notified in writing of any changes to be made to any of these terms.

Details about sick pay, notice periods and pension arrangements may be given to employees by referring them to other documents, but again any subsequent changes in these documents must be notified directly to individual employees. Employees should also be referred to documents outlining the disciplinary rules, procedure, named person or position of person to whom appeals against decisions can be made, grievance procedures and name or position of person to whom a grievance should be referred in the first instance.

### Notice of termination of employment

Employers may have their own schedule of the notice they require from employees and are prepared to give to employees, but the statutory rights as stated in part IX of the ERA are:

➤ 1 week's notice after 1 month and up to 2 years' service

➤ 2 weeks' notice after 2 years and up to 3 years' service, continuing to increase by one week for every completed year of service to a maximum of 12 weeks' notice.

### Employee rights to time off work

The ERA provides for employees to have a right to time off work in various circumstances. This may be unpaid or paid, depending on the circumstances, and includes time off for:

➤ union officials, in a union recognised by the employer, to complete certain duties such as taking part in negotiations with the employer (paid)

➤ members of a recognised union to participate in certain activities (unpaid)

➤ public duties such as acting as a justice of the peace (unpaid)

➤ employees selected for redundancy to look for work or make arrangements for training (paid; 2 years' service required)

➤ antenatal care (paid).

This is not a comprehensive list, but gives you some idea of existing entitlements to time off. The phrase that is applied to the entitlement to time off is that it should not be unreasonably refused, and in some circumstances, for instance those related to the performance of public duties, employers are entitled to give consideration to business needs in assessing what a reasonable amount of time off work would be.

### Rights relating to maternity

The employment rights of pregnant workers is a complex area and one in which there will be many individual circumstances to be taken into account. We shall outline the basic rights here, but remember that you will have to study this topic in more depth if you are responsible for interpreting maternity rules and policies in the workplace. The Department of Trade and Industry (1997) booklet on maternity rights is a good starting point. The key points are as follows.

*Antenatal care*
As mentioned earlier, pregnant employees have a right not to be unreasonably refused paid time off work for antenatal care regardless of length of service and hours worked.

*Maternity leave and maternity absence*
The major point is that all pregnant employees are entitled to at least 14 weeks' leave regardless of length of service and hours worked. The right to 14 weeks' leave implies the right to return to work. Two further points are that there are entitlements to additional absence for women with qualifying service, and that women who wish to take maternity leave and/or return to work afterwards must give proper notice to their employers. You should check the regulations that are in force whenever you have to deal with these matters, as the rules are complex and they could also be subject to change. At the time of writing, for instance, the Government has included in its White Paper, *Fairness at Work*, a proposal that maternity leave be increased to 18 weeks to correspond better with the period of entitlement to maternity pay. You should check to see whether this proposal has subsequently been accepted as a new regulation or within an Act of Parliament.

Two Court of Appeal rulings in 1998 (*Greaves* v *Kwik Save Stores Ltd* and *Crees* v *Royal London Mutual Insurance Society Ltd*) clarified the position of women who are not able to return to work at the agreed end of their maternity leave because of illness. As long as the employee has given proper notice of her intention to return and acceptable evidence of illness, she is deemed to have returned to her post, even if she cannot be physically present at the workplace due to illness. The dismissals that had occurred in these cases were held to be unfair.

The entitlement to maternity leave is one area where employers often provide contractual enhancements in recognition of the fact that it is desirable to retain valuable employees, but that family commitments can sometimes conflict with workplace obligations.

*The right to return on a part-time or job-sharing basis*
Increasingly there is an onus on employers to give serious consideration to any request for a part-time or job-share arrangement from an employee returning to work from maternity leave. Refusal to do so could be construed as indirect sex discrimination since women with young children are less likely than men to be able to accept a contract requiring full-time hours of work.

> **DID YOU KNOW?**
> Between 1995 and 1998 a number of settlements ranging between £20,000 and £35,000 were paid to women in cases involving companies' refusal to allow them to work part-time or to job share after maternity leave. (Clare Dyer, *Equal fights*, Guardian, *April 28 1998, p. 17.)

*Maternity pay*
An employee on maternity leave continues to benefit from all the terms and conditions of her contract except for remuneration. This means, for instance, that she continues to accrue holiday entitlement, payments into the pension scheme should continue, and the maternity leave period counts as continuous service.

All qualifying pregnant employees are entitled to 18 weeks of statutory maternity pay. The qualifications are that they have worked for at least 26 weeks for their employer before the qualifying week (i.e. the fifteenth week before the week of expected childbirth) and their average weekly earnings in the eight weeks up to and including the qualifying week have been equal to the lower earnings limit for National Insurance contributions (currently £64). SMP is 90% of the employee's average weekly earnings during the first six weeks of the maternity leave, and the remaining weeks are paid at the flat rate, which is currently £57.70 per week. Employers can recoup 92% of the SMP they have paid out, and small employers can recoup 100% plus compensation of 7%.

### Dismissal or selection for redundancy

Dismissal for a matter related to pregnancy or childbirth is automatically unfair. There is no qualifying period of employment or threshold of hours worked to acquire this right. It is also unlawful to select a woman for redundancy on grounds of pregnancy or childbirth.

### Written statement of reasons for dismissal

An employee dismissed during pregnancy or maternity leave is entitled to receive a written statement explaining the reasons for the dismissal. The employee does not have to request the statement in these circumstances, and again there is no qualifying length of service or number of hours worked.

## Part-time employees

The treatment accorded to part-time employees in the UK has traditionally been inferior to that given to full-time employees. However, as employers have come to depend more on employees to be flexible, and to recognise the benefits companies can gain from employing people on non-standard contracts, they have also had to recognise the necessity of addressing the needs of these employees and treating them fairly. The statutory rights of part-time employees were strengthened in the mid 1990s by a ruling from the House of Lords, and current developments are also bolstering their position.

Prior to 1994, part-time employees had to work for considerably longer than full-time employees to acquire the employment protection rights then enshrined in the Employment Protection Consolidation Act 1978. In March 1994 the House of Lords held that the UK had been in breach of Article 119 of the Treaty of Rome and the Equal Pay and Equal Treatment Directives. The existence of differing thresholds to obtain a variety of employment protection rights amounted to indirect sex discrimination since the majority of part-time employees are women. The right of part-time employees to claim statutory protection against unfair dismissal and redundancy should be the same as that of full-time workers, i.e. a two year qualifying period. In response to this judgement, the Government implemented the Employment Protection (Part-Time Employees) Regulations 1995 (now incorporated into the Employment Rights Act 1996) which created equality between full- and part-timers in terms of statutory employment rights.

Part-time staff also have rights to membership of pension schemes as outlined in the Pensions Act 1995 ss 62–66 and Occupational Pension Schemes (Equal Treatment) Regulations 1995. Their rights have been strengthened more recently by the adoption of the EU Part-Time Workers Directive which will be implemented by December 1999 and will give part-timers equal rights to the full array of contractual terms, including rights to staff discounts, and access to training and promotion opportunities. A major aspect of the directive is that it will be unlawful to discriminate against a person because of his or her part-time status; cases of discrimination against part-time employees will no longer have to be presented as sex discrimination.

### Transfer of undertakings

Briefly, the Transfer of Undertakings (Protection of Employment) Regulations 1981 (TUPE) protect the terms and conditions of employees in cases of a transfer of ownership of a trade or business, and dismissal because of the transfer is unfair. This protection was restricted to commercial undertakings and TURERA 1993 removed this restriction. There were many implications from this change for the process of competitive tendering in local authorities, where some contracts had been won on the basis that current employees would accept inferior terms and conditions if this was necessary to win an in-house bid or if they were transferred to the new contractor.

TUPE continues to be a very complex area of legislation, illustrated by the fact that *People Management* devotes a monthly column to an update on the issues and court cases involved.

### Guaranteed pay

Under the ERA, employees are entitled to five days' pay within any three- month period for workless days if the employer cannot provide work as contracted.

### Written statement of reasons for dismissal

Employees are entitled to receive a written statement of reasons for dismissal on request. Under the EPCA, an employee had to have six months of employment to acquire this right, but the Employment Act 1989 increased this to two years for those employed on or after 26 February 1990. Remember, however, that different rules apply to anyone dismissed during pregnancy or maternity leave, and that this right has now been incorporated into the ERA.

### Parental leave

As a signatory to the Treaty of Amsterdam (1997), the UK Government committed itself to the implementation of the European Directive on Parental Leave. This was one of the directives that had been established as part of European social policy at Maastricht and was also one of the directives vetoed by the then Conservative Government.

The basic right to leave is established in the Directive, but details such as duration

**DID YOU KNOW?**
*Parental leave entitlements are already well established in some other European countries. Examples are: two weeks' paid leave in three Scandinavian countries; three days' paid leave in Belgium and France, and two days in Spain.*
*(Guardian, 4 April, 1998, p. 9.)*

and payment or non-payment will be addressed in national legislation. The entitlement can therefore differ among the member states. The proposals for parental leave entitlements in the UK are outlined in the *Fairness at Work* paper, and include:

> the right to time off work to look after a sick child
> three months' planned, unpaid parental leave
> the rights of adoptive parents to these provisions

A further provision that is being considered is an entitlement for fathers to paid paternity leave (one week funded by the Department for Social Security).

ACTIVITY **6.1**

Remember that what you have just read about are *proposals* for parental leave entitlements. The actual provisions have yet to be decided at the time of writing, but are meant to be in force by December 1999. Check in the appropriate issues of legal journals and *People Management* to ascertain the final shape of these entitlements. Have any cases gone to Employment Tribunals, and what was the outcome? Be prepared to report your findings to your class.

## Working time

In 1998 the Government published a set of draft regulations related to the EU Directive on Working Time with the intention of implementing them by October 1998. The major issues are the rules about limits on working hours, entitlement to rest breaks, the right to annual leave, and exceptions or derogations from the regulations. We shall give you a simplified description of the most important issues, but there are many complex and detailed clauses in the regulations. For a fuller understanding you can refer to the *Industrial Relations Law Bulletin* or to the IDS briefing paper on the *Implementation of the European Working Time Directive in the UK* (available on the Internet at http://www.incomesdata.co.uk/brief/wtime.htm).

*Working hours*
Essentially the regulations provide for a maximum of 48 weekly working hours averaged over a period of 17 weeks. It should be noted that employers and employees can reach agreement to work longer hours; the legislation protects employees from being obliged to work longer hours.

*Rest breaks*
Employees should have 11 consecutive hours of rest in any 24 hour period, and a 24 hour rest in every seven days. There is also an entitlement to a 20 minute break if the work day exceeds six hours.

*Annual leave*
Until the advent of this legislation there was no legal obligation for employers to provide paid annual leave for their employees, other than arrangements for statutory holidays. Of course, the vast majority of employers did make such provision, and annual leave has often been part of collective bargaining agreements between employers and trade unions. Even now, many employers will

provide more than the basic entitlement, but at least this legislation will guarantee a basic entitlement which is three weeks in the first year that the legislation is introduced and four weeks after November 1999.

*Derogations*

There are some groups of workers who are not covered by these regulations, including workers involved in air, sea and road transport, junior hospital doctors, and people who have autonomous decision making powers, such as senior managers. Remember, too, that employees can opt out of the provisions regarding working hours by voluntary agreement.

## Data protection

Employers gather and keep a wide range of personal information about employees, and employees have a right to expect that those data will be kept confidential and that a high standard of accuracy will be maintained. The Data Protection Act (1984) provided for some assurances with regard to computerised information, and more recently, paper documents have been covered by the 1995 EU data protection directive which is to be implemented in member states by October 1998. The main thrust of the legislation is that:

➤ documents should be kept in a secure system which allows only for authorised access
➤ every effort should be made to record information accurately and to keep the documents up to date
➤ employees should have access to information about themselves.

The requirement that employees should have access to information about themselves raises several issues that should be explicitly addressed in company policies and procedures:

➤ how is a system of allowing access to be administered, e.g. should employees give notice that they wish to inspect documentation and, if so, how much notice would be a reasonable requirement;
➤ what are the implications for documents that also give information about others, e.g. lists showing salary details of individuals by department or function;
➤ what is to be done about documents that are meant to be confidential to the employer, e.g. references provided by former employers or references written by the current employer when the employee has applied for other jobs.

ACTIVITY **6.2**

Questions such as these are addressed in a number of publications such as the article by Anat Arkin (1997). Read this article and any other information you can find on this topic, and see if you can find the solutions to these problems. Be prepared to report back to your class.

### *Statutory rights: a concluding statement*

As well as understanding the rights and obligations of both employers and employees already established in law, it is essential to be aware that this is an area where issues develop and change very rapidly. These changes can arise, as we explained earlier, from formal consideration of statutes in Parliament or because new understanding of various circumstances arises when judgements are handed down on cases in the courts. In 1995 the Walker case, among others, focused attention on employer obligations with regard to the mental health of employees. Lobbying on behalf of disabled people engendered changes in the mid 1990s in statutory law regarding their rights to equal opportunity in employment. You will find more information on these two issues in the counselling and recruitment chapters (Chapters 11 and 3). One way of staying informed about developments in employment law is to read the legal update articles that appear in journals such as *People Management, Personnel Today, Equal Opportunities Review* and *Industrial Law Journal*.

It is essential to review and update policies and practices to reflect the law as new requirements come into effect. The willingness of employers to offer employees more than the minimum that is required by the law might also contribute to improved employee relations and so enhance the contribution that employees are willing to make.

## Working conditions

Most people still have an image of traditional working patterns which involve spending Monday to Friday in a workplace with contractual provisions for a 36–40 hour work week and three or four weeks' holiday. There are, however, many new patterns evolving to suit the changing requirements of businesses. These include the increased prevalence of part-time employment; contracting-out of work; arrangements for flexi-time, and contracts based on annual or even zero hours. Supermarkets now open on Sundays, and the restrictive Sunday licensing hours for public houses have also been relaxed. Some people are working fewer hours to provide flexibility, and some are working more to cope with the pressures of work. All this variety and change suggests that for some part of your working life you are as likely to be working under flexible conditions as in a traditional arrangement.

**DID YOU KNOW?**

*Men in Britain are more likely to work longer hours than their counterparts in the rest of Europe. (TUC figures quoted in 'Yardstick',* Personnel Today, *28 March 1995.)*

Even the traditional idea of a hierarchical structure with well-defined roles and responsibilities has been subject to much change. Charles Handy (1989) outlined his ideas about new organisations by drawing an analogy with the shamrock leaf. The basic concept is that within an organisation there would be a core of employees consisting of the specialists and managers dedicated to the essential business of the organisation. These are the people who are likely to be working longer hours than the standard 40 per week. In fact, some contracts even contain clauses that mention 'the number of hours necessary to fulfil the requirements of the job'. Other types of work that are needed to keep the organisation going, but are not a part of the organisation's central work, are contracted out to others who specialise in them. This contracting-out of work is the second leaf of the shamrock. The third group consists of part-time and temporary employees who are hired on a flexible basis as required. If everyone in an organisation is a full-time employee, the inevitable fluctuations in business needs imply that you will have slack times when you are paying people to do little work, and times when overtime is required. The mix of working arrangements that Handy identified means that you have the flexibility to call on people's services only when you need them. The emphasis is on developing arrangements to increase flexibility and the organisation's ability to respond rapidly and well to changing requirements.

**PAUSE FOR THOUGHT 6.4**  *Can you think of examples where companies may be employing people to perform tasks that are peripheral to the company's core activities, and where services could therefore be contracted from outside providers specialising in those areas?*

Your examples may have included some of the following. As we have already mentioned, compulsory competitive tendering has now been in place in local government for several years. Services for which external providers can bid include refuse collection, school dinner services, and some professional services, including parts of HRM. Third-party provision of transport for the distribution of goods from manufacturers to wholesalers and retailers is well established, and many manufacturers contract out the distribution of their goods rather than maintaining their own fleet. The provision of counselling by outside agencies is discussed in Chapter 11, and external provision of outplacement services is mentioned in Chapter 15. Cleaning or cafeteria services are often bought in, and payroll services can be provided by banks.

If a company intends to look to external provision of services such as these, rather than creating posts and having its own employees perform this work, then the relationship changes from employer–employee to client–service provider. This relationship requires new skills of managers, who must ensure that a service is delivered to their satisfaction rather than managing employees. Usually, service contracts with exact specifications of the required standards are drawn up, and performance is measured against these.

### Flexible working

As we described above, many employers are developing new arrangements of working conditions in order to meet business requirements, but sometimes these meet the needs of individual employees too. In fact, meeting the needs of business can be synonymous with meeting employee needs if a company wishes to retain valuable staff, whether they are members of the core staff or more peripheral workers. We shall review some of the important developments, looking specifically at annual hours contracts, part-time work, fixed-term contracts, job share arrangements, and teleworking.

## Annual hours

Instead of contracting employees to work, say, a 40 hour week throughout the year, which might entail periods of underemployment and periods of overtime for which the employer pays at an enhanced rate (usually one a half times or double the normal rate), the employer estimates the number of hours he or she will need an employee over the period of a year, and contracts the employee to work those hours at the standard rate. This means that, subject to agreed arrangements, the employer can call on the services of employees when they are needed, and most importantly does not pay employees for their presence at times when they are not needed. Employees are guaranteed payment for the hours that they have been contracted for, and normally the salary would be paid in equal amounts spread over the year.

Terms that would usually need to be imposed on this arrangement would be agreements on things such as the maximum number of hours an employee could be expected to work in a given number of days, entitlement to a consecutive number of days off, notice of a call in to work. The arrangements should be such that employers are able to cover both scheduled and unscheduled requirements.

A number of companies have found that annualised hours work to their advantage. One of the companies that has used this innovative approach is Welsh Water. Managers from Welsh Water presented their system as a case study to the IPM conference in November 1993. Employees were scheduled for new shifts which included some weeks with 40 hours of work and some with 48, weekend and on-call requirements were covered, and employees were also rostered to have one week in six off. The company saw improvements in productivity and a more controlled use of overtime. As this example shows, annual hours arrangements reduce the need for overtime working and strengthen management's ability to control them, but an element of flexibility to use overtime when needed has to remain.

## Job share

The concept of having two people share the tasks designated as constituting one post probably grew out of the recognition that some women did not wish to return to full-time work after maternity leave but would prefer to continue in their careers, working a reduced number of hours. Some employers developed job sharing schemes partly to accommodate this desire, but also because they recognised that this was one way of retaining scarce talent and benefiting from the investment they had made in employees who no longer wished to work full-time. As we explained in the section on maternity rights, it has also recently become increasingly clear that there is an obligation on all employers to at least consider the viability of such arrangements.

Job sharing requires additional arrangements to ensure coordination between partners, which has implications for the managers of job share partners, but there are numerous benefits: it can bring additional flexibility in terms of availability of staff when required for extra work; it shows that the employer is willing to consider new arrangements that accommodate staff needs; the talents and ideas of two people are applied to one job; and it is good for morale. In fact, it is an arrangement that can clearly bring mutual benefit. Also, although we stated earlier that the arrangement probably grew out of the wishes of women returning from maternity leave, job share is not just of bene-fit to women. Men can also have responsibilities as the primary care givers in their families and welcome the opportunity to work part-time, and job share is also attractive to people who wish to combine a steady income with consul-tancy activities.

### Part-time employment

The use of part-time employees has also grown to provide employers with the flexibility they need. The retail sector has always used a proportion of part-timers, but a number of employers, including BHS and the Burton group, increased this proportion substantially in the early 90s. The move to part-time work increases the numbers of jobs for those who wish to work part-time, but it affects the morale of those who really want full-time work.

The improved employment protection rights of part-time employees may have an effect on employers' preference for part-timers over full-timers, since sim-ilar levels of flexibility in terms of hours worked could be achieved by developing a system of annual hours. For example, rather than employing a number of part-timers to cover peak retail hours, a retailer could employ a number of full-time people who work more hours at their standard rate of pay at peak times. Since some of the regula-tions on part-time employees' rights have been in effect for a relatively short time only and others have yet to be imple-mented, it will be a while before any changes in trends are noticed.

> **DID YOU KNOW?**
> The TUC claims that the number of people taking part-time work because they could not find full-time work rose by 62% between 1984 and 1995. The TUC's analysis of government figures showed that of 1.37 million part-time employees, 850,000 would prefer to work full-time.
> (reported in Guardian Careers, 24 June 1995, p. 3.)

### Fixed-term contracts

Fixed-term contracts are addressed specifically in part XIII, s 197 of the ERA 1996, but other sections of the act also apply, such as the need to issue a writ-ten statement of employment particulars to anyone hired for longer than one month. The major features of fixed-term contracts are:

> they state the maximum period of the contract, giving the date on which the contract will end
> non-renewal at the end of a fixed-term contract is a dismissal
> a contract for a specific purpose is not a fixed-term contract; i.e. the contract is discharged by performance and there is no dismissal at its conclusion
> service over a series of fixed-term contracts can be aggregated to constitute continuity of service
> employees on fixed-term contracts can sign written waiver clauses to forego statutory employment rights regarding unfair dismissal and redundancy pay.

There are a number of potential pitfalls that employers may succumb to in drawing up fixed-term contracts. The situation, particularly with regard to waivers of statutory rights, is recognised as being very complex and in need of review. Unfair dismissal waivers are only allowable if the initial term is for one year or more and renewals are for one year. Waivers of the right to redundancy pay are permissible if the initial term is for two years or more; renewals may be of any length. The Government has promised in its *Fairness at Work* paper to review this complex situation.

Another recognised pitfall lies in the wording about the length of the contract. If a fixed-term contract is issued for a period of two years, but the employer discovers after six months that the employee is unsuitable or the expected volume of work does not materialise, a poorly worded contract could see the employer liable to pay the full two years' salary.

### Teleworking/homeworking

The work arrangements we are referring to as teleworking are not to be confused with the kind of low-paid piece work that involves activities such as stuffing envelopes. Teleworking has evolved with the rapid developments in information technology and telecommunications. With the advent of the fax and e-mail, people do not need to be in the same building to transmit written documents and reports instantaneously. Distance working is also used as a term for employees who no longer need to go into an office to do their work, 'tele' being the Greek root meaning 'far'. In other words, the term can be used for people who mainly use technology to produce reports, but also for people out on the road seeing customers. Orders can be relayed using information technology, and often it is more sensible for such employees to use their home as their base rather than an office in a town centre. Jobs are no longer equated with a desk in the office.

**PAUSE FOR THOUGHT 6.5**     *Make a list of what you think the advantages and disadvantages of teleworking are. For every disadvantage you identify, suggest a solution.*

*Advantages*
- ➤ A wider range of people can be gainfully employed, for instance those who have care duties and cannot leave home for prolonged periods of time but who can organise their time at home to include periods of work.
- ➤ Flexibility in working hours: some people like to work at three in the morning while others sleep, and teleworking gives them the opportunity to do so.
- ➤ Working at home cuts down on travelling time, and costs of office accommodation and furniture.

*Disadvantages*
- ➤ Social factors may be the source of disadvantages, but the social system simply needs to be managed properly. Teleworkers may suffer from isolation and a feeling of not being part of a company. An antidote for this is to arrange training sessions and regular briefing sessions when employees can get together and review common problems, and to use communication channels to keep people in touch. If some isolation cannot be avoided, recruiters should attempt to select people who will be suited to the type of work.
- ➤ Some managers, particularly those who adopt a control style, may be uncomfortable supervising teleworkers. It is possible to institute regular reporting mechanisms and control the volume of work done in a period of time, but on the whole the development of teleworking calls for a different

style of management and a higher level of trust. The emphasis is definitely on the fact that the work gets done rather than on imposing controls on when and where it is done.

ACTIVITY **6.3**
...............

Your class will conduct a survey to establish what kinds of working patterns are in existence and whether these meet the needs of the employees concerned. You should decide who your target population will be. For example, you may wish to survey only local businesses and residents, or to include the friends and relatives of students to extend your geographical coverage. You may wish to target a particular industry, for example, the manufacturing sector or retail outlets. You should probably exclude full-time students from your survey, as they have an obvious need to work only part-time.

**DID YOU KNOW?**

*The manufacturing sector is reported to be the sector making the most use of teleworking ('Yardstick', Personnel Today, 28 March 1995).*

1 Work out in class what you want to find out and what questions you need to ask to gather this information. You will want to include some of the following issues. Establish what basis each person is employed on: part-time, permanent, temporary, etc. Establish whether they are satisfied with this or would prefer some other arrangement. If they are not satisfied, why not?

2 Each student will conduct a survey of 5 to 10 people who have some sort of employment and make an analysis of this small sample. Compare your findings with those of others in your class.

3 Work in groups of five and compile an analysis of your pooled information. Report your results to the class and compare your results with those of the other groups in your class.

4 Establish which patterns of employment and employee attitudes have emerged.

5 Discuss how this information might be used by employers to improve their human resource management practices.

The concept of flexible working arrangements is directly connected with the HRM approach in that these innovations lead to empowerment (as must be the case with teleworkers), and the flexibility that is necessary to become a high-performance organisation.

## Termination of employment
.....................................

Employees leave their organisations in a variety of ways and a number of circumstances, and for a number of reasons. Stop for a moment and make a list of as many of these circumstances as you can think of.

In making your list you may have categorised the reasons for employee exit into those that signify voluntary exit and those that are involuntary. Voluntary reasons include:

➤ to take up another post

➤ retirement or voluntary early retirement (although not everyone welcomes retirement at the normal retirement age)

➤ voluntary non-employment, often due to a change in circumstances including parenting or studying.

The involuntary reasons you have listed may include:

➤ redundancy or early retirement as an option to redundancy
➤ dismissal, including dismissal due to ill health.

For each of these reasons for exit, there is a range of circumstances that apply, except perhaps for retirement, which usually occurs for everyone at the company's normal retirement age. People taking up another post, for example, may be doing so for a number of reasons, such as:

➤ personal reasons for moving to another geographical area
➤ because they have been offered more pay or better conditions for doing the same work with another employer
➤ opportunities for promotion
➤ to escape from uncongenial managers or colleagues
➤ a desire for a change of career.

If you have read the chapter on human resource planning (Chapter 2), you will realise that it is essential for employers to understand why people leave their organisations so that appropriate recruitment and retention plans can be devised to maintain the workforce necessary for them to achieve their goals. For this reason, many employers gather information from staff who are leaving for voluntary reasons and conduct an exit interview with them.

### Exit interviews

It is important to gather data on any problems connected with aspects of the employment relationship so that employers can take action to remedy any arrangement that might potentially cause more valuable employees to leave. The areas usually covered in an exit interview include:

➤ the reason for leaving, particularly if the person is going to another job – is it for pay/opportunity/some other benefit
➤ relationships with supervisors and co-workers
➤ working conditions in general and specific ones that might be problematic, such as shift work.

Exit interviews are usually conducted by someone in the human resource management department since employees, even when they are leaving an organisation, may be more willing to talk about problems with a person who does not work directly with them. The interviewer should ensure confidentiality and explain that information gained from exit interviews is used to identify trends rather than to act on information from any individual. These reassurances can make people open up. A good process will include a form that the employee can complete in advance of the interview, and the interview can then be used to clarify details. You will find a similar process recommended for appraisal interviews in Chapter 9.

ACTIVITY **6.4**
••••••••••••

Design an exit interview form and process, either generic or for a company of your choice. Try to apply the questioning techniques you have learned from studying Chapter 4.

### *Retirement*

One of the benefits that employers can offer their employees is preparation for retirement through some kind of formal pre-retirement programme. Moving from working life to retirement requires a big adjustment, and can be achieved more successfully with careful planning, in terms of coping with a changed financial situation as well as increased leisure time. Financial advice on pensions is a complex subject beyond the scope of this text. It is sufficient to note that this is another area that can be affected by changing legislation.

Employers can further consider programmes for keeping in touch with people who have retired from employment with them. It can be a low-cost benefit to arrange occasional social gatherings for past and present employees and to send the company newsletter to past employees, and the returns in terms of morale and commitment from current employees who witness this evidence of their employer's concern for employee welfare may well repay these costs many times over.

### Conclusion
••••••••••••••

We have seen that the relationship between employer and employee consists of rights and obligations on both sides, and that these are determined by law and various other agreements. Innovations in terms and conditions are a signature of the times as businesses attempt to respond to increasing competitive challenges, and the expectation of further developments in European law guarantees that this will continue to be an area of change in the future.

**REVIEW QUESTIONS**

You will find brief answers to review questions 1 and 3 on page 424.

1   Peruse the 'Law at work' sections in *People Management* or the court cases listed in the *Industrial Case Reports* for the last three months or so. Select the articles or cases that are concerned with contractual issues, and review them. Summarise the major hot topics of the day. Have these issues arisen because of any changes in legislation?

2   Find out what the current rate of statutory maternity pay is. How long is basic maternity leave? What are the service requirements to be eligible for extended maternity leave and parental leave?

3   We mentioned that employment legislation usually sets out minimum provisions for employee rights. Can you identify a number of areas where some employers are known to provide more than the minimum?

**SELF-CHECK**
**QUESTIONS**

Answer the following multiple choice and short answer questions. The correct responses are given on page 424 for you to check your understanding of this chapter.

1  Which of the statements below best describes the psychological contract?
    (*a*)  Managers will do nothing to destroy the relationship of trust they have with their subordinates.
    (*b*)  Employers will do all they can to promote the mental well-being of employees, for instance by providing facilities for counselling on personal problems.
    (*c*)  The expectations that managers and employees have of each other can lead to a relationship based on coercion, a calculation of reward for effort, or cooperation.

2  Explain the difference between implied and express terms in a contract.

3  Name the terms that are implied in an employment contract on the part of an employee.

4  Joe Biggins has worked for Actwell Company for nine years. There is nothing in his contract about how much notice he should get if his job is terminated. The company is now moving to another location and has had to dismiss all its employees. How much notice should Joe receive?

5  Annie Creston has been with Actwell for only two months. How much notice should the company give her?

6  What does the acronym ERA mean?

7  How many weeks' maternity leave constitutes the basic entitlement of pregnant employees?

8  A woman needs to have two years of service before the expected birth in order to qualify for the 14 weeks of maternity leave. TRUE or FALSE?

9  An annual hours contract means that employees are not allowed to work over-time. TRUE or FALSE?

10  What major problems were identified related to teleworking?


## References
**· · · · · · · · · · · · · ·**

Argyris, C. *Understanding Organisational Behaviour*. Dorsey Press, 1960.

Arkin, Anat. Data protection: secrets out. *People Management*, 28 August 1997, 26–31

Department of Trade and Industry. *Maternity Rights: A Guide for Employers and Employees*. DTI, 1997.

Dyer, Jackie, Hayes, Nicky and Hayes, John. *The Psychological Contract: Theory and Reality*. Unpublished research presented at the OB Network meeting at Leeds University, 20 May 1998.

*Fairness at Work*. Government White Paper, May 1998. (The paper can be viewed on the Internet at http://www.dti.gov.uk/IR/fairness/fore.htm)

Guest, David and Conway, Neil. *Issues in People Management No 21: Employee Motivation and the Psychological Contract*. IPD, 1997.

Handy, Charles. *The Age of Unreason*. Hutchinson, 1989.

Handy, Charles. *Understanding Organizations*. 3rd edition, Penguin, 1985.

Schein, E. H. *Career Dynamics: Matching Individual and Organisational Needs*. Addison Wesley, 1978.

## Further study
·················

### *Books*

Advisory, Conciliation and Arbitration Service. *Annual Report.* (The annual reports contain a section outlining the legislation that has been created in that year, together with a comment on its likely impact.)

Advisory, Conciliation and Arbitration Service. *Effective Organisations: The People Factor.* ACAS, 1997.

Advisory, Conciliation and Arbitration Service. *Hours of Work.* ACAS, 1997. (Reviews a number of ways of structuring hours of work, including annual hours and job sharing.)

Advisory, Conciliation and Arbitration Service. *Personnel Records.* ACAS, 1997. (An advisory booklet, this reviews the types of information an employer may need to obtain from employees, and explores ways of storing the data.)

Aikin, Olga. *Contracts (Law and Employment Series).* 2nd edition, IPD, 1997. (An excellent reference book for anyone who needs more practical information about various forms of employment contracts.)

Cuthbert, Mike. *Nutshells: E.U. Law in a Nutshell.* 2nd edition, Sweet and Maxwell, 1997.

Department of Trade and Industry. *Written Statement of Employment Particulars.* PL 700 DTI, 1997.

Handy, Charles. *Beyond Certainty: The Changing World of Organisations.* Hutchinson, 1995.

Handy, Charles. *The Empty Raincoat. Making Sense of the Future.* Hutchinson, 1994. (Handy makes interesting observations on the world of work and the ways in which organisations and their requirements change.)

Huws, Ursula. *A Manager's Guide to Teleworking.* Employment Department, 1995.

Pitt, Gwyneth. *Cases and Materials in Employment Law.* Pitman, 1994. (An excellent source of information about the legal aspects of the employment contract and recent court cases in this area.)

Rollinson, Derek. *Understanding Employee Relations: A Behavioural Approach.* Addison-Wesley, 1993. (Chapter 2, 'The individual and workgroups', contains sections on the employment relationship.)

Slade, Elisabeth and Giffin, Nigel. *Tolley's Employment Handbook.* Tolley Publishing Company. (An excellent source of information on employment law. Make sure you refer to the latest edition available.)

Taylor, Simon. Competitive success through participation: the John Lewis Partnership. In: Bradley, Keith (ed.). *Human Resource Management. People and Performance.* Dartmouth Publishing Co., 1992. (A brief review of one employer's relationship with its employees, the underlying philosophy, and the contribution this makes to the company's success.)

### Articles

Ewing, K. D. Swimming with the tide: employment protection and the implementation of European labour law. *Industrial Law Journal*, Vol. 22, No. 3, September 1993, 165–180.

Fowler, Alan. How to draft an employment contract. *Personnel Management Plus*, December 1993, 23–24.

Fowler, Alan. How to draft and use fixed-term contracts. *Personnel Management Plus*, September 1994, 23–24.

Fowler, Alan. How to operate an annual hours contract. *Personnel Management Plus*, April 1994, 26–27. (Alan Fowler provides succinct guidelines on drafting a range of contracts with suggestions for good terminology.)

*Human Resource Management Journal*, Vol. 7, No. 1, 1997. (This issue contains several articles on the psychological contract.)

'Law at work' is a regular feature in *People Management.* (The authors offer readable interpretations of employment laws and regulations, addressing specific issues that are of current concern to HR practitioners and line managers.)

McMullen, John. Flexible working practices. *Croner's Industrial Relations Briefing*, No. 30, 13 June 1995, 12–15.

Syrett, Michel and Lammiman, Jean. Developing the peripheral worker. *Personnel Management*, July 1994, 28–31. (Examines the importance of the contribution of flexible workers and the need to provide them with developmental opportunities.)

### Internet

Law Rights – Employment Questions and Answers  **http://www.lawrights.co.uk/empq2.htm**

As it stood at 15 June 1998, questions 1–9 and question 17 on this page provide an additional self-test for you on the content of this chapter. If you have read Chapter 3, you should also be able to answer question 3 on sex and race discrimination.

There are many Internet sites which can give you access to legal information. We have listed only a selection here for you to try. Most of them have numerous linked sites which you can click on to get more specific information.

European Union Law, UK law online  **http://www.leeds.ac.uk//hamlyn/european.htm**

Eclipse Group: Industrial Relations Law Bulletin  **http://www.irseclipse.co.uk/publications/irlbtext.html**

Implementation of the European Working Time Directive in the UK  **http://www.incomesdata.co.uk/brief/wtime.htm**

Acts of Parliament  **http://www.hmso.gov.uk/acts.htm**

### Audio-visual

BBC2. *Working All Hours: Brave New World*. A Money Programme Special. BBC News and Current Affairs, 1995. (The second of two programmes examines tele-working and other responses to technological developments in the workplace.)

# CHAPTER 7

# Training and the learning process

**Objectives:**

*By the end of this chapter you will be able to:*

➤ state what is meant by learning
➤ appreciate the relevance of various theories of learning to training and development
➤ understand the training cycle
➤ appreciate when to use a variety of training techniques.

In any organisation there are a great many things that the people employed need to learn in order to become competent in their jobs. They learn some of the things they need to know unconsciously, such as the way people speak to each other and the acceptable style of dress or behaviour. At its simplest they are learning about the common view within that organisation of 'the way we do things around here' – the organisation culture.

Anyone who leaves one organisation and goes to work in another will appreciate that things are done differently in different organisations, and people sometimes suffer a feeling of culture shock if behaviour that had been acceptable in their previous organisation is not viewed in the same way in the new one. The new person picks up clues from the behaviour of others as to what is acceptable and what is not. Supervisors and managers will be seen to praise certain types of behaviour but will frown on others.

Managers and supervisors will be keen that the new employee learn certain aspects of their job, and may use a variety of approaches to encourage this learning to occur. They need to be aware, however, that you cannot make people learn, and on the other hand you cannot stop them. People are learning all the time, even if they do not appreciate it: when people join an organisation and learn in an informal way what behaviour is acceptable, the speed with which they learn depends on their motivation, their perceptiveness in picking up clues as to what is acceptable and the examples they see around them. Unfortunately, this may also result in learning bad habits or having incorrect perceptions of situations at work.

Although employees will learn a great deal in this informal way, it is also a good idea for organisations to try to ensure that they have the opportunity to learn things that will enable them to perform to their best ability. This will mean that the organisation will need to:

➤ assess what it thinks people need to learn
➤ plan opportunities to facilitate learning experiences
➤ evaluate what has worked well, and what has been less successful.

Before we actually start to consider what people need to learn we shall examine some of the ways in which people learn. The ways in which people learn have been a subject of interest for thousands of years, and many theories seek to explain how people actually learn. A basic understanding of the learning process is important in order for us to be able to provide appropriate training techniques which will enable people to learn most effectively. In this chapter we shall examine different learning theories and the contribution that they have made to our understanding of the learning process. A range of training techniques will then be discussed as well as some approaches to learning, which may also help you to learn more efficiently.

The next chapter is closely linked to this chapter, and in it we shall discuss methods of assessing training needs and examine some specific groups and the training that they require.

## Learning theories

In order to appreciate more fully the most effective methods to use in training and development, and in order to understand current debates in education or training, it is a good idea to also know a little about learning theories.

### Definitions of learning

There are in fact innumerable definitions of learning, and few are likely to satisfy everyone. Some of the different theories of learning are, however, reflected in the way we use the word 'learning', and these are shown in the following definitions.

The *Shorter Oxford Dictionary* defines learning as:

> 1. 'The action of the verb TO LEARN 2. What is learnt or taught.
> 3. Knowledge ... got by study.'

This dictionary definition seems to indicate that learning is a process in which people are involved, and that they will somehow end up with a certain degree of knowledge as a result of this. Bass and Vaughan (1966), in a definition which has become widely used, said that

> Learning is shown by a relatively permanent change in behaviour that occurs as a result of practice or experience.

This definition sees learning as being shown by a change in behaviour which has resulted from activities or experiences in which the individual has been involved.

In the view of Honey and Mumford (1986), learning has occurred when someone:

> ➤ 'knows something they did not know earlier, and can show it
> ➤ is able to do something which they were not able to do before.'

The last of the three definitions implies that learning could be about acquiring knowledge, which could be tested, or it could be about acquiring a new skill, which similarly could be demonstrated.

These three definitions of learning serve as a useful starting point to examine some of the major theories of learning. They illustrate three differing approaches to learning. The first definition implies that learning is about acquiring knowledge; we call this approach cognitive. The second implies that it is about changing behaviour, so we refer to this perspective as behaviourist. The third definition describes learning as being about both knowledge and behaviour; we might refer to this as an experiential approach.

### Cognitive theories

Cognitive theorists would say that learning occurs within the mind. Ancient scholars such as Plato and Aristotle saw that the exercise of mental faculties, such as reason, memory and willpower, were important to the development of the individual. From this came the notion of the importance of the trained mind. Much education and training in Europe and the United States, especially in the first half of this century, was based on this approach. This meant that learning was structured, teaching methods tended to be by telling and directing (didactic), and the subject matter was perceived to be important in its own right, with memorising facts and learning rules seen to be of great importance. This resulted in the 'chalk and talk' approach to learning, with formal classrooms and lectures where information went from the teacher to the pupil.

This traditional approach to learning can still be seen at work much of the time, and you will see later in this chapter that it relates closely to some people's preferred style of learning. It can, however, be criticised as being too theoretical, and lacking in stimulus for learners of a practical bias. It was in the search for a more practical, active form of learning that the following modern developments in cognitive theory took place. The approach that follows came to be known as discovery learning.

Relatively recent cognitive theorists have been concerned to discover how we solve problems: whether this is by trial and error, by deductive reasoning, by seeking more information or help from someone, or by using a mixture of all these approaches. Sometimes the solution comes with a flash of sudden insight, as in the case of Archimedes' discovery of how to find the weight of irregularly shaped objects when he realised that he himself displaced by his presence a certain amount of bath water and that the amount of displaced water could be measured.

In fact, you do not have to be a genius to have moments of insight. Köhler in 1925 studied how an ape would solve the problem of getting a banana, which was just outside its cage but which was just beyond its reach. The initial attempts by the ape resulted in it stretching its arms as far as possible towards the banana, and of course failing in its task. After a short period of time, however, it reached through the bars of its cage to grasp a short stick and with the aid of the stick brought the banana into its cage. In a later experiment the banana was placed even further out of reach. This time the ape reached through the cage for the short stick which was within its reach and then used this stick to drag a longer stick, which was previously not within reach, into its cage. Then, using the longer stick, the ape was able to reach the banana and drag it into its cage. This showed that the ape was discovering how to use the sticks to get the reward of the banana.

**PAUSE FOR THOUGHT 7.1**  *If apes can have flashes of insight, so can you. Can you give an example of a time when you had a sudden flash of insight and realised that you had learnt something new?*

Köhler's approach to learning relates clearly to discovery learning, where students or trainees are given tasks to achieve but have to find clues or stimuli to show them how to proceed. They learn by working through a process of trial and error to see what does and what does not work. This method aims to provide a means of unassisted learning in which appropriate experiences are provided and by which the student or trainee will gain insights into the best method of achieving the task. This is a very powerful method of learning, as an individual is usually quite rightly proud of what they have learnt, especially since they have been actively involved in discovering for themselves the solution to a problem.

This method, although very effective, cannot always be used. Time can be a constraining factor, as it takes time to allow people to make discoveries for themselves. There is also the related problem of costs. Can you afford as an organisation for all of a group of trainees to waste valuable materials in order to discover for themselves something that their manager could have told them about more quickly and cheaply? There is also the problem of safety to consider: it is not always practicable to allow people to experiment with equipment or materials, even if this is a very powerful aid to learning, if they endanger themselves or others in the process.

### Behaviourist theories

The work of cognitive psychologists that we have examined so far focused on what was going on in the brain, and how we learn and memorise things. In contrast, many learning theorists felt it important to focus on observable behaviour, as they believed it impossible to study the workings of the mind in a scientific manner. The behaviourists, like Köhler, generally studied the behaviour of animals in order to gain insights into how people learn; they were concerned with studying changes in behaviour and said that learning occurred if you could see such a change. The behaviourists made no assumptions about what the animal was thinking or what was going on in its mind; they were concerned only with behaviour that they could see.

**PAUSE FOR THOUGHT 7.2**  *Look again at the definitions of learning given earlier. Which of these definitions reflect the behaviourist view of learning?*

The definition by Bass and Vaughan (1966) – 'Learning is shown by a relatively permanent change in behaviour that occurs as a result of practice or experience' – would seem to reflect the behaviourist view of learning. This definition focuses on the change in behaviour. It does not relate to what the person might be thinking, and unlike the definition from the *Shorter Oxford Dictionary*, it contains no reference to the idea of acquiring knowledge. This latter definition seems to reflect a cognitive approach, while the definition of Honey and Mumford (1986) shows that both gaining knowledge and demonstrating a change in behaviour can be important in the learning process. Their definition encapsulates very neatly elements from both the cognitive and the behaviourist school of thought.

### Behaviourist concepts

Although work with pigeons and dogs may not appear at first sight to be very relevant to training that occurs within organisations, this work does, in fact, raise a great many important issues, of which trainers should be aware.

Early in this century Pavlov (1927) trained dogs to salivate when he rang a bell. He noticed that dogs salivated naturally as a reflex response when food was put in front of them. For his experiment he rang a bell every time the dogs were fed; after a time, the dogs would salivate when the bell was rung, whether there was food or not (Figure 7.1). He deduced that the dogs had learnt to salivate by associating the bell with the food, and came to see the learning process as the development of responses to the new stimuli given by the world. He called them conditioned responses, as opposed to the unconditioned or natural responses that came before. His term for the process of learning was 'conditioning'.

Later, Skinner (1953) took the theory further. The limitation of Pavlov's work was that it showed that animals (or people) could learn to apply instinc-

*figure 7.1*
**Pavlov's dogs**

1.
Bone
stimulus

Dog salivates
unconditioned
response

2.
Bell          Bone
Association

Dog salivates

3.
Bell
conditioned
stimulus

Dog salivates
conditioned
response

tive responses to new sets of circumstances, but it did not show how totally new responses could be learnt. Skinner in fact succeeded in teaching pigeons to play ping-pong by a process that he called operant conditioning. In this process, the pigeons were watched for any patterns of behaviour that might be useful when playing ping-pong, and whenever they performed one they were rewarded with food. Not surprisingly, the birds soon learnt to do certain movements, and they retained their learning better if the reward was repeated regularly, a process Skinner called 'reinforcement'. In human learning, Skinner believed, reinforcement mainly took the form of feedback – information telling the learner whether he or she is getting the task right.

Skinner believed that all learning took place in this associative manner, and that all complex patterns of behaviour, such as learning ping-pong or learning to speak, could be broken down into small steps that could be taught one by one in a simple fashion. He applied this theory both to training workers and to the education of his own children, and his work is still very influential. It obviously makes sense to break down routine tasks into their component parts, and to provide methodical training to cover them. In addition, his emphasis on the visible or objective side of learning led to the practice of setting learning objectives or statements of what a learner had to achieve in terms of action.

On the other hand, you might be wondering whether Skinner's account of the pigeons' learning process was complete. Did insight play no part in their grasp of the rules of the game? In human learning insight often seems to enable people to cut the corners on the road to knowledge, and experience of behaviouristic attempts to teach complex matters suggests that they can lead to a slow, mechanical set of activities. Many psychologists have challenged Skinner's view, particularly with regard to the learning of complex behaviour such as speech.

Scientists such as Pavlov and Skinner referred to the instinctive need that led to learning as 'the drive'. In animals this was normally provided by a desire for food, but in people the drive or motivation might be to pass an exam or just the satisfaction derived from mastering something new. This aspect of their work is important in itself, in that it points to the importance of considering people's motivation to learn. If we can find out what makes them want to learn, we will be able to tailor our instruction better.

ACTIVITY **7.1**
. . . . . . . . . . . . . .

Make a list of a range of situations where you feel that you have learnt something.

➤  In each case consider what was your drive, or motivation, to learn.
➤  Was there a stimulus to increase your drive to learn? What was this?
➤  Was there any form of reinforcement of your learning? What was this?

### Discussion of Activity 7.1

People are motivated to learn by a variety of things, so you may have listed quite a few drives to learn. These may take the form of incentives, encouragement or rewards. Some people may be motivated by the need to do well in an examination or they may perhaps be motivated to learn a new skill because it may provide an improved opportunity of getting a better job or more pay. In other cases the motivation may be the pleasure of learning something new for its own sake or for the respect that other people may feel towards you when you have learnt something impressive. Other people may be motivated to learn by a sense of curiosity or by anxiety and fear of failure.

The tests and exercises should help you to prove to yourself that you are learning. They are one way in which you can show your response to learning. Your response shows what you have learned by giving you the opportunity to demonstrate a new skill, or by your acquisition of new knowledge on which you could be tested.

Programmed learning and computer-based training courses were developed from the behaviourists' work: in them the correct response is immediately rewarded by praise from the manual or computer and you are told that you have given the correct answer or pressed the correct key and can progress to the next stage.

## Reinforcement and feedback

The behaviourists used reinforcement to indicate a correct behavioural response. The reinforcement could be negative or positive. Rewards such as food for animals or praise for people are positive forms of reinforcement of the desired behaviour, while punishments aim to eliminate incorrect behaviour. Research tends to suggest that positive reinforcement is generally more effective than negative reinforcement in gaining a change in behaviour in the long term, as with negative reinforcement the desired change often occurs only as long as there is the threat of punishment. When this threat is withdrawn then behaviour often reverts to the original behaviour.

Reinforcement of your learning could occur by your reading or viewing something and being tested on this and praised by your tutor for your efforts, or by your completing a self-check exercise and giving yourself a pat on the back if you have done well. This will reinforce correct behaviour or show you that you have the right answers, but won't necessarily give you any detailed understanding of what you have done well or of what you did wrong. For that you also need knowledge of results or feedback

Knowledge of results or feedback is important if we are to learn effectively. In a training situation this could be by the trainer giving comments on the person's progress, or perhaps by a manager appraising the work of one of their staff. Giving feedback successfully is a very important skill to develop. Feedback is a way of learning more about ourselves and the effect that our behaviour has on others. If feedback is given in a constructive manner it should result in the individual becoming more self-aware, being aware of differing options and feeling encouraged to develop and grow. Feedback could be given in a destructive way, in which case the individual would end up feeling bad about themselves, with a feeling of hopelessness that there were perhaps no alternatives available to them, and a sense of failure.

When giving constructive feedback one should start with the positive, and focus first on the behaviour that has been done well before giving feedback about behaviour that has been done less well. Feedback about incorrect behaviour, if given skilfully, is extremely important; it doesn't have to be destructive, and here it is important to focus on specific aspects of behaviour that can be changed. General statements such as 'that was awful' are much too vague to be helpful in changing behaviour. It would be easy for the person receiving the feedback to feel that they are just being criticised unless the person who is giving the feedback also suggests alternative ways of behaving. For example, you might say 'The fact that you seemed preoccupied with your paperwork when Rosalind walked into the room, and took some time before you greeted her, seemed a very unwelcoming start to an interview. I think that if you had acknowledged her presence immediately and got up and walked towards her to greet her, it would have been a much more welcoming start to the interview, and would have been likely to have made Rosalind feel much more at ease.'

Feedback is, as we have shown, a very important part of the learning process. The saying 'Practice makes perfect' could well be modified to 'Practice with appropriate feedback makes perfect', since without the feedback the person could just carry on with the same inappropriate behaviour over and over again.

### *Experiential learning*

Behaviourist and cognitive theories are useful, but each tells only part of the story. Other theories try to use elements of both to produce a more holistic view of the learning process. Such an approach is taken in the work of Kolb *et al.* (1974) in America, and of Honey and Mumford (1986) in Britain. They have focused on learning from experience – experiential learning – and have recognised the importance of both behaviourist and cognitive theory and integrated these into the learning cycle shown in Figure 7.2. Their theory also suggests that different people may have different preferred styles of learning.

#### The learning cycle

People learn in a variety of ways, and over the years may develop certain learning habits which enable them to benefit from certain types of experience more

*figure 7.2*
**The learning cycle**

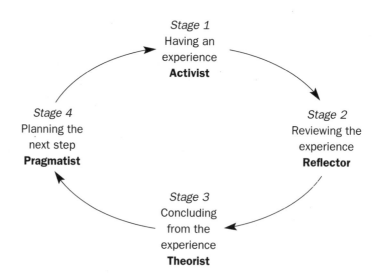

Stage 1
Having an
experience
**Activist**

Stage 2
Reviewing the
experience
**Reflector**

Stage 3
Concluding
from the
experience
**Theorist**

Stage 4
Planning the
next step
**Pragmatist**

than other types. Students in college and people learning in the workplace are both likely to meet a range of different learning opportunities. Many students nowadays will work to supplement their student grant and will themselves have a range of work experiences from which they can learn. Some will be mature students who have already worked for a number of years, some will be part-time students combining study with a career, and yet others will be on sandwich course degrees where they have the opportunity of gaining work experience in a placement for a period of time. Knowing about their own learning style preferences may help them to understand and they may become more efficient in learning from these experiences.

### Stage 1 – Having an experience

Most people have plenty of experiences from which they could learn, but age does not necessarily mean that people have learnt more. Some people do not use the experiences that they have. One way of learning is to let experiences come to you (reactive), and the other is to deliberately seek out new experiences (proactive). Trainers need to provide suitable experiences from which their trainees can learn (in the form, for example, of case studies, role plays and other simulations), but trainees also need to appreciate the need to be proactive and seek for themselves suitable experiences from which to learn. The use of suitable individuals who are willing to act as mentors, or forming a supportive study group of friends, can assist in this process by:

➤ helping to identify suitable experiences from which to learn
➤ reviewing with individuals what they have actually done and helping to draw out what they have learnt
➤ encouraging the individual to be proactive and to seek for themselves suitable learning experiences.

### Stage 2 – Reviewing the experience

If we are to learn from an experience it is important to review what has happened. Unfortunately we are often too busy to do this, and some people never develop the habit of reflection. The individual should be encouraged to:

➤ think about what actually happened
➤ think of other ways in which the situation could have been handled
➤ make comparisons with what happened in other similar situations
➤ read about the subject
➤ compare theory and practice.

### Stage 3 – Concluding from the experience

There would be little point in reviewing the experiences unless we then drew some conclusions from them. This involves scanning the raw material for lessons to be learned and reaching some conclusions. The individual should be asking:

➤ What have I learnt from this?
➤ What could I have done differently?

*Stage 4 – Planning the next stage*

Having reached a conclusion, it is important to try to do things better next time. In order to be able to do this we need to be able to plan, and this involves translating at least some of the conclusions into a basis for appropriate action next time. The individual should be encouraged to:

➤ state what they would actually do next time
➤ draw a plan of action for handling such a situation again.

The four stages in the process of learning using experiences are mutually dependent. The whole process is summarised in the learning cycle (Figure 7.2).

## Learning styles

Most people only use one or two learning styles. Honey and Mumford have developed a questionnaire so that individuals can establish their preferred learning style. They developed this approach as a result of their work with managers, as they became concerned to discover why one person will learn from a particular experience but another does not appear to learn anything from the same experience. Further details of their approach are given in the recommended reading. They say that there are four types of people with differing learning styles which clearly link with the four stages of the learning cycle. These are activists, reflectors, theorists and pragmatists and these will be discussed in turn.

*Activists*

Activists tend to throw themselves into whatever is happening. They seek out new experiences and tend to be enthusiastic about anything new. They tend to be open-minded and not sceptical, and this tends to make them enthusiastic about novelty. They tend to act first and then consider the consequences later. Their days are filled with activity and they often tackle problems by brainstorming.

*Reflectors*

Reflectors tend to stand back and observe experiences from different perspectives. The thorough collection and analysis of data are what are important to them, so that they try to put off reaching definite conclusions for as long as possible. They prefer to take a back seat in meetings and discussions. They listen to others and get the drift of the discussion before making their own points. When they act it is as part of a larger picture which includes the past as well as the present and takes into account other people's observations as well as their own.

*Theorists*

Theorists tend to adapt and integrate observations into complex but logically sound theories. They think problems through in a vertical, step by step, logical way. They assimilate disparate facts into coherent theories, and tend to be perfectionists who will not rest easy until things are tidy and fit into a rational scheme. They value rationality and logic.

*Pragmatists*

Pragmatists are keen to try out new ideas, theories and techniques to see if they work in practice. They positively search out new ideas and take the first opportunities to experiment with applications. They are the type of people who return from a training course full of ideas that they want to try out immediately. They like to get on with things and act quickly and confidently on ideas. They hate long ruminating discussions.

### Individuals' barriers to learning

We all know of people who say that they have years of experience but really seem to have had the same experience over and over again for many years and to have not learnt much from it. Age or length of service does not guarantee that any greater learning has occurred for these people than for someone who has worked for a much shorter period of time, as some people create their own barriers to learning, and are not willing to try anything new or even slightly different.

Some of the barriers that individuals create for themselves to prevent themselves from learning at each of the stages of the learning cycle are discussed next.

➤ People may be afraid that they will lose face or be laughed at if they do something wrong, so they justify their unwillingness to experiment to themselves by saying that the old ways are the best and have always worked well enough in the past – so why change now? In this case, fear of making a mistake will prevent them from using the activist approach.

➤ In order to learn, people need to allow themselves time for reflection. Some people are too busy coping with crisis after crisis to stop and reflect on what they have learnt, and so they are unable to prevent the next crisis from occurring. If this is the case then they will not be using the reflective style of learning.

➤ Some people think that they are unable to learn from books and are unwilling to sit down quietly and try. They may have had bad experiences at school and may reject this as an approach to learning. These people are unlikely to be theorists or to see benefits in this approach to learning. They are unlikely to make connections between theory and practice.

➤ Other people enjoy studying theories but are less interested in whether they will actually work in practice, and so do not ever try to learn in this way. They are not interested in what happens in practice and so the pragmatist approach to learning will not be for them.

An understanding of which learning style seems to work best for you will give you the opportunity either to choose experiences that enable you to learn effectively using your preferred learning style, or enable you to decide to practise and develop the use of other learning styles and so increase the range of ways in which you learn. Using their questionnaire will help you to identify your preferred learning style or styles: how you use then this knowledge is up to you.

ACTIVITY **7.2**

1 Read the description of the four learning styles again.

2 From the descriptions given, which learning style do you think you use most frequently?

3 List the barriers that prevent you from learning using other learning styles.

4 Take this opportunity to practise using all four learning styles. Look at the references at the end of this chapter. Be pragmatic and try out these ideas in a practical way. You could do this by testing whether your view of the way in which you learn matches an analysis of your learning style by using Honey and Mumford's questionnaire. This will involve you in being an activist and seeking out a new experience by finding and answering for yourself Honey and Mumford's learning style questionnaire.

Then, see for yourself whether your analysis of your preferred learning style matches what you discover by using their questionnaire. Reflect on your findings.

Examine the theory by rereading the description of the styles outlined earlier. You might want to look at a more detailed account of how people learn, and this will also reinforce what you have already learned. Further readings to encourage you to do this are included at the end of this chapter.

Then, once you have established your preferred learning style or styles, you can be a pragmatist again and look for practical opportunities to learn in differing ways or seek out more opportunities to learn using your preferred learning style or styles.

You might take your studies further and complete the same exercise using Kolb's learning style inventory, the original learning style questionnaire from which Honey and Mumford developed their work, and then compare your results on the two questionnaires.

### Discussion of Activity 7.2

You may have discovered that you are equally at home learning in each of these styles. Two per cent of the population use all four styles. The majority of the population – 70% – tend to prefer to use just one or two learning styles. You can use the understanding that you have gained about your learning styles in various ways. You might choose to seek out opportunities to use the learning styles that you use less, and in this way you may become a more rounded learner who is able to make use of a wider range of learning opportunities.

You might, on the other hand, choose to make use of the learning styles that you know you prefer to use, so that if learning opportunities are presented to you in ways that you don't like, you may look for alternative ways to learn about the topic which are more in line with your learning style preferences.

### Summary

Whenever we are designing training for individuals or groups, we need to consider learning theory and build into the training as many conditions as we can to ensure effective learning. Not only is it important when learning from experiences for the individual learner to be aware of their preferred learning style, it is also important that the trainer should be aware of differing training styles in individuals in order to provide a learning experience which will be congruent with the way in which the trainee will learn best.

## Practical issues relating to learning
..........................................

We have examined some of the theories about learning, and will now consider some practical issues relating to learning which may be of some use to you in improving your own learning.

### *Learning curves*

Many people think that if they keep working solidly at something that they are trying to learn they will master it. They are convinced they will continue to learn at the same pace as long as they are persistent. This approach is generally counter-productive, as people do not continue to learn at the same rate all the time. The learning curve shown in Figure 7.3 illustrates the main stages that may occur in the learning process. Each person's curve is likely to be different, but will display many of the same features.

The learning curve illustrated here shows the rate at which someone mastered a physical task in a factory environment. At first there was no output at all, as the initial training was being undertaken(a). This means not that learning wasn't actually happening, but that at that stage it could not be demonstrated by any output. After a short time the learning that occurs is rapid(b), but then it seems to reach a plateau where little learning occurs(c). The rapid learning that occurs initially shows an initial mastery of the training. Learning could still be occurring when the plateau is reached, but it is not shown by an increase in output. It could be as a result of moving on to mastering a more difficult stage of the production process, or it may just reflect a need to consolidate what has been learnt. Once this has been achieved the learning is likely to be rapid for a short time before slowing down(d).

In the above case the learning that has occurred can be demonstrated by the level of output produced. The learning that a student or a trainee does, if they have to learn a certain amount of information, may reflect a similar pattern. For a short time the learning may be rapid, but it does not continue at this pace. There may be a stage where the student or trainee seems to reach a plateau and feels that they are not learning anything more. This may be because they need to master more difficult concepts, and once again it does not mean that no learning is occurring. Once this stage has been mastered the stu-

*figure 7.3*
**The learning curve**

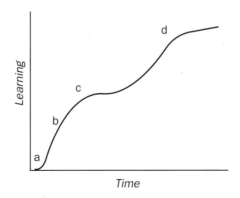

dent or trainee may progress to learning more rapidly again. This can also be demonstrated using computer games. After some initial confusion where the person may seem to make little progress with the game, there is usually a stage where progress is rapid and mastery of the game seems assured. Progress to a new level, however, may introduce new skills to be mastered or new ideas to think about, and a plateau in the learning may occur.

### Effective learning

If we are trying to learn a set of information, we tend to learn most effectively at the beginning of the learning period when we are fresh. We may also find that we can recall most easily things that we learnt at the beginning as well as the most recent things that we learnt at the end of the learning period. There may be a great deal of information that we thought we learnt in the middle of the learning session which we cannot recall.

It is not possible to keep learning at the same pace all the time, and besides reaching a plateau where they feel that they are not progressing, people also need to have breaks from the concentration involved in learning. It will be more effective to have a short break after studying for about half an hour than to continue to try to work at the same pace, as this will mean that when they return to study they will be fresh again and should learn rapidly once again for a short period of time. If the students keep trying to learn without taking any breaks their increase in learning is likely to be extremely slow and their concentration will probably lapse so that they will probably have to learn everything all over again.

### Forgetting

With a physical task in a factory the trainee can demonstrate what they have learnt by their improvement in output. Since they are normally using what they have learnt again and again in the course of their job, it is unlikely that they will forget what they have just learnt. Their learning will be reinforced as they will be repeating the learned action again and again, and it will be reinforced by praise or recognition from their supervisor, or just by the fact the right quality of product is produced. On the other hand, if knowledge or skill is not used for a long time then there is a danger that what had been learnt will be forgotten. This does not mean that this has vanished from their minds forever, just that they may have a problem in recalling it.

Figure 7.4 shows how we often seem less able to recall something that we have learnt a few days later. The diagram shows that recall is excellent just after we have learnt something, but that the amount we can recall then drops rapidly and we may be unable to recall as much as 80% of the information we had learnt.

This means that we need not only to pay attention to how we learn, but also to practise recalling what we have learnt. If the individual does not go over the material again there is a danger that they will gradually forget what they have learnt. Going over material that has been learned later that day and then on the following day, and also a few days later, is likely to minimise this effect and to reinforce what has already been learned.

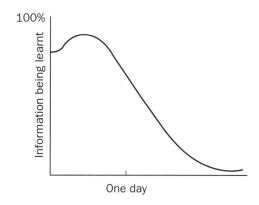

*figure 7.4*
**The forgetting curve**

Figure 7.5 shows how recall of what has been learnt can be improved by recalling it at different times (reviews) so that it becomes easy to remember the information. This could involve the students testing themselves on what they can recall by rewriting what they have learnt in different words and then going over the information again.

*figure 7.5*
**Ways of improving recall**

### Techniques to improve learning and recall

The way in which people were traditionally taught or trained in the past tended to value memorising many facts. It is still important in some circumstances today. In some examinations you may need to recall factual information accurately. This subject will be considered briefly here, but further guidance on how to improve learning and recall can be found in the recommended reading.

Some people use special techniques to help them to learn effectively and to improve their ability to recall what they have learnt. Mnemonics, number rhymes and stories can all help here.

Mnemonics provide a system for remembering lists of information by associating each word with a key letter and creating a word which you would find easy to remember from this. A simple example of this is the term SWOT analysis. This stands for Strengths, Weaknesses, Opportunities and Threats, and is a way of examining an organisation or department under these four headings.

Number rhymes can also prove to be very effective ways of remembering a list of words. In this case you have a rhyming word for each number in the list, which you then associate with the word that you are trying to remember, e.g. 1 = gun, 2 = shoe, 3 = tree. In each case the rhyming word and the word that is to be remembered need to be made as memorable in your mind as possible. Work by Tony Buzan listed at the end of the chapter will provide detailed guidance on memorising extremely large lists of factual information in this way.

Many people invent a story about a set of words that they need to memorise. Once again this needs to be as vivid as possible. A well-known example of this, which also rhymes, is: 'In fourteen hundred and ninety-two Columbus sailed the ocean blue'.

**PAUSE FOR THOUGHT 7.3**   *What techniques have you been using in memorising what you have been reading in this book?*

### Mind mapping techniques

Psychologists are finding out more about the ways in which we think and learn. Some psychologists have studied which part of the brain governs logic and rationality and which side of the brain uses creativity. Psychologists now say that our minds work in patterns and that several ideas can be developing at once. The brain then goes through a process of integrating ideas, but this doesn't necessarily happen in a linear order.

**DID YOU KNOW?**

*It is generally believed that the two sides of the brain are used for different things. The left side of the brain is used mainly for analysis, words, planning and dealing with things in a logical, rational way. The right side of the brain is better at the synthesis of ideas, presenting information in pictorial form, spatial competencies, and creativity and the generation of new ideas.*

Tony Buzan (1982) developed the idea of mind maps to allow people to express themselves freely and encourage creativity, without being necessarily governed by the linear form. Many people, when presenting information in the form of a mind map, show a very detailed grasp of the subject which they were not be able to demonstrate in a traditional written form. The mind maps (some examples are used as chapter summaries in this book) start with the central subject, which can be presented pictorially. Lines then lead from this subject by straight lines to other connected topics. This gives more freedom for ideas to appear without worrying at first about the connections, and it allows for several links to be made between related parts of a topic.

The mind map shown in Figure 7.6 illustrates our view of the key points with which this chapter has been concerned so far. Mind maps encourage creativity, and if they are to be used in a way that helps someone to remember and learn effectively then they should be very visual. The central topic should be written clearly, preferably in capital letters, and underlined. A pictorial representation of that topic is also useful, as it encourages easier recall. Lines should then be drawn from this key word, and the main areas relating to the subject area should be drawn.

Further diagrams or pictures can be useful to make the mind map of the topic memorable. Further lines and words should branch from each of these, and the pattern is then developed. Groups of ideas can be linked by the use of different colours. Links can be made easily, by using arrows or lines, between

*figure 7.6*
**Partial mind-map of
the chapter**

TRAINING &
DEVELOPMENT

related topics. Relationships and links with other subjects can also be made and
identified at the edges of the mind map.

ACTIVITY **7.3**
• • • • • • • • • • • • •

The mind map in Figure 7.6 is incomplete, since it is being used part-way though this
chapter. When you have read the rest of this chapter complete the remainder of the
mind map in a way that will make it memorable for you. Draw links with other
subjects or topics around the edge of the mind map.

### *Discussion for Activity 7.3*

You should have included further sections on:

➤  the training cycle
➤  the role of the organisation
➤  the value of learning theories for training and development.

You may have included other things that you considered relevant, and in order for it to be useful and memorable you should have made the mind map as visually attractive as possible. Further links could also be made with the next chapter to draw connections with

➤ the learning organisation
➤ recent developments in education and training
➤ training for specific groups

## Training

We have examined the way in which people learn, and will now move on to consider how they should be trained and the various training techniques or strategies that may be used.

### The training cycle

All the people who are involved in training and development at work need to be aware of the key stages in the training process. This is often referred to as the training cycle. The training cycle is shown in Figure 7.7, and each of the stages will now be discussed in more detail.

### Assessing training needs

It is important, as we said earlier, for organisations to plan the training that employees may need. While there is much to be gained from training in terms of improved skills and productivity for the workforce, it is nevertheless a costly activity, so it is important to provide training of the right type for the people who need it. An understanding of how the individuals or groups learn, and their preferred styles of learning, is important here, but it is even more important to identify first whether training is needed at all. There is little point in designing a programme that will suit the individuals' learning styles if there is not a need for training.

*figure 7.7*
**The training cycle**

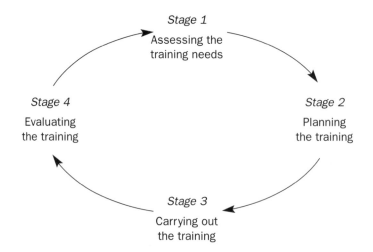

Stage 1
Assessing the
training needs

Stage 2
Planning
the training

Stage 3
Carrying out
the training

Stage 4
Evaluating
the training

This stage of the training cycle is referred to as assessing training needs. Training needs can be assessed in many ways, but one of the easiest ways is to examine the job that has to be done and the knowledge, skills or competencies needed to it. Job analysis needs to be undertaken to establish what is involved in the job. Refer back to Chapter 2 to refresh your memory of the ways in which to carry out job analysis. The usual result of job analysis is a job description, and a training specification can be written from this. In many organisations, where employees are encouraged to work towards National Vocational Qualifications (NVQs), there will already be a national standard for the employee to work towards.

Once the organisation knows the standard of work it needs from the employee, the next stage is to assess the work of the employee concerned and see the extent to which they meet those standards. This can be part of the appraisal process, where the employee and their manager have together identified an area where further work is needed. It could also be assessed by asking the person or people concerned what training they feel they need, by using questionnaires, or by an analysis of mistakes (faults analysis). If there are any gaps where they do not meet these standards then there is a possible need for training to help to close the gaps, and so a training need has been identified.

### Planning the training

Once a training need has been identified, there are a number of choices to be made about how the training should be carried out. Firstly, should the training be carried in the organisation (in house) or by an external organisation such as a college or other training provider? Secondly, the trainer needs to consider which training techniques should actually be used, and thirdly, the training programme needs to be designed.

### Internal or external training

ACTIVITY **7.4**

Make up your own list in which you compare the advantages and disadvantages of providing training in-house with the possible advantages or disadvantages of using an external training provider.

**In-house training**
   **Advantages**                                             **Disadvantages**

**External training provider**
   **Advantages**                                             **Disadvantages**

### Discussion for Activity 7.4

Your lists are likely to contain several advantages and disadvantages for both approaches. Among the points you should have considered are the cost and resources available to carry out the training. It is likely that in-house training will be cheaper and will be tailored perfectly to meet your training needs. However, if the particular training need identified is very specialised and is required for only one or two people, or if there is no-one available able to carry out the training, then it may be better and more cost-effective for them to join a course run by an external training provider. This, although it may not be tailored to meet the organisation's specific needs, will have the advantage of providing a wider experience and opportunities to find out how other organisations do things.

In the past when people were trained they were often just made to sit next to someone and told to do what they did. This is often referred to as 'sitting by Nellie', and the effectiveness of the training depended on how good Nellie was at her job. If she was good at it, and a naturally good instructor, then it could work well, but there was always a danger that the trainee would learn faults as well as good practice. This was one of the main disadvantages of using 'on-the-job' training. In more recent times the emphasis in a great many organisations has switched back to on-the-job training with the introduction of (NVQs). This time, however, the person who does the training and assesses what has been learnt is trained themselves, and there are national standards to work towards, so there should be much greater consistency in approach. This aims to harness the benefits of on-the-job training, in terms of low cost and relevance to the organisation, while ensuring that standards are high and consistent. In this case using on-the-job training could be beneficial, as the training has been planned, there is a trainer who knows how to train, and a qualified person will test whether the individual is competent in that job. NVQs will be discussed in more detail in the next chapter.

### Training techniques

We stated earlier that once the decision has been made about where the training is to take place, it is also important to decide on the most appropriate training techniques to use. The training method used must be chosen to be appropriate for the particular training need that has been identified. Table 7.1 lists some of the available training methods, with suggestions as to training situations in which they might be suitable.

Many other training techniques could also be used. Spaces have been left at the end of Table 7.1 for you to add your own suggestions for different training techniques.

Some of these training methods are much more participative than others, and it is a good idea to use a variety of techniques to avoid the trainee becoming bored and also to give opportunities to practise skills if a skill is being taught.

**DID YOU KNOW?**
*I hear, I forget*
*I see, I remember*
*I do, I understand.*
*(Old Chinese proverb)*

*table 7.1*
**Training
techniques and
their suitability**

| Training technique | Suitability |
| --- | --- |
| Lecture | This is suitable when a large amount of information needs to be given to a large number of people at the same time. The information can be prepared in advance but a disadvantage is the lack of participation from the audience. |
| Role play | Here a small group of people have the chance to act as if they were in a real work situation. They have a problem or situation to deal with which would be similar to a situation that they might experience at work. They can practise their responses and receive help and support from the trainer and from the others in the group. This can help in developing awareness of interpersonal skills and can give confidence, as there is an opportunity to practise skills in a protected environment where it does not matter if mistakes are made. There can sometimes be a problem if the role play is not taken seriously or if trainees are too nervous or embarrassed to perform their roles. |
| Group discussion | This can lead to a free exchange of knowledge, ideas and opinions on a particular subject among the trainees and the trainer with the opportunity to air various viewpoints. It can be useful when there are varying opinions about an issue, or a range of ways in which a situation could be handled. There is a danger that the trainees may wander too far from the subject if it is not handled skilfully by the trainer, and that important points may not get discussed. |
| Video or film | These can be used to show a real situation and differing ways of handling that situation, or to give information to several people at once. They can show examples of good and bad use of interpersonal skills to a large number of people at once and be used as the basis for a group discussion. They do not demand much involvement from the audience, although the trainer could add to this by use of discussion or questions after each showing. |
| Project | Normally a task is set by the trainer which will give an individual or group general guidelines to work to, but will also leave a great deal of scope for them to show creativity or initiative. This is a good way of stimulating creativity or initiative but, in order to do so, the project has to be about something that will interest the trainee. |
| Case study | A case study is a history of some event or situation in which relevant details are supplied for the trainee to get an overall picture of the situation or organisation. Trainees are then asked to diagnose the problems or suggest solutions. A case study provides the opportunity to examine a situation in detail yet be removed from the pressures of the real work situation. This allows for discussion and provides opportunities to exchange ideas and consider different options. Since a case study can limit the number of factors or issues that should be discussed, it may sometimes seem too easy and trainees may not fully appreciate that in the real-life situation there may be other more complex issues to take into account. |
| Computer-based training | This allows the trainee to work at their own pace through a series of questions or exercises using a computerised training program. The trainees get immediate feedback from the computer program and can cover a range of work in a short space of time, going back over exercises if necessary and learning at a time that is convenient for them. Trainees can learn without the need for a trainer to be present, although since some trainees may be nervous of the technology or may experience |

*table 7.1*
**(contd)**

| | | |
|---|---|---|
| | | difficulties, it is normally useful to have easy access to help or advice at least via a telephone. |
| | Guided reading | A series of recommended reading is provided on a topic, perhaps graded according to difficulty. The trainee is able to work at their own pace through this. Since the reading has been selected by someone else to highlight points on that subject, this can save the trainee time, since they know that the materials will be relevant to the subject. It doesn't encourage the trainee to research further around the subject or seek materials for themselves. |
| | In-tray exercise | Trainees are given a series of files, memos and letters similar to those that they might have to deal with in a real work situation. They need to decide on the appropriate action to take and the priority for action. This gives an opportunity for trainees to experience the sort of issues that can arise, but it is important that the contents of the in-tray are realistic. |

**DID YOU KNOW?**

*It is often claimed that the average rate of retention when learning new material is as follows:*

*10% of what is read*
*20% of what is heard*
*30% of what is seen*
*50% of what is seen and heard*
*70% of what the trainee says*
*90% of what the trainee says and does.*

This will also mean that if you are training a group of people and you utilise a variety of techniques, you are likely to use the preferred learning styles of different individuals at various times. Learning is an active process, and even if it is a list of facts that needs to be learnt, most people learn more effectively when they test themselves, or rewrite information in their own words. This also improves their recall of the information.

These points emphasise the importance of providing some opportunities for the trainee to practise what they are supposed to be learning, and underline the value for you of completing the exercises as you go through this book so that you continue to learn effectively.

ACTIVITY **7.5**
• • • • • • • • • • • • • •

Consider each of the training techniques listed in Table 7.1. Make four new lists as shown below, naming the training techniques you think will suit activists, reflectors, theorists and pragmatists. (Some of the techniques may suit more than one style of learning.)

**Training techniques to suit people who prefer each of the four learning styles**

| Activist | Reflector | Theorist | Pragmatist |
| --- | --- | --- | --- |
| | | | |

## *Discussion of Activity 7.5*

Your list is likely to include a variety of different training techniques, some of which we listed earlier and some that you have added for yourselves. We will consider in turn each of the preferred learning styles.

*Activist*

The training techniques that allow activists to participate fully in the learning experience will be the ones that appeal most to them. These could include: role play, group discussion, project work, case studies, computer-based learning and in-tray exercises. The role play is especially likely to appeal to the activist, as it provides plenty of opportunity for them to become involved in a leading role. Activists are likely to be bored by the lack of involvement required from them in techniques such as lectures, videos or films.

*Reflector*

Reflectors are likely to appreciate learning techniques where they are presented with information that they can then think about, so lectures, films, videos and guided reading are likely to appeal to them. They will probably also appreciate to some extent group discussions and case studies, as long as they do not have to take too active a part and have plenty of time for reflection afterwards. Computer-based training courses, in which they can progress at their own speed and go back to examine again points that they want to look at in more detail, may also prove popular.

*Theorist*

Theorists welcome opportunities to examine new theories and compare them with other points of view. Lectures and guided reading are likely to appeal most to them as training techniques. The lecture is likely to be preferred by theorists, especially if it has a fairly academic content so that ideas gained from the lecture can be compared with other ideas and theories. If the guided reading covers a suitable range of material this could also be useful to a theorist, although if the material is not extensive or theoretical enough for them, they are likely to want to delve further into other areas.

*Pragmatist*

The pragmatist wants to know how things will really work in practice, so they are likely to find training techniques that are close to reality useful. Case studies, role plays and in-tray exercises will appeal to them if they think that they are realistic and of immediate use to them at work.

## Designing the training programme

It is not enough just to choose the training techniques to be used and hope that these will develop into a course. When you are designing a training programme you should have in mind clear objectives for the course. What do you want the trainees to be able to do and what do you want them to know by the end of the course?

**PAUSE FOR THOUGHT 7.4**
➤ *What were the objectives for this chapter?*
➤ *What should you know by the end of the chapter?*
➤ *What should you be able to do by the end of the chapter?*
➤ *What opportunities were provided for you to practise things you learnt?*

The objectives for this chapter were stated at the beginning. By the end of the chapter you should know something about all four objectives. You should be able to demonstrate this by stating various definitions of learning. You should also be able to demonstrate that you appreciate the relevance of various theories of learning to training and development by being able to discuss these. You should be able to show your understanding of the training cycle and that you appreciate when to use a variety of training techniques, even if you have not yet had an opportunity to use them.

A variety of opportunities have been provided for you to achieve these objectives. Firstly, you have had the opportunity to read the text itself. Secondly, opportunities have been provided for you to undertake exercises to practise some of the things you have read about. In one exercise you covered every stage of the learning cycle, and you have been encouraged to be actively involved in learning and to reflect on what you have learnt. The Pauses for Thought also provide the opportunity for you to be actively involved in your own learning process and to practise recall of information.

Once you have decided your objectives for the course, you are then able to plan a programme that uses a variety of training techniques in order to achieve this aim in the most effective way. The next chapter will focus on the provision of training courses, but first we need to discuss briefly the other stages in the training cycle.

If the training is to be effective it cannot be left to chance and a great deal of planning needs to happen first. Who are the people that you are going to involve in this training? Will you do all the training yourself or will you involve managers from other departments? When you have decided these points you need to decide on the most logical order for the training and plan the course. Some parts of the course will be obvious – for example the introduction, perhaps stating your objectives for the course, is likely to be at the beginning – but you have considerable freedom after that, although you will be constrained by the amount of time each part of the course takes. Some examples of the design of specific training programmes will be discussed in the next chapter. Remember that people do need to have breaks, as their attention spans are not limitless and they will learn more when they are refreshed, so you should timetable tea, coffee and lunch breaks if the course runs for full days. Remember also to give opportunities for people to be actively involved in their own learning, and allow time to practise skills and time to go over points so that recall is enhanced. Specific training programmes for particular groups of workers will be considered in the next chapter.

### Carrying out the training

You need to ensure that everyone is aware of the training course in plenty of time. Letters should have gone to the course participants, people involved in running the course, and the supervisors and managers of those who will be on the course so that there is time to arrange cover for their absence from work if necessary. Those who are to carry out the training should themselves have some training in running training programmes. Although specialised training officers or human resource managers with responsibility for training will be trained in training techniques, line managers or other members of staff will often be involved in actually training individuals. Everyone at some time has the experience of showing a new employee what to do in a job. At the very least an appreciation of what is involved in giving job instruction on a one-to-one basis is useful. The techniques required to instruct on a one-to-one basis will be described fully in Chapter 8.

### Evaluating the training

This is an extremely important stage in the training cycle, and one that is often neglected by organisations. If no evaluation of training is carried out then the organisation does not know whether the training has been successful or not and may waste money and resources on training that is not the most effective, and it will not know whether or not its original objectives have been met.

Evaluation should be carried out at several different times. First, at the end of the training course, the course participants should be asked their views on the effectiveness of the training. This could be done by means of a simple questionnaire to the course participants, which will at least give clear views as to whether the people concerned liked the course, what they felt would be useful, and what they felt was less useful. Consequently it should yield a great deal of valuable material, which the manager responsible for the design of the course should be able to incorporate usefully in the next course.

However, this only establishes what the participants say they feel about the course. It may also be useful to establish what they have learned on the course, and so both knowledge and skills may be tested at the end of the training.

It is also useful to find out what effect the training has had on the person when they actually get back to work. This can be done by questionnaires or interviews of the course participants and their supervisor a few weeks later, or a review of the person's work and the effect that the training has had on him or her.

## The role of the organisation in learning

Some organisations do not seem to encourage learning. They put up barriers at different stages of the learning cycle. If people are to learn from experience then sometimes they will make mistakes. An organisation that does not tolerate some mistakes will not encourage learning to take place, as people will be too frightened to take risks and will not experiment with the way they do things. There are also organisations where the emphasis is on practical experience and where life is so action-packed that there is no time to stop and reflect on what has been learnt.

In some organisations the culture is for management to pride themselves on having got on without the benefit of much education, so that people who enjoy referring to books or theoretical ideas are looked down upon. In others the reverse may be true and only academic approaches are valued.

A culture where there is a preference for distance and detachment is unlikely to encourage people to be active in their learning style, whereas an organisation in which people are secretive or mistrustful, or with an emphasis on living for today, will be unlikely to encourage a reflective style of learning.

## Conclusion

We have tried in this chapter to provide a brief account of several different learning theories and to show how an understanding of learning theory is important for trainers in order to understand the way in which people learn, and in order that they provide appropriate training which is geared to the employees' needs. Although no one theory provides all the answers to the question of how people learn, the various theories we have discussed suggest a variety of ways of helping people to learn knowledge and skills more effectively.

Feedback of how a person is performing is necessary in training and development, and individuals need to know how they are doing in order to continue to learn effectively. Computer-based training uses some of the ideas of the behaviourist school of learning, and rewards a correct behaviour such as pressing the correct key with praise or by allowing you to progress to the next stage.

We have also shown that people learn in a variety of ways and that they often have one or two preferred learning styles. In order to cope with groups of trainees with varying learning styles and to help individuals develop and use other styles, a variety of training techniques need to be used, and we have considered when different approaches would be appropriate.

Learning can be improved by breaking the learning periods up into short sessions with breaks. There are also techniques, such as mnemonics and number rhyming systems, that can help when it is necessary to memorise facts. Recall can be improved by going over the information at regular intervals.

Rationality and logic are not the only important qualities, and people should also be encouraged to develop creativity and to use the right side of their brain more. For many people the use of mind mapping techniques provides an opportunity to display knowledge that they have not always been able to demonstrate using traditional approaches to learning. Mind maps also give the opportunity to plan topics in a creative way, and can make it easier to remember the key points of a topic.

We have examined the stages in the training cycle, training techniques, and the design of training programmes. The next chapter will consider approaches to developing training courses for specific groups, and will also consider some recent developments in education and training.

**REVIEW QUESTIONS**

1 Plan a series of learning activities to develop your own ability to learn using a learning style that is not normally one of your preferred styles. Then, working in pairs, get a friend/colleague to suggest additional learning activities for you so that you can further develop this learning style, while you suggest and plan a variety of learning activities for them.

2 Get further ideas for developing your learning styles from the suggested reading at the end of the chapter.

3 Plan a revision session for one topic in this book by designing your own mind map to cover the key points.

**SELF-CHECK QUESTIONS**

Answer the following multiple choice questions. The correct responses are given on page 424 for you to check your understanding of this chapter.

1 The illustration in Figure 7.8 shows what happens when Caroline makes a cup of tea. She often chooses to feed the cats at the same time as putting the kettle on. Thus the kettle and the tin of cat food being opened are linked in the cat's minds. Sometimes she puts the kettle on but doesn't open a can of cat food. However, the cats now appear when they hear the sound of the kettle.
   (a) What is this effect known as?
   (b) According to Pavlov, how should we label the cat food in diagram 1?
   (c) According to Pavlov, what is the link between the kettle and the cat food known as? Label diagram 2.
   (d) According to Pavlov, what should the kettle be labelled in diagram 3?

2 According to Honey and Mumford:
   (a) learning has occurred when knowledge has been acquired by study
   (b) learning has occurred when a person knows something that they did not know earlier and can show it, or is able to do something that they were not able to do before
   (c) learning has occurred when a person knows something that they did not know earlier but can't show it, or is able to do something that they were not able to do before
   (d) learning is shown by a relatively permanent change in behaviour that occurs as a result of practice or experience
   (e) learning is shown by a change in behaviour which occurs just as a result of experience.

3 Which of the following terms best describes Köhler's approach to learning?
   (a) Experiential learning
   (b) Experimental learning
   (c) Discovery learning
   (d) Holistic learning
   (e) Cognitive learning

*figure 7.8*
**Caroline's cats**

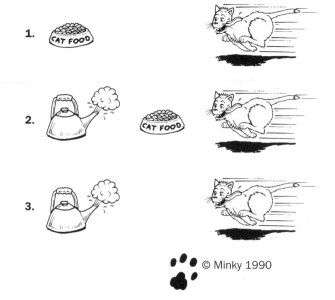

© Minky 1990

4 The *Shorter Oxford Dictionary* defines learning as: ' the action of LEARN v. 2. What is learnt or taught. 3. Knowledge ... got by study.' This definition is an example of which of the following views of learning?
(*a*) Cognitive
(*b*) Behaviourist
(*c*) Experiential
(*d*) Holistic
(*e*) Experimental

5 According to Honey and Mumford, a pragmatist is someone who
(*a*) seeks out new experiences and is open-minded, not sceptical, and enthusiastic about novelty
(*b*) integrates and adapts observations into logically sound theories
(*c*) thinks problems through in a step-by-step, logical way
(*d*) collects data in a very thorough way and analyses them
(*e*) is keen to try new ideas, theories and techniques to see if they work in practice.

6 Which of the following is NOT one of the stages in the training cycle?
(*a*) Assessing training needs
(*b*) Having an experience
(*c*) Planning the training
(*d*) Evaluating the training
(*e*) Carrying out the training

7 Computer-based training and programmed learning were developed from the work of which of the following schools of thought?
(*a*) Cognitive psychology
(*b*) Experiential psychology
(*c*) The holistic school of thought
(*d*) Behaviourist psychologists
(*e*) The pragmatic school of thought.

## References
..............

Bass, B.M. and Vaughan, J.A. *Training in Industry – the Management of Learning*. Tavistock Publications, 1966.

Buzan, Tony. *Use your Head*. BBC, 1982.

Honey, Peter and Mumford, Alan. *The Manual of Learning Styles*. 1982.

Köhler, W. *The Mentality of Apes*. Vintage Books, 1959.

Kolb, David *et al*. *Organisational Psychology: An experiential approach*. Prentice Hall, 1974.

Pavlov, I. *Conditioned Reflexes*. Oxford University Press, 1927.

Skinner, B.F. *Science and Human Behaviour*. Macmillan, 1953.

## Further study
................

### *Books*

Bee, Frances and Roland. *Training Needs Analysis and Evaluation*. IPD, 1994. (This is excellent at linking training needs and the needs of the business and discusses also how corporate strategy must be developed.)

Boydell, Tom and Leary, Malcolm. *Identifying Training Needs*. IPD, 1996.

Bramley, Peter. *Evaluating Training*. IPD, 1996.

Buzan, Tony. *Use your Head*. BBC,1982.

Gough, Jacqui. *Developing Learning Materials*. IPD, 1996.

Hackett, Penny. *Introduction to Training*. IPD, 1997.

Hardingham, Alison. *Designing Training*. IPD, 1996.

(The above all form part of the IPD's Training Essentials Series and each covers in some detail the stages in the training cycle described in this chapter.)

Harrison, Rosemary. *Employee Development*. Institute of Personnel and Development, 1998.

Honey, Peter and Mumford, Alan. *The Manual of Learning Styles*. Peter Honey 1982. (The learning style questionnaire comes as part of this package and provides a useful start to establishing your preferred learning styles.)

Honey, Peter and Mumford, Alan. *Using your Learning Styles*. 2nd edition, Peter Honey, 1986. (Gives clear information about ways to improve effectiveness of particular learning styles. Useful mainly for those concerned with designing training programmes.)

Honey, Peter and Mumford, Alan. *The Opportunist Learner*. Peter Honey, 1990. (This guide complements the manual of learning styles and is written for the use of learners.)

Kolb, David *et al*. *Organisational Psychology: An Experiential Approach*. Prentice Hall (1974). (This contains the American test which led Honey and Mumford to develop their version of the learning style questionnaire. It also relates clearly to the stages of the learning cycle.)

Reid, M., Barrington, H., and Kenney, J. *Training Interventions*. 5th edition, Institute of Personnel and Development 1997.

Siddons, Suzy. *Delivering Training*. IPD, 1997.

### Articles

Mumford, Alan. Sources for courses. *People Management*, Vol. 4, No. 40, 14 May 1998, 48–51.

### Audio-visual

BBC Enterprises. *Use your Head* (first broadcast 1974), 1987. (The video to accompany the book of the same name, by Tony Buzan. Presented by Tony Buzan, the video shows excellent techniques for improving memory and recall, using mind mapping and other learning strategies.)

Island World Videos. *Get Ahead: a Short Cut to Straight* As, 1992. (Presented by Lana Israel, a young student who adopted Tony Buzan's ideas and dramatically improved her grades. Introduction provided by Tony Buzan. Clear explanation of the uses of mind mapping for effective note taking, improving study and enhancing creativity.)

Video Arts. *You'll Soon Get the Hang of It.* 1995

### Internet

Tony Buzan and Mind Mapping
**http://www.ozemail.com.au/~caveman/Creative/Mindmap/buzan2.htm**

# CHAPTER 8

# Training and development programmes

## Objectives:

*By the end of this chapter you should be able to:*

➤ understand the meaning of the terms training, education and employee development

➤ understand the role of the human resource manager, line manager and training manager in training and developing the people in the organisation

➤ understand the importance of induction training

➤ design a simple training programme to meet the needs of a particular group of employees

➤ instruct a person in a particular skill by training on a one-to-one basis

➤ understand recent developments in training and development.

We showed in the last chapter that there are several definitions of the term 'learning', each of which reflects the view of a particular school of thought and makes a useful contribution to our understanding of the learning process. We showed how some understanding of the learning process is necessary to trainers and to those being trained. In this chapter we shall examine some aspects of training and development in more detail, but before doing so it would be useful to define three important terms: employee development, education and training.

## Employee development

Reid *et al.* (1997), referring to employee development, say that it is:

> essentially about making learning happen – any form of learning, although usually in the service of some work goal or goals.

As we said in the previous chapter, people will learn naturally in a random way, and you cannot stop them from learning. This definition implies that employee development will be concerned with the way the learning process is structured and gradually expanded in order to ensure that it does fulfil the organisation's goals.

Rosemary Harrison (1993) expands on this by providing a useful definition of employee development for human resource managers and for training or human resource development practitioners. She says:

> Employee development as part of the organisation's overall human resource strategy means the skilful provision and organization of learning experiences in the workplace in order that performance can be improved, that work goals can be achieved and that, through enhancing the skills, knowledge, learning ability and enthusiasm of people at every level, there can be continuous individual

growth. Employee development must, therefore, be part of a wider strategy for the business, aligned with the organisation's corporate mission and goals.

This shows employee development to be an extremely important process to the organisation through which both individual and organisational growth can be achieved over a period of time so that both can fulfil their full potential. It can also be clearly seen here that education and training are both ways in which planned learning experiences are provided, and that they contribute to employee development.

## Education

The (now defunct) Manpower Services Commission's *Glossary of Training Terms* (1981) defined education in the following way:

> as activities which aim at developing the knowledge, skills, moral values and understanding required in all aspects of life rather than a knowledge and skill relating to only a limited field of activity. The purpose of education is to provide the conditions essential to young people and adults to develop an understanding of the traditions and ideas influencing society in which they live and to enable them to make a contribution to it. It involves the study of their own cultures and of the laws of nature, as well as the acquisition of linguistic and other skills which are basic to learning, personal development, creativity and communication.

This definition shows that education is mainly, although not exclusively, relevant to the young and is about preparing them with the necessary foundations in knowledge, skills and moral values as a preparation for the rest of their lives.

## Training

The *Glossary of Training Terms*, further defined training as:

> a planned process to modify attitude, knowledge, skill or behaviour through learning experience to achieve effective performance in an activity or range of activities. Its purpose, in a work situation, is to develop the abilities of the individual and to satisfy the current and future needs of the organisation.

This shows that training is specifically about providing a range of learning experiences in a work situation.

## Comment

Although there appear to be clear distinctions between education and training, with education being a general foundation for life and training being specifically related to work, it is not in fact as simple as that. Learning opportunities are nowadays provided in a wide range of places, in differing formats and for all age groups. It is not always easy to distinguish whether a particular learning opportunity is education or training. Some adults may decide to improve their education later in life, and may take courses, e.g. one in languages, that might be regarded as education. If their language course is relevant to their need to speak another language for their job, then this might be viewed as training. Some young people who are in the mainstream educational system may study for vocational courses such as General National Vocational Qualifications (GNVQs) which could have large elements which we would consider to be training.

Education and training can no longer be regarded as being in watertight compartments, and there is often considerable overlap between the two. Employee development is concerned to utilise all learning opportunities whether they are regarded as education or training, or some combination of both. There are a wide range of ways in which this may be brought about, and besides formal education and training there are many sources of developmental opportunities which will be discussed later in this chapter. Employee development also concerns all employees and not just human resource or training and development managers.

### Strategic human resource development and the people involved in training and development

People are an organisation's most precious resource, and so it is extremely important that they work to their optimum level of performance. Employee development makes an important contribution to this, but in order to be most effective it should be part of the strategic plan for the organisation and must very clearly relate to the organisation's objectives. In this way the contribution of all those involved in employee development will be seen to be aimed at specific organisational objectives thus making a vital contribution to organisational effectiveness, rather than, as has sometimes been the case, being viewed just as an expensive luxury. Too often in the past training has been regarded as an unnecessary expense rather than as an integral part of achieving organisational effectiveness.

ACTIVITY **8.1**

With reference to any organisation of your choice examine the organisation's strategic objectives and list the ways in which training and development might help contribute towards the achievement of these objectives.

### Discussion of activity 8.1

This will obviously depend on the organisation chosen and its objectives, but may include, for example the provision of language training for marketing managers for an organisation which aimed to diversify into new European markets, or the provision of training about information technology for supervisors, where the stated aim was to improve efficiency by introducing new technology.

It may be that the strategic level of activity described above is performed by someone at director level. Others involved may include the human resource manager, the training specialist, the line manager and the individuals themselves

Many human resource managers will be directly responsible for the training and development of the people in their organisation, though this does not, of course, mean that they necessarily do all the training and development work themselves. It may be that all the records of training and development are held within the human resource department, or there may be a separate training and development section with a training manager or human resource development manager as head of department. If there is a separate department there will need to be strong links between the two departments, as they need to work very closely together. Since the merger of the Institute of Personnel Management and the Institute of Training and Development in July 1994, all their members have become members of the same institute and a joint qualification has been developed. This merger emphasises the closeness of training and development to human resource management, together with the importance to the organisation of training and development and the need for both human resource management and training to work together, if they are separate.

Besides the human resource manager there may also be, as we have already seen, training officers or human resource development officers. They are trained in the same way as human resource managers, but are likely to have chosen to specialise in training and development. It is unlikely that even they will do all the training or development work within the organisation, as line managers have an increasing role to play in training and developing their own staff. Human resource managers and training officers are, however, likely to provide specialist courses and advice and also to ensure that managers are trained adequately to carry out the level of training required for their own staff.

Not only are line managers likely to be involved in employee development for their own staff and to be trained and encouraged to seek a range of suitable developmental opportunities, but the staff themselves will also be encouraged to actively seek opportunities for their own development. In organisations where there is often little room for promotion, and where the future of the organisation itself is insecure, it is in employees' own interests to keep themselves as up-to-date as possible and to seek out new opportunities for developing new skills or new knowledge.

We emphasised in the previous chapter the importance of identifying training needs. A training need is often viewed as the difference between what a person knows or is able to do, and what his or her job description indicates he or she should know or be able to do. Clearly, the identification of a gap between these two might indicate a training need. In this case training would be needed to bring the person's work up to the standard required. Employee development could also be about ensuring that people are not only able to do the jobs that they are employed to do, but also developing in ways to meet future organisational needs and to cope with the pace of change today.

### *Training and development for particular groups of employees*

Although all employees are likely to have training needs, and should be concerned to develop themselves fully to meet future needs and the pace of organisational change, there are also likely to be many groups with specific training needs, such as new employees, women returning to work after a break, supervisors and managers. This section will focus on one group who have particular training needs, namely new employees.

**New employees**

New employees are likely to have their own individual learning needs, but in some respects may be treated the same, as they all have to learn certain things about the organisation and its culture. New employees need to learn a great deal of information when they join an organisation. This can be learned informally, but this may take a long time and the employee may learn the wrong things. Consider the following example.

ACTIVITY **8.2**
................

Read the following story. Comment on what happened because informal methods were being used in this organisation to train new employees.

Danielle is just home from her first day at work at Denby Transport. She set off this morning feeling very enthusiastic about her new job as a clerk in the despatch section in this large motor transport company. The scene opens when she walks into her home.

| | |
|---|---|
| Danielle | Hello Mum, I'm home. I'm really tired, when will dinner be ready? |
| Mum | I expect you are tired. It's a big change from school to work. How did things go? |
| Danielle | Dunno really. OK I suppose. |
| Mum | Why do you never tell me anything? I always have to drag things out of you! Now tell me what happened while I get dinner ready. Your father will be home soon. What happened when you got there this morning? |
| Danielle | It was odd really. I don't think anyone knew I was coming. The man on the gate didn't seem to be expecting me and I was left waiting in a room for half an hour while he found someone to collect me. They gave me this pink card here. They said it was a clock card or something. I expect someone will show me what to do with it if I go back tomorrow. |
| Mum | Well I expect the Despatch Office Supervisor looked after you. He seemed a nice man when we met him at your cousin's engagement party. Strange that he didn't tell you what to do with the clock card. It's important so make sure you take it back tomorrow. |
| Danielle | Haven't met him yet but Anwar seemed all right. I work next to him but he's been too busy to tell me much yet. |
| Mum | So who does tell you what to do? |
| Danielle | Well I suppose it must be Anwar. He asked me to go to the stores section with some figures that needed checking. I tripped up on the way there and hurt my foot. The storeman shouted at me and told me I wasn't allowed in that area wearing sandals and that I should always wear safety shoes when I have to go into the factory. |
| Mum | Are you sure your foot is all right now? Didn't you even go to the First Aid room? |
| Danielle | I didn't know they had a first aid room and I felt such a fool I didn't like to mention it to anyone. Anyway I don't know where to get these special safety shoes. |
| Mum | Are you hungry? Did you get a good lunch in the canteen? |
| Danielle | It was fine but it cost £1.50. |
| Mum | That's strange. I'm sure the woman who interviewed you said it would only be 80p until you are 18. |

*Enter Dad*

| | |
|---|---|
| Dad | Hi. How's it going? Have they promoted you yet? |
| Danielle | Don't be silly Dad. |
| Dad | Well what exactly did you do? Do you think you're going to like it there? |
| Danielle | I don't really know what I'm supposed to do. Anwar talked about credit notes and despatch notes and there are blue cards and green cards to complete but I don't know what he was talking about. I expect I'll understand it eventually. That's if I don't get the sack first. I'm not sure that I want to go tomorrow. It's all too difficult. |
| Dad | Hey, what's all this about getting the sack? What have you done? |
| Danielle | Well nothing really. I just lit a cigarette while I was in the factory delivering notes to stores. Some man in a white coat was really angry when he saw me with a cigarette. I only saw the No Smoking sign later. I've had enough of work. It's all too difficult and you feel such a fool when you don't know what to do. |

### Discussion of Activity 8.2

Danielle was not made to feel welcome in her new job, since no-one was prepared for her arrival. She didn't know who to ask for information and had very little information to act on. She ended up feeling foolish because of this lack of information. The organisation needs to take more care to ensure that this does not happen, as there is a strong possibility that Danielle might never return to work after a first day like this. A more structured approach is needed, with individuals being clear about what a new recruit needs to know and also who is going to give him or her this information. This organisation needs a good induction programme.

### Induction

We define induction as the process of helping a new employee to settle quickly into their job so that they soon become an efficient and productive employee. The actual process of induction starts before the person's first day at work, and generally starts as part of the recruitment and selection process. The impression the interviewers create about the organisation, and the letters and information sent to the prospective employee, can all be regarded as part of the induction process.

ACTIVITY **8.3**

If you were the training and development manager at Denby Transport and you were to design an induction course for Danielle, what would be your objectives for the course? List what you would like Danielle to know, and what you would like her to actually be able to do, by the end of her induction period.

### Discussion of Activity 8.3

You are likely to have listed some of the following points and your objectives, in terms of knowledge, are likely to include the following.

At the end of the induction training programme the trainee will:

➤ know the layout of the main building in which she works, including entrances and fire exits, toilet and washroom areas, canteen areas, and where she will actually be working
➤ know the names of her supervisor and people working near her
➤ understand safety procedures and company rules about safety
➤ understand the company's disciplinary and grievance procedure
➤ understand the company's sickness and welfare procedures
➤ know in general about the company's pension scheme
➤ know about the trade unions she could consider joining
➤ know about the company's first aid and welfare facilities
➤ know where to find information about these in the relevant staff handbook or staff notice board.

You might also want the trainee to be able to do certain things, such as:

➤ find her way unaided around the main working area
➤ carry out certain aspects of her job to a specified standard
➤ clock in and out correctly.

Danielle's first day at work was far from successful, and many employees who feel as badly as she did on that day would probably not return to work for a second day. This would be a very expensive waste of resources, which the human resource manager should be concerned to eliminate. The loss of new employees soon after they have started work is known as the induction crisis.

In order for Danielle to settle quickly into her new work environment there was a great deal of information that she needed to know. An induction course could have helped, and the design of a suitable induction programme would help in that process. You may have included other information that you feel Danielle needs to know. If all the information is given at once, then there is a danger that much will be forgotten. An induction training course needs to be designed in order to meet your objectives.

In order to do this you should decide what information the new person is required to know, over what time scale, the length and training methods to be used, and the role of the line managers and human resource staff in the programme. Some information needs to be given immediately, such as layout of the building, names of workmates and supervisors and points about safety. Other information may be necessary later, such as pension rules or details of the sports and social clubs.

Other staff need to be prepared and aware of their roles also so that, for example, the person on the gate should expect Danielle and know exactly where to take her, and the supervisor and human resource manager should also know their roles.

### Induction training

As we have just shown, there is a need for induction training to help new members of staff settle into their new job as quickly as possible. Induction also helps to create a favourable image of the organisation in the mind of the new employee, and is therefore also a valuable public relations exercise. Part of the induction process starts at the time of interview, with the information and impression of the organisation that is given at that stage. Any letters or booklets given after this also form an important part of the induction process.

When new employees actually start work, they will need to get to know the people with whom they will be working, become familiar with their surroundings, learn about their new job and learn about the organisation in which they will be working. Although there is a great deal of information to impart to the new employee, not all of it is needed immediately and in fact there is a danger of overloading the individual with information if it is all given at once. If formal induction courses are run for all new starters then these could be spread over parts of several days, imparting the most urgent information, such as the geography of the building, canteen arrangements and introductions to supervisors and work colleagues, first. It may be that the formal courses do not even need to start on the first day, especially if recruitment is sporadic. Small groups of employees may be gathered perhaps once a month for the formal induction course, providing of course that their immediate induction needs such as information on safety rules have been adequately covered.

A formal induction course is useful, as several new starters can be given information at the same time. However, the new employees are likely to be starting different jobs in various departments, so that there is still an important role for their line managers to play in their induction. A checklist indicating which topics will be covered, when they will be covered and who will cover them is also extremely useful. This can be signed by the employee when he or she has gone through all the topics and then stored with his or her training records. It also provides a useful reminder to all of the need to cover these topics.

Table 8.1 gives an indication of the type of things that need to be covered during an induction period. It is useful to indicate who is responsible for dealing with each topic and when it should be covered. A section for the trainee to sign to say that she or he has completed each topic would also be useful.

Some of the information will need to be given in a written form, perhaps in a company handbook. Although much of this information may also have been given orally in the formal induction course, it is useful to have a source of reference for things such as what to do when you are ill. This might not have seemed particularly relevant to a new starter, and indeed may not be needed for a year or two, by which time it may have been largely forgotten unless there is a company handbook to refer to.

It is important not to give too much information, as the new starter may feel overwhelmed. It is better to spread the information over a period of time and alternate with periods where the person is introduced to his or her new job and given a chance to settle into this. After all, that is the reason they have joined the organisation. In some organisations new recruits are asked to arrive later than the rest of the workforce on their first day, so that those who will be involved in their induction can get things organised and deal with any crisis that may occur, and then have time to spend on the new recruit.

*table 8.1*

**Sample induction checklist**

| Topic | Person responsible for covering this topic | Day 1 | First week | First month |
|---|---|---|---|---|
| Reception | Human Resource Manager | * | | |
| Documentation and introduction to Manager | Human Resource Manager | * | | |
| Hours, clocking on, flexitime, lunch breaks, overtime. | Human Resource Manager | * | | |
| Layout of department, outline of function and introduction to staff | Supervisor | * | | |
| Tour of main work areas, staff restaurant, toilets, fire exits | Person delegated by supervisor | * | | |
| Health and safety rules | Supervisor | * | | |
| The company – products, services, the company handbook | Training Officer | | | * |
| Rules and procedures – discipline and grievance | Human Resource Manager | | * | |
| Payment, holiday pay and sickness pay | Human Resource Manager | | * | |
| Communication and consultation | Training Officer | | | * |
| Training and Development | Training Officer | | | * |
| Performance appraisal | Training Officer | | | * |
| Pensions | Training Officer | | | * |
| The trade union | Shop Steward | | | * |

## Job instruction on a one-to-one basis

Managers, supervisors and experienced members of the workforce, as well as human resource professionals and training specialists, are all likely to be involved in training at some time. Even if they are not specialists in this area, many people are asked to give introductory instruction to others in a new skill, so a basic understanding of the process is likely to be useful to everyone. In this section we shall discuss ways in which you can be more effective if you have to instruct someone in a simple task.

Once again, there have to be systematic stages that the instructor works through relating clearly to the training cycle and you should go through stages 1–4 described in the last chapter (see Figure 7.7).

### Stage 1: Assessing the training needs

**PAUSE FOR THOUGHT 8.1** *The first stage should, as always, be to assess the training needs of the individual. What methods might you use to assess the training needs here? (Refer back to the previous chapter if you cannot remember.)*

### Stage 2: Planning the training

1   Set objectives.

- ➤ State what the trainee must be able to do.
- ➤ State the standard they must achieve.
- ➤ State any time limits in which this must be achieved.

2   Break the instructions down into key stages.

- ➤ Do the job or rehearse the subject yourself.
- ➤ Divide the job into stages.
- ➤ Select the main or key points for each stage of the instruction.

3   Get everything ready and material and equipment organised before you start to instruct.

- ➤ Pay attention to layout.
- ➤ Have the correct materials.
- ➤ Have all the correct equipment working properly.
- ➤ Decide on training aids you will use: charts, diagrams, overhead transparencies, videos.
- ➤ Decide where the training will take place.

4   Make a training plan.

- ➤ How will the trainee's absence from the job be covered?
- ➤ What standards of performance are required?
- ➤ Do any targets have to be reached?
- ➤ Select who is to be trained.
- ➤ Arrange a date for completion of training.
- ➤ Use the trainee's abilities to best effect.
- ➤ Keep the plan up to date.

### Stage 3: Carrying out the training

1   Prepare the trainees for instruction.

> ➤ Put him or her at ease.
> ➤ State clearly the job or subject.
> ➤ Check the existing knowledge of the trainee.
> ➤ Create an interest in learning the skill.
> ➤ Ensure that the trainee is positioned correctly to see and hear all your instructions.

2   Present the training material.

> ➤ Tell, show and demonstrate the task one step at a time.
> ➤ Emphasise key points, especially points about safety or quality.
> ➤ Give instructions clearly and patiently.
> ➤ Encourage the trainee to ask questions.

3   Allow the trainees to try to complete the task by themselves.

> ➤ Get the trainee to show and explain each stage of the task to you.
> ➤ Ensure that you correct errors as they occur.
> ➤ Check on the trainee's understanding of the key points as they demonstrate them.
> ➤ Continue until satisfied that the trainee has mastered all stages.

4   Put the trainees to work.

> ➤ Ensure that they are aware of targets and safety.
> ➤ Tell them who will help them if they have a problem.
> ➤ Encourage questions.
> ➤ Check at intervals that progress has been maintained.

**PAUSE FOR THOUGHT 8.2**   *What should the fourth and final stage of the training cycle be? (Refer back to the previous chapter (Figure 7.7) if you are unable to remember.)*

Throughout this process of instructing on a one-to-one basis we have emphasised the need to break the task down into small manageable sections and to go through them in a systematic manner, giving clear instructions and giving the trainee opportunities to practice the new task for themselves.

ACTIVITY **8.4**
· · · · · · · · · · · · · ·

Think about a simple task that you can do well. It might be a part of a sport or hobby. Prepare to instruct someone else in this task. As part of your planning for instruction, break the task down into stages using the columns below.

| **Stage** | **Step** | **Key points** |
| --- | --- | --- |

### *Discussion of Activity 8.4*

Even a fairly simple task usually has several stages. The following example gives the stages that one might go through when instructing a person in the simple task of refilling a stapler.

| Stage | Step | Key points |
|---|---|---|
| Overview | 1. Describe equipment | ➤ used everyday |
| | 2. Point out parts | ➤ base |
| | | ➤ arm |
| | | ➤ striking plate |
| | | ➤ staple track |
| | | ➤ staples |
| | | ➤ spring |
| Loading | 1. Open stapler | ➤ Hold lower part in left hand with thumb and index finger (if right-handed). With right hand grasp top firmly and pull up until you hear the click. BE CAREFUL. |
| | 2. Insert staples | ➤ Place them in track facing points down wards. Ensure they are straight and slide them to the front of the track. |
| | 3. Close | ➤ Reverse the second stage as described in 1 for opening the stapler. |
| Using | 1. Decide on style of stapling | ➤ Swivel the base plate according to whether you require permanent staples or temporary staples |
| | 2. Rotate plate | etc. |

This shows an example of a simple task being broken down into stages. It is important to provide an overview at the beginning so that the person knows how this particular task fits into the wider context of the job. This may help to prevent them from making obvious mistakes, as they will have some understanding of why they are doing the task and of its importance.

ACTIVITY **8.5**
• • • • • • • • • • • • •

When you have chosen a task for yourself and broken it down into stages like this, you can practise instructing someone in the task you have chosen. Sometimes, as in the example above, it may be necessary to check whether the person is right- or left-handed before you start to instruct. In the example of refilling a stapler, even though staples are sharp, there are not a great many safety points to pay attention to. Make sure in your example that you stress important factors such as safety or quality.

## Recent developments in training
• • • • • • • • • • • • • • • • • • • • • • • • • • • • • • • • • • • • •

Although the human resource is the organisation's most important resource and consequently its full development is essential for the organisation's future success, many have traditionally not been very good at developing it and this has resulted in various government-led initiatives to encourage employers to train their staff. In the 1960s and 1970s there were Industrial Training Boards which aimed to encourage this. They imposed a levy on organisations depending on their size, which could be repaid to the organisation fully or in part depending on the amount of training that they did. Some of these became bureaucratic and most were disbanded. More recently the government has encouraged Training and Enterprise Councils (TECs) or, in Scotland, Local Enterprise Councils (LECs) to take responsibility locally for encouraging training and development. TECs and LECs administer the Youth Training and Employment Training schemes in their area but can also develop local training initiatives with employers, often in partnership with them. TECs and LECs are an excellent source of advice and information for employers who need help in providing training.

### The Qualifications and Curriculum Authority (QCA)

The Qualifications and Curriculum Authority came into being on 1 October 1997 and brought together the work which had previously been undertaken by the National Council for Vocational Qualifications (NCVQ) and the School Curriculum and Assessment Authority (SCAA). In the previous chapter we showed how often in Britain training and education has been treated in differing ways with newer competence-based qualifications sometimes suffering lack of parity of esteem when compared with more traditional academic qualifications. This can be traced back, as we said in Chapter 7, to the underlying theories of learning such as cognitive or behaviourist, but it has resulted in the creation of two education and training systems in Britain. The creations of the QCA is a move to integrate these two education and training systems and end the academic/vocational divide.

The QCA is responsible for establishing a comprehensive qualifications framework. This means everything ranging from the curriculum for those of pre-school age, to the National Curriculum, GCSEs and A levels, NVQs and GNVQs, through to higher-level vocational qualifications. The QCA has a series of priorities for action identified in their corporate plan for 1998–2002. These have been summarised by QCA as the following broad strategic aims:

> ➤ By its review of the school curriculum, QCA will define the structure and content of teaching and learning that will enable all pupils to develop and demonstrate their knowledge, skills and understanding. A rigorous curriculum will equip pupils with the knowledge and skills needed for adult life.

> ➤ Through development and management of the assessment system, QCA will define the way in which schools can demonstrate their contribution to national and local targets.

> ➤ As the regulatory body for public examinations and publicly funded qualifications, QCA will take the lead in designing and developing a coherent national framework of qualifications which meets the needs of education, training, individuals and employers. It will define and maintain clear and high standards of quality assurance expected of awarding bodies.

> ➤ As one of a number of bodies committed to enhancing quality in education, QCA aims to help raise national standards of achievement. This includes promoting greater access to and participation in education and training, enhancing lifelong learning opportunities creating ways of giving credible national recognition for all learners, and developing ways of increasing achievement in literacy, numeracy and key skills generally. (The Qualifications and Curriculum Authority, 1998.)

Besides ending the two education systems, the QCA also has a very clear role to develop new initiatives, monitor existing ones and ensure the highest quality standards in training and education. The QCA forms part of the government's strategic plan for improving the quality of the education and training of the country. Like many other organisations the QCA has a corporate plan translated into broad strategic aims and as mentioned earlier it will also help other bodies such as schools to develop to achieve targets, both national and local, just as sections of a business or individuals will work towards achieving the targets that contribute to their organisation's strategic objectives. Targets will be discussed in more detail a little later in this chapter.

### National Vocational Qualifications (NVQS)

An NVQ is a statement of competence clearly related to work, and is intended to facilitate entry or progression in employment, further education or training. This qualification must be issued by a recognised body to an individual, and the statement of competence must include specified standards in the ability to perform in a range of work-related activities and the skills, knowledge and understanding that underpin such performance in employment.

NVQs have to meet certain criteria.

> ➤ They must be competence-based and must therefore be concerned with the outcomes of learning.

> ➤ They should be based on a statement of competence, which should include the performance standard as well as the underpinning knowledge and understanding.

> ➤ An NVQ qualification must be relevant to the needs of industry and must have requirements that are found in the real workplace. It should reflect the actual competencies that are needed in a real job.

➤ The qualification should be independent of any particular course or programme, so that individuals could gain their qualification by studying in a variety of ways including open learning, or by showing that they have gained experience, or by formal training.

➤ The qualification should be based on national standards so that everyone throughout the country works towards the same standards and competencies and the performance criteria will be the same for everyone.

➤ Every qualification should provide equality of opportunity of access and provide equality of learning opportunities for everyone, regardless of age, sex, race, or special needs.

➤ An NVQ should be broad-based and should cover a range of activities, with scope for progression between levels.

➤ Industry must have been involved in defining the standards, which must ensure that the needs of the workplace are met in full. This is to ensure that everyone has confidence in the value of the qualification.

➤ Assessment is important to the quality of the NVQ, and all elements of competence should be assessed to national standards.

➤ Competence must be shown and assessed.

There are five levels of qualification.

*Level 1* recognises competence in a wide range of work activities that are likely to be routine and predictable.

*Level 2* recognises competence in a broader and more demanding range of work activities, some of which may be non-routine.

*Level 3* recognises competence in a broad range of work activities, of which many are complex and non-routine and which may be performed in a variety of contexts. There is likely to be a need to demonstrate responsibility and autonomy at this level and it may also be necessary to prove competence in guiding others.

*Level 4* recognises competence in the performance of complex, technical and professional work activities which are performed in a wide variety of work settings. There is likely to be a substantial degree of personal autonomy and responsibility and it is usually necessary to demonstrate competence in allocating resources and in management or supervision.

*Level 5* recognises competence in applying fundamental principles and complex techniques across a wide range of situations which may often be unpredictable. At this level there will be a need to demonstrate a great deal of personal autonomy as well as showing significant levels of responsibility for the work of others and the allocation of resources. There will be a need to be able to analyse, diagnose, design, plan, execute and evaluate issues and solutions.

### National training organisations (NTOs)

These are new, independent employer-led organisations which aim to work strategically both within their own particular sector and with the Government on matters relating to education and training in Britain. They are recognised, for this purpose, by the Department for Education and Employment (DfEE) and they have replaced Industry Training Organisations, Lead Bodies and Occupational Standards Councils. They bring under their umbrella a diverse range of organisations including professional bodies, trade unions and trade associations, and also those involved in education and training. NTOs have responsibilities for National Occupational Standards and the frameworks for Modern apprenticeships. According to the Department for Education and Employment (1998), NTOs have five main aims:

➤ identification of skill shortages and training needs for the sector,
➤ influencing the provision for education and careers guidance,
➤ advising on the structure of national qualifications and developing occupational standards such as NVQs/SVQs,
➤ giving advice about training solutions,
➤ providing an effective means for communication between employers and their other key partners to implement strategies.

Notice that we said that NTOs aim to work *strategically* within their sectors. This shows the importance that the government places on education and training and the part that these play within the government's strategic plans for the country. The role of education and training is fundamental to the Government if they are to meet the targets they have set for an increasingly skilled and better-educated workforce. Here, once again, as with the QCA, we can see that it is not only employers that need to think strategically with regard to education and training, but also the Government; the establishment of NTOs is part of the Government's strategic plan for the country.

**The Employment National Training Organisation (ENTO)**
This is the national training organisation for those involved in development, management and representation of employees. It aims to develop and improve national standards in these areas and develop NVQs/SVQs which reflect these standards. The NVQs that have been developed focus on outcomes rather than the processes or tasks that individuals need to complete and thus can be linked closely to the needs of the organisation. There are a range of NVQs/SVQs which have been developed specifically for people in training and development and these range from level 3 to level 5. The titles of these NVQs/SVQs are listed below:

➤ Level 3: Training and Development
➤ Level 4: Human Resource Development
➤ Level 4: Learning Development
➤ Level 5: Training and Development Strategy

Some of you may be working towards these qualifications yourself perhaps as part of your own career plan to enhance your competencies in these areas or to help towards gaining Graduate Membership of the IPD. You will notice once again the importance of training and development strategy for those working towards the level 5 qualification. Remember that people operating at level 5 should be able to demonstrate substantial personal autonomy, responsibility for allocation of resources and for the work of others . They are likely to be operating at a fairly senior managerial level and so must be able to demonstrate that they are competent in thinking strategically and developing training and development strategies.

In order to maintain the quality of NVQs those involved as either assessors or verifiers also need to have qualifications. These qualifications are sometimes referred to as the 'D Units' and comprise units D31–36. These are not full NVQs/SVQs but are nevertheless national standards and anyone involved with the assessment or verification process for NVQs/SVQs must have completed the appropriate 'D Unit'.

**PAUSE FOR THOUGHT 8.3** *What do ENTO, NVQ and IPD stand for? (Look back earlier in the chapter to find the answer if you are unsure.)*

### Criticisms of the NVQ system

There have been many criticisms of the NVQ system, notably by Professor Alan Smithers (1994) of Manchester University. It has been claimed that the NVQ system in Britain is not as rigorous as similar systems in other countries, and that a wide range of assessment standards are being used, varying between one institution and another. The procedures have been criticised as over-bureaucratic, and assessment has proved to be a very time-consuming process. Many of the same criticisms have also been applied to GNVQs (General National Vocational Qualifications) the full time, school or college based, pre-vocational courses which teach people about a broad area of work, rather than a specific job. Employers may consequently lack confidence in the standards which are claimed to have been achieved and has led some employers to develop their own competence based systems of training.

## The national targets for education and training
● ● ● ● ● ● ● ● ● ● ● ● ● ● ● ● ● ● ● ● ● ● ● ● ● ● ● ● ● ● ● ● ● ● ● ● ● ● ● ● ● ● ● ● ● ● ● ● ● ● ● ● ● ● ● ●

In 1991 in order to develop a more competitive and better-trained workforce the government, as part of its strategic plan for the nation, set a series of targets. In 1995 the government endorsed more demanding revised targets, and three Foundation Learning Targets plus three Lifetime Learning Targets were set to be achieved by the year 2000. The intention is for employers, individuals, training providers and the government all to work together to improve the skills of the existing workforce and to develop the potential of young people.

### Foundation learning targets

1   By age 19, the aim is for 85% of young people to achieve 5 GCSEs at grade C or above, an intermediate General National Vocational Qualification (GNVQ) or a National Vocational Qualification (NVQ) Level 2.
2   It is intended that 75% of young people should achieve level 2 competence in communication, numeracy and IT by age 19; and 35% should achieve level 3 competence in these core skills by age 21.
3   By age 21, 60% of young people should achieve 2 GCE A levels, and advanced GNVQ or an NVQ level 3.

### Lifetime learning targets

1  60% of the workforce to be qualified to NVQ level 3, advanced GNVQ or 2 GCE A level standard.

2  30% of the workforce to have a vocational, professional, management or academic qualification at NVQ level 4 or above.

3  70% of all organisations which employ 200 or more employees, and 35 per cent of those employing 50 or more, to be recognised as Investors in People.

These targets are currently being revised and new targets will be set for 2002 which are likely to incorporate further targets for both education and training. As mentioned earlier in the chapter the QCA will also have an important contribution to make in setting standards for an integrated qualifications structure for the nation and in setting and monitoring the standards achieved.

Various other government initiatives have been introduced to encourage employers to provide training and development for employees and to help in achieving these targets. These include:

**DID YOU KNOW?**

Statisticians at the DfEE predict that the Government's Foundation Learning Target 2 is likely to be nearly achieved and estimate that between 53% and 59% will have reached this level by the year 2000.

However, there is still a huge gap in achieving some of the other targets. (Employment Development Bulletin, 97, January 1998.)

➤ Modern Apprenticeships
➤ National Traineeships
➤ New Deal

### Modern Apprenticeships

Modern Apprenticeships were launched in 1995 as part of the attempt by the Government to revitalise education and training. They are usually aimed at 16–17 year olds but there are also Accelerated Modern Apprenticeships which extend the scheme to those leaving school at 18. The key features of a Modern Apprenticeship are:

➤ They lead to NVQ level 3 or above.
➤ There must be a written pledge between the employer and the young person which is underwritten by the TEC.
➤ As well as the emphasis on skills training, there is also a requirement to meet certain standards of literacy and numeracy.
➤ There is a framework for different sectors which sets the minimum standards required but this is sufficiently flexible to meet company needs.

Modern Apprenticeships have been very successful and have helped contribute to the percentages of young people achieving Foundation Learning Target 3. The government needed something similar to encourage school leavers and employers to invest in training at NVQ level 2, and in 1997 they introduced National Traineeships.

### National Traineeships

These, like Modern Apprenticeships, are also aimed at school and college leavers aged 16 and over. They aim to attract young people who might otherwise not pursue any formal training by encouraging them to 'earn while they learn'. Their main features are:

- They lead to NVQ level 2
- They aim to develop quality training to industry standards.
- They have a written training agreement and a formal training plan.
- Although normally the young persons will be employed and earning wages, they could alternatively be linked to an employer or group of employers and be a paid a training allowance.
- As well as the emphasis on skills training, there is also a requirement to meet certain standards in information technology, solving problems and communication, handling numbers, team working and managing future developments.

New Traineeships should do much to improve the level of skills in this country and they are likely to provide an important boost to the achievement of the other Foundation Learning Targets, which at present are a long way from being achieved.

### New Deal

New Deal is a scheme for 18–25 year olds (from late 1998 it will also be made available for those over 25). While it is not solely a training scheme, there are nevertheless important training provisions within it, particularly in 'the Gateway', an introduction to and intensive preparation for work which clients undertake before they go to an employer. There is also a requirement for training to be provided either by the employer or by a third party to bring the person up to the required standards. The key features of the scheme are:

- The Gateway: a period of intensive training and preparation for work before the person actually joins an employer.
- Applicants must have been unemployed for at least six months before being eligible to join the scheme.
- A subsidy to the employer. At the time of writing there is a subsidy of £40.00 for those employed between 24 and 29 hours per week and of £60.00 for those employed 30 or more hours per week.
- The employer can choose who to take into the placement within their organisation.
- There is a full-time education and training option for those who are in need of preparation before beginning on-the-job training.
- Training in placements through voluntary work is also possible where places in employment are not available.

## Management training and development

We discussed earlier the term 'employee development', and stated that this applies to all groups of people within the organisation. In the past this term was often used with reference to management. The term implied that formal training is not neccesarily required but that the individuals need to develop and grow, not just to meet existing training needs but also to help them to develop for some future role. While this term is often used when discussing managers, it can be argued that it should also apply to any other individuals who may need to be developed, in order perhaps to be ready for promotion, or just to reach their potential. Many opportunities for management development exist, and people involved in employee development need to be aware of these opportunities. Opportunities to deputise for the manager in his or her absence or to act as secretary to a meeting can provide a useful developmental opportunity.

As well as the numerous changes that have occurred in vocational training and development, there have been several new initiatives relating to management training and development.

The above were two of the findings of a report, *The Making of Managers*, by Professor Charles Handy *et al.* (1987). This was one of two influential reports published at that time, the second being *The Making of British Managers* by Constable and McCormick (1987). These reports together showed that there were not many educational or management training opportunities available to the British manager. Compared with training opportunities for managers in many other nations, the training available in Britain was not of sufficiently high quality. Also, managers who are uneducated, untrained and undeveloped themselves are hardly likely to see the value of training or developing their own staff.

**PAUSE FOR THOUGHT 8.4** *Think of some well-known fictional managers in TV soaps, sitcoms and dramas (e.g. Mike Baldwin in* Coronation Street, *Grant Mitchell in* EastEnders, *Gordon Brittas in* The Brittas Empire, *Basil Fawlty in* Fawlty Towers *or one of the NHS managers in* Casualty). *What training needs can you identify for each one?*

These reports helped to generate discussion about the need for more and better management training and development opportunities, and resulted in the setting up of the Management Charter Initiative (MCI) supported by the Confederation of British Industry (CBI), the British Institute of Management (BIM) and the Foundation for Management Education. A Council for Management Education and Development (CMED) was established with Bob Reid, Chairman of Shell UK, as its Chairman. It was intended that its membership should be wide, with representatives of management education and training as well as managers being included. In 1988 the CMED widened its operations, becoming the National Forum for Management Education and Development (NFMED), a policy-making, standard-setting and accrediting body. The NFMED was the Industry Lead Body for developing and setting management and supervisory standards. The MCI is the operating and marketing section of the NFMED. In 1988 the MCI launched a ten-point Code of Practice, and by 1990 over 530 organisations from all sectors had joined the initiative.

The MCI has in turn promoted the establishment of national professional management qualifications at three levels: certificate, diploma, and degree and master's level qualifications. National Standards of Competence were developed and launched by the MCI in 1990, and a national framework of competences has subsequently been devised.

The idea of competencies forms the basis of management training courses endorsed by the MCI. Managers need to prove that they are competent in a wide range of tasks and are assessed against national standards.

There are many critics of this approach, who argue the role of managers is very diverse and that you cannot break it down into measurable units of competence and then use these for a National Qualification.

### The learning organisation

Another popular recent idea is the idea of the learning organisation. In some ways the term is confusing, since people actually do the learning, but it is good that people have started to see learning within organisations as being of importance. According to Jones and Hendry (1992), the term at its simplest means an organisation where there are 'a lot of people learning' and according to Pedlar *et al.* (1988) it means 'an organisation which facilitates the learning of all its members and continuously transforms itself'.

If an organisation is to encourage learning to occur, then it must develop a culture which recognises that people learn in different ways and must provide a range of experiences from which they may learn. Many organisations, as we have already shown, create situations where people learn all the things that the managers don't want them to learn. In the learning organisation, human resource managers and training and development specialists have an important role in ensuring that the organisation develops in a way which facilitates the learning that the organisation does want to occur, and that a suitable environment is created in which continuous improvement is actively encouraged. Line managers also need to be involved in encouraging learning to occur, and the organisation should try to minimise barriers that may hamper learning and development and encourage individuals to seek learning opportunities for themselves. The training and development that occurs should clearly link with the objectives of the organisation, and its efficiency and effectiveness should be regularly evaluated.

### The Investors in People award (IiP)

This award is a Government initiative to try to improve British training practices and to try to ensure that every organisation becomes or strives to become a learning organisation. Responsibility for IiP was initially divided between the TECs and the central unit of the Employment Department's Training Enterprise and Education Directorate in Sheffield, but in 1993 a new business-led body, Investors in People UK, was established to be responsible for ensuring a consistent national standard. To achieve the Investors in People award an organisation, or even a branch of that organisation, must demonstrate that it can meet four criteria:

- ➤ a written business plan, including information on how employees will contribute to achieving it
- ➤ regular agreements between line managers and employees on their training needs

> evidence of induction training and continuous development of all employees
> evaluation of training against business goals.

Although standards may vary between large and small organisations, the main criteria for every organisation appear to be that the organisation can show that it has become a learning organisation in which training plays an integral part, is linked to business needs and is regularly evaluated. A more formal approach to demonstrating that this is the case is likely to be expected from a large organisation.

## BS5750/ISO9000

Originally developed as a quality standard for industry, the British Standards Institute standard BS5750 has in recent years been applied to training. This lays down procedures for producing a particular product and requires a great deal of paperwork to prove quality. Some organisations have used BS5750 as a measure of the quality of their training, while others have decided to try to achieve the Investors in People award.

Standards are increasingly being set for other areas of work practice besides quality and training and recently a new standard has been developed to address the issue of exploitation. The Ethical Standard is a new independent code designed to protect workers in developing countries from exploitation by their richer western neighbours. The code establishes standards for a minimum age of 15 for employment; basic health and safety standards to be provided; union rights; rights against unfair discrimination; no corporal punishment, coercion or verbal abuse to be used; a 48 hour maximum working week with at least one day off a week; a level of pay that should do more than just provide for basic needs. There have to also be systems of management in place to ensure continued compliance and six-monthly monitoring visits by independent auditors.

### Approaches to training adopted by learning organisations

Specific training techniques have been discussed in the previous chapter. A few others, which might be used by an organisation that wants to encourage the culture of a learning organisation, will be discussed here.

### Mentors

Rather than just leaving learning experiences to chance, many organisations now use mentors to help individuals to learn. Mentors need to be prepared to guide and suggest suitable learning experiences for their protégé. They may encourage reflection on these learning experiences by asking for reports, and may suggest books to read on the subject. They may also sometimes provide opportunities for the individual to demonstrate what he or she has learnt by, for example, reviewing a presentation before the learner makes it to its target audience. While their main aim is to encourage individuals to learn, the mentors are also likely to learn a great deal themselves by their involvement in this learning experience. In effect, the mentors will be encouraging the individual to learn in different ways according to their development needs and to practice using different learning styles and different stages of the learning cycle.

### Learning logs

Another way in which individuals may be encouraged to learn from their experiences is by the use of a learning log. Learning logs are ways of keeping track of a person's development, with emphasis on unstructured, informal activities. This is likely to involve individuals in describing events that they feel are important for their own development process. They would then need to comment on what they had learnt from the experience and how, if a similar situation were to arise again, they would handle that situation. The idea is that because individuals have to write up their learning experiences, they will be likely to do things better in the future. Learning also ceases to be a haphazard process, as it becomes conscious and increasingly learner-centred. This means that the individual will have used several of the stages of the learning cycle.

Keeping a learning log should encourage activists to be more reflective and encourage reflectors/theorists to take action and to do things after reflecting on them. This could be undertaken with a mentor or as a totally self-directed method of gaining insights into your own learning processes. This method is very subjective but tends to encourage an analytical approach to problems. It can also be therapeutic to get a problem sorted out on paper, with clear targets for how you would handle a similar situation in the future.

The main headings likely to be used for a learning log will be:

➤ Description of a significant learning experience.
➤ What actually happened.
➤ What you concluded/learnt from this experience.
➤ What action you will take now or how you would handle a similar situation in the future.

In order to ensure that all stages of the learning cycle are covered a further section could be added:

➤ How what you learnt relates to the theory on this subject.

### *Continuing professional development*

The Institute of Personnel and Development strongly encourages the use of a form of learning log as a means for members to continue to update their professional knowledge. This is to ensure that individuals will stay up to date not only on facts but also on opinions and skills. The IPD aims to ensure that the reputation of its members remains high and that they aspire to high levels of performance, and that its members devise and manage learning methods appropriate to their needs and the circumstances in their own organisation.

The IPD acknowledges that continuing professional development opportunities will take many forms, but suggests that a balanced mix which includes some of the following might be appropriate.

**Professional activities**
➤ Seeking opportunities to contribute to strategic planning in their own organisation.
➤ Developing an understanding of business outside the remit of human resource management.
➤ Project management.
➤ Secondments and visits to other organisations' personnel units.
➤ Involvement with IPD and other professional bodies; committee work at branch, regional and/or national level.
➤ Part-time activities, e.g. writing, lecturing, mentoring, examining.
➤ Education/industry liaison, e.g. as a governor or careers adviser.
➤ Working party membership.

**Courses, seminars and conferences**
➤ Professional education courses leading to recognised qualifications.
➤ Degree, higher degree, research and post-graduate qualifications.
➤ Flexible learning courses.
➤ Courses and conferences, especially in human resource management and general management topics.

**Self-directed learning/informal learning**
➤ Reading of professional journals and books.
➤ Updating of knowledge (e.g. via television, press, newsletters).
➤ Use of management-related audio and video tapes.
➤ Learning new languages.
➤ Part-time responsibilities, e.g. membership of a political party, voluntary work or club/committee membership.
➤ Observation of events in the course of one's own work and reflection on their significance.

(adapted from *IPM Policy on Continuing Professional Development*, 1993)

This list provides for both formal and informal learning opportunities. Evidence of continuing professional development is required for changes in grade of IPD membership. The IPD suggests that all its members keep a personal record of their professional development, and IPD branch meetings and national conferences provide the participants with forms to complete a record of what they have learnt on each occasion.

The suggested outline for the IPD continuing professional development personal record gives the following headings.

Key date
What did you do?
What did you learn from it?
How might you use this now and in the future?

The IPD suggests that as a minimum an individual's continuing professional development should equate to between 5 and 30 days' development per annum.

## Conclusion
..............

In this chapter we have provided an introduction to employee development and what this means today. We have focused on the training needs of new employees and also discussed techniques of training on a one-to-one basis which you will probably find some opportunities to apply whatever environment you work in. We then examined some of the recent changes affecting employee development today. This is a constantly changing area where many new developments and government-led initiatives are occurring, and we have outlined some of these. If you want to explore these areas further then newspaper or journal articles and internet sites will provide you with the most up-to-date information. Employee development is a very important subject for human resource managers today, as it is vital if we are to be competitive with other nations that we find ways to help people and organisations to work at their optimum levels. Further useful materials are listed at the end of this chapter as suggestions for you to use if you want to examine particular areas in more detail.

**REVIEW QUESTIONS**

You will find brief answers to these review questions on page 425.

1  Find out the current National Targets for Training and Education and establish the extent to which they are likely to be met.

2  Use the Internet, government publications or your local TEC to find out more about one of the following topics: Investors in People, Modern Apprenticeships, National Traineeships, New Deal. Using this information describe how you would persuade a sceptical line manager of the benefits to be gained from introducing the initiative into an organisation of your choice.

3  Interview a manager about his or her organisation's strategic plans and objectives and try to assess the extent to which training and development in that organisation contributes to the achievement of those strategic plans.

4  Many organisations do not provide an adequate induction programme for new employees. Comment critically on the benefits to be gained from implementing a good induction programme, and outline what should be contained in that programme.

5  Evaluate the relative effectiveness of on-the-job training and off-the-job training.

**SELF-CHECK QUESTIONS**

**Answer the following multiple choice questions. The correct responses are given on page 425 for you to check your understanding of this chapter.**

1  **Does the definition we have quoted from Rosemary Harrison define employee development in the following way? (Yes/No)**

   **Employee development should be separate from the organisation's overall human resource strategy and as such there should be skilful provision and organisation of learning experiences in the work place in order that performance of individuals can be improved.**

2  **Should employees themselves be involved in determining the context of employee development? (Yes/No)**

3 When there are very few new recruits to an organisation, should induction be left for several months until there are sufficient to form a group? (Yes/No)
4 Do the initials ENTO stand for Employing National Training Officers? (Yes/No)
5 Does NVQ award qualifications? (Yes/No)
6 Is an NVQ a statement of competence clearly related to work, intended to facilitate entry or progression into further education or training? (Yes/No)
7 In the 1980s, were only 5% of all managers found to have no management training at all? (Yes/No)
8 Does MCI stands for Management Charter Initiative? (Yes/No)
9 Are mentors always training managers? (Yes/No)
10 Does CPD stand for continuous personal development? (Yes/No)

## References

Constable, J. and McCormick, R. *The Making of British Managers: A Report for the B.I.M. and C.B.I.* British Institute of Managers, 1987.

Roger Cowe. Code breaks the ethics ploys. *The Guardian*, 13 June 1998, p. 30.)

Employment Department. *Investors in People: A Brief for Top Managers.* Employment Department, 1991.

Handy, C. *et al. The Making of Managers: A Report on Management Education, Training and Development in the USA, West Germany, France, Japan and the U.K.* National Economic Development Council, 1987.

Handy, C. *et al. Making Managers.* Pitman, 1988.

Harrison, Rosemary. *Employee Development.* IPM, 1993.

IPM. *Continuous Development, People and Work – The IPM Code.* IPM, 1987.

*IPM Policy on Continuing Professional Development.* IPM, 1993.

Industrial Relations Services. Employee development. *IRS Employment Review*, No. 648, January 1998.

Jones, A. M and Hendry, C. *The Learning Organisation: A Review of Literature and Practice.* The HRD Partnership, 1992.

Management Charter Group. *The Management Charter Initiative.* MCI, 1987.

Manpower Services Commission. *Glossary of Training Terms.* HMSO, 1981.

Pedlar, M., Burgoyne, J. and Boydell T. *The Learning Company Project.* Training Agency, 1988.

QCA, About QCA. The Qualifications and Curriculum Authority, http://www.crownbe.com/qca/ovover.htm (7 June 1998).

Reid, M. Barrington, H. and Kenney, J. *Training Interventions.* IPM, 1993.

Smithers, Alan. Whither competencies? Reported in *Times Higher Education Supplement*, 22 April 1994.

## Further study

### Books

Advisory, Conciliation and Arbitration Service. *Recruitment and Induction.* ACAS, 1997. (A very useful guide to this subject.)

Fowler, Alan. *A Good Start: Effective Employee Induction*, 2nd edition. IPM, 1990. (Extremely useful on the subject of induction training.)

Harrison, Rosemary. *Employee Development*. IPD, 1998. (An excellent textbook for those who wish to study the subject of employee development in more depth.)

IDS Study 608. *Training Strategies*. Income Data Services Ltd, August 1996. (This describes, using case studies in eight organisations, how more organisations are linking their training strategies to the business objectives.)

IDS Study 620. *Modern Apprenticeships*. Income Data Services Ltd, February 1997. (This study examines the ways in which seven organisations organised their modern apprenticeship schemes.)

IDS Study 570. *NVQs in Practice*. Income Data Services Ltd, January 1995. (This examines the NVQ programmes in six very different organisations and looks at benefits gained by those employers and the problems experienced.)

*IRS Employee Development Bulletin.* This is published monthly and is to be found within the IRS Employment Review which is published twice a month. (It contains articles and facts and figures relating to training and development.)

Ollin, Ros and Tucker Jenny. *A Practical Guide to Units D32, D33, D34 and D36.* (A clear guide to assessment processes for those who want to be involved in the assessment of NVQs.)

Parsloe, Eric. *The Manager as a Coach or Mentor*. Training Extras Series. IPD, 1995. (Another book in the IPD Training Extras series, designed to cover specific management skills. In this book the similarities and differences between coaching and mentoring are explored by the author who uses a lively, easy to read style.)

Reid, M. and Barrington, H. *Training Interventions*. IPD, 1997. (Another excellent textbook for those wishing to explore more fully the whole subject of employee development.)

### *Articles*

(We have covered a wide range of issues relating to training and development in this chapter, and there are innumerable articles published on these topics. We include a selection of articles that you may find useful if you want to start to discover more about a particular aspect of training and development.)

Beardwell, Ian. On the record. *People Management*, Vol.4, No. 8, 16 April 1998, 43–46. (An account by three senior personnel practitioners of their learning experiences and the completion of their CPD record.)

Crawley, Rick. Personnel NVQs a big step forward – a pragmatic truce between knowledge and compromise. *Personnel Management*, Vol. 26, No. 10, August 1994, 31.

Fowler, Alan. How to plan an induction programme. *Personnel Management Plus*, September 1990, 20–21.

Greene, Melanie and Gibbons, Andrew. Learning logs for self development. *Training and Development*, February 1991, 30–32.

Honey, Peter. The learning organisation simplified. *Training and Development,* July 1991, 30–33.

Littlefield, Dave. Getting to grips with the GNVQ. *Personnel Management,* Vol. 26, No. 10, October 1994, 89–90.

Lowe, Kate. Test pilots. *Personnel Today,* August 9, 1994, 26–28.

Marshall, Vivien. Employers beware: don't lose your control of NVQs. *Personnel Management,* Vol. 26, No. 3, March 1994, 30–33.

Pickard, Jane. What does the 'investors in people' award really mean? *Personnel Management Plus,* March 1991.

Pickard, Jane. New Training bodies focus on skill gaps. *People Management,* Vol. 4, No.40, 14 May 1998, 15. (A brief analysis of the role of the new NTOs.)

Pickard, Jane. A slice of the action. *People Management,* Vol. 4, No. 40, 14 May 1998, 36–43. (A more detailed account of the role of the new NTOs.)

Roche, Peter. Personnel NVQs a big step forward – how standards help us to outperform the opposition. *Personnel Management,* Vol. 26, No. 10, August 1994, 30.

Sparrow, Stephanie. The Right Chemistry. *Training: The Personnel Today Magazine for Training Professionals,* May 1997, 12–13. (An interesting account of BP Chemicals' experiences of NVQs and of the need to develop similar training schemes for older workers.)

Welch, Jilly. National firms raise team spirit to offset local bias. *People Management,* Vol. 4, No. 8, 16 April 1998, 14–15. (A description, from the perspective of several large employers, of their experiences of the Government's New Deal.)

### Audio-visual

*You'll Soon Get The Hang of It.* Video Arts, 1995. (A humorous video which examines instruction on a one-to-one basis and provides plenty of sound advice.)

*Supporting Modern Apprenticeships.* National Extension College for the Department for Education and Employment, 1996. (This is designed as an open learning resource for people involved with Modern Apprenticeships and comprises audio-tape, computer discs and a workbook.)

### Internet

| | |
|---|---|
| Department for Education and Employment | **http://www.dfee.gov.uk/dfeehome.htm** |
| Investors in People | **http://www.iipuk.co.uk/iipuk/main.html** |
| New Deal | **http://www.newdeal.gov.uk** |
| Qualifications and Curriculum Authority | **http://www.open.gov.uk/qca/index.htm** |

# CHAPTER 9

# Performance appraisal and performance management

**Objectives:**
. . . . . . . . . . . . . .

*By the end of this chapter you will be able to:*

➤ state what is meant by the terms performance management and performance appraisal

➤ explain the differences between these terms

➤ give examples of techniques used in the management of performance at work

➤ design a simple performance appraisal system.

It is always important for managers and supervisors to get the best performance from their workforce in terms of levels of production and quality of output. They are concerned to motivate and encourage their employees to work effectively, in pursuit of the strategic objectives of the organisation and one way of trying to achieve this involves managers in designing systems to give employees feedback about their performance. We have discussed the importance of feedback in Chapter 8, and in this chapter we shall be looking at a specific way of giving feedback called performance appraisal.

Although, as we have said, it is important to motivate employees, this is often difficult to achieve, and if the organisation or manager handles the complex process of performance appraisal in an inappropriate way, then instead of feeling motivated, the employee may end up feeling totally demotivated by the experience. We aim to show in this chapter how to avoid the main pitfalls associated with the introduction of performance appraisal, so that the organisation and manager get it right.

We shall also examine what is meant by the term performance management, a relatively new term for a sphere of management activity that began to take shape in the 1980s and steadily increased in popularity during the 1990s. It is widely held to have grown out of performance appraisal, and also to have absorbed some of the newer techniques used in performance appraisal such as emphasis on setting objective standards of performance. Like performance appraisal, performance management is concerned to get the best performance from the individual, but goes further in that it also aims to get the best performance from the team and from the organisation as a whole. While performance appraisal will form part of the performance management approach there is more to it than this, and each of the topics covered in this book also makes a contribution towards performance management. Performance management is a process for sharing an understanding about what needs to be achieved and then managing and developing people in a way that enables such shared objectives to be achieved.

Performance appraisal is often one of the techniques used to encourage, motivate and help employees improve their performance. This chapter will examine first what is meant by the term performance appraisal and the development of different systems of performance appraisal before going on to examine the topic of performance management itself.

## Definitions
••••••••••••••

Before going any further it would be useful to define exactly what we mean by the terms 'performance appraisal' and 'performance management'.

### *Performance appraisal*

We have already said that performance appraisal is one way of giving employees feedback about their performance at work. According to ACAS (1997):

> appraisals regularly record an assessment of an employee's performance, potential and development needs. The appraisal is an opportunity to take an overall view of work content, loads and volume, to look back on what has been achieved during the reporting period and agree objectives for the next.

This definition clearly shows that the employee does get feedback about his or her past performance, but indicates that in performance appraisal there is the opportunity to assess or judge various aspects of an employee's work performance by looking back at how they have performed in the past and then by looking forward to agree future objectives or work load.

Fletcher and Williams (1985) have gone further than this in their definition of appraisal, and have said that the assessment of people is not the only thing that we do when we appraise a person's work performance. They feel that there are in fact two conflicting roles involved in appraisal – those of judge and helper.

We shall consider each of these facets of appraisal in turn. Firstly, we do all act as judges when we make informal judgements about the way people talk, what they wear and how they behave. These informal judgements may be objective or subjective and we may not even be aware that we are making them. They may not have much effect on people in everyday life, as we don't normally have any right to try to change these things in others, and we don't usually have any power to influence the way people behave. If we start to judge people in a work situation in this informal way with regard, for example, to the way they dress, we are likely to be accused of being too subjective and we might, quite rightly, be accused of treating people unfairly according to our own whims and prejudices. This sort of appraisal is not likely to encourage people to feel motivated about work. In this sense the term 'appraisal' means judging the worth, qualities or value of something, and in a work situation especially it is important that any judgements are fair and are based on objective job-related criteria.

Secondly, the term 'appraisal' is also used in another way, as Fletcher and Williams (1985) have indicated. When we appraise people in the work situation, we not only judge them but we usually also try to help them to improve aspects of their performance. We may suggest alternative ways of behaving or suggest training courses or provide developmental opportunities in order to help employees improve their performance and assess their own developmental needs.

Performance appraisal is therefore about giving feedback to the employee, but also involves the appraiser in being both judge and helper to an individual employee. The performance appraisal interview represents the organisation's provision of a formal opportunity in which to give feedback and be both judge and helper to that employee.

### Performance management

Michael Armstrong (1994) defines performance management as 'a process which is designed to improve organisational, team and individual performance and which is owned and driven by line managers'.

As such, performance management is a much broader concept than performance appraisal, which as we have seen has traditionally been concerned with judging the individual's performance, giving the individual feedback about this performance and helping that individual to improve by systematically trying to motivate them to work harder or more effectively. Performance management is concerned with improving not only the performance of the individual, but also the performance of the team and the organisation. Some traditional appraisal schemes have been accused of being run for the benefit of personnel managers or top managers, with many other people in the organisation not really understanding or appreciating what the performance appraisal scheme was trying to achieve. This may be true of some poorly designed schemes, but is a rather harsh judgement on many excellent appraisal schemes and personnel managers and on the contribution they make to their organisation's effectiveness. In order that the same criticisms cannot be made of performance management, there is an increased emphasis on the role of the line manager and on the involvement of teams and individuals. Performance management forms part of the human resource management approach to managing people, and performance is basically a shared process between managers, individuals and teams in which objectives are agreed and jointly reviewed and which aims to integrate corporate, individual and team objectives.

Since performance appraisal schemes form part of the techniques used in a performance management system, and are still perhaps more widely known, we shall start by examining performance appraisal systems before going on to consider performance management in detail.

## Performance appraisal schemes

Performance appraisal schemes may be used for a wide range of reasons, some of which may conflict with each other, but the main reasons are likely to include the following:

➤ to improve current performance
➤ to provide feedback
➤ to increase motivation
➤ to identify potential

> ➤ to identify training needs
> ➤ to aid career development
> ➤ to award salary increases
> ➤ to solve job problems
> ➤ to let individuals know what is expected of them
> ➤ to clarify job objectives
> ➤ to provide information about the effectiveness of the selection process
> ➤ to aid in career planning and development
> ➤ to provide information for human resource planning
> ➤ to provide for rewards.

Randell *et al.* (1984) suggest that for most employers there are three main uses for appraisal schemes: *performance, potential* and *reward*. All the reasons listed above fall into one of these three categories, and we shall examine each category in turn.

### Performance

Managers seek to review an individual's past performance and assess strengths, level of effort and areas where further development would be useful. Here the focus is on what the employee has actually done in the past, and an attempt is made to build on the employee's strengths and make improvements in other areas so that the employee can perform more effectively in the future. Many managers claim that they give this sort of feedback all the time informally, and if they do this well there may indeed be no need for a formal appraisal scheme. However, it is unlikely that all managers in a particular organisation will appraise their staff constantly and effectively. It is more likely that without a formal system and proper training, many managers will be appraising infrequently or not at all, using subjective criteria or not appraising fairly, so a formal appraisal system is necessary.

### Potential and development needs

From an examination of past performance many employers wish to identify as part of their human resource planning process, or for individual career development, individuals with potential to take up new or more responsible or challenging positions within the organisation. The concern here is not just with what the person has done in the past, but with trying to predict the level and type of work that employees will be capable of doing in the future, and then helping them to reach their full potential, so that the organisation can also benefit fully from their talents and abilities.

### Reward

This use of performance appraisal basically entails trying to reward employees for their past work, while hoping that the incentive of a reward will encourage other employees also to strive to work harder in the future. In recent years many organisations have sought to motivate their employees by linking rewards, using a system like performance-related pay, to excellent performance at work.

Many organisations try to get too much from one appraisal scheme, and try to use one scheme to fulfil all three purposes. This is unlikely to work, and usually results in the scheme falling into disrepute.

**DID YOU KNOW?**

*It is often suggested that as many as two-thirds of all appraisal schemes are abandoned or altered substantially within two years of their creation. This, to a very large extent, is due to organisations' not being aware of, or not paying enough attention to, a range of problems that can be avoided with sufficient forethought and planning, and to trying to make one scheme serve too many incompatible purposes.*

## Problems

A number of problems may prevent the appraisal schemes from being as effective as they should be. These include:

➤ the organisation not being clear about the purpose of the appraisal system and consequently trying to use the appraisal scheme to fulfil too many different purposes
➤ links with pay preventing open discussion of problems or of areas where improvement could be made
➤ keeping information secret from the employee
➤ the appraiser attacking the appraisee's character
➤ being too subjective in judgements
➤ using appraisal as part of the disciplinary process.

### Lack of clarity

We have already shown that most appraisal schemes fall into one of three categories, i.e. they are concerned with performance, potential or reward. An organisation should not attempt to use one appraisal scheme to fulfil all three categories. The particular objectives of an appraisal scheme should be clarified before the scheme is designed in detail, and should have been discussed with employees, trade unions and managers in order to take account of their views and to gain their commitment to the new appraisal scheme. Everyone should then be clear what the particular scheme is trying to achieve. Any scheme, however good the design, is unlikely to succeed if the managers and the workforce are suspicious of the reasons for its introduction and are opposed to making it work effectively.

While there are good reasons why employers should seek to appraise performance potential or give rewards to good employees, problems can also occur if employers try to achieve too much from their performance appraisal scheme. It is difficult, if not impossible, to devise a scheme that will appraise successfully all three areas, and there is a grave danger that the performance appraisal scheme will be rejected if it fails to live up to all that is claimed for it. This can easily happen if the scheme is poorly designed or if the managers show a reluctance to impart critical assessments, or if people are not trained properly in the appraisal process.

### Linking appraisal with pay

In particular, it is difficult to imagine that a person being appraised is likely to admit to any developmental need, or be willing to accept any help in their performance, if their salary increase depends on a good appraisal. It is therefore recommended that employers should in general try to keep reward considerations separate from the other areas of appraisal.

In spite of this advice and research evidence which suggests that performance-related pay (PRP) does not always motivate everyone in a workforce, many employers think that the offer of an incentive or reward is the only way to motivate employees to work harder, and this is often their main reason for introducing performance appraisal. The motivational aspects of pay will be discussed in more detail in Chapter 10, but the important point is that great care needs to be taken if appraisal systems are linked to pay. It will be especially important to ensure that the criteria being appraised are objective and free of unfair bias, and that there are genuine opportunities for all employees to be rewarded for their efforts. In many organisations financial constraints mean that the number of people who are awarded PRP is severely restricted and there is a serious danger that if the vast majority of the workforce do not feel they have any opportunity to receive a reward, they may feel much more demotivated than they did before the appraisal scheme was introduced. Only the select few who receive the reward will then feel positive about the experience and about the organisation, and even they will not necessarily be motivated to work harder.

### Keeping information secret from the employee

Appraisal involves, as we have already said, being both a judge and helper for an individual employee. In order that we can help the individual it is also important that they know about the judgements that have been made about them and that they receive feedback about these. Therefore if people are to be helped to develop, there must be discussion about problem areas, and any judgements made about employees should not be kept secret from them. Obviously the appraisal interview and reports of it do need to be confidential from other employees, but not so confidential that they are a secret from the employee concerned.

### Subjectivity or attacks on the appraisee's character

If the person doing the appraising feels insecure about his or her own performance, there could be a tendency to try to ensure that the employee being appraised doesn't become a threat to them by focusing solely on the aspects of the job that have not been handled well and failing to show recognition for jobs that have been done well. In some cases, subjective judgements may be made because there are no clear criteria on which to appraise the employee, and the appraiser may resort to attacking aspects of the person's character that the person cannot do anything about. In the past many appraisal schemes were based on assessing personality traits that were thought to be important to a particular job, but that in fact were very broad categories that could only be judged subjectively. These included personality traits such as enthusiasm, application, intelligence and resourcefulness.

**PAUSE FOR THOUGHT 9.1** *How would you feel if one of your tutors said that you lacked integrity or that your intelligence was inadequate?*

We imagine that you would not feel very happy with comments about your lack of integrity or poor level of intelligence, and would want to know on what criteria these comments were based.

If appraisal schemes are to be credible to employees, great care must be taken that judgements made are objective and have some basis that can be discussed with the employee. Integrity is likely to mean slightly different things to different people, and judgement of a person's integrity is likely to be fairly subjective. Rather than focusing on subjective topics such as this or on aspects of an individual's personality which they cannot alter, it is better to examine aspects of the job that the person actually does, and make an objective judgement about the person's effectiveness at carrying out each aspect of the job.

Appraisers should also concentrate on seeking to help to bring about an improvement in areas of the employee's work where the appraisee can do something to make an improvement. Criticising someone for not being intelligent enough is similar to criticising them for being too short. There is really not much that they can do about it, so it is pointless to judge them on it and impossible to help them to change.

### Appraisal as part of the disciplinary process

We have already said that appraisal is partly about making judgements about an employee's performance, and that areas where performance is not as effective as it should be need to be discussed. However, this does not mean that disciplinary matters should be saved for several months to be dealt with at the appraisal interview. If a disciplinary offence occurs, then it should be dealt with immediately and not saved for discussion at the time of the appraisal interview. The appraisal interview should be about seeking to motivate employees, not an opportunity to discipline them.

### *The manager in performance appraisal*

Traditionally the people who are involved in the appraisal process are most likely to be the person who is to be appraised and his or her immediate manager. This has the advantage that the managers or supervisors should know their subordinates and should also know about each subordinate's job and the way in which he or she carries out his or her duties. Managers and their subordinates will see each other every day but may be too busy to discuss performance. The performance appraisal interview provides the time for the individual and the manager to sit down together to discuss the individual's progress. This should enable the manager to feel that he or she is helping the career of one of the staff, and prove to be a motivating experience for the employee, who has the undivided attention of the manager listening to his or her views and focusing attention on his or her development.

There can, however, be some disadvantages in having the employee's immediate manager carry out the appraisal, especially if there is a conflict of personalities, or if the manager perceives the employee to be a threat and is therefore unwilling to look for positive aspects of the employee's performance. If the appraisal scheme allows a high degree of subjectivity in comments made by the manager, then there is a danger that more will be learnt about the manager's attitudes to work and managing employees than about the employee's performance. Training in performance appraisal techniques is obviously extremely important here. We shall return to this subject later in this chapter.

ACTIVITY **9.1**

. . . . . . . . . . . . . . .

In spite of these problems, the appraisee's immediate supervisor or manager is usually the person most often involved in the appraisal process, although in some organisations other people may be involved. Using Table 9.1, write a list of people who you think might be involved in the appraisal process. For each of them, list the advantages and the disadvantages of their involvement.

*table 9.1*

**People involved in the appraisal process**

| People who may be involved in the appraisal process | Advantages | Disadvantages |
| --- | --- | --- |
| | | |
| | | |
| | | |
| | | |

### Discussion of Activity 9.1

*table 9.2*
**Discussion of Activity 9.1**

| People who may be involved in the appraisal process | Advantages | Disadvantages |
|---|---|---|
| The appraisee's manager's immediate manager | Often used as well as the appraisee's manager to check that the manager is being fair. When used as sole appraiser there is the possible advantage of being more objective about employee's work and of not being directly threatened by their success. | Not likely to know the appraisee well and likely to have to obtain information about the individual's performance from their immediate manager. |
| The personnel manager | Often used as a check that the manager is being fair and as a monitor of consistency of approach throughout the organisation. Personnel managers are sometimes used as sole appraiser for reasons of fairness and consistency and because they are not perceived to be a threat to the manager. | Not likely to know the appraisee well and likely to have to obtain information about the individual's performance from their immediate manager. |
| Colleagues | This can be especially useful where team work is important or in an organisation with a matrix organisation structure where the individual may report to more than one manager. The main advantage is that colleagues are likely to have a clear idea of how effective the individual is at working with them and the views of several people are likely to provide a balanced perspective. | The colleagues concerned may not know about all aspects of the individual's job. They may be reluctant to express an honest opinion about a colleague, and may be influenced by whether they have a good or poor relationship with that person, or by jealousy or rivalry. |
| Subordinates | People who work for the individual who is being appraised will certainly have a different view of that individual's abilities and performance and can therefore provide valuable information about the person's performance. | They may be too frightened to express their real opinion, if they feel that their manager might hold this against them at some future date. The person being appraised may be reluctant to accept the views of his or her subordinates. |

*table 9.2*
**Contd.**

| | | |
|---|---|---|
| Self-appraisal | Often used as part of the appraisal process, as in many systems the appraisers and the appraisee complete forms independently of each other and then use them as the basis of discussion. The individual will have a more detailed knowledge of the standard of their own work performance than their manager. Since individuals should be encouraged to take a great deal of responsibility for their own development, this increased self-awareness will be useful. | Some people may find it difficult to analyse their own work performance and may have unrealistic views of how well they have actually done. They may not be willing to admit to weaknesses, although in many cases the opposite is true, and people are more critical of themselves than their manager would be. |
| 360° appraisal (not actually a person, but gathers information from all the people mentioned so far) | This form of appraisal gathers information from all the above sources to gain an all-round view of the person's performance. This is extremely thorough and will provide information on different aspects of the individual's performance, so that it is possible to compile a total picture of the person's job performance. | It can be very time-consuming to collect information from so many people, and may not always be cost-effective. It is also subject to all the disadvantages listed above. |
| 540° appraisal (not actually a person but gathers information from all the people mentioned so far, as in 360° appraisal, but also gathers and uses additional information from people outside the organisation, such as customers or clients) | Once again an extremely thorough way of gathering information as those outside the organisation, such as clients or customers, may be able to provide very valuable insights into how an individual is performing. | This can be difficult to organise as customers or clients may not wish to spend time participating in questionnaires and cannot be coerced into doing so. Many employers will also be hesitant to use this approach as they may not wish to give their clients or customers any cause to think that they, or any of their employees, might ever provide a less than perfect service or product. |
| Assessment centres (not actually a person, so you may not have included assessment centres in this list, but we include them as they form yet another important way of assessing performance) | Individuals undertake a battery of tests to measure aspects of personality; verbal, numerical and reasoning skills; and ability to lead and work in a team. This provides an all-round view of the person's talents and abilities. Particularly useful when assessing future potential and in the appraisal of potential supervisors or managers. | Expensive and time-consuming to carry out for all employees. |

### Design of documentation

In most appraisal systems it is necessary to have some type of documentation to record what has been agreed. At its simplest this could just be blank sheets of paper for both the appraiser and appraisee, on which they both assess the performance of the appraisee. This provides a means for jotting down ideas and views on performance which can then be used as a basis for discussion at the time of the performance appraisal interview. The disadvantage of this system is that there may be little basis for agreement about the topics to be discussed.

In order to provide for a systematic and consistent approach to performance appraisal, many organisations design an appraisal form. In this case, the manager and the person being appraised both complete a form prior to the appraisal interview. They then exchange forms and at the interview use both the forms as a basis for discussion. This has the advantage of both parties having focused on similar topics and saves time at the interview, as both should have already done quite a bit of preparation for the interview. When designing such a form, there should be clear guidelines explaining what is meant by each section, and the points already discussed in the section on problems must be borne in mind. The criteria to be appraised should not be subjective and should be fair. They should relate to things that employees could improve, and there should be opportunities for the employee to see the appraiser's comments and a section in which to respond to those comments. There should also be a right of appeal. The guidelines should indicate what should then happen to the appraisal forms. Where will they be kept? Who will ensure that action is taken on key points?

The actual content of such a form will be influenced by the type of appraisal scheme adopted by the organisation. This will now be discussed.

### Types of performance appraisal

#### Management by objectives (MBO)

We have already said that appraisal schemes are most likely to succeed if the criteria to be appraised can be assessed objectively rather than subjectively, and that the appraisal of aspects of a person's personality should be avoided. One way of achieving this is to set clear objectives for the employee to achieve before the next appraisal, and then to focus the discussion at the appraisal interview on the extent to which these objectives have been achieved. An appraisal interview also provides an opportunity to look forward, so the next stage would be to set and agree objectives for the next review period.

One way in which to achieve this would be to look first at the job description and then agree specific objectives for some of the main tasks. This has the additional advantage that the objectives can be linked very clearly to the organisation's strategic goals, so that the individual can see exactly what to do to help the organisation to meet its objectives. A sample form for this type of performance appraisal is shown in Figure 9.1.

In this example there is an opportunity to look at past objectives and consider the extent to which they have been achieved, and also a chance to look forward and agree future objectives. Here the appraisee has an opportunity to write comments, as do the manager and countersigning manager. This type of

*figure 9.1*

**Sample form for performance appraisal using management by objectives**

---

NAME ............................. JOB TITLE .......................

DATE OF APPRAISAL ................ DEPARTMENT/SECTION ..............

---

**JOB DESCRIPTION** (To be agreed with employee)

---

**REVIEW PERIOD** ...........

1. Objectives agreed for this last review period. (This should include special tasks, personal training and development.)

2. To what extent have these objectives been achieved?

3. Were there any other major achievements?

4. Were there any obstacles which prevented achievement of agreed objectives?

5. What steps need to be taken to overcome these obstacles?

6. What training development and education were undertaken during the review period?

---

**NEXT REVIEW PERIOD** ............

1. What specific objectives have been agreed for the next review period?

2. What training development and education should be undertaken during the next review period?

3. What follow-up action is needed?

---

**COMMENTS OF APPRAISER.**


Signed ................... (Appraiser)

---

**COMMENTS OF APPRAISEE.**


Signed ................... (Appraisee)

---

**COMMENTS OF COUNTERSIGNING MANAGER.**

appraisal can also link with overall company objectives, and is often used as part of a performance management system, as we shall show later.

### Rating scales

This is another form of performance appraisal scheme that seeks to encourage objectivity by focusing on aspects of the employee's job and then indicating by graded statements how successfully the employee has fulfilled each of the main duties listed in his or her job description. The statements would be linked to the job description, and the team of writers would provide a series of statements for each category of the job description, indicating levels of performance in that duty ranging from excellent to poor. The appraiser would discuss the person's performance using these scales during the appraisal interview, and would then tick the statement that he or she and the appraisee agreed best summed up the appraisee's performance.

ACTIVITY **9.2**
• • • • • • • • • • • • •

Do you remember the job description which we gave in Chapter 2? The main duties for this are listed in Table 9.3. For each of these duties write a series of statements to indicate the possible degrees of success of someone who is working in this job. It is intended that these statements will form the basic information with which the individual's performance in that job is compared by the appraiser. We have started this for you by suggesting some graded statements for the first row.

### *Discussion of Activity 9.2*

This gives a simple way of rating the employee's behaviour in the job that is clear and easy to use, as the appraiser simply ticks the box containing the comment that most nearly reflects the actual performance of the employee. It also means that there is a common standard which all appraisers would use when appraising a person doing that job. In this case, examples of four types of behaviour had to be provided for each aspect of the main duties listed in the job description. This was because many appraisers tend to rate employees as average just to avoid upsetting people or to avoid giving too much praise: by not allowing a middle category, they are encouraged to be more decisive. There may still be a tendency to go for the middle two boxes (and for many employees this will be highly appropriate), but appraisers must be encouraged by training to use the full range of categories if and when this is needed.

In this Activity you were the only person to choose the descriptions for the criteria to be rated, so there could still be some degree of subjectivity involved, as you may have described the performance of each duty in a different way to other people. It would be more usual to involve a team of people to provide the descriptors for each main duty and to get consensus about the descriptors to be used.

### Behaviourally anchored rating scales (BARS)

If this appraisal system were to be introduced in a large organisation, it would not rely on just one person's ideas of a suitable range of categories. In the first section of the ratings exercise we have used the following terms as descriptors of the first of the major duties listed in the job description:

*table 9.3*
**Job rating**
**(Activity 9.3)**

Name of Job holder: _____

Job title: Receptionist_____

Date of appraisal: _____

| Main duties | Appraiser's comments | A (Well ahead of standard performance) | B (More than satisfactory, slightly above job requirements) | C (Less than satisfactory, needs slight improvement) | D (Requires constant supervision) |
|---|---|---|---|---|---|
| Greet walk-in visitors and ascertain purpose of their visit. Handle or redirect queries as appropriate. | | Always quick to greet visitors and ascertain purpose of visit, dealing with queries extremely rapidly and effectively so visitors are always highly satisfied. | Greets visitors, ascertains purpose of visit and deals effectively with queries. | Normally greets visitors promptly and ascertains purpose of their visit; sometimes slow to redirect queries. | Slow to notice walk-in visitors, does not always greet them promptly, and is not always able to deal with queries or redirect them to the appropriate place. |
| Answer phone queries as above. | | | | | |
| Answer all initial queries about receipt of payments using the on-line payment receipts system. | | | | | |

*table 9.3*
**Contd.**

| | | | | | |
|---|---|---|---|---|---|
| Open and sort incoming post by department. Organise delivery of post by assistant receptionist. | | | | | |
| Perform clerical tasks assigned by department in agreement with the Office Services Manager. | | | | | |
| Supervise assistant receptionists and delegate work as appropriate. | | | | | |
| Perform other duties as assigned by the Office Services Manager or other authorised manager. | | | | | |

Comments of appraiser

Signature .......................................(Appraiser)

Comments of appraisee

Signature .......................................(Appraisee)

Comments of countersigning manager

Signature .......................................(Manager)

➤ always quick to greet visitors and ascertain purpose of visit, dealing with queries extremely rapidly and effectively so visitors are always highly satisfied

➤ greets visitors, ascertains purpose of visit and deals effectively with queries

➤ normally greets visitors promptly and ascertains purpose of their visit; sometimes slow to redirect queries

➤ slow to notice walk-in visitors, does not always greet them promptly, and is not always able to deal with queries or redirect them to the appropriate place.

These were purely our own subjective choices, and we had not checked whether or not other people would describe this aspect of the job in the same way. You could find other descriptors that may be more effective than these. We may have chosen terms to describe each level of performance that are different from the way in which other people would describe the same task.

One way to try to get round the subjectivity of having just one person writing the descriptions of behaviour is to use a newer technique, known as behaviourally anchored rating scales. In this case a group of other raters would also be asked to suggest descriptions for a range of behaviour for each aspect of the main duties, so that a wide range of behavioural examples could be collected.

These descriptions are then collated and returned to the sample raters, but this time there is no indication of the scale point for which they were suggested. The sample raters are asked to indicate a scale point from A to D, where A represents excellence and D represents bad work, to which they think each descriptor most aptly relates. The descriptors that are consistently located at the same point of the scale are then used in the final version of the behavioural anchored scale. This is intended to remove the subjectivity inherent in the simpler rating method and ensure that descriptions used are likely to mean the same thing to most people.

ACTIVITY **9.3**

What do you see as the main advantages and disadvantages of this system of behaviourally anchored rating scales? Make a list of advantages and disadvantages.

### Discussion of Activity 9.3

Compare your list of advantages and disadvantages with the following one.

*Advantages*

➤ Objective rating of each of the main duties listed in job description.

➤ Agreement over suitable descriptors for each category of behaviour.

➤ Easy to use.

➤ Useful if lots of people have the same job descriptions so that the amount of time involved in designing the system will be repaid.

*Disadvantages*

➤ Time-consuming, as it takes a long time to get agreement on descriptors for each job.

➤ Only takes account of existing job performance; does not allow for discussion of future potential.

**Behavioural observation scales (BOS)**

These form another way of rating performance in a job. These scales are also developed as a result of lengthy procedures, and indicate a number of dimensions of performance with behavioural examples for each. Job analysis is used to identify the key determinants of performance and the performance dimensions are once again related to the job description, but in this case the appraiser is asked to indicate a point on a scale by a numerical value.

An example of such a scale in relation to selected aspects of a lecturer's job is given below. The appraisers simply circle the number that they think relates most closely to the usual behaviour of the appraisee.

ACTIVITY **9.4**

You can try this for yourself by selecting a lecturer that you know well and assessing him or her on this scale. Circle the number that most closely relates to the lecturer's normal behaviour.

1 Provides clearly structured lecture that is easy to follow

| Almost never | 5 | 4 | 3 | 2 | 1 | Almost always |
|---|---|---|---|---|---|---|

2 Provides up-to-date and interesting material in lectures/tutorials

| Almost never | 5 | 4 | 3 | 2 | 1 | Almost always |
|---|---|---|---|---|---|---|

3 Explains to students exactly what is expected of them when they complete written work

| Almost never | 5 | 4 | 3 | 2 | 1 | Almost always |
|---|---|---|---|---|---|---|

4 Is willing to give advice and guidance

| Almost never | 5 | 4 | 3 | 2 | 1 | Almost always |
|---|---|---|---|---|---|---|

5 Gives detailed and helpful feedback concerning written work that students have completed

| Almost never | 5 | 4 | 3 | 2 | 1 | Almost always |
|---|---|---|---|---|---|---|

### *Discussion of Activity 9.4*

We hope that you were fair in your assessment and were not influenced by personality or past grades given to you! In this case you were assessing the lecturer from the position of a student, and you are likely to have a very different view of his or her work performance to the lecturer's manager or the human resource manager. You may not, however, be able to assess all aspects of the lecturer's job such as his or her ability to carry out research, or an individual's administrative capabilities, but this exercise is similar to assessment by a person's subordinates which we mentioned earlier. It has the same type of limitations that we discussed then, but it gives you some idea of the way in which different points of view can be important and shows that if this were combined with appraisal from other perspectives, as in a system such as 360° or 540° appraisal, it could contribute to developing a full picture of a person's effectiveness and provide valuable feedback.

### The appraisal interview

Interviews have already been discussed in some detail in Chapters 4 and 5, and most of the points made there with regard to selection interviews also apply to appraisal interviews. Preparation, privacy and confidentiality, good questioning technique, avoidance of bias, good records and attention to the style of interview will also be important in the appraisal interview.

### Preparation

There is a need, as we explained in Chapter 4, for careful preparation before the interview and employees should be given adequate notice of the date of the appraisal interview to allow them time to prepare. In the appraisal interview this is also likely to mean that care needs to be taken with the layout of the room, so that the person being appraised will not be intimidated by a formal set-up with barriers such as a big desk, and so that he or she feels comfortable and at ease. There is also a need to avoid interruptions and to ensure that telephone messages are taken elsewhere and that there are no unnecessary distractions.

If the person has been appraised in the past, then the last appraisal record will need to be read to check what objectives, if any, were agreed for the current appraisal period. The individual's job description will also need to be checked and the training and development records examined to discover what training and development has occurred since the last interview. In some cases, if the person who is to be appraised works for several people, it may also be necessary to obtain information from other managers, or in the case of other types of performance appraisal from subordinates or peers.

It is also useful for both parties in the appraisal to prepare for the meeting, and both the appraiser and appraisee need to have received training so that they know what to expect in order that they can both handle what is potentially a difficult interaction skilfully. A constructive approach used by many organisations is to give both the appraiser and appraisee a form to complete prior to the appraisal interview. In some organisations these are then exchanged, and this has the advantage of focusing the attention of appraiser and appraisee on common issues. In other organisations these forms are simply used as an aide-mémoire for the individuals concerned, but if they are exchanged prior to the interview, they can help to clearly identify areas where there is broad agreement so that more time can be allowed to discuss other topics where there are differences of opinion.

### Privacy and confidentiality

We have already indicated that the appraisal is an important way of giving feedback to the employee about his or her work performance. In the past some organisations did not allow the appraisee to see the records of their appraisal, but we feel that this misses a valuable opportunity for providing feedback from which the employee could learn. On the other hand, the appraisal form and interview have to be kept confidential from other people as there will probably be very personal information on the form, and no one who feels that half the department can hear every word of the conversation is likely to feel willing to discuss his or her performance openly.

## Good questioning technique

The appraisal interview has, as we have already said, much in common with all other types of interviews. Once again the type of questions asked will be important. As this is an opportunity to provide feedback to the employee there will perhaps be slightly more opportunity for the interviewer to do more talking than in some other forms of interview, but this should be treated with caution. It is certainly not the time for the appraiser to do all the talking.

There should be an introductory phase where the interviewer tries to put the person being appraised at ease. It is generally better to follow this with a discussion of the employee's strong points and then try to get information, especially about any areas of perceived weakness, from the employee by asking open questions and teasing out the information. Areas of weakness need to be raised and discussed fully, and open questions are important here. If the interviewer uses closed questions that merely need yes or no answers, he or she will end up doing most of the talking. Leading questions, which put words in the appraisee's mouth or indicate what the appraiser wants him or her to say, should also be avoided.

Appraisers should also take great care not to be unduly influenced by a high assessment in one particular area, and should not allow this to cloud their judgement so that they rate all other areas of the employee's performance highly, even though these may not deserve such a high rating. This is known as the 'halo' effect. Similarly, care should be taken to avoid being unduly influenced by one very poor assessment. This is known as the 'horns' effect.

## Interview style

Interviewers can adopt a variety of interview styles. According to Wright and Taylor (1984), these different styles can involve varying degrees of participation and involvement from the appraisee, and are called, tell, tell and sell, tell and listen, ask and tell, joint problem-solving, and ask and listen. These are shown in Figure 9.2 and are now described.

### Tell

As can be clearly seen in Figure 9.2, at this end of the scale the tell approach allows for very little involvement by the individual who is being appraised. This is normally portrayed as a style used by a fairly autocratic manager who tells the appraisee about their strengths and weaknesses, but who doesn't really listen to what they have to say for themselves. From the manager's point of view there is an advantage to this style in that interviews are fairly short, but the employees are likely to feel that their views do not really matter in appraisal, and they won't be encouraged to think about their own continuing development.

*figure 9.2*
**Appraiser/appraisee involvement**

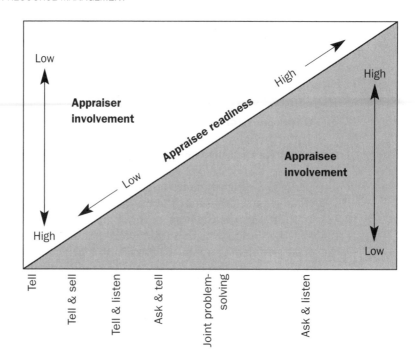

*Tell and sell*
The manager still does most of the talking, but this time tries to persuade the employee of the correctness of the manager's judgements about the employee. This still allows for very little involvement from the employee, and there is once again a danger that employees will feel that their views don't really matter.

*Tell and listen*
The manager starts by doing most of the talking and expresses most of the views about the employee's performance, but is then prepared to listen to what employees have to say for themselves. Here the employee is allowed more involvement and more opportunity to take control of his or her own assessment, but more control is still in the hands of the employer.

*Ask and tell*
The manager will ask questions of the employee and will appear to allow them much greater involvement in the appraisal process, but will then finish by making most of the decisions about future objectives and will end by telling the employee what he or she should do.

*Joint problem-solving*
This is the style which is generally recommended in appraisal interviewing, as it allows the appraiser and the appraisee an equal say both in the review of the past and in setting objectives for the future. Here the manager does not dominate the interview but allows the appraisee opportunities to assess his or her own work performance, and encourages opportunities for individuals to take charge of their own career and development and to express their views on what they hope to achieve in the future.

*Ask and listen*

In this last example of an interview style, the manager asks the questions and listens to the responses of the appraisee. Here the balance of control has shifted clearly to the appraisee, who will do most of the talking and who will be giving clear indications about their views of their past performance and future aims. This style of interview would be appropriate if self-assessment were being used to quite a large extent. It is possible in this scenario that the appraiser may not broach the subject of areas of weakness, as too much control of the interview could be said to be in the hands of the appraisee.

*The contingency approach*

While it is fair to say that the style of interview that is generally recommended for appraisal interviewing is the joint problem-solving approach, it is also possible that some of the other styles of interview may be appropriate in certain circumstances.

**PAUSE FOR THOUGHT 9.2** *Can you think of some circumstances in which one of the alternative styles might be more appropriate than joint problem-solving?*

The contingency approach says that it all depends on circumstances, and the choice of style depends on factors such as the manager's own style, the organisation's culture and the behaviour of the appraisee themselves. In an autocratic organisation where people are not used to having their views considered, there may be a high degree of suspicion if at the time of the appraisal interview the manager suddenly adopts a joint problem-solving approach and actually asks for the views of the employees. This can be a problem for many organisations, because if the organisation normally conducts its affairs in such a way that the employees don't trust the managers to treat them fairly, then it is going to be extremely difficult, if not impossible, for the employees suddenly to start to trust the person who is conducting their appraisal, and to talk in an open and honest way to them. This shows that appraisals should not be used just as an isolated technique to try and motivate the workforce. They need to be an integral part of the way the organisation treats people, and fundamental issues such as the culture of the organisation and its normal style of management also need to be addressed.

Figure 9.2 is adapted from the work of Pryor (1985), and indicates situations where other styles of appraisal interview may be appropriate. In this case the important consideration is the amount of experience of the job and of appraisal that the appraisee has, which is called appraisee readiness.

Figure 9.2 shows that even the tell style of approach could be appropriate if the person being appraised was inexperienced in the job and had little experience of being appraised. In such circumstances it would seem logical that the appraiser should do most of the talking and should guide the person being appraised. At the other end of the continuum, the ask and listen approach could be useful if the appraiser was interviewing a very experienced member of the workforce who had been appraised many times before, who was ready to take responsibility to a very large extent for his or her own future development and was able to use self-assessment in an appropriate way.

In conclusion, although the style of appraisal interview that is generally recommended is the joint problem-solving approach, we have shown here that the contingency approach indicates that in some circumstances other interview styles could also prove to be useful, and the style chosen should depend on factors such as employee experience and readiness, the manager's own preferred style of interviewing and the culture, or the way things are done, in that organisation.

## Performance management

Although the aim of performance appraisal is undoubtedly to improve individual and consequently organisational performance, in poorly designed systems this may not be as effective as it should be. We shall now examine the topic of performance management, and establish the extent to which it differs from traditional performance appraisal.

Armstrong's (1994) definition of performance management, which we used at the beginning of this chapter, says that it is 'a process which is designed to improve organisational, team and individual performance and which is owned and driven by line managers'.

We said earlier that performance appraisal should not be used just as an extra technique to be attached to an organisation's systems when the organisation wants to try to motivate employees, but that rather it needs to be integrally linked with the whole ethos and culture of the organisation in question. Performance management attempts to do just this, and highlights the use of performance appraisal as a central activity in the good management of employees. A good system of performance appraisal is therefore still important as a part of performance management. Figure 9.3 shows the way in which performance appraisal contributes to performance management.

Performance management is a process concerned with the effectiveness of the individual, the team and the organisation. It seeks to find ways to get the best performance from all, to motivate them to achieve the organisation's objectives. In addition to performance appraisal, performance management uses a range of other techniques mentioned in other parts of this book, to encourage improvements in performance. These include team building, quality circles, Total Quality Management, improving quality of working life, and working towards the Investors in People award. It must also be remembered that while performance management systems seek to get the best from individuals and motivate them to perform better, they also need to address ways of integrating the employee into the workforce and ensuring that they are aware of the contribution that they make towards achieving the organisation's strategic objectives, while also providing ways of dealing with poor performance. Motivation and integration will form part of the induction and of the training and development process, while the techniques to address poor performances are more likely to be included in an absence management system and as part of the grievance and disciplinary procedure. Both are dealt with in more detail in other chapters.

Typical features of a system for performance management include:

➤ clear links with the organisation's objectives
➤ clear links with job descriptions

figure 9.3
**Performance
management: a
dynamic
approach**

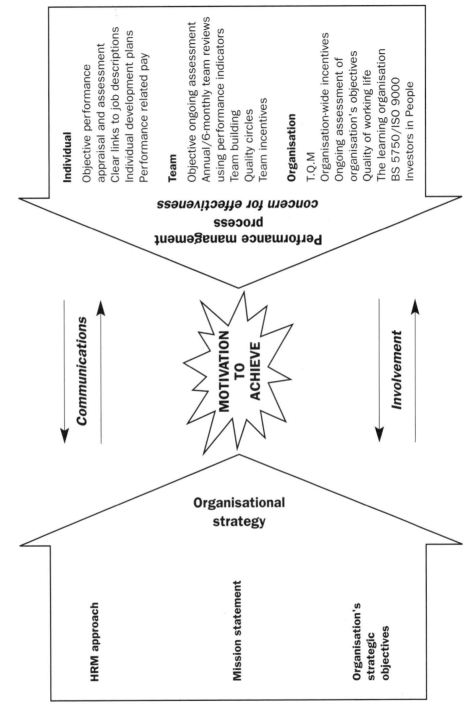

**Individual**

Objective performance
appraisal and assessment
Clear links to job descriptions
Individual development plans
Performance related pay

**Team**

Objective ongoing assessment
Annual/6-monthly team reviews
using performance indicators
Team building
Quality circles
Team incentives

**Organisation**

T.Q.M
Organisation-wide incentives
Ongoing assessment of
organisation's objectives
Quality of working life
The learning organisation
BS 5750/ISO 9000
Investors in People

*concern for effectiveness*

**Performance management
process**

*Communications*

**MOTIVATION
TO
ACHIEVE**

*Involvement*

**Organisational
strategy**

**HRM approach**

**Mission statement**

**Organisation's
strategic
objectives**

> ➤ rigorous and objective assessment process
> ➤ emphasis on individual development plans
> ➤ ongoing assessment
> ➤ links between assessment and pay.

We shall consider each of these in turn and relate them to the definition of performance management already given.

### Clear links with organisation's objectives

The objectives for work groups and individuals are derived from the organisation's strategic objectives, so that work groups and individuals can clearly see what they have to do to make their contribution to the organisation's overall effectiveness. In addition to individual performance the team is also considered to be important here and will have clear objectives which the members will help to set. Team achievements can also be assessed in the same way as individual performance. The objectives need to be clear and measurable and should be agreed after discussion between the team, the individual and the manager concerned. In this way the goals of the team and of the individual are both clearly related to those of the organisation. Both good communications and involvement are extremely important aspects of performance management, as the organisation's objectives and mission need to be clearly communicated to all employees in order that they can participate in setting objectives and contribute to the fulfilment of the organisation's objectives. Moreover, communication should not just be from top to bottom within the organisation, but should also provide for upward and lateral communication so that everyone can make a real contribution to the achievement of the organisation's objectives.

### Clear links with job descriptions

Individuals have clear job descriptions which they will have agreed, and which are reviewed regularly as the job changes. Some of the types of performance appraisal that we discussed earlier in the chapter were also closely linked to the individual's job description, such as behaviourally anchored rating scales, behavioural observation scales and use of management by objectives. In performance management the job descriptions are reviewed regularly and are also agreed between the manager and the subordinate, which may not always be the case in some of the other systems.

### Rigorous and objective assessment process

The objectives for the individual, which are derived from the organisation's strategic objectives, will be jointly devised by the appraiser and the appraisee and will have clear, measurable targets intended to contribute to the individual's development needs by providing a challenge, as well as contributing to the achievement of the needs of the organisation as a whole. Clearly, a management by objectives approach to performance appraisal would fit easily within this framework. The assessment process is not just a top-down approach but increasingly uses assessment of managers by their subordinates, 360° or 540° assessment.

The team or work group may also have objectives to achieve, and the individual needs to be aware of the need to play a part in these. Performance indicators may be used for an office or team, to set standards and to measure the team's effectiveness in meeting those standards. The following is an example of some possible performance indicators for the operational staff in a human resource department:

1 a staff presence will be provided in the human resource department between 8.30 a.m. and 5.00 p.m. (Monday to Friday)

 Percentage achieved =

2 all telephone calls will be returned within two working days, and all callers will be allocated a time or date to be contacted or to call again

 Percentage achieved =

3 the answer machine will be switched on outside normal office hours, and all messages will be cleared from it by 9.30 a.m. each day

 Percentage achieved =

4 all urgent letters will be dealt with within two working days

 Percentage achieved =

5 all non-urgent letters will be dealt with within five working days

 Percentage achieved =

It might be agreed with the team that standards 1, 2 and 3 should be achieved 100% of the time, but, perhaps because of staffing difficulties, performance standards 4 and 5 should be achieved 90% of the time during the first six months, with the aim being to then meet them 100% of the time.

### Individual development plans

Each individual will have an individual development plan which is designed to give detailed goals and provide for activities to enable that individual to achieve his or her goals. This is jointly designed by the manager and the employee, and the manager will provide support and coaching to help the employee to meet his or her goals. This relates very closely to the idea of the organisation being a learning organisation, discussed in Chapter 8, where everyone is encouraged to learn and to develop themselves so that the organisation will also change and develop over a period of time.

### Ongoing assessment

There is, as in performance appraisal, a regular annual assessment but there is also assessment on a more frequent basis as part of an ongoing process. This is likely to involve the manager, the individual and the team. This is intended to motivate employees and help them to focus on developmental issues. Clearly this once again relates to the idea of a learning organisation and continuous development for the individual and the team. In order for this to happen, communication is also extremely important and the organisation culture should be such that feelings of openness and trust are encouraged.

### Links between assessment and pay

In a performance management system, the annual performance appraisal is often linked with pay and is intended to reward those who have done well in meeting their objectives. Relating assessment to pay suffers from the same problems as in other forms of performance appraisal scheme, in that there is a potential conflict between the need for employees to talk frankly about their performance and a reluctance to do so because it would jeopardise their pay award. Performance development interviews and performance reward interviews are consequently often held separately in order to try to minimise this effect.

### Performance management summarised

Performance management derives from the human resource management approach as a strategic and integrated approach to the management and development of people. It emphasises the important role of line managers to take responsibility for the management of the performance of the people in their department. With its emphasis on the need for continuous performance review, performance management also relates clearly to the ideas of continuing development and the learning organisation discussed in Chapter 8. It uses the techniques of performance appraisal but prefers to use the more objective types, such as management by objectives. It does, however, go further than performance appraisal as what is appraised is clearly derived from the strategic plan and both individuals and teams are involved in setting objectives for themselves and in evaluating their success in achieving these objectives. Line managers also have responsibility to review progress and development throughout the year, not just at the time of the annual appraisal interview. Both individual and team objectives are clearly derived from the corporate strategic objectives, and everyone is aware that management of performance is the concern of all in the organisation, and not just personnel management or the senior management team. Performance management is above all a process for sharing an understanding about what needs to be achieved, and then managing and developing people in a way which will facilitate this so that excellent communications, in all directions, and employee involvement are also extremely important.

**REVIEW QUESTIONS**

You will find brief answers to these review questions on pages 425–427.

1 From your knowledge of organisational behaviour, what would you say are the main motivation theories that influence and underpin the ideas of performance management?

2 'It (appraisal) has a long history of being damned for its ineffectiveness at the same time as being anxiously sought by people wanting to know how they are doing. It is difficult to do, it is frequently done badly with some serious results, but on the occasions when it is done well it can be invaluable for the business and literally life-transforming for the individual.' Torrington and Hall (1998). Discuss this statement.

**3** Performance appraisals are intended to motivate employees towards greater productivity and improve communication/relations between managers and their team members. Explain why performance appraisals often fail to achieve this goal, and comment on the skills that managers need to make performance appraisal work.

**4** Performance management is described by Michael Armstrong as a 'systematic approach to the management of people, using performance, goals, feedback and recognition as a means of motivating them to realise their full potential'. Explain how performance appraisal systems operate as a performance management technique in terms of this definition.

**5** Describe three different approaches to performance appraisal, and comment critically on the benefits to be gained from these systems.

**SELF-CHECK QUESTIONS**

Answer the following multiple choice and short answer questions. The correct responses are given on page 427 for you to check your understanding of this chapter.

**1** Figure 9.4 shows our interpretation of a mind map summarising the key points in this chapter. We have left some key headings blank. Complete the mind map by inserting the missing headings.

**2** According to ACAS, performance appraisal is
  (*a*) an assessment of an employee's performance, potential and disciplinary needs
  (*b*) an assessment of an employee's performance, potential and development needs
  (*c*) an assessment of an employee's personality, potential and development needs
  (*d*) an assessment of an organisation's performance, potential and development needs
  (*e*) an assessment of an organisation's performance, potential and disciplinary needs.

**3** In this chapter we said that when we appraise someone there are three key, but sometimes contradictory, roles. Which of the following are the three roles to which we referred?
  (*a*) Giving feedback and being friend and helper
  (*b*) Giving feedback and being judge and source of discipline
  (*c*) Giving feedback and being judge and helper
  (*d*) Giving a subjective assessment of performance and being judge and helper
  (*e*) Giving feedback and being judge and critic

**4** Which of the following is a good reason for organisations to introduce a performance appraisal scheme?
  (*a*) To improve current performance
  (*b*) To provide a check on their staff's integrity
  (*c*) To check on the honesty of their employees
  (*d*) To clarify the employee's contract
  (*e*) To discipline individuals

**5** Appraisal schemes may not be as effective as they should be because of a number of problems. Which of the following is not one of the problems associated with the introduction of performance appraisal schemes?

*figure 9.4*
**Mind map of this chapter**

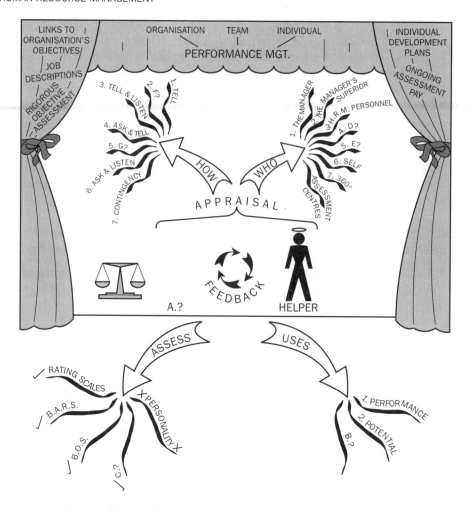

(*a*) The organisation is not clear about the purpose of its appraisal scheme
(*b*) The performance appraisal scheme is too objective in the judgements made
(*c*) Information is kept secret from the employee
(*d*) The performance appraisal scheme is too subjective in the judgements made
(*e*) Appraisal is used as part of the disciplinary process

6   Which of the following best describes what is meant by the term 'performance management'?
(*a*) A process designed to improve organisational, team and individual performance which is owned and driven by line managers
(*b*) A process designed to improve organisational performance which is owned and driven by line managers
(*c*) A process designed to improve individual performance which is owned and driven by line managers
(*d*) A process designed to improve organisational and individual performance which is owned and driven by personnel managers
(*e*) A process designed to improve organisational, team and individual performance which is owned and driven by personnel managers

## References
·············

Advisory, Conciliation and Arbitration Service. *Employee Appraisal*. ACAS, 1997.

Armstrong, Michael. *Performance Management*. Kogan Page, 1994.

Fletcher, C. and Williams, R. *Performance Appraisal and Career Development*. Hutchinson, 1985.

Pryor, R. A fresh approach to performance appraisal. *Personnel Management*, June 1985, 37–39

Randell, G. A., Packard, P. M. A., Shaw, R. L. and Slater, A. J. P. *Staff Appraisal*. IPM, 1984.

Torrington, Derek and Hall, Laura. *Human Resource Management*. 4th edition, Prentice Hall Europe, 1998.

Wright, P. L. and Taylor, D. S. *Improving Leadership Performance*. Prentice Hall International, 1984.

## Further study
··················

### *Books*

Advisory, Conciliation and Arbitration Service. *Employee Appraisal*. ACAS, 1997. (An excellent clear guide to performance appraisal.)

Advisory, Conciliation and Arbitration Service. *Appraisal-Related Pay*. ACAS, 1997. (Another excellent guide, this time to the complex task of linking performance appraisal to pay.)

Advisory, Conciliation and Arbitration Service. *Teamwork: Success through People*. ACAS, 1997. (This booklet concentrates on one very important aspect of performance, teams.)

Advisory, Conciliation and Arbitration Service. *Effective Organisations: The People Factor*. ACAS, 1997. (This booklet focuses on getting the best from people and this is what performance management is all about. It examines a wide range of measures that may contribute to an improvement in the organisation's performance.)

Armstrong, Michael. *Performance Management*. Kogan Page, 1994. (A very thorough examination of the whole topic of performance management.)

Income Data Services Limited. *Study 626: Performance Management*. IDS, May 1997. (This examines new issues in performance management such as 360° appraisal and includes six case studies about the operation of performance management systems in six organisations.)

Randell, G. A., Packard, P. M. A., Shaw, R. L. and Slater, A. J. P. *Staff Appraisal*. IPM, 1984. (A classic work on how to manage staff appraisal effectively.)

Walter, Mike. *The Performance Management Handbook*. IPD, 1995. (This text provides an excellent introduction to the subject of performance management.)

### Articles

Dugdill, Gerard. Wide angle view. *Personnel Today*, 27 September 1994, 31–32. (An interesting account of the uses of 360° appraisal.)

Fletcher, C. What's new in performance appraisal? *Personnel Management*, February 1984, 20–22. (A review of objectivity in appraisal and of the use of self-appraisal.)

Fowler, A. New directions in performance pay. *Personnel Management*, May 1986.

George, J. Appraisal in the public sector: dispensing with the big stick. *Personnel Management*, May 1986, 32–33. (A discussion of the problems caused by the need for trust in appraisal.)

Long, P. and Gill, D. *Performance Appraisal Revisited*. Third IPM Survey. IPM, 1986.

### Audio-visual

Video Arts. *How Am I Doing?* Video Arts, 1978. (Entertaining and informative views about performance appraisal with some humorous examples of how *not* to interview.)

Open College Interviewing. Programme 5, 'Appraisal Interviews'. Produced by Yorkshire Television for the Open College with Channel Four, 1988. (Interesting examples of appraisal interviews and discussion about the appraisal process.)

### Internet

Income Data Services Limited (Some very useful articles on a range of HRM topics, including a section on management pay and remuneration, are published on line plus lists of contents for IDS publications.)

**http://www.incomesdata.co.uk/**

# CHAPTER 10

# Payment systems

**Objectives:**

*By the end of this chapter you will be able to:*
➤ explain the main factors that influence the choice of a particular payment system
➤ understand the relationship between motivation theories and pay systems
➤ state the advantages and disadvantages of different types of payment systems
➤ understand and explain the process of job evaluation
➤ appreciate how to use a particular job evaluation system.

We have indicated in previous chapters that human resource management is concerned that people should work as effectively as possible for the organisation, and that one of the ways in which the organisation attempts to achieve this is by using an appropriate system of payment to encourage and reward them. The payment system that is adopted must, as stated in Chapter 2, be in line with and support the key elements of the strategic plan.

In this chapter we shall be examining a variety of payment systems and discussing the philosophies on which they are based, and the links with motivation theory, as well as the circumstances in which particular payment systems may prove appropriate.

## Definitions

Before we proceed, it will be useful to define some of the words we shall use throughout this chapter. Several words are commonly used to refer to the wages or salaries paid to people at work, and these include the terms compensation, remuneration, reward and pay. We shall examine these definitions and then define other terms used in connection with payments, such as harmonisation and job evaluation. We shall then examine the different types of payment system that are available for an employer to use.

*Compensation* is frequently used to refer to payment, but implies that the employee somehow has to be compensated for a loss or injury caused through work, rather than that they are actually being paid to work. This seems to reflect a theory X viewpoint on work (see 'Did You Know' page 256), and to imply that people do not enjoy work and so have to be compensated for working at all.

*Reward* is frequently used nowadays to refer to payment systems, especially since many payment systems try to motivate people to work harder and then reward them for their extra effort. The word 'reward' is useful in this sense, and could apply to either monetary or non-monetary award, but it also implies that something special is being rewarded. While it is true that many payment schemes do seek to reward extra effort, this is normally only one part of the payment system. The term 'reward' also seems to have theory X overtones, as it implies that it is

*Douglas McGregor (1960) stated that the way managers perceived work and employees would affect the way in which the employees actually carried out their work. He said that there were two contrasting assumptions that managers made about the behaviour of employees, which he called theory X and theory Y.*

**Theory X**

*A manager who adopts the theory X viewpoint would tend to assume that the average worker will dislike work and avoid it if she or he can, and will only be made to work by a mixture of control and threats. A 'carrot or stick' approach is what is generally seen to be appropriate here. The use of the words 'compensation' and 'reward' would seem to fit this perspective, and to lead to the idea of management needing to provide either control or incentives to motivate the employee to work effectively.*

**Theory Y**

*Theory Y assumes that work is a natural and welcome activity which need not be controlled by the manager, as the employee will seek responsibility and will be motivated by the work itself. Managers who hold a theory Y view are not going to be particularly interested in providing control or incentives, and so the words 'reward' and 'compensation' seem less appropriate for them. Instead these managers are more likely to be concerned with having a fair, easy to understand payment system and are also more likely to involve workers in the design of this.*

always necessary to dangle a carrot in order to get good work from an employee.

*Remuneration* means broadly the same as payment system, but is a more cumbersome term to use (and more difficult to spell!).

*Payment* is the most straightforward of the four terms, and seems to us to be the most appropriate term to use. It can include monetary or non-monetary payment. This is therefore the term we shall use in general throughout this chapter. We include under this heading various types of both monetary and non-monetary payment, as well as sickness pay, maternity pay and pension arrangements.

Although distinctions between wages and salaries are decreasing as many organisations move towards harmonisation of terms and conditions for different groups of workers, it is also useful to define the differences that do still exist.

*Wages* tend to be paid weekly and may be based on an hourly rate of pay, with possible deductions for lateness or absence, and this hourly rate is often the rate that is referred to in negotiations. Wage-earners are often still paid in cash and are less likely to have fringe benefits such as luncheon vouchers, company cars or expenses. Organisations paying wages expect short-term thinking from their employees, and incentives for wage-earners are also usually quick and precise. There has traditionally been less job security for wage-earners than for salaried employees, and the emphasis is on a short-term relationship with the employing organisation. The peak of wage-earners' earning capacity is comparatively early, perhaps while they are still in their twenties. Wage-earners perceive themselves as doing a totally different type of job from management, and expect jobs to be short-term, with some degree of insecurity.

*Salaries* tend to be paid monthly, and these monthly payments are normally expressed as an annual salary, this being the figure that is normally referred to in negotiations on salary. Those who are salaried normally have their salaries paid directly into a bank or building society and they are also likely to have several fringe benefits, such as company cars, extra payments for additional qualifications, or luncheon vouchers. Some salaried workers get immediate incentives added to their incomes, but generally the most widely held incentive is supposed to be a much longer term consideration, that of good prospects. Salaried employees either are in managerial posts or tend to identify very closely with management, and they perceive themselves to be on a lengthy career progression with the peak of their earning power achieved relatively late in life. In addition, until fairly recently they have expected to have long-term job security.

### Harmonisation

There are differences in organisations' attitudes towards those paid wages and those paid salaries, but as mentioned earlier, many organisations have tried to get away from the problems that this sometimes causes, and have moved towards a common system of payment with the harmonisation of terms and conditions of employment for both groups of workers. This means that there is an expectation that all employees can be treated in the same way and will expect the same benefits. In these organisations, everyone is paid a monthly salary rather than a weekly or hourly rate of pay, and everyone gets the same sick pay and redundancy arrangements, works the same hours and eats in the same canteen.

Nowadays there is also much less job security, and career progression for salaried employees and promotion or even job security cannot be regarded as automatic, as many organisations in which salaried jobs were normally secure have moved to remove whole strata of managers. The growing trend towards the acquisition of a flexible workforce with increasing numbers of part-timers and contract workers has also led to a blurring of distinctions between the two groups.

### Job evaluation

A further term that is relevant to payment systems and will be discussed fully later in this chapter is 'job evaluation'. ACAS (1997) defines job evaluation in the following way.

> The aim of job evaluation is to provide a systematic and consistent approach to defining the relative worth of jobs within the workplace, single plant or multiple site organisation. It is a process whereby jobs are placed in a rank order according to overall demands placed upon the job holder. It therefore provides a fair basis for a fair and orderly grading structure. Job evaluation does not determine actual pay. That is a separate operation, normally the subject of negotiation between management and trade union representatives. Only the job is evaluated, not the person doing it.

As you can see here, job evaluation doesn't actually determine rates of pay that any individual employee should receive, but it can be used as a systematic basis for determining differences in jobs and subsequently the different pay levels for those jobs. As such it seems to us to be an appropriate topic to discuss in this chapter.

## The main influences on payment systems

What the organisation decides to pay staff will depend on many factors, some of which are under the control of the organisation and some of which are external.

ACTIVITY **10.1**

We have provided you with a selection of job titles and you have to decide how much to pay these staff. You are to consider who you think *ought* to be paid the most rather than considering what actually happens in reality.

(a)  Put the jobs listed below in order of importance, i.e. with number one being the job that you judge should be paid the most.

(b)  List the factors that will influence how much you will pay these staff.

| | |
|---|---|
| Nurse | _____ |
| Sales assistant (clothes shop) | _____ |
| Car park attendant | _____ |
| Office cleaner | _____ |
| Accountant | _____ |
| Police officer | _____ |
| Receptionist | _____ |
| Teller (bank) | _____ |
| Warehouse supervisor | _____ |
| University lecturer | _____ |
| Truck driver | _____ |
| Secretary | _____ |
| Traffic warden | _____ |
| Security guard | _____ |
| Safety officer (manufacturing company) | _____ |
| Warehouse picker | _____ |
| Doctor | _____ |
| Personnel manager | _____ |
| Church minister | _____ |
| Ambulance driver (paramedical) | _____ |
| Transport manager | _____ |
| Computer services officer | _____ |
| Lawyer | _____ |
| Undertaker | _____ |
| Professional football player | _____ |

(c)  Compare your order with others and try to reach agreement about a list of factors that should be taken into account when you are making these decisions.

### Discussion of Activity 10.1

The relative worth of these jobs is likely to vary according to the type of organisation, and your ranking of worth is likely to vary compared with that of your colleagues because you have been highly subjective. You should think about what influenced your choice of each job's worth. Did you have knowledge of some jobs? Did you value strength, skill, level of responsibility or a caring response most, or were you influenced by people you know who do some of these jobs, or by your own career aspirations? There will be many highly subjective influences on your decision.

Many other factors may influence the relative worth of jobs. Your list is likely to include at least some of the following:

➤  what the organisation can afford to pay
➤  what other organisations in the area are paying for similar jobs
➤  national or international rates of pay within the organisation

➤ legislation
➤ trade unions or employee demands
➤ government initiatives
➤ the scarcity of particular skills
➤ the state of the economy
➤ the introduction of new technology
➤ the relative worth of jobs as rated by a job evaluation exercise
➤ the actual performance of the person in the job.

As you can see from this list, an organisation doesn't have a completely free hand when it decides how to pay someone. Many factors influence the decision of how and what to pay, and we shall discuss these more fully in turn.

### What the organisation can afford to pay

Obviously, no organisation can afford to put itself out of business by paying more than it can afford, so this has to be one of the first factors that influence how much an organisation will pay.

### What other organisations in the area are paying for similar jobs

Most organisations will at least take account of the rates that other local organisations are paying. The organisation may refer to published pay surveys or do its own survey of the local area to establish rates that others are paying for similar jobs. If it can afford to, and if they want to be able to select the best employees, they may choose to pay slightly more than the going rate. This can cause a spiral of wage increases as other employers retaliate by increasing their wages. When labour is scarce this is one way in which many employers will behave.

Even when employing people on a small scale, the rate of payment can have quite an effect locally. A recent television programme looked at people from London with second homes outside London, and the problems they caused locally by paying someone to clean their second home each week so that it was ready for their arrival at the weekend. Those with the second home obviously could afford to pay good wages and were used to paying the going rate in London. When they paid these same rates to local cleaners they obviously attracted good staff, but were then accused by other locals of poaching their cleaners and of setting rates that the locals could not afford to match. In this situation the second home owners got excellent cleaners but didn't make many friends.

### National or international rates of pay within your organisation

If the organisation is part of a larger organisation, there may be national or international agreements that will affect what is actually paid, and the human resource manager needs to assess these rates also.

### Legislation

All organisations are affected by the law of the country in which they operate. In Britain they will also be affected by European Union legislation. The legislation that will have most effect on payment or reward systems is:

➤ The Equal Pay Act 1970
➤ The Equal Pay Amendment (Regulations) 1983
➤ The Employment Rights Act 1996
➤ National Minimum Wage Act 1998

#### The Equal Pay Act 1970

The Equal Pay Act 1970 actually came into effect in December 1975, at the same time as the Sex Discrimination Act 1975, which is discussed in Chapter 3. It was part of a two-pronged attack on inequality and specifically aimed to ensure that men and women who were doing the same job, or jobs that were broadly similar in nature, would receive the same pay. Consequently it is now illegal to pay men and women doing the same or broadly similar jobs different amounts of pay.

Under the Equal Pay Act 1970 it is also illegal to pay different rates to men and women who do different jobs, but whose jobs have been rated the same under a job evaluation scheme. The whole topic of job evaluation and problems of fairness and equality within job evaluation will be discussed later in this chapter.

#### The Equal Pay Amendment (Regulations) 1983

This legislation added to the Equal Pay Act 1970 a further category, that of equal value. It is therefore now possible for men and women who are doing totally different jobs and who are paid differently to bring a case against their employer if they feel that their job is of the same value to the organisation as the job done by the higher paid group. The legislation is complex, and most who have brought cases have been supported by their trade union or the Equal Opportunities Commission. Criteria such as the level of qualifications required, the level of effort or skill involved, and the amount of responsibility and decision-making involved in each of the jobs are factors that are likely to be taken into account. In a tribunal hearing of this type, the person of the opposite sex with whom the claimant wishes to compare himself or herself must first be identified. If the tribunal decides that there are reasonable grounds for determining that the work is of equal value, a report will be commissioned by an independent expert as to the relative worth of each of the jobs. The tribunal will then convene once again after receiving the report of the independent expert, and will make a decision.

> **DID YOU KNOW?**
>
> *In spite of the legislation that has just been discussed, in 1995 male manual workers' average earnings were £281.00 per week while those of female manual workers were £182.00 per week. Male non-manual workers' average earnings were £428.00 per week, while those of female non-manual workers were £278.00 per week. (New Earnings Survey 1994, quoted in* Personnel Today, *11 May 1995.)*

#### The Employment Rights Act 1996

The Employment Rights Act 1996 is a consolidation act which consolidates previous legislation relating to employment rights. Under the Employment Rights

Act 1996 an employer is not allowed to make deductions from an employee's wages except in the following circumstances:

➤ When deductions are authorised by law, such as Tax or National Insurance contributions or orders such as a court order relating to the provision of maintenance.

➤ When there is a statement in the employee's written contract which specifies that certain deductions may be made from wages and when the worker has already given consent in writing to the deduction, e.g. to pay membership fees for a sports or social club or when deductions are agreed for lateness or poor work.

➤ Accidental overpayment of wages, or of expenses, even though this is likely to be the fault of the employer.

➤ When the employee has been absent from work due to strike or other industrial action it is permissible for the employer to deduct money from the employee's wages.

➤ In retail organisations, employers may also deduct money from wages to make good any cash deficiency in the till or any shortfall in stock. This deduction should not exceed 10% of the wages due to the employee concerned on a particular day and the deduction must also be made within twelve months from the date that the discrepancy or shortfall in stock was discovered.

### The National Minimum Wage Act 1998

The Government published details of its National Minimum Wage Bill in 1998 with the intention of establishing a single national minimum rate with no variation for regions, jobs, size of organisation or industrial sector. Differences will be allowed, however, based on age. The National Minimum Wage should provide some protection for the lowest paid groups of workers but does provide for a lower rate, at least initially, for those who are aged between 18 and 21. Margaret Beckett, Secretary of State for Trade and Industry at that time, announced to the House of Commons on 18 June 1998 that the initial rates would be £3.60 per hour for people aged over 21 but only £3.00 per hour rising in time to £3.20 per hour for those aged 18–21. There will be no minimum wage at all for apprentices and those who are under 18. Employers will have to keep records for National Minimum Wage purposes and employees should have access to these records with a right to complain to an Employment Tribunal if the employer fails to give them the required access to the records. The Bill received Royal Assent and became an Act towards the end of 1998.

### Trade union and employee demands

In recent years, with a framework of legislation that has sought to curb the power of the unions and against a background of high unemployment, trade unions have not been particularly powerful forces in bargaining on wages. Nevertheless it is important to consider the views of both trade unions and employees in general, and any payment system that an organisation may design needs to be introduced after full discussion and consultation with employees and trade unions. The most effective payment systems will have been selected to meet the needs of both the organisation and the workforce, will have the commitment of all groups and will have been developed, introduced and updated with the participation of employee representatives, whether or not they are members of a trade union.

### Government initiatives

The government can have an effect on the supply of labour as it introduces various training initiatives for adults or young people who are facing unemployment. This should have the effect of providing people with relevant skills that employers need, but it also has an effect on wage expectations, since if people are used to receiving a very low training allowance they are likely to feel pleased if they get a job that pays more than this, even if it is still a comparatively low wage.

### The scarcity of particular skills

Although in recent years there has been high unemployment, there has also been a scarcity in some industries of particular types of skilled workers. This may be due to failure in the past to train people adequately, but it appears that there is often a mismatch between the skills that employers require and the skills that those who are without jobs can offer. In a situation such as this, the relatively small number of people who do have the necessary skills can command high wages or salaries and may move from one organisation to another as different employers try to outbid each other for their scarce skills.

### The state of the economy

We have already mentioned that the availability of labour and the scarcity of particular skills will have an effect on the wages paid. Other economic factors such as inflation will also have an effect, as in times of high levels of inflation there will be increasing pressure from workers to increase salaries to keep pace with or get ahead of inflation.

### New technology

The relative pay levels of people in different jobs can change over time, for example, when new skills have to be learnt with the introduction of new technology, so that a particular group of workers change from being of low skill level to needing a high level of technical expertise. This change in skill level is likely to be reflected in a demand for higher wages.

### The relative worth of each job as rated by a job evaluation exercise

Job evaluation is a way of rating the value to the organisation of the jobs that people do. It does not in itself decide what pay should be awarded to each job, but it is a systematic way of comparing different jobs so that this can be used as the basis for a payment system. The various ways in which job evaluation can be carried out and the different types of scheme will be discussed later in this chapter.

### The performance of the individual employee in the job

In many organisations it will also be important to assess the effectiveness of the person doing the job. Whether this happens will depend on the type of payment system used and the organisation's views on collectivism or individualism with regard to payments. Organisations that favour collectivism will want to minimise differences in pay between employees as this may avoid costly or time-wasting disputes, while other organisations will want to pay everyone individual rates as far as possible in order to reward each person for his or her efforts, and these two perspectives will result in a variety of differing types of payment system.

It is clear that the last two factors are of great importance to payment systems, so we shall now go on to discuss each in detail.

## Job evaluation schemes

Very few organisations will pay all the people who work for them exactly the same regardless of the job they do or how well they do that job. Most organisations therefore seek to find ways to compare the worth of different jobs to the organisation, as well as a person's performance in each job. We shall consider later in this chapter the ways in which individual performance may be assessed, but first we shall concentrate on ways of comparing the relative worth of different jobs. If organisations were to base decisions about the relative worth of different jobs on managerial whims, they would be accused, quite rightly, of being unfair. That is why many organisations use a system for assessing the worth of different jobs based on job evaluation.

Job evaluation does not determine the correct payment level for a job, but rather provides a possible ranking of a job relative to other jobs. This has the merit of being systematic and of appearing objective, although in reality there is normally some degree of subjectivity in all job evaluation schemes. There are normally three stages involved when an organisation is deciding how much to pay for each job:

➤ evaluate the jobs in the organisation and get a ranking for them
➤ decide which jobs are similar in terms of the job evaluation exercise and group them together
➤ decide what pay to attach to these jobs, partially on the basis of market value.

There are a variety of job evaluation schemes in existence, and discussion of these could occupy a full chapter in its own right. We shall seek to give a brief outline of some of the more commonly used types of job evaluation scheme. They can be divided into non-analytical and analytical schemes, and we shall consider each of these groups in turn.

### Non-analytical schemes

Non-analytical job evaluation schemes compare whole jobs rather than analysing the components of each job and assessing them factor by factor. There are three main types of non-analytical scheme:

➤ whole job ranking
➤ paired comparisons
➤ job classification.

In order to understand the basics of each of these approaches, you should complete the following activities. For both activities you need to consider the job descriptions we have provided and imagine that you had to evaluate the jobs as part of a job evaluation exercise, which will ultimately be used as the basis of the organisation's payment system. You are being asked to evaluate only three jobs, whereas in reality there would be far more jobs than this in most organisations.

**Whole job ranking**

ACTIVITY **10.2**

(a) Consider each of the three job descriptions given below and decide which job you feel is worth most to the organisation, which is the next in value and which is of least value to the organisation.

**Job description A**

| | |
|---|---|
| Job title: | Receptionist |
| Reports to: | Office Services Manager |
| Responsible for: | Assistant Receptionists (2) |
| Purpose of post: | To ensure that visitors to the company are received in a welcoming fashion, answer routine queries and ensure that all other queries are handled expeditiously by the appropriate staff member. To ensure that all telephone queries are handled in the same manner. |
| | As the first point of contact for the company, the receptionist must maintain high standards of customer care. |
| Contacts: | All customers and other visitors, to deal with initial and routine queries. All members of staff, to pass on queries as appropriate. |

Major duties:

➤ Greet walk-in visitors and ascertain purpose of their visit. Handle or redirect queries as appropriate.
➤ Answer phone queries as above.
➤ Answer all initial queries about receipt of payments using the on-line payment receipts system.
➤ Open and sort incoming post by department. Organise delivery of post by assistant receptionists.
➤ Perform clerical tasks assigned by departments in agreement with the Office Services Manager.
➤ Supervise assistant receptionists and delegate work as appropriate.
➤ Perform other duties as assigned by the Office Services Manager or other authorised manager.

**Job description B**

| | |
|---|---|
| Job title: | Human Resource Assistant |
| Reports to: | Human Resource Manager |
| Responsible for: | No one |

| Purpose of post: | To provide a day-to-day advisory service for the managers in the company on matters of human resource management policy and procedures, and to monitor and implement procedures. |
| --- | --- |
| Contacts: | Managers from head office and throughout the branches. Employees, to deal with initial and routine queries. Prospective employees, to deal with initial enquiries regarding job vacancies. Outside organisations such as employment agencies, training organisations and newspapers. |

Major duties:

➤ Greet visitors and ascertain purpose of their visit. Handle or redirect queries as appropriate.

➤ Answer phone queries as above.

➤ Answer all initial queries about applications for employment.

➤ Pass all rejected applications to typist for standard rejection letters and check and sign these letters.

➤ Monitor application for employment forms submitted by line managers on behalf of candidates selected by them.

➤ Agree salary details, in accordance with company pay scales, with line manager.

➤ Enter agreed salary, contract, job title and joining details on successful applications and pass to typist for documentation.

➤ Sign joining documentation on behalf of the company.

➤ Advise line managers on the interpretation of the organisation's human resource policies and procedures.

➤ Advise line managers on the interpretation and implementation of the organisation's sickness pay and pension schemes.

➤ Advise line managers on the interpretation of relevant employment legislation.

➤ Advise line managers on employees' salary entitlements.

➤ Ensure that the human resource management records are kept up to date on the computerised information system, and that there is no unauthorised access to these and any manually produced records.

➤ Provide up-to-date reports or data for use by managers.

### Job description C

| Job title: | Sales Assistant |
| --- | --- |
| Reports to: | Buyer of China Department |
| Responsible for: | No one |
| Purpose of post: | To sell china goods and assist customers with their purchases and with any queries or problems that they might have. |
| Contacts: | All customers and other visitors to make sales of china and deal with routine queries. |

Major duties:

➤ Sell china goods to customers.

➤ Provide expert advice about the various products on sale.

➤ Provide a high standard of service and customer care.

➤ Unpack with care valuable merchandise and pack customers' purchases carefully, including packing them for export.

➤ Display products attractively to encourage sales and promote certain special offers.
➤ Perform clerical duties associated with the work of the department, e.g. completion of orders, forms for returns or breakages.
➤ Handle accurately and honestly cash and credit transactions.
➤ Total cash and credit transactions and deliver money to Cash Control Office.

When you have read the three job descriptions, rank the jobs in order with the job you feel is worth more to the organisation being ranked as number 1.

1 _____
2 _____
3 _____

(*b*) What are the advantages and disadvantages of this approach?

### *Discussion of Activity 10.2*

This is the simplest form of job evaluation exercise and we have ranked the three jobs in the following order: 1, Human Resources Officer; 2, Sales Assistant in China Department; 3, Receptionist. You may have reached a different rank order to us or to other students. This is because this is a very subjective way of ranking the jobs, and the criteria we took into account may be different to those that you have used. There is nothing in this method to indicate what criteria have been chosen. We have asked you to make decisions about only three jobs, and it would be more difficult to use the whole job ranking system in a large organisation where there were many different jobs to rank. In that case, the jobs would probably have to be grouped into categories first for ease of comparison and so that the appropriate criteria were used, e.g. for clerical jobs, as it could be a problem to identify suitable criteria if the jobs were very dissimilar.

We could make this system slightly more objective by agreeing the criteria to be considered in advance of the exercise, but even this would not help us to identify the extent of difference in the value of the different jobs to the organisation, so we would still have difficulty deciding how much more to pay the job that was ranked first compared to the job that was ranked second. In reality, job evaluation schemes should not depend on the subjective judgements of just one person. It would be better to involve more people in an exercise such as this and then get a consensus view from this job evaluation panel about the ranking of each job.

*Advantages of whole job ranking*
➤ Simple
➤ Cheap to operate
➤ Easy to understand

*Disadvantages of whole job ranking*
➤ Subjective
➤ No analysis of jobs to explain reason for ranked order
➤ Difficult to use with large number of jobs

ACTIVITY **10.3**
...............

(a) Refer to the three job descriptions given in Activity 10.2, but this time compare pairs of jobs and decide which you feel is worth more to the organisation, so that each job is compared with the other jobs in turn. Use the following points system to work through this exercise.

➤ If you feel that a job is worth more than the job it is being compared with, give it 2 points.
➤ If you feel it is worth the same as the job it is compared with, give them both 1 point.
➤ If you feel it is worth less than the other job, give it zero points.

Enter the values that you give each job in the chart below, and then add the scores for each job. The job with the highest value will be the one that you decide to pay the most, followed with the job with the next highest value and the job with the lowest value.

|        | JOB A | JOB B | JOB C |
|--------|-------|-------|-------|
| JOB A  | –     | ——    | ——    |
| JOB B  | ——    | –     | ——    |
| JOB C  | ——    | ——    | –     |

Total points for each job – A:          B:          C:

1st job  _____
2nd job  _____
3rd job  _____

(b) Did you rank the jobs in the same order as before? What are the advantages and disadvantages of this approach?

### Discussion of Activity 10.3

This is also a simple method of job evaluation, but it is slightly more systematic than whole job ranking. It still does not analyse particular jobs in detail and, although the numerical values attached to each job create an impression of objectivity, this is really not the case as again there is nothing to indicate what the criteria used might be. A large number of calculations may need to be made – for an organisation that intends to analyse 50 or more jobs, 1,225 calculations would need to be made. There are, however, computerised systems that work on this basis and solve this particular problem. Once again, an improvement to this approach would be to involve a job evaluation panel, drawn from various sections of the workforce, and then try to get agreement about the rating of various jobs.

*Advantages of paired comparisons*
➤ Simple
➤ Easy to understand
➤ Slightly more systematic than whole job ranking
➤ It is easy to fit new jobs into this system

*Disadvantages of paired comparisons*

➤ Subjective

➤ No analysis of jobs to explain reason for ranked order

➤ The need for an enormous number of calculations if it is to be used with a large number of jobs.

## Job classification

The exercises you have just completed indicate in a very simple way the main stages and the main problems with two forms of non-analytical job evaluation. The third non-analytical form of job evaluation is known as job classification. It is similar to job ranking but uses a different approach. In this case the number of groups of jobs, or pay grades, is decided first and a general job description is then produced for all the jobs in each of these groups. An individual job that is considered to typify this group of jobs is then used as a benchmark. Each job is compared with the benchmark jobs and the general job description, and placed in an appropriate grade.

*Advantages of job classification*

➤ Simple to operate

➤ Easy to understand

➤ It is easy to fit new jobs into job classification structure

*Disadvantages of job classification*

➤ Difficult to use with a wide range of jobs

➤ Not analytical

### Analytical methods of job evaluation

## Points rating

This is probably the most commonly used type of job evaluation scheme, and is regarded as analytical because instead of comparing whole jobs, the jobs are broken down into a number of factors such as skills, responsibility, physical requirements, mental requirements, working conditions. Each of the factors is awarded points based on a predetermined scale, and the total points determine the position of that job in the rank order. A weighting is often attached to the particular importance of each attribute to the organisation.

Although this scheme is analytical, there is, as we said earlier, an element of subjectivity in all job evaluation schemes, as subjective decisions are made about which factors will be weighted most highly to show their importance to the organisation. Care should be taken to avoid sex bias in the choice of factors for high weighting. Many older schemes based on this system were biased against women as characteristics such as physical strength, normally associated more with male employees, were given higher weighting than factors such as dexterity, which is more often associated with women.

Points rating schemes are easy to understand and are more objective than the non-analytical schemes. Because they are analytical, they can be used to explain the extent of differences between jobs and hence to justify subsequent differences in pay. They can, however, be time-consuming and costly to develop. Once again a panel of people are likely to be involved. An example of this type of scheme is given at the end of this chapter so that you can apply the concepts you have read about.

### Proprietary schemes

Faced with the time and costs involved in designing and validating their own job evaluation scheme and checking that it is free of unfair bias, many organisations decide to buy a proprietary scheme or employ a consultant to design a scheme specifically for them. A scheme designed specifically for one organisation is obviously a good idea and is likely to have a great deal of credibility with the workforce, but buying a proprietary scheme has the advantage of giving access to extensive comparative data on job markets and rates of pay which designers of proprietary schemes also collect. This can provide much more comprehensive data on which to base decisions about payment levels to relate to jobs than any one organisation could collect.

## Different types of payment system

There are, as we have shown, many factors that affect what the organisation pays its workforce, but whatever payment system is chosen will give a different message to the workforce about the issues and values that the organisation feels are important. In this section we shall consider some of the different payment systems that the organisation might choose. There are many variations in systems of payment: some of the more common types will be considered here.

➤ Time rates
➤ Individual payment by results (piece work)
➤ Group payment by results
➤ Measured day work
➤ Plant- and enterprise-wide schemes
➤ Profit sharing
➤ Performance-related pay or merit rating
➤ Cafeteria-style payments or flexible pay.

### Time rates

This is the simplest of all payment systems: as the name implies, people are paid according to the time they spend at work. This may be based on an hourly rate, a weekly rate or an annual salary. In spite of all the talk of incentive schemes and movement towards a human resource management approach with performance-related pay systems, this is still an extremely popular way for many organisations to pay people. This is largely because it is a simple system that is easy to understand and doesn't result in a great many industrial relations disputes. On the other hand, organisations that have moved away from this system of payment have done so because it provides little incentive to improve productivity or efficiency.

As we said earlier, employers vary in their beliefs about what motivates employees. Those who say that employees can be motivated by the satisfaction gained from the job itself will be concerned to provide a reasonably competitive level of pay for all employees and won't want to pay bonuses or divide the workforce by performance-related pay systems, so that time rates and harmonisation of terms and conditions of employment are likely to appeal to them. The basic rate paid must be sufficiently high that it is adequate for most people's needs. If the rate of pay falls behind this level then the workforce are likely to be demotivated.

**PAUSE FOR THOUGHT 10.1** *What do you think about this philosophy? Does it link with anything you have studied on other modules about motivation theory?*

The idea that pay is necessary at a certain level to provide for an employee's basic needs, but that to increase pay beyond this is not likely to result in increased performance at work, links very clearly with the work of another motivation theorist, Frederick Herzberg (1966), whose ideas you may have studied, and with his motivation/hygiene theories. Herzberg said that certain things, such as pay and good conditions at work, which he referred to as hygiene factors, were necessary to prevent employees from becoming dissatisfied with work, but that an improvement in these things would not necessarily motivate employees to work harder although it would remove the dissatisfaction. He said that these were the sort of things that people moan about, but that when the dissatisfaction had been removed and the pay or working conditions improved, these people would still not be actually motivated to work harder. The motivators, according to Herzberg, were factors such as making the job more interesting or giving the employee more responsibility.

Payments on time rates, as we have said, don't normally vary from week to week and people are paid for going to work, regardless of how hard they actually work when they are there. In the next Activity we would like you to consider a particular example of a time rate payment system, where there are some variations in the payments people receive.

ACTIVITY **10.4**

Imagine that you are a branch manager in a large building society. You are talking to one of your staff, a graduate who is regarded as being bright and a hard worker and who should have an excellent future with the organisation. You ask how things are going and are rather dismayed when she replies, 'OK, but I'm getting a bit disillusioned. I seem to work hard and yet it will take me at least six years to get to the top of the pay scale. Most people around here seem to be at or near to the top of the pay scale already and they seem to take life easy and don't work nearly as hard as I do. I'm thinking seriously about looking for another job.'

1  What is an incremental pay scale supposed to achieve for the organisation?
2  What are the advantages and disadvantages of this type of payment system?
3  How does this payment system relate to what you know about motivation theory?

### Discussion of Activity 10.4

1   An incremental pay scale is a form of time rate payment system, as people are still paid for the time that they spend at work regardless of the amount of effort they put into their work. In this case they are also paid an extra amount or increment for each year that they work for the employer. This is supposed to encourage employees to stay with the same employer for a long period of time, and so result in a stable workforce. There is also an implication that people will become more knowledgeable and effective in their job as they work for more years and gain more experience. This is not necessarily true, and although some people do learn from experience and will become more valuable employees the longer they are employed, you may be able to think of people that you know who have done the same job for years and who seem to have stopped learning from experience, and who do not appear to be any more effective in their job than they were on the day they started.

2   Advantages of incremental payment schemes:

> ➤ Simple
> ➤ Easy to calculate wages
> ➤ Reward long service and lead to stable workforce.

Disadvantages of incremental payment schemes:

> ➤ No incentive to work harder
> ➤ Slow progress for high fliers
> ➤ No incentive at top of the scale.

3   This approach tends, like other forms of time rates, to reflect a collectivist view that everyone should be treated the same and that to pay people differently would be divisive. With incremental pay scales such as this, differences that are taken into account are usually about non-contentious things such as length of service. Everyone can see that people are treated fairly and that they will get the same treatment.

   This approach tends to be favoured in relatively large, impersonal, bureaucratic organisations, which place emphasis in determining pay on the jobs rather than the people. This form of payment system will also work best where the pace of change is slow and where there is little scope for individual initiative. An incremental pay system doesn't tend to work well in a fast moving organisation where it is likely to stifle initiative and innovation.

We shall now examine a group of payment systems that reflect a more individualised approach, where individuals are rewarded for their contribution. We shall consider both individual payment by results and performance-related pay.

### Individual payment by results (piece work)

This approach, based on individualism, reflects the view that since some people work harder than others they should be paid different amounts to reflect the differences in effort that they have made. In this system the amount that people are paid depends on how much they produce, so there are very clear criteria and a strong link between earnings and effort. This system is most common in types of manufacturing environment where it is easy to identify the products that each individual has made, or to identify clearly an individual's contribution to a manufactured product.

The main advantages to the employer of payment by results can be summarised as follows:

➤ there is a strong incentive to increase effort, as there is a very clear link with earnings
➤ if an increased number of tasks are completed in the same amount of time, using the same equipment, the costs per unit of output will be lower.

Like all payment systems, there are disadvantages as well as advantages. The main disadvantages are that:

➤ it can be expensive to install and maintain
➤ it can result in many disagreements about standards or levels of production
➤ production may increase at the expense of quality
➤ the emphasis on personal performance can cause friction between employees.

This payment system is expensive to install and maintain, as there needs to be a fair system for assessing the norm for levels of production so that production over and above this level can be paid. Work study engineers are often employed to find the most efficient method of carrying out a task, and managers and trade union officials may spend a great deal of time timing different stages in the production process. There is an emphasis in the payment by results system on providing an incentive, but also on control and measurement. Even with controls in place there can be problems, as Activity 10.5 shows.

ACTIVITY **10.5**

Imagine that you are the human resource manager in a knitwear manufacturing company. You are about to negotiate with the trade union on the current round of pay talks. The sewing machinists are paid on a piece work system but there is a great deal of absenteeism, particularly on Fridays. It seems to you that many workers increase their levels of production on the other days of the week so that they can have Fridays off. The company wants to ensure regular high levels of production on every day of the week in order to meet its full order books.

1   What is the underlying message that a piece work system, such as this one, intends to give to the employees?
2   Why is this system not working as well as the organisation wants?
3   How does the situation within this organisation link with motivation theories?

### Discussion of Activity 10.5

1   The underlying message that a piece work system is intended to give is that a person will be rewarded for working hard, and the more they produce, the more they will be paid.

2    The system is not working as well as management had hoped because management have assumed that the workforce are only motivated to work harder for money, and that they will continue to work harder and harder for more and more money. Remember the factors that Herzberg (1966), for example, suggested as motivating factors.

3    This situation relates to the view that people may be motivated by a variety of things. In this case the workers wanted a high level of income, but they also wanted some time to relax and spend that income. Some people may be motivated by the opportunity of earning more money, especially if they are saving for some large expenditure. However, not everyone will attach the same degree of importance to financial rewards all the time, and the organisation needs to find out what its employees will value. The employees here seem to be sending a message that leisure is something they value, but other people might be motivated by promotion, a company car, increased responsibility or the increased respect of colleagues.

Individual payment by results is not always particularly appropriate, as we have seen in Activity 10.5. This payment system is most appropriate where:

➤    it is possible to measure work
➤    it is easy to attribute it to individuals
➤    the pace of work is under the employee's control
➤    management can provide a steady flow of work for the employee to do
➤    the work is not subject to constant changes in method, materials or equipment.

There are a variety of payment by results schemes. These include:

➤    group incentives
➤    individual time saving
➤    measured day work.

### Group incentives

These are based on the same principles as the individual payment by results system, but are used when the individualistic approach is not wanted by the organisation. For example, in order to try to encourage team working or to take into account support workers who contribute to overall output, but whose contribution may be difficult to assess, some organisations introduce a system of group payment by results.

The size of the group may vary from small teams or work units to the whole plant or enterprise.

ACTIVITY **10.6**

Make a list of the advantages and disadvantages of plant- and enterprise-wide payment by results schemes.

### Discussion of Activity 10.6

You may have suggested some of the following advantages and disadvantages.

Advantages:

➤ Employees see how they contribute to the whole organisation's effectiveness.
➤ Employees are usually encouraged to find ways to improve performance and productivity.
➤ Employees become interested in how the organisation is managed.
➤ It is cheaper to install plant- or enterprise-wide payment by results schemes than individual payment by results schemes.
➤ There is usually a need to discuss financial information with employee representatives and this can result in an improved understanding of how the company is run.

Disadvantages:

➤ There is a weaker link in employees' minds between the bonus and the level of their effort, so it may not be a strong incentive.
➤ Schemes can be difficult to understand.
➤ Bonus payments could be affected by factors such as inflation which the workforce can do nothing about.

### Individual time saving

Individual time saving is a further example of an individualised payment scheme. In this case, instead of basing payment on $x$ pence per piece produced, an incentive is paid for the amount of time saved by the worker when he or she performs a specific task. There is normally a standard amount of time allowed for the workers to perform a particular task or sequence of tasks, and they get an extra payment when they manage to improve on this time. This has the advantage of being able to take account of situations where the worker is not able to complete tasks because there is no work to do, for example, because of a machine breakdown. In this situation the time involved is not counted in the calculations for the incentive payment.

### Measured day work

Measured day work is another individualised payment scheme. In this case pay rates are agreed at a higher rate than would normally have been paid for a time worker doing the same job, but there is an agreement that the workers will work at a specified level of performance. These levels of performance are agreed using work study techniques and then management carefully monitors the actual level of performance. A further variation of this is the stepped measured day work system, where a number of levels of performance are specified and workers can choose at which level to work. If their work improves they can progress to higher levels and increased pay. These systems have the advantage that the employees' pay will not fluctuate wildly on a daily or weekly basis, and so they provide for stability, but they do not allow individual workers as much flexibility as to how hard they want to work each day.

### Profit sharing

This is a form of payment scheme where the focus is on the group rather than the individual. Employees all receive a bonus whose size depends on the profits made by the organisation that year. Once again there is little direct incentive for individuals to work harder, as it is difficult to see how their contribution actually relates to the profit made, but many profit sharing schemes encourage employees to get involved with how the scheme is run. Sometimes, bonus payments are made in shares rather than cash. This is also intended to give employees an interest in the enterprise, but can result in a risk to both shares and job if the organisation doesn't do as well in the future. It is difficult to see this as a strong motivational force.

### Performance-related pay or merit rating

Performance-related pay, which is sometimes referred to as merit rating, is also a way of linking an individual's pay progression to his or her level of performance or to a rating of competence. It is once again an individualistic approach which favours rewarding people differently according to level of performance or competence, and it aims to motivate all employees and give clear indications of what the organisation expects from employees. Performance-related pay differs from payment by results as it doesn't relate just to the quantity of a product that is produced, and may apply to workers where there is not even any end-product to measure.

Initially, performance-related pay was used as a motivational tool primarily for non-manual employees, but in recent years it has been extended to shop floor workers and has been discussed as a tool for use in the health service and in education. It is increasing in popularity, and is often introduced even when organisations are aware of the fact that money is not necessarily a motivator to all employees in all circumstances, as it is felt to be fair to pay people according to the contribution that they make to the organisation.

Performance-related pay is often regarded as a key feature of performance management, as outlined in the previous chapter, and although some performance management schemes do not operate performance-related pay, most do use it. While the motivational theorists cast doubt on the value of money as a motivator, many managers instinctively feel that money will motivate employees. Some organisations, even if they do not feel that it will have a strong motivational effect, introduce performance-related pay as a way of being fair and rewarding high performers' past performance, and so argue that equity is the rationale for the introduction of such a scheme. The fact that performance is considered at all can also have positive effects, in that it helps to create a culture in which performance is valued and recognition of good performance can be a reward in itself. It is important once again to emphasise that performance-related pay needs to be based on what can be seen to be a fair and just system of allocation, with clear objective criteria being used.

**DID YOU KNOW?**

*Although an IPD survey in 1998 found there to be a growth in recent years in the use of performance pay it was still the case that only 43% of the organisations surveyed indicated that they used performance pay for managers or non-managers. (IDS, Focus 85, March 1998, pp. 5–6.)*

ACTIVITY **10.7**
• • • • • • • • • • • • • • • •

Imagine that you work in an organisation where performance-related pay has recently been introduced. You are appraising one of your subordinates, a man in his fifties who has been with the organisation for about 15 years. You have discussed most of the rating criteria, which have all been satisfactory. You say, 'Your work has been good but are there any areas where you feel there could be improvements?' He replies, 'I'm happy in the job but I don't really see much point in working a great deal harder. The mortgage is paid off now, the children have finished their education and if I earn more money I will only have to pay more tax on it. I want to take life a bit easier now and spend more time at home or away in the caravan. I don't always want to be taking work home with me.'

1    What are the advantages and disadvantages of performance-related pay?
2    How does the situation here link with what you know about theories of motivation?
3    Suggest alternative ways of motivating this employee to work to his full potential.

### Discussion of Activity 10.7

1    Advantages of performance-related pay:

➤    Rewards the individual by linking systematic assessment of their performance to their level of pay or to a bonus.
➤    The factors taken into account may be weighted to reflect their relative importance to the organisation.
➤    It can be used where an incentive is needed but the actual work rate is difficult to measure.
➤    It can reward factors not easily taken into account in other payment systems.

Disadvantages of performance-related pay:

➤    There may be disagreements about the performance factors to be assessed, and if great care is not taken in the choice of the factors there may be claims that they are too subjective or even of sex bias.
➤    Bonus payments may be too infrequent to provide a direct incentive.

2    This is another example of the view that individuals will be motivated by different things and that we value different things. This would link with Maslow's (1954) hierarchy of needs mentioned earlier in the chapter.

3    The situation described reflects the view that there needs to be a range of different forms of incentive so that individuals can choose what will motivate them. In this case the employee might well be motivated if he was offered the opportunity to work for increased holidays.

Performance-related pay can be paid in several ways, and may even involve non-financial rewards. The most commonly used financial rewards are:

➤    salary increases within the normal salary scale
➤    salary increases above the maximum point of the normal pay scale
➤    where each employee is paid on an individual fixed rate, with good performers getting something above the normal rate
➤    lump sum payments that are not included in salary.

### Salary increases within the normal salary scale

This is a commonly used form of performance-related pay, and gives a clear message that although there is a fixed scale for the job and everyone's pay depends on performance, exceptional performers can progress through this scale more rapidly than others.

### Salary increases above the maximum point of the normal pay scale

This is sometimes used when the organisation wants to maintain its existing incremental pay scales but also wants to reward excellent performance. In this case high performers benefit as everyone else progresses along the normal scale until they reach the maximum, but it is of no benefit to average employees who have reached the top of the scale because of the length of their employment.

### Each employee is paid on an individual fixed rate, with good performers getting something above the normal rate

In this case the individual is paid on a particular rate, but there is no automatic annual salary increase. The organisation budgets for a percentage increase each year, but then allocates this money according to assessments of employee performance, with excellent performers receiving most, good performers getting some allocation of award and poor performers receiving nothing at all. This gives a very clear message to all concerned, and may result in those who are assessed as being poor performers leaving the organisation.

### Lump sum payments that are not included in salary

This can be added to most payment systems, and it can be argued that a lump sum payment will have more impact than if the same amount were included in normal salary. This provides the opportunity to draw attention to the organisation's policy for rewarding excellence, especially if the opportunity is used for a special presentation ceremony.

### *Non-monetary awards*

As shown in Activity 10.7, people may be motivated by a range of different factors and may not always be motivated by being paid more money directly in their pay, especially if they lose a great deal in tax. Although we are all pleased to get more money, there is no public recognition of a job well done in that approach. This view is recognised in many organisations, which now seek to provide both monetary and non-monetary awards. Some of the non-financial awards we have selected will also have a monetary value. We have included them as non-monetary awards as the fact of an award being special, in recognition of a job well done or special effort made, may have a motivating effect larger than purely monetary value. Saying 'thank you' is a much overlooked form of non-monetary award in many organisations. The most commonly used non-financial rewards are:

➤ commendation
➤ overseas travel
➤ gifts
➤ gift vouchers.

### Commendation

The opportunity to commend someone for the efforts that they have made can be extremely important as a way of rewarding and motivating them, whether this is done through the normal performance appraisal interview or at a public ceremony at which a letter or certificate of commendation is presented. The latter situation, with the attendant publicity, will serve as a reinforcement of the values that the organisation wishes to encourage and may also motivate others to improve their work performance.

### Overseas travel

This type of reward used to be used primarily to reward sales staff for improvements in sales, but in recent years it has become an incentive on offer to many other individuals. Sometimes overseas travel is used as an incentive for team effort, with the whole team being rewarded with a trip abroad.

This type of reward can be in the form of overseas holidays or the opportunity to attend a high-profile training course held at an exotic destination.

### Gifts

Other gifts awarded to people who have made significant improvements in their performance include consumer items such as cameras, microwave ovens or jewellery. Once again there is the problem of choosing an appropriate range of gifts, as individuals are not likely to be motivated by the opportunity to acquire a new microwave oven, for example, if they already own one.

### Gift vouchers

Gift vouchers are perhaps the most flexible form of incentive payment and are also very popular with individuals, as they offer real choice. Many high street stores promote the use of their gift vouchers to organisations that are thinking of establishing this type of scheme.

### Cafeteria or flexible pay systems

An even more flexible approach to pay is sometimes referred to as the 'cafeteria approach', because employees can choose their own preferred reward or combination of rewards. It gives an opportunity for employers to find a pay package that will suit a diverse range of staff, whether male or female, full-time or part-time, and who come from a wide age range. This can prove attractive for recruiting and retaining labour. In the cafeteria approach the workforce are told what rewards or benefits they can choose from each year. This could mean that they select from gift vouchers, gifts or holidays or they may prefer to choose from other benefits such as improved health care options, health or life insurance, an improved pension scheme, longer holidays or even additional cash. Companies that have introduced flexible schemes such as this have done so not to cut costs but to tailor their benefits to the needs of their workforce, and they have found that younger staff prefer cash or a second car, older staff often prefer to improve their pensions or health cover, while staff with young families may prefer longer holidays.

In order for a flexible system to work there has to be an excellent system established for administration, and improvements in computer technology help here. There must also be an appropriate culture within the organisation and excellent communication with members of the workforce and their representatives. Not all organisations have moved towards a complete menu of options: some have felt that staff might be confused by too much choice and have gone for schemes that offer core benefits to all staff with some additional choice over certain options.

### The Equal Opportunities Commission Code of Practice on Equal Pay

In May 1997 the Equal Opportunities Commission published a Code of Practice on Equal Pay which suggests that whatever payment system is adopted should be 'transparently clear' to all concerned. They also suggest that, although not required by law, organisations should regularly carry out reviews of their pay systems to ensure that they are not unwittingly guilty of perpetuating sex bias.

## Conclusion

We have examined some of the types of payment systems that are available to employers and related them briefly to motivation theory. No scheme is perfect for all organisations, and all schemes have advantages and disadvantages. Each scheme gives a clear message about the values of the organisation and should be a reflection of its mission statement. The choice of payment scheme will depend on the wishes of the workforce as well as the culture of the organisation, and these should be taken into account before any scheme is introduced. The workforce should be involved in discussion, design, implementation and review of whatever payment scheme is introduced. With the increasingly diverse workforces of the 1990s, and moves towards a flexible workforce, many organisations have introduced flexible approaches to the pay and benefits that they provide for employees, using their payment systems as one mechanism for achieving their strategic goals.

**REVIEW QUESTIONS**

You will find brief answers to these review questions on pages 427–428.

1   Imagine that you are the human resource manager for an organisation that is considering the introduction of a points rating system of job evaluation. The job evaluation committee with whom you are working has specified that the following criteria should be used in evaluating jobs:

➤   skill
➤   responsibility for people, e.g. in a job caring for children
➤   responsibility for equipment and materials
➤   responsibility for other employees
➤   mental effort
➤   physical effort
➤   working conditions.

Rate the three jobs, as described in their job descriptions (see pp. 264–266), according to these criteria. You can give up to 10 points for each of these factors for each job.

10 exceptional
7–9 high
4–6 medium
1–3 low
0 negligible

Then add the total scores for Job A, Job B and Job C.

For example, if you feel that a medium level of skill is required by a receptionist as described in job description A you will give that job between 4 and 6 points in that category. If you feel that Job B, the human resource assistant, shows a high level of responsibility for people, you will give it between 7 and 9 points. Remember that in job evaluation it is the job you are evaluating, not the person, so you do not need to know how effective a person actually is in that job.

Compare your evaluation of the three jobs using this points rating method, with your evaluations of the same jobs completed earlier in this chapter, using the whole job ranking method and then the paired comparison method.

Were your rankings of the jobs the same or different in all three cases? Why was this?

2  Find out how much the minimum wage actually is at the present time. How much is the rate for adults aged over 21?
How much is the rate for those aged 18–21?
What are the rates being paid to those who are on government training schemes such as National Traineeships or New Deal?

3  Interview managers or employees from three organisations of your choice from different industrial sectors to establish what effect, if any, the introduction of the National Minimum Wage has had on that organisation/industrial sector.

4  Explain the process of job evaluation and comment on how a points-rating job evaluation scheme can contribute to perceptions of fairness from the point of view of employees.

5  Fairness in pay is an objective of both employers and employees. Describe briefly the issues that need to be considered with reference to fairness, and evaluate critically the approaches that employers could adopt to achieve fairness.

6  Imagine that you are a consultant employed to select a job evaluation scheme for an organisation that employs 500 employees in a large range of clerical jobs. Write a report to the human resource manager in which you outline the advantages and disadvantages of the various types of job evaluation scheme and recommend what you consider to be a suitable job evaluation scheme for this organisation.

**SELF-CHECK QUESTIONS**

**Answer the following multiple choice questions. The correct responses are given on page 428 for you to check your understanding of this chapter.**

(a) **Does harmonisation of wages and conditions of employment mean that managers and other employees get different payment systems and conditions of employment to each other? (Yes/No)** (*b*) Does job evaluation determine the amount of pay for a person doing a particular job? (Yes/No)

(*c*) Are the following all types of non-analytical job evaluation schemes: whole job ranking, paired comparisons, points rating? (Yes/No)

(*d*) Are all of the following advantages of the whole job ranking method of job evaluation: it is simple, cheap to operate and easy to understand? (Yes/No)

(*e*) Is the points rating system of job evaluation an analytical method of job evaluation? (Yes/No)

(*f*) Does job evaluation take account of the individual's performance in the job? (Yes/No)

(*g*) Does an incremental pay scheme provide an incentive for people to work harder? (Yes/No)

(*h*) Does a payment system based on time rates reflect an individualistic approach to the way people are paid? (Yes/No)

(*i*) Is piece work another name for individual payment by results? (Yes/No)

(*j*) Is performance-related pay a way of linking an individual's pay progression to their length of employment with the organisation? (Yes/No)

## References

Advisory, Conciliation and Arbitration Service. *Job Evaluation: An Introduction*. ACAS 1997.

Equal Opportunities Commission. *Code of Practice on Equal Pay*. EOC, 1997.

Herzberg, F. *Work and the Nature of Man*. Staples Press, 1966.

The New Earnings Survey 1994, quoted in *Personnel Today*, 11 May 1995.

Maslow, A. *Motivation and Personality*. Harper and Row, 1954.

McGregor, Douglas. *The Human Side of Enterprise*. McGraw-Hill, 1960.

Income Data Services. *Focus 85*. IDS, March 1998.

*Personnel Today*. Yardstick 4 June 1998.

## Further study

### Books

ACAS Advisory Booklets, particularly *Introduction to Payment Systems* (1997), *Job Evaluation: An Introduction* (1997) and *Appraisal-Related Pay* (1997).

Armstrong, Michael. *Employee Reward*. IPD, 1996. (This provides an in-depth coverage of all aspects of employee reward.)

Equal Opportunities Commission. *Code of Practice on Equal Pay*. EOC, 1997. (A very useful booklet which provides guidance on how to ensure that payment and job evaluation schemes are free of sex bias.)

Institute of Personnel and Development. *The IPD Guide on Team Reward*. IPD, 1997. (An excellent source of information for organisations which are seeking to find ways to reward teams in the workplace.)

Torrington, Derek and Hall, Laura. *Human Resource Management.* 4th edition, Prentice Hall Europe, 1997. (There are four chapters devoted to employee reward which are useful for the reader who wants to explore this subject in a little more detail. Chapter 31 provides an excellent coverage of the strategic aspects of payment, Chapter 32 describes job evaluation processes and systems, Chapter 33 examines incentives, performance pay and fringe benefits while Chapter 34 provides information on pensions and sick pay.)

### Articles

Brading, Liz, and Wright, Vicky. Performance related pay. *Personnel Management,* Factsheet 30, June 1990.

Fowler, Alan. How to choose a job evaluation scheme. *Personnel Management Plus*, October 1992.

Fowler, Alan. How to reward performance. *Personnel Management Plus*, July 1991. (Two extremely useful short articles giving practical suggestions for job evaluation and reward management.)

Hogg, Clare (ed.). Incentive programmes. *Personnel Management*, Factsheet 33, September 1990.

Industrial Relations Services. We're in this together: profit sharing schemes, *Pay and Benefits Bulletin 444. In IRS Employment Review*, 652, March 1998. (A useful article relating to profit sharing schemes.)

Institute of Personnel and Development. *Key Facts: Team Reward*. IPD, 1997. (IPD Key Facts sheets are useful as they succinctly present the main information about the topic, in this case how to reward teams.)

*(Pay and Benefits Bulletin*. (The Contained in the *IRS Employment Review*, is published twice a month and is an extremely useful source of articles and up to date information about pay and benefits in various sectors and organisations.)

Platt, Sally. Take your pick. *Personnel Today*, 13 September 1994.

### Internet

Income Data Services Ltd
(Some very useful articles on
a range of HRM topics, including a
selection on management pay and
renumeration, are published on-
line plus lists of contents for
IDS publications).

**http://www.incomesdata.co.uk/**

# CHAPTER 11

# Counselling and employee welfare

As described in Chapter 1, the main focus of personnel management has changed over the years. One of the earliest roles for personnel specialists included that of the welfare officer (Fowler, 1994). The focus of this role was on the well-being of employees and it sometimes meant taking a paternalistic viewpoint, i.e. adopting a moral stance and telling people what was best for them. Although the personnel function has changed and become more complex, most people would probably still expect a concern for employee welfare to be part of what a human resource management division would promote. Even if the paternalistic elements are not acceptable in our modern culture, employers are expected to care about their employees, and responsibility for this may be held by line managers as well as human resource and other specialists. There are also business reasons for saying that an employer has not just an obligation but also a right to be involved in employee welfare.

The focus of this chapter will be on the provision of counselling as a response to employee welfare problems, although other possible responses will also be discussed. To develop an understanding of the need for counselling and how it should be provided, we shall address the following issues:

➤ the role of the employer
➤ the types of problem involved and their sources
➤ the implications of these problems for the workplace
➤ what to consider when drawing up policies and procedures
➤ who should be involved in providing counselling
➤ counselling skills and techniques.

## The role of the employer
.....................................

One area of debate on the subject of welfare is whether this is a personal and private matter. Should an employer have a right to enquire into the well-being of employees?

**PAUSE FOR THOUGHT 11.1** *Before you read on, take a few minutes to think about your position on this issue. Make a list of arguments for saying that employers should be concerned about the personal welfare of their employees, and a list of reasons why they should not.*

The major argument for employers to concern themselves with the welfare of individuals is that personal problems may affect an individual's performance at work. These may be problems in their private lives, but also problems that arise in the workplace. When people are upset or angry or suffering from anxiety, this can manifest itself in a variety of behaviours, such as:

➤ tiredness due to lack of sleep or poor diet
➤ loss of appetite or eating more (particularly chocolate and cream cakes!)
➤ drinking more alcohol or coffee
➤ smoking more
➤ mood swings, particularly a tendency to be more irritable
➤ changed attitudes, loss of interest in work
➤ inability to concentrate.

These are just some examples of the changes in behaviour you might expect to see. Their impact on work standards is obvious: productivity may decrease; standards of work are likely to fall; there is a heightened probability of absenteeism and turnover.

Even if personal problems are affecting work performance, the question remains as to what the employer's role is and how far the employer should go in assisting people to solve these problems. Many feel that it is intrusive, an invasion of privacy, to ask about events in a person's life outside work, i.e. that this is not the employer's business even if the effects are being felt within the workplace.

**PAUSE FOR THOUGHT 11.2** *Where do you think the balance lies between these two points of view?*

Employers do hold some responsibility for ensuring employee health, as discussed more fully in Chapter 14. This responsibility is partly addressed in the Health and Safety at Work Act 1974 which is intended to ensure the health, safety and welfare of persons at work. Much of this act is directed at the prevention of accidents and physical injury to people in the workplace, and it could be argued that an employee distracted by personal problems is more likely to cause or be the victim of accidents. This, then, would be one argument for an employer's right and obligation to pursue a resolution of an employee's problems.

The principles of common law are also relevant. These dictate some of the factors that are implicit in a contract of employment. You will find a full discussion of this in Chapter 6. The issue that is important here is the expectation that employers will show due care for their employees. This obligation entails not exposing employees to known hazards. Historically, most discussion of this issue has centred around the physical environment and work methods that might have a direct impact on physical health. A court case in 1994, however, brought the issue of employee stress into the limelight.

In November 1994, John Walker, a senior social worker with Northumberland County Council, won his case in a high court, claiming that the employer had been negligent in its handling of this employee's stress. Mr Walker had returned to work after suffering a nervous breakdown. After his return to work the employer failed to make adjustments in his work load, and Mr Walker was dismissed on ill-health grounds after he had a second nervous breakdown. The fact that Mr Walker had suffered a first nervous breakdown meant that it could reasonably have been foreseen that the workload was a potential hazard for this employee. Mr Walker received an out of court settlement of £175,000 (Midgley, 1997, 36).

An additional factor to do with employer obligations is that Employment Tribunals hearing cases of unfair dismissal would expect employers to have conducted a full investigation of the circumstances surrounding an incident of misconduct or incompetence, particularly in the case of a person who previously had a good work record, and to take any extenuating circumstances into consideration. You can read more about this in Chapter 14. The point about legal obligations could be summarised in the statement that employers have a duty of care.

A further point should be made here about the link between counselling and discipline. If an employee's personal problems result in falling standards at work, or even in an event that could be construed as misconduct, this could result in formal disciplinary action. On the whole, managers prefer to handle conflict in an informal manner to preserve good working relationships, and regard formal discipline as action to be taken if the informal approach fails. This approach is encouraged by the ACAS guidelines on discipline (1990). Again, you will find a fuller discussion of this in Chapter 14. It should suffice to make the point here that the proper use of counselling may obviate the need to embark on formal disciplinary action.

Finally, we can justify an employer's interest in the well-being of employees with reference to the basic need to develop good working relationships, on the part of individual employees, individual managers, and from a corporate point of view. Abraham Maslow (1954) was one of the first writers to describe motivation in terms of human needs, and these concepts have often been applied to the workplace. One of the needs that Maslow identified is the social need for relationships. A number of surveys on motivation have identified the importance of good relationships at work, and specifically the relationship between supervisor and subordinate. It is not inappropriate to care about the people we work with. Much has also been written about corporate image, and many employers wish to be recognised as 'good employers', especially since corporate image can affect a company's ability to attract and retain good employees and therefore can have a major impact on the success of the organisation.

The reasons for employers to be involved with employees' problems can be summarised as follows:

➤ to address problems with productivity, standards of work, attendance and turnover
➤ legal obligations to ensure the health, safety and welfare of employees
➤ to avoid the development of disciplinary problems
➤ to maintain good employee relations.

## Types of problem and their sources

Stress has already been identified as a major area of concern, and can be regarded as an umbrella term for a range of problems. Stress is manifested when people are dealing with so many pressures that their normal behaviour patterns become affected. Hans Selye (1956 and 1974), a noted writer on stress, used the terms eustress and distress to explain that stress is not always a negative concept. Sometimes people are stimulated by having to deal with a number of issues; this can be exciting and motivating. When it becomes too much and one cannot cope and at the same time continue to behave within the range of one's normal behaviour patterns, this is what Selye refers to as distress. This is what we normally mean when we refer to stress these days.

What are the causes of stress? There are a wide range of factors that cause stress both in personal relationships and health and in work relationships; these factors are referred to as stressors. Holmes and Rahe (1967) identified a number of life events as being sources of stress. Ranked at number one as a source of stress was the death of one's spouse, and other factors identified included divorce, taking on a high mortgage, and taking a vacation.

It is also recognised that circumstances at work such as poor relationships, especially with one's manager or supervisor, and overwork or underemployment can contribute to stress. The case of John Walker mentioned earlier is an example of too high a workload combined with the demanding nature of the work contributing to stress.

*figure 11.1*
**Some causes of stress**

The symptoms of stress are the behavioural changes we previously identified that might alert you to the fact that a colleague is under pressure. If not dealt with, the end-result can be physical or mental illness leading to mental breakdown.

## Implications of personal problems for the workplace

People who are worried, stressed or upset because of problems in their personal lives cannot automatically put these emotions to one side when they enter their companies' premises. Being at work might sometimes provide some relief from having to think about personal problems, but more often it will be the case that an individual's powers of concentration are disturbed by the existence of personal worries. These preoccupations may manifest themselves in several ways, including:

➤ short temper and impatience
➤ emotional outbursts
➤ lack of attention to duties
➤ decreased productivity
➤ increase in number of accidents
➤ increased absence, lateness and turnover.

All of these obviously have a deleterious effect on a person's work and a company's performance.

*DID YOU KNOW?*
*According to the Department of Health, 80 million days are lost from work every year because of mental health problems. This is estimated to cost £3.7 billion annually, and makes mental health problems one of the three most frequent causes of absence from work. (ABC of Mental Health in the Workplace, 1994.)*

## Company policy and procedures

Policy statements and procedures provide guidelines for all employees. They let managers know how to handle problems, and inform everyone about the help, assistance and support they can expect to receive. There is a dual role for policies as far as situations requiring counselling are concerned. First there is a need for policies relating directly to the provision of counselling, and second a company should have policies dealing with workplace behaviours or events that have been identified as causing distress. For instance, in a *Guardian* Careers Section article, Professor Cary Cooper was quoted as saying that bullying probably accounted for a third to a half of all stress-related illness (Venning, 1995).

Policies on bullying and sexual/racial harassment can help to eliminate these unwanted behaviours and promote a less stressful working environment. Many companies such as banks and retail outlets, where staff handle cash and at the same time have direct contact with the public, have recognised that specialised counselling is necessary to deal with the trauma their employees can suffer after an episode involving violence or a threat of violence. This is true when they have either been directly threatened or witnessed an incident. Employers will obviously have to decide which issues are most important for their organisations, and this may involve surveying employees to discover which issues are of concern to them, and which solutions the employees would most like to take advantage of. The package of welfare policies, procedures and benefits an employer offers to employees is often referred to as an Employee Assistance Programme.

Policies should also address the following issues:

➤ who will be involved in providing counselling, and what are the parameters of their roles
➤ what type of services will be offered
➤ issues of confidentiality.

### *Who should be involved*

**PAUSE FOR THOUGHT 11.3** *Before you read on, stop to consider who might be involved in providing counselling to employees, and why. Make a list of at least three potential sources of counselling, and compare it with lists made by other students in your class.*

A number of people can be identified as providers of counselling within a company's employee assistance programme. They may themselves be employees of the company or the assistance may be available from external agencies. The possibilities include the following:

➤ *Direct line managers.* Line managers know their subordinates well and are in a good position to spot the initial signs of stress. They should be the first to observe or be affected by the existence of a problem in their work area. It is a fundamental part of a manager's job to ensure the smooth running of the organisation, so it is reasonable to expect that line managers should take appropriate action when counselling is needed.
➤ *Human resource managers.* Human resource specialists are often identified in companies as capable of providing counselling and the natural choice to do so. Employees may prefer to talk to personnel staff, regarding them as disinterested parties who understand the company but have some distance, being outside their own department.
➤ *Occupational health unit/trained counsellors.* An employer may decide to employ professional staff to provide a dedicated service within the organisation's formal structure.
➤ *Trained volunteers.* One possibility is to develop a network of trained volunteer contacts throughout the organisation. Interested contacts with aptitude can be trained to provide initial counselling. This has the advantage of employees being able to talk to someone outside of their own work area, but within the company. Such a system is, however, probably feasible only in large organisations.
➤ *External agencies.* Provision of counselling can be contracted out to an external agency specialising in employee assistance programmes. Contracts can specify a range of services, and these variations are discussed in more detail later.

With the methods of providing employee assistance that involve non-specialists, there is a need for training for anyone involved at any level, at least in the basics of counselling. As well as covering counselling skills, this training should enable people to recognise when the boundaries of their capabilities have been reached. That is, although we are maintaining that people throughout an organisation should be capable of offering initial counselling, we recognise that this is only one part of their job; they will not become professional counsellors. Part of the skill of basic counselling is knowing when to refer someone for further help and how to do this.

In deciding for any particular company which particular methods of providing counselling are appropriate, you may wish to draw up a table showing the advantages and disadvantages of each, and indicating key issues to be considered. Table 11.1 presents an example of a generic assessment, but this could, of course, be tailored to the circumstances in an individual company.

*table 11.1*
**Assessment of methods of counselling provision**

| Provider | Advantages | Disadvantages | Key issues |
|---|---|---|---|
| Line manager | Low cost/duty is part of job Knows employees well Knowledge of company | Employees may be reluctant to open up to someone they work with | Need for training and development of skills Company culture and employee relations |
| Human resource specialist | Low cost/duty is part of job Knowledge of company | Employees may not wish to be seen approaching HRM office | Need for training and development of skills |
| Volunteer counsellor | Low cost | Employees may doubt confidentiality Suitable only for large companies | Need for training and development of skills |
| Internal specialist | Availability of person dedicated to task Confidentiality | Higher cost Employees may not wish to be seen approaching internal specialist | Range of expertise required |
| External specialist | Confidentiality Distance from workplace Flexible choice between telephone and face to face counselling | Higher cost Reluctance to admit need for specialist help | Determine selection criteria and selection process |

## *Types of service*

Employers need to decide what level of employee assistance they wish to offer, particularly if they are negotiating a contract with a specialist agency. Options include:

➤ telephone consultations
➤ referrals to specialist agencies such as Alcoholics Anonymous, debt counsellors, Relate (for guidance on marriage and other intimate relationships)

➤ face-to-face consultations

➤ agreement on the number of times any individual may use the service.

Usually the cost of an external service is based on a flat fee per employee with a service contract for an agreed array of services.

### *Confidentiality*

Obviously there must be guarantees of confidentiality if any counselling system is to work. No-one will reveal details of their personal lives to someone who they suspect will go away and reveal the information to other people, and anyone who provides counselling should be aware of the need to respect confidences. However, the decision about what can be treated confidentially versus the right to disclose or act on information obtained during a counselling session is not necessarily straightforward. What if someone admits within the framework of a counselling session to theft from the company, and the penalty for theft in the disciplinary code is instant dismissal?

There is a need to clarify what can be handled confidentially and what cannot. This should be addressed explicitly in the relevant policy statement and communicated to all employees.

## Counselling skills
• • • • • • • • • • • • • • • • • • • •

Before you read about the range of skills and techniques required for effective counselling, you may benefit from carrying out the following activity to assess your approach to counselling.

ACTIVITY **11.1**
• • • • • • • • • • • • • •

You are the personnel manager in a large company with many divisions. An administrative assistant asks to see you about a problem at work. She tells you that her manager is always picking on her, criticising her work and the way she talks to clients. She has asked him to be specific, but she can never tie him down. The criticism always takes the form of throwaway, sarcastic comments. She also complains that this manager is totally disorganised, which creates a lot of work for other people as he does not plan ahead, so people in his department are always rushing to meet deadlines. Inevitably this leads to mistakes. The administrative assistant tells you that she is so distressed by this that she feels unwell most of the time and is often close to tears.

Think about how you would handle this situation and then choose from the following actions the one that most closely resembles what you would do.

(*a*) Refer the administrative assistant to the grievance procedure, and suggest that she either discuss the situation with her manager or put it in writing to him. Agree a date to review progress.

(*b*) Tell the administrative assistant about stress management techniques and suggest that she gives them a try. Agree a date to review progress.

(*c*) (*a*) and (*b*) together.

(*d*) Ask questions to get a clearer picture and ask the administrative assistant what she thinks the solutions are. Agree actions to be taken and fix a date to review progress.

After you have read more about counselling techniques you can look at this scenario again and consider whether you have adopted the most effective approach.

### *The importance of communication skills in counselling*

The techniques that are emphasised for effective counselling are all to do with some aspect of communication such as listening, questioning, providing feedback. To ensure a full understanding of the impact of these techniques, it is a good idea to review a general model of interpersonal communication first. You can later examine how the counselling techniques fit into the communication model.

Figure 11.2 is a simplified model, of the major stages of interpersonal communication, using terms developed by Berlo (1960), among others.

If one simply reads this model as a representation of the communication process, it gives the impression that the process is very uncomplicated. Someone, the sender, has some information to communicate. The sender decides how to formulate the message (encoding) and how to pass it on to the receiver (choosing a channel). The target person, the receiver, gets the message and takes appropriate action which provides feedback to the sender of the message. This seems very straightforward, but a more detailed examination of what is happening at each stage of the model will reveal its hidden complexities, highlighting why communications so often fail and how an understanding of the process can help you to improve your communication skills.

*figure 11.2*
**A model of interpersonal communication**

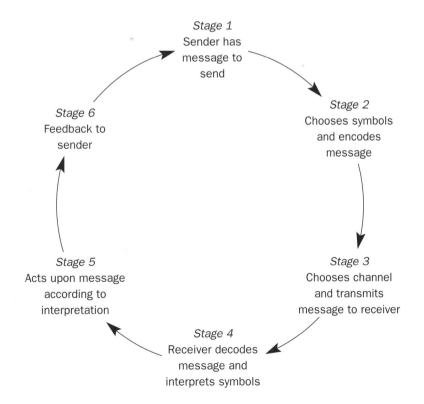

Stage 1
Sender has message to send

Stage 2
Chooses symbols and encodes message

Stage 3
Chooses channel and transmits message to receiver

Stage 4
Receiver decodes message and interprets symbols

Stage 5
Acts upon message according to interpretation

Stage 6
Feedback to sender

We shall examine the processes that occur at each stage of the communication process, paying particular attention to two things:

➤ the barriers to communication that can arise at each stage
➤ considerations that will help you to avoid these barriers.

*Stage 1*: the sender has a message to send. Usually in discussions about the communication model it is assumed that the sender wishes to inform, persuade or give direction to the recipient of the message. In the case of counselling, the initiator of the communication will probably have recognised a need to elicit information rather than a need to pass information on. The same principles of communication apply, however, whether it is a matter of framing questions or statements.

Many people who have something to communicate focus exclusively on what it is they wish to say. That is, they concentrate on the content of the message when they formulate it. This is the first source of failure in communication. The model shows that every communication involves at least two parties; every message is intended for the person who will receive it. It makes sense, therefore, to take the receiver into consideration when you formulate a message. If you do not, you run the risk of putting together a message that although objectively correct will not be understood. Your knowledge of the receiver should be the major influence on the decisions made in the next two stages of the communication model.

*Stage 2*: the sender encodes the message. At this stage the sender has to choose symbols that are appropriate to the message, but he or she must also incorporate knowledge about the level of understanding of the receiver. Symbols can be words, mathematical symbols, sign language, gestures, tic-tac, etc. The content of the message obviously influences which symbols will be chosen. For instance, it is much easier to describe financial data with numbers than with words. However, if the level of understanding of the receiver is low, then the use of mathematical symbols will not convey the message and it may be necessary to explain various concepts in words. Another example of the constraints that the sender's level of understanding places on the encoding stage is the use of technical language. Experts in any field become very comfortable with specialised terms, but if they wish to communicate effectively with someone outside their field, they must be careful not to overuse such terms.

*Stage 3*: the sender transmits the message. Considerations include the effect that the content of the message is likely to have on the receiver. The more important and contentious the message is, the more personal the channel should be. Channels include face-to-face conversation, written memo, telephone, fax, e-mail, etc.

*Stage 4*: the receiver interprets the message. The receiver reacts not only to the words contained in the message but to the perceived intentions of the sender too. Figure 11.3 shows how one message might be interpreted in different ways depending on the perceptual set of the receiver, and this will obviously have an effect on the receiver's response.

The major barriers to communication that may occur at this stage are interference due to status differences and anxiety occasioned by the content or expected content of the message. Anxiety makes people hear what they expect to hear.

*figure 11.3*
**The receiver
interprets the
message**

'George, I'd like to assign Mary to help you with some of your work. What do you think?'

**POSSIBLE REACTIONS FROM GEORGE**
Yes, please. I need some help with this rush work.
What's she trying to get at? Is she saying I'm incompetent?
Here she is, trying to promote Mary again.
Thank goodness she's realised I've got too much work, but I'd just have to spend time training Mary, so I'll say 'No, thanks'.

*Stage 5*: the receiver reacts to the message. This reaction can take many forms, including spoken or written responses or actions.

*Stage 6*: the feedback loop. This is a very important part of the communication process for two reasons:

➤ it shows that communication is not a one-way process; it is dynamic, two-way and ongoing.
➤ it highlights the fact that the sender should receive information about whether or not the communication was successful.

It is important to understand that feedback does not only mean a verbal message sent back to the original sender. Any reaction on the part of the receiver can provide feedback to the sender. Physical reactions such as frowning, laughing, crying, shaking of the head or fist send obvious signals that the message has been understood or misunderstood. If the original message was a request to do something and the receiver fails to do it, this lack of action too provides feedback to the sender about how the message has been interpreted.

This understanding of the role of feedback in the communication model places the major responsibility for the success of communication firmly on the shoulders of the sender. The sender should actively look for signs of whether or not the message has been understood, and take further action if necessary.

The communication model requires you to allocate the roles of an initiator of the communication and a recipient of the communication. This raises the question in the counselling context as to who is the initiator of the communication. You may feel that this depends on whether a person decides they have a problem and seeks help with it, which would mean that the counsellee was the initiator of the process. An alternative scenario would be that a manager, for example, notices that an employee has a problem and decides to broach the topic. This would make the manager the initiator. There is another way of looking at these situations, however, and that is to say that whoever initiates the counselling, it will be the person with the counselling skills, i.e. the person in the counselling role, who will actively seek to structure the communication towards a successful outcome. In terms of the communication model, then, this puts the counsellor in the position of the sender, even if the event that starts the process off is the counsellee's sending a message requesting help.

As you read more about counselling skills, you will become aware that a counsellor's role is fulfilled much more by careful use of questioning techniques, soliciting rather than giving information, seeking to understand rather than providing input for another person to understand. This almost suggests a need for a redesigned model that shows that communication often starts with the need to obtain more information. Many concepts from the model still apply, particularly:

> ➤ the need to gear communication to the receiver
> ➤ the need to eliminate barriers to communication
> ➤ the need to look for, interpret and react to feedback.

We can return to an examination of these issues within the framework of a communication model after we have examined specific counselling techniques in more detail.

## Counselling techniques

Now that we have a general understanding of the communication process, we can turn our attention specifically to the counselling process. Although most basic counselling in the workplace may be provided by people who are not professional counsellors, some of the concepts of clinical counselling provide the basis for an understanding of what might be an appropriate approach to any situation requiring counselling. One of the major contributions to our understanding of effective counselling is the work of Carl Rogers, and two of his works are listed at the end of this chapter as suggestions for further study. Rogers is identified with a client-centred approach to counselling; he emphasised that there are two components that counsellors must master, and these are to adopt an appropriate general approach to counselling and then within this framework to utilise a specific method of questioning. The major concepts of importance to anyone providing counselling at any level are the need for empathy and the use of reflective responses.

### The counsellor's approach and attitude

Rogers explored three concepts that must be contained in the general approach to counselling if it is to be effective. In general, the counsellor must wish to help and the counsellee must perceive this. To achieve this, the counsellor must display empathy, acceptance and congruence.

### Empathy

Empathy is displayed when the counsellor attempts to understand the situation from the point of view of the person with the problem. This means not super-imposing one's own views and avoiding being judgemental, both in trying to understand and in one's response. Let us apply this concept to an example to understand it better.

*A problem situation*

You have always been very ambitious, and have worked your way through the ranks to a senior position. You have also acted as a mentor to a junior colleague and have promoted him as you have progressed. Now you are moving with the company to a new location, and you want your colleague to go with you. You foresee brilliant opportunities for both of you in the future. Your colleague tells you, however, that he is not happy with this, and he is worried about moving his family to another part of the country.

From *your* perspective this is wrong. If you respond by saying: 'You'd be a fool to give up this chance', what reaction would you be likely to get? This response is judgemental and superimposes your view. Your colleague is likely to be defensive; feeling that he is being judged, he may try to justify himself, or alternatively he may decline to discuss the issue further. Either way, it is not likely that the problem will be discussed further.

**PAUSE FOR THOUGHT 11.4** *What would be a more empathic response? How would the conversation be likely to continue following a display of empathy?*

An empathic response would be anything that focuses on trying to understand the situation from the other person's point of view. You might say: 'What is it that worries you about moving the family?', or 'So you're not happy about moving with the company?' Such responses would encourage further discussion of the problem and might lead to the discovery of underlying reasons that have not yet been expressed.

### Acceptance

Acceptance means showing that whatever the person decides to do, you accept the person's right to make these decisions. This does not mean that you necessarily agree, but you accept without making judgements. Again, the statement above, 'You'd be a fool ...', shows a lack of acceptance of another person's right to think and act differently from you.

### Congruence

Congruence means showing that you are genuine in your concern. If the counsellee felt you were faking interest, the relationship of trust would be destroyed. Congruence occurs when there is agreement between the way you feel and your outer behaviour. This may be difficult to achieve if, for instance, you feel angry or disappointed. Showing this would be being judgemental and would inhibit the other person from opening up. It is obviously difficult to combine congruence with acceptance and empathy in all circumstances; the way to achieve it is to focus on your underlying genuine interest in the person, even if your own ultimate aim is the smooth running of the workplace.

Athos and Gabarro (1978) developed aspects of Rogers' work specifically for the use of managers, and highlighted the fact that this caring attitude is not necessarily encouraged in the development of managers. In fact many of you may be thinking that you have not chosen to go into a caring profession, and that what is valued in the occupation of your choice is 'hard-headed business skills.' Counselling certainly requires the use of a specific attitude and specific communication skills that may vary from the day-to-day skills used by managers. Business efficiency, however, for reasons outlined earlier in this chapter, does require that these skills and attitudes be a part of the manager's repertoire. Athos and Gabarro provide reassurances that an understanding of the techniques of reflective responses will reinforce the manager's ability to adopt an empathic stance.

## Reflective and directive responses

Essentially, directive responses are those that reflect the viewpoint of the person directing the conversation, let us say for our purposes the manager, and reflective responses are used when the manager is trying to gain a better understanding of his or her subordinate. Interview skills are important in a range of circumstances; for instance, this text discusses interviewing in selection, performance appraisal and discipline. Different circumstances may call for different responses, but the counselling situation calls predominantly for reflective responses.

In order to explore and fully understand the types of responses one may make in a counselling situation, let us design a scenario to which we can apply each type of response and evaluate the usefulness of the potential reaction each may engender.

Imagine you are a manager in a bank. One of the cashiers has asked to speak to you privately. She tells you that she is having problems concentrating at work and is afraid she is going to make mistakes. What she does not tell you is that she has just left her husband and is living with her sister, although she doesn't get on with her sister's husband and this is causing a lot of arguments and bad feelings.

As we review the types of responses you might make, consider what effect each of them is likely to have in the above scenario. Remember that all the cashier has said is 'I am having problems concentrating at work and I'm afraid I'm going to make mistakes' and that at this stage you know nothing of the underlying problems.

### Reflective responses

Reflective responses, focusing on gaining a better understanding of the cashier's point of view, include silence; non-committal conversational sounds; paraphrase; clarification. It is also important to respond to apparent feelings and emotions expressed by the cashier and not just to her words.

*Silence; conversational sounds; non-verbal cues*
These techniques are meant to encourage the other person to continue talking so he or she may go on to tell you what the problem really is. Consciously practising these techniques also ensures that you do not do too much of the talking. Silence must be used judiciously, since a prolonged silence could lead to embar-

rassment and would inhibit communication rather than promoting it. Using silences merely means not jumping in too quickly to fill a pause; allow the other person to gather his or her thoughts. The term 'conversational sounds' refers to those companionable sounds we make to reassure someone who is talking that we are in fact listening. We use phrases such as: 'Yes, I see', 'Mmm', 'Oh, right', often accompanied by a nod of the head, a questioning frown or a smile.

*Paraphrase:*
'So you think because you're thinking of something else, you might make mistakes.' This might lead the cashier into talking about what the something else is.

*Clarification:*
'So there's something that's bothering you and making you afraid it's going to make you make mistakes?' The response should clarify whether there is something specific that is disturbing the concentration.

*Respond to feelings:*
'You seem upset by something that's affecting your concentration.' The cashier may respond by revealing what it is that is upsetting her. Note that in responding to feelings, you have to sense what is the most important underlying emotion. Whatever is upsetting the cashier is more important, in terms of understanding the problem, than her fear of making errors.

Many inexperienced people feel a natural reluctance to 'pry into other people's affairs' and deal with sensitive situations, especially if it means picking up on emotional cues. If you wish to become a good counsellor, you must conquer these inhibitions. You can develop greater ease with such situations by taking part in role play exercises.

**Directive responses**
Directive responses shift the focus from trying to understand the perspective of the counsellee to expressing the viewpoint of the counsellor. Directive responses include making suggestions; expressing approval or disapproval; trying to persuade or sell a course of action. These are more likely to occur once some of the hidden problems are revealed, so some of the examples below address this situation.

*Making suggestions:*
'You're probably drinking too much coffee and not getting enough exercise.' This kind of response reflects the manager's interpretation of the situation and doesn't attempt at all to encourage further revelations about the true problem. It is not a solution to the core problem.

*Approving/disapproving*
Let us now assume in this case that the cashier has now told you about her leaving her husband, and you respond, 'Well, I think it's a good job you left your husband since you weren't getting on with each other.' This does not encourage further exploration of the problem that now exists and needs to be solved.

*Trying to persuade:*

'Why don't you take a week off to find your own apartment. You'll be all right when you have your own place. Go on, why don't you try that?' This has the same effect as making a suggestion, but is an even more effective communication barrier as the counsellor is obviously committed to this solution and not ready to explore others.

It is also important to avoid challenging questions that make a person defensive, particularly questions beginning with 'why': 'Why can't you concentrate?'; 'Why are you having arguments with your sister's husband?' In response to questions of this nature, people usually become very defensive and attempt to justify their actions. This does not help people to be open about their problems and diverts them from trying to find solutions.

ACTIVITY **11.3**

Practise responding to counselling situations by creating a paraphrasing, a clarifying and a directive response in the following situations.

1   My partner has been offered a good position 200 miles away. It would mean finding new schools for the children and I would have to give up my job here.
2   My teenage son/daughter has started staying out late at night and I think he/she may be taking drugs. What do you think I should do?
3   My father has just died and my mother is now living on her own. She's getting on in years, and I don't think she'll be able to cope on her own for much longer.
4   My boyfriend/girlfriend has just told me that he/she is HIV positive. What would you do in my position?
5   I just can't get on with this new colleague in the office. You've got to do something about it.
6   A colleague tells you that her husband has been becoming more and more violent, and she admits that the bruises you have noticed on her arms and face resulted from his hitting her. (You feel very strongly that battered women should leave their husbands.)

ACTIVITY **11.4**

1   Assess the usefulness of each of the responses you created for the situations described above. How is each response likely to help or otherwise affect the person seeking assistance?
2   Compare your responses with those of other students in your class, and choose those that you think would be most helpful in counselling.

A final word is necessary about the choice between directive responses and reflective responses to a request for advice. Activity 11.4 should have led you to choose and recognise the value of reflective responses. Also, if you watch the Video Arts film recommended in the suggestions for further study, you will find that you are very firmly advised not to offer your own opinions and solutions but rather to encourage the persons seeking advice to think the problem through themselves and arrive at their own solutions.

This is sound advice, but a directive response may sometimes be called for to solve workplace problems. This is particularly the case if there is a policy setting out the procedures to be followed to resolve certain issues. Examples of this include instances of sexual or racial harassment, where an employee would rightly expect the employer to handle the issue rather than expecting the complainant to find a suitable solution.

ACTIVITY **11.5**

You should take the role of the Human Resources Manager in the following two scenarios. Examine each of the scenarios, and decide which one you feel calls for a reflective response and which calls for a more directive response. List your reasons for each choice, and compose suitable responses.

### Scenario 1

A male cook who works in a company restaurant kitchen is quite open about the fact that he lives in a homosexual relationship. Most of the other people who work in the kitchen are women. One day the cook jokingly said in the kitchen that they'd better not kiss him under the mistletoe or they might get infected with HIV. Now the women will not speak to him, and he has heard that some of them would like him to be dismissed. He has come to ask you as the personnel manager what he can do about it.

### Scenario 2

One of the secretaries from the wages department has been newly promoted to the post of Administrative Assistant, supervising 15 office staff in the invoicing unit. She calls you at home one evening to ask how much notice she needs to give in order to leave her job.

### *Discussion of Activity 11.5*

Scenario 1 would probably call for a more directive answer, since employees could expect an organisation to have a policy on how to deal with issues related to HIV and AIDS. Since it is the behaviour of other employees that is causing the problem, it is the responsibility of the organisation to take appropriate action. A reflective response such as 'So you feel uncomfortable with the atmosphere in the kitchen?', aiming to get the cook to explore the situation more fully, would not be helpful in these circumstances. A directive response, outlining the steps recommended in the relevant policy, would be more appropriate.

Although it would be possible to respond to Scenario 2 with direct information about notice requirements, the situation seems to require a more reflective response to uncover the underlying problem. A suitable response might be 'Does this mean you're unhappy with the new job?'

### *Practical counselling techniques*

The abilities to be empathic and to use reflective responses are two mainstays of counselling. There are, however, a number of other techniques you can use in combination with these to ensure your effectiveness as a counsellor. Many of these are similar to skills we have identified in other interviewing situations and for effective communication in general. First we have set out guidelines for counselling, followed by more detailed discussion of the major techniques.

➤ Create the right environment.
➤ Listen actively.
➤ Identify the real problem.
➤ Clarify expectations and roles.
➤ Get the person to:
  – talk
  – recognise the existence of a problem
  – identify solutions
  – identify the preferred solution
  – accept responsibility
  – decide what to do.
➤ Follow up on actions agreed.

## Create the right environment

As in other interview situations, the right environment is important to reassure the counsellee that you are prepared to give your full attention to the matter in hand and to ensure privacy and confidentiality. You will want to find a quiet room, ensure that there will be no interruptions, and arrange the seating to create an informal atmosphere.

## Listen actively

Active listening is another concept that is connected with the work of Rogers and Farson (1976). In general, active listening refers to the development of listening skills to promote better communication. It includes the use of reflective responses to develop and check understanding, but also involves a range of techniques to reassure the partner in conversation that he or she is being listened to. These techniques include looking for clues in facial expressions and general demeanour; eye contact; body language such as leaning forward and appearing relaxed.

**DID YOU KNOW?**

*The Samaritans regard listening skills as an important part of counselling. They offer one-day training courses to organisations wanting to develop counselling skills. The courses will help you to deal with a range of problems and not just suicidal feelings.*

*You can obtain more information by calling the Samaritans on 01753 532 713.*

## Identify the real problem

Even if a person actively seeks help, it may be necessary to investigate what the real problem is. The core of the problem may be hidden for several reasons.

➤ People often suffer from what is known as free-floating anxiety. They know that something is making them unhappy, but they are unable to pinpoint exactly what it is.

➤ In information services it is a well-known fact that people do not know how to ask for exactly what they want. A person in Wakefield wanting to arrive in Huddersfield in time for a job interview at 10.30 a.m. may call railway enquiry services and ask how frequently the trains run from Wakefield to Huddersfield. If the answer to this question were 'once an hour', the enquirer would still not have adequate information to plan the journey. For this person to get the information he or she really wants, the information provider would have to ask a series of questions to ascertain what the true query is.

➤ Even when people recognise that they need help, it may be difficult for them to talk about their problems. A popular TV series about a doctor's practice ran an episode which showed that people very often only reveal the true reason for their visit to the doctor when they have their hand on the door knob as they are about to leave the room.

Counsellors should be alert to signals given at any time in a counselling interview, and they should develop skills in questioning, listening and reacting to consciously or subconsciously revealed cues in order to reach the true nature of the problem.

## Clarify expectations and roles

It is natural to feel that you should come up with solutions, especially if someone has approached you with a problem. Most counselling guidelines, as you now know, will urge you very firmly to resist this temptation. One way to help relieve this tension is to ask persons seeking counselling what they expect from you, how you might help them in solving their problem. The answer to this question may very often clarify the situation for both the counsellor and the person being counselled. If the person responds that you cannot do anything, they simply need someone to talk to, then this diminishes that natural inclination to come up with solutions. If the person asks you for direct action or to offer solutions, you can begin a discussion about what the appropriate role for you is, and again this will clarify for both parties what the options are and may lead towards the formulation of acceptable solutions.

## Get the person to

➤ talk
➤ recognise the existence of a problem
➤ identify solutions
➤ identify the preferred solution
➤ accept responsibility
➤ decide what to do.

Again, it cannot be stressed too strongly that ultimately the solution to a problem has to be owned and pursued by the person with the problem. In terms of technique, as with most interview situations, the interviewer should be sure not to do most of the talking.

## Follow up actions agreed

Although the emphasis has very definitely been on the counsellor's not taking responsibility for the solution to a problem, he or she should still want to know that the problem has been resolved satisfactorily. Just because a solution is agreed in discussion doesn't guarantee that someone will go away and actually take action. There may be hesitation to take the action agreed, there may be a change of heart . . . any number of things might happen to impede progress. The counsellor should check on progress to ensure that agreed improvements are being achieved. This will also be further evidence of genuine concern, but any queries made after a counselling session must be carried out in a discreet and sensitive fashion; the counsellor must not give the impression of interfering or wishing to force the issue.

**PAUSE FOR THOUGHT 11.5** *Think about the interview skills we have identified in other chapters, for instance with reference to selection or performance appraisal. There is one important factor that we have omitted in the case of counselling interviews. What is it?*
*If you cannot remember, you should refer to chapters 4 and 9 before you read on.*

In other applications of interviewing and communication skills one of the major factors emphasised over and over again is preparation. In a counselling situation, however, a more spontaneous reaction is often called for. Also, if you adopt the reflective approach you cannot really prepare before a conversation, as the emphasis is on finding out what the other person thinks and feels and responding to this rather than following your own prepared agenda. You cannot prepare for these revelations. The only form of preparation you can undertake is to practise the techniques so that you will be more at ease with them when you are called on to use them.

A further reason for practising your counselling skills is to overcome the inhibitions that most of us feel when confronted with a person in obvious emotional distress. This is why much of the training provided to counsellors consists of role play exercises and why a number of practical exercises are given at the end of this chapter. Your lecturer will also have access to two major role play exercises contained in the Lecturer's Guide companion to this textbook. The more you practise, the better your counselling skills will become.

ACTIVITY **11.6**

Watch a counselling video of your choice, and read Alan Fowler's article on 'How to provide employee counselling' and the IPD Guide on Counselling at Work. List what you consider to be the five most important guidelines for counselling.

## Cost and evaluation

As with any other human resource management programme, the provision of employee assistance should be costed and then monitored and evaluated for its effectiveness. A cost–benefit analysis can then be performed, and an assessment of the contribution of the programme to the organisation's effectiveness can be made. This is a difficult exercise, as the benefit from counselling is an absence of secondary problems. It is hard to account for savings achieved through the avoidance of problems. However, after the introduction of a counselling service 'before and after' measures of absenteeism, turnover, etc. can be used, and at least a proportion of improvements in these areas can be attributed to counselling. Employee opinion surveys can also be used judiciously to monitor the value that employees place on the availability of such services. It must be borne in mind, however, that existing benefits are sometimes taken for granted and people do not always value them at their true worth.

The costs of an employee assistance programme can be fairly easily estimated and would consider the following factors:

➤ time of internal counsellors and counsellees spent in counselling sessions
➤ training costs

➤ administrative costs
➤ fees to external employee assistance providers.

## Conclusion
..............

As with any organisational problem, there is probably not just one solution to the range of problems identified in this chapter. Counselling is not a panacea, and providing a counselling service once a problem is identified may not be sufficient to eradicate or alleviate the problem: a range of complementary solutions should be considered.

**PAUSE FOR THOUGHT 11.6**  *What initiatives do you think a company could undertake to complement counselling services in resolving human problems in the workplace?*

Some suggestions are:

➤ training in areas such as stress management, time management, dealing with conflict
➤ development of policies to cover areas such as sexual and racial harassment, bullying
➤ management programmes to deal with absenteeism
➤ culture change programmes aimed at management style, employee empowerment
➤ job design related to reasonable work loads and expectations; flexible work patterns
➤ performance management systems
➤ communication and consultation systems to lessen the stress associated with insecurity
➤ employee opinion surveys followed by action in response to areas of concern identified by employees.

Effective human resource management necessitates an integrated approach towards best practice in all these activities. The provision of appropriate employee assistance programmes to enhance the personal effectiveness of every employee is just one facet of a complex picture. It should be remembered that counselling can play a vital part in maintaining the morale of employees, and consequently makes an important contribution to helping the organisation to achieve its objectives.

**SELF-CHECK QUESTIONS**

**Answer the following multiple choice questions. The correct responses are given on page 429 for you to check your understanding of this chapter.**

1   **Which of the following has not been identified as a justification for employer involvement in employee welfare and counselling?**
    (*a*) **Improved productivity**
    (*b*) **Decreased absenteeism**
    (*c*) **Improved discipline**
    (*d*) **Reduced wage demands**

2  Which of the following do Holmes and Rahe identify as the source of the greatest stress?
   (*a*) Overwork
   (*b*) Divorce
   (*c*) Death of one's child
   (*d*) Death of one's spouse

3  Which of the following describes encoding?
   (*a*) The sender telephones the recipient of the message.
   (*b*) The sender chooses words to frame the message.
   (*c*) The receiver interprets the meaning of the message.
   (*d*) The receiver acts on the message.

4  Which of the following issues is NOT likely to be addressed in a policy on counselling?
   (*a*) Whether to respond directively or reflectively
   (*b*) Issues of confidentiality
   (*c*) Who is responsible for providing counselling

5  Which of the following are components of the interpersonal communication model?
   (*a*) Encoding, reflection, feedback
   (*b*) Description, reflection, interpretation
   (*c*) Direction, transmission, feedback
   (*d*) Encoding, transmission, feedback

6  Which of the following comes after the encoding stage of the communication model?
   (*a*) Interpretation
   (*b*) Feedback
   (*c*) Transmission
   (*d*) Direction

7  Carl Rogers' term for trying to understand another person's point of view is:
   (*a*) Sympathetic listening
   (*b*) Active listening
   (*c*) Empathy
   (*d*) Reflection.

8  Joan tells you that she cannot manage with the new machines in the packing unit. A paraphrasing response would be:
   (*a*) Well, why don't you ask for a transfer?
   (*b*) I see. So you don't want to work there any more?
   (*c*) What exactly is causing you a problem?
   (*d*) So you're having problems with the new machines?

9  Tom tells you he has been very unhappy with his work. You respond by saying: 'So you're saying that you'd like to look for another post?' This is an example of:
   (*a*) Clarification
   (*b*) Paraphrasing
   (*c*) A directive response
   (*d*) A suggestion.

10 According to this text, is the following statement true or false? A directive response is never appropriate in a counselling situation.

## Major assignment: personal problems and productivity

It has long been recognised that personal problems that employees experience either at work or at home can have an impact on their effectiveness and productivity in the workplace. Problems of this nature arise from a wide range of sources and include issues such as alcohol or drug dependence, gambling, debt, care duties, sexual/racial harassment, and aspects of personal relationships. Employers can respond to this with a variety of policies, procedures and programmes.

You are a personnel assistant working at the regional headquarters of an insurance company. The senior managers of the company recognise that they have never investigated the possible effect of such problems on the productivity of employees either at headquarters or in the branches. They have asked your personnel management team to write a report and make a presentation about one or more of these problem areas. They have asked you to report on how other employers are tackling them and to make recommendations for your own company.

Your report should include evidence from published materials and from analysis of primary data that your team of four or five personnel management professionals have collected yourselves. You should take a critical, analytical stance, and you may wish to address one or more of the following factors:

➤ what employers should consider when deciding which issues to pursue
➤ range of issues/specific issue
➤ role of policies, managerial attitudes, employee attitudes
➤ benefits/costs
➤ available programmes/support mechanisms
➤ personnel/line manager/other roles
➤ innovative solutions.

Your team will produce a report of approximately 5000 words excluding appendices and prepare a presentation of the major points. Your presentation should last approximately 15 minutes to allow time for questions, and each person should take an active part in the delivery of the presentation. This will test your ability to produce a polished and focused presentation, and you will be penalised for overrunning.

## References

Advisory, Conciliation and Arbitration Service. *Discipline at Work. The ACAS Advisory Handbook.* ACAS, 1990.

Athos, Anthony G. and Gabarro, John J. *Communication and Understanding in Relationships.* Prentice Hall, 1978.

Berlo, David K. *The Process of Communication.* Holt, Rinehart and Winston, 1960.

Fowler, Alan. How to provide employee counselling. *PM Plus*, May 1991, 24–25.

Fowler, Alan. Personnel's model army. *Personnel Management*, September 1994, 34–37.

Holmes, T. H. and Rahe, R. H. The social readjustment rating scale. *Journal of Psychosomatic Research*, August 1967, 216.

Institute of Personnel and Development. *IPD Guide on Counselling at Work*. IPD, 1998.

Maslow, Abraham. *Motivation and Personality*. Second edition. Harper & Row, 1954.

Midgley, Simon. Pressure points. *People Management*, 10 July 1997, 36–39.

Rogers, Carl R. and Farson, R. E. *Active Listening*. Industrial Relations Center of the University of Chicago, 1976.

Selye, Hans. *The Stress of Life*. McGraw-Hill, 1956.

Selye, Hans. *Stress without Distress*. Lippincott, 1974.

Venning, Nicola. Taking the bull by the horns. *The Guardian*, Careers Section, 15 April 1995, 2–3.

## Further study

### Books

Advisory, Conciliation and Arbitration Service. *Health and Employment*. ACAS, 1997. (Outlines good practice for employers in dealing with health problems at work, and focuses specifically on issues to do with smoking, alcohol, drugs, AIDS and stress.)

Athos, Anthony G. and Gabarro, John J. *Communication and Understanding in Relationships*. Prentice Hall, 1978. (Chapters 8–11 deal with counselling techniques, including an in-depth discussion of Carl Rogers' concepts. Two interviews are reproduced as case studies, giving some excellent examples of the reflective technique.)

Beehr, Terry A. *Psychological Stress in the Workplace*. Routledge, 1995. (An in-depth examination of stress emanating from issues in the workplace. Beehr examines stressors such as role ambiguity and role conflict, the workplace outcomes of stress, and methods of treatment.)

Burley-Allen, Madelyn. *Listening: the Forgotten Skill. A Self-Teaching Guide*. 2nd edition, Wiley, 1995. (An easy-to-read guide on how to improve your listening skills to promote better communication. Includes self-assessment exercises, cases and anecdotes.)

Cooper, Cary L. *Creating Healthy Work Organizations*. Wiley, 1994.

Cunningham, Gloria. *Effective Employee Assistance Programs. A Guide for EAP Counselors and Managers*. Sage, 1994. (This book provides a detailed overview of the development of employee assistance programmes in the United States, and current issues including types of problems encountered, assessment and treatment. Notwithstanding the US context, the book will be valuable to those who want in-depth information about employee assistance programmes.)

Department of Health. *ABC of Mental Health in the Workplace*. 1994. (A resource pack of fact sheets for employers, giving, among other things, guidance on how to recognise mental health problems, how to prevent them developing, what to include in a health policy, and how to get further information.)

Earnshaw, Jill and Cooper, Cary. *Stress and Employer Liability*. IPD, 1996.

Fisher, Dalmar. *Communication in Organizations*. 2nd edition, West Publishing Company, 1993. (A good introduction to the topic of communication in general and various aspects of workplace communications in particular. Chapter 15 deals with counselling, listening and feedback skills.)

Harris, Jeff O. and Hartman, Sandra J. *Human Behavior at Work*. West Publishing Company, 1992. (Chapter 12 deals with counselling employees and Chapter 14 with stress. This textbook includes useful self-test exercises and interesting case studies.)

Institute of Personnel and Development. *Stress and Bullying in Workplace*. IPD, 1998.

Institute of Personnel Management. *Substance Misuse at Work. An IPM Guide* (no date given).

Rasberry, Robert W. and Lemoine, Laura Fletcher. *Effective Managerial Communication*. Kent Publishing Company, 1986. (A thorough introduction to the topic of communication and an examination of its importance in a variety of managerial roles.)

Ross, Randall R. and Altmaier, Elizabeth M. *Intervention in Occupational Stress*. A *Handbook of Counselling for Stress at Work*. Sage, 1994.

Torrington, Derek and Weightman, Jane. *Effective Management: People and Organisation*. 2nd edition, Prentice Hall, 1993. (Chapter 21, on interpersonal communication, examines in detail the effect of various types of questioning in a number of situations.)

### *Articles*

Hegarty, Sarah. It's good to talk. *Personnel Today*, 27 September 1994, 25–27. (This article examines the benefits to employers of providing counselling in the workplace, including companies where staff may be vulnerable to traumatic incidents, and highlights the difficulty of evaluating these benefits against the costs involved. Contact numbers are given for a number of organisations providing help with a variety of problems.)

Rogers, Carl R. The characteristics of a helping relationship. *Personnel and Guidance Journal*, Vol. 37, No. 1, September 1985, 6–16.

Rogers, Carl R. and Roethlisberger, F. J. Barriers and gateways to communication. *Harvard Business Review*, August 1952, 46–50.

When the going gets tough. *People Management*, 29 June 1995, 22–28. (Three articles exploring various aspects of current employee health concerns.)

### *Audio-visual*

Executive Business Club. *Valuing People No. 7: Coaching and Counselling*. Management TV International Limited, 1992. (Video.) (Presenters describe the place of coaching and counselling in the framework of modern business demands, and outline the basic stages and skills required for successful counselling. The video demonstrates the usefulness of taking part in role play exercises to develop these skills. Several company representatives outline the importance of counselling and coaching in their companies.)

Open College. *Interviewing. Programme 3.* Produced by Yorkshire Television for the Open College with Channel Four, 1988. (Video.) (This is the third programme in a series of five on interviewing skills in the workplace. The programme covers counselling interview skills, including the reflective technique, responding to hidden messages and how to ask the right questions.)

Video Arts. *Can You Spare A Moment?* Video Arts, 1987. (The focus of this video is on the dos and don'ts of counselling, presented with humour and making some very good points. It is also accompanied by a useful set of notes.)

# CHAPTER 12

# Health and safety

## Objectives:

*By the end of this chapter you will be able to:*

➤ explain what is meant by the terms 'health' and 'safety'
➤ explain the human resource management approach to health and safety at work
➤ explain the key points in the main legislation relating to health and safety at work
➤ explain the role of various people and groups in health and safety at work
➤ design a health and safety policy
➤ demonstrate the need for occupational health programmes
➤ undertake a simple risk assessment exercise.

In Chapter 1 we traced the history of personnel management and examined several approaches to welfare. Some people who have adopted the 'hard' human resource management approach have tried to distance themselves from all these welfare approaches, as they felt that these approaches show a lack of business awareness.

In Chapter 11 we showed that even though the focus of the work of the personnel department has changed over the years, from the earlier welfare approaches to the more cost-conscious, hard-headed approach of the human resource manager of today, the importance of counselling and employee welfare remains. Welfare can be defined as 'well-being', and health and safety are both aspects of welfare as they are both important to the employee's well-being. In this chapter we shall examine the topics of health and safety in the workplace and discuss the reasons why we feel that health and safety are important in the management of people.

## Definitions

### Safety

We define safety as absence from danger and avoidance of injury.

According to this definition, we should expect employers to do everything in their power to keep employees away from danger and free of injury while at work. This does not sound like a great deal to expect from an employer, but there is often a conflict in the employer's mind between increased production, which sometimes may involve some risk-taking, and the necessity to keep employees safe and uninjured, which may cost money. Legislation has developed over a number of years to protect workers, and was initially designed to protect those who were weak and particularly vulnerable to exploitation from any employers who, tempted by the lure of increased production, might put their employees at risk of injury.

### Health

Here the concern is for good health. We define good health as being physically and mentally well with body and mind in excellent working order.

This goes further than safety in that the employer is no longer just expected not to do anything to injure his or her employees, but should seek to promote activities that encourage the good health of the employees. We shall return to a discussion of health promotion activities later in this chapter.

## Safety

The Health and Safety Commission's Annual Report (1997) gives provisional figures during the reporting year 1996/7 as 219 fatalities among employees in the United Kingdom. This is a little higher than in the previous year but is very similar to the figure for 1994/5. The provisional figures also show that during this period 83 self-employed people suffered fatal accidents at work. The Health and Safety Commission's Annual Report (1997) also indicates a decrease in the number of employees suffering injuries which require them to have more than three days absence from work from 130,582 in 1995/6 to 127,219 in 1996/7. This does, however, seem to be mainly as a result of changes in the regulations for reporting accidents introduced in RIDDOR 1995 which will be discussed later in this chapter.

ACTIVITY **12.1**

Sometimes employers are reluctant to spend money on safety improvements as they don't feel this is justified. There are, however, costs associated with accidents. List the possible costs to the employer of accidents at work.

### Discussion of Activity 12.1

Obviously, depending on the severity of the injury, there are costs to the injured person in terms of pain and suffering, and possible loss of earnings. There are also costs to the employer, and your list is likely to include at least some of the following:

➤ cost of lost time and production due to absence caused by injury
➤ cost of lost time and production due to dealing with the injury
➤ cost of replacement worker or of training the replacement
➤ cost of replacing broken machinery or unsafe machinery or equipment
➤ cost of compensation to injured employee
➤ higher insurance premiums if the organisation's accident record is not good
➤ cost involved in carrying out a full investigation into the causes of the accident
➤ cost of paying fines or even facing imprisonment if the employer was to blame for the accident
➤ cost of poor morale within the workforce
➤ cost of people not being willing to work for the organisation because of its poor reputation for safety.

You may have found some other costs involved in accidents as well. Employers should be aware of the hidden costs of accidents: if they carried out a cost-benefit analysis they would probably be amazed at how much accidents were costing them and be more prepared to spend money on accident prevention. In their studies of accidents, the Health and Safety Executive (1995) identified one organisation where the costs of accidents amounted to as much as 37% of profits. This organisation did not have a particularly bad record on health and safety, nor had it suffered any major disasters, fatalities or prosecutions.

Various approaches can be adopted in relation to health and safety at work. The human resource management approach has tended to distance itself from the topics of health and safety, even though, as we have shown, the costs of this lack of interest can be high. We feel that this neglect of health and safety issues is not wise, especially since the organisation's objectives will not be attained if the workforce are not in good shape or suffer from poor morale. We believe that health and safety is an important area of concern for all HRM practitioners, since it is in the organisation's interest to pursue any initiatives that will provide benefits and services which the employees will want and value but that will also fit with the strategic needs of the organisation by enhancing levels of employee performance.

Much of the interest that has been shown in health and safety by personnel practitioners has traditionally been as a response to health and safety legislation, and has indicated a desire to meet the minimum legal obligations as shown in the legal–reactive approach we discussed in Chapter 1. Human resource management tends to emphasise individual initiative, flexibility and adaptability, which are clearly not likely to fit very well with a legal–reactive approach. However, while we would argue that the approach adopted to health and safety should not just be satisfied with achievement of the legal minimum standards, we nevertheless feel that we must discuss some of the legislation since HRM specialists and line managers will still need to be aware of the legislation and of the bodies set up under the legislation to enforce it, and will need to comply with the law. There is scope for innovation, but there is also legislation that must be complied with.

**DID YOU KNOW?**

*Since 1992 the maximum fine (in the Magistrates' Courts) for a serious offence is £20,000 or six month's imprisonment, or both. In 1993/1994 the average penalty for a conviction was £3061. More serious cases may be heard in Crown Court, and there can be an unlimited fine or imprisonment for up to two years, or both. (Health and Safety Commission Annual Report, 1993/1994, p. 62.)*

## Legislation
••••••••••••••

Much of the early development of legislation to protect employees at work was closely linked to the historical development of personnel management. The more enlightened employers were concerned to improve working conditions for their employees and appointed industrial welfare workers to help with this. Less enlightened employers were compelled to pay some attention to the protection of selected groups of employees, and as early as 1840 legislation designed to limit the hours that children worked was passed. In more recent times several new acts have been passed and regulations issued, which were designed to protect employees. This legislation includes:

➤ The Factories Act 1961
➤ The Offices Shops and Railways Premises Act 1963
➤ The Fire Precautions Act 1971
➤ The Health and Safety at Work Act (HASAWA) 1974
➤ The Control of Substances Hazardous to Health Regulations (COSHH)1988
➤ Management of Health and Safety at Work Regulations 1992
➤ Workplace (Health, Safety and Welfare) Regulations 1992
➤ Provision and Use of Work Equipment Regulations 1992
➤ Personal Protective Equipment at Work Regulations 1992
➤ Health and Safety (Display Screen Equipment) Regulations 1992
➤ Manual Handling Operations Regulations 1992
➤ Reporting of Diseases and Dangerous Occurrences Regulations (RIDDOR) 1995

The Management of Health and Safety at Work Regulations 1992 and the next five regulations listed here are often referred to collectively as the 'six-pack'. Many parts of the earlier legislation, such as parts of the Factories Act and parts of the Offices Shops and Railways Premises Act, have been revoked by the 'six-pack'. Much of this earlier legislation was very prescriptive and laid down minimum standards for temperature and space for workers. It is not our intention here to give a complete guide to the law on health and safety, but we shall focus on some key aspects of more recent legislation such as the Health and Safety at Work Act and the 'six-pack', since these embody some fundamental principles that HRM practitioners need to understand.

### The Health and Safety at Work Act 1974 (HASAWA)

HASAWA is mainly an enabling measure which states general principles of safety but also provides the power for the Secretary of State to make detailed safety regulations, based on advice from the Health and Safety Commission. This power may be used to update previous health and safety legislation and streamline it. One of the intentions was to enable older laws to be progressively replaced by a system of regulations and approved codes of practice which would operate in conjunction with the Act itself. It also enables future legislation to be incorporated into HASAWA. Before HASAWA, the legislation that could be used to protect employees at work was patchy and applied to vulnerable groups such as women or children, or to particular industries where there were thought to be high risks. The vast majority of the working population before 1974 were not actually protected by any health or safety legislation. The Health and Safety at Work Act 1974 set up some new bodies and reinforced the power of others:

➤ The Health and Safety Commission (HSC)
➤ The Health and Safety Executive (HSE)
➤ The enforcing authorities.

HASAWA was the first piece of legislation designed to protect everyone at work, and also to protect others who were not at work, such as customers or even passers-by. It is estimated that it brought an extra 3 million people under the scope of protective safety legislation for the first time.

The main aim of the Act was to provide a comprehensive system of law which would raise standards of safety and health for all persons at work and also protect members of the public who might be affected by their actions.

## The Health and Safety Commission (HSC)

The Commission was set up under the Health and Safety at Work Act 1974 and is a quango responsible for carrying out the policy of the Act and for providing advice to local authorities and others about how to implement the provisions of the Act. It is largely independent and acts on behalf of the Crown, but reports to Parliament primarily through the Secretary of State for Employment. It has a chairman and between six and nine other members drawn from bodies representing employers, employees and local authorities, who are appointed by the Secretary of State for Employment. The Annual Report 1993/4 of the Health and Safety Commission states that the mission statement for the HSC and HSE is:

> to ensure that people's health and safety from work activities are properly controlled. This involves:

- providing a framework of laws and standards to ensure that people are protected on a comparable basis at reasonable cost, and to standardise hazardous plant and substances for international trading purposes
- protecting the health of workers and the public and protecting them from risks of accidents through inspection and assessment of hazardous processes and plant
- protecting all people from catastrophic accidents even when the risk is remote
- assuring the public that risks are properly controlled, through information and responsiveness to public concerns.

The Commission can

- assist and encourage people involved in furthering the purposes of the Act
- arrange for research to be done and publish the findings
- provide information for government departments, employers and employees
- submit proposals for making regulations.

## The Health and Safety Executive (HSE)

The Secretary of State and the Health and Safety Commission jointly appoint three people to lead the Health and Safety Executive, and together they have responsibility for ensuring that there are adequate staff for the performance of the HSC functions. They are responsible for making provision for enforcing the legislation, for dealing with daily administration and conducting research, and for identifying the range of information necessary to enable the HSC to remain properly informed. Local authorities also have responsibility for enforcement of health and safety in over 1,250,000 workplaces. Under HASAWA the Secretary of State can make regulations for local authorities to take on responsibility for certain activities and to ensure that there is no duplication of effort between them and the Health and Safety Executive. The local authority inspectors, normally known as environmental health officers, are responsible for health and safety mainly in the services sector, while the HSE tends to concentrate on the more hazard-prone industries. There is a liaison committee which ensures consistency of approach between the HSE and local authorities. The HSE publishes a wide range of material each year explaining its role and the practical implications of legislation.

### The enforcing authorities

As we said earlier in this chapter, the inspection of workplaces and investigation of accidents is shared between HSE inspectors and local authority enforcement officers. Basically the HSE inspectors cover work conducted primarily in factories, building sites, mines, fairgrounds, quarries, railways, chemical plants, offshore and nuclear installations, schools or hospitals. The local authority enforcement officers cover retailing, some warehouses, most offices, hotels, catering, consumer services, sports and leisure activities and places of worship. Both have similar powers of enforcement. These include a right to:

➤ enter employers' premises
➤ carry out inspections/investigations
➤ take equipment or materials on to premises
➤ take measurements, photographs or recordings
➤ carry out tests on articles or substances
➤ examine books and documents
➤ issue improvement notices
➤ issue prohibition notices.

The last two points are of particular importance, and we shall consider each of them in turn.

*Improvement notices*
If the inspector feels that an organisation is contravening one of the relevant provisions of legislation then he or she can issue an improvement notice which will specify that improvements must be made within a specified time limit to bring the equipment or process up to the required standard of safety.

*Prohibition notices*
If when the inspector visits he or she feels that there is serious danger or risk of injury to employees, he or she can issue a prohibition notice which will stop work activity immediately until the risk has been dealt with. In some circumstances a deferred prohibition order may be issued: this would occur, for example, if it would be difficult to stop a process in mid-cycle or if there was no immediate risk of injury. The Health and Safety Commission's Enforcement Policy Statement (1995) states the approach which both the Health and Safety Executive and local authorities should take in relation to law enforcement. The overall aims of the HSC are to protect the health, safety and welfare of employees and to safeguard others such as mem-

**DID YOU KNOW?**
*In 1996/7 the HSE carried out 115,728 inspections of workplaces. They issued 7,333 improvement and prohibition notices and prosecuted 1,256 employers. (Summary of HSC Annual Report 1996/7, pp. 1 and 10.)*

bers of the public who may be exposed to risk from the workplace or activity. In order to achieve this the enforcing authorities need to:

➤ seek speedy compliance with legislation,
➤ provide advice and guidance as to how employers and employees should go about achieving health and safety goals,
➤ use the principle of proportionality so that the enforcement action taken is related to the amount of risk,
➤ show consistency in their approach by using similar approaches in similar circumstances to achieve similar ends,
➤ show transparency so that people are clear about what to expect when an inspector visits and are also clear about their rights,
➤ use a targeted approach so that organisations or activities which are likely to cause the most risk are well controlled and that there is a system of priorities for visits.

*Recent developments*
New procedures were introduced in February 1996 covering the way in which both HSE inspectors and local authority inspectors issue improvement notices. The improvement notices will still be used for exactly the same purposes as we have just outlined. However, if an inspector states that he or she intends to issue an improvement notice to an organisation, that organisation will then have a right to request a written explanation of what is wrong, and an outline of what steps need to be taken, prior to the improvement notice being issued. The organisation has two weeks in which to respond if it feels that the proposed notice should be changed or not be issued. At this point the enforcing inspectors would look again at the proposed action in the light of the organisation's representation and may or may not decide to issue the improvement notice. If there is no representation from the organisation within the prescribed two weeks then the enforcing officer would issue the improvement notice as planned. There are no alterations to the way in which prohibition notices are issued (HSE, 5 February 1996).

## Effects of health and safety legislation

**ACTIVITY 12.2**

Both employers and employees have responsibilities under HASAWA. List what you would expect to be the duties of employers and employees with regard to health and safety.

**Duties of employers** | **Duties of employees**

Compare your lists with the following duties, taken from the Health and Safety at Work Act 1974 itself.

### Outline of the responsibilities of employers and employees

General duties of employers to their employees: 'It shall be the duty of every employer to ensure, so far as is reasonably practicable, the health, safety and welfare at work of all his employees.' (HASAWA 1974, S2)

Particular duties: the employer is given responsibilities for:

(a) the provision and maintenance of plant and systems of work that are, so far as is reasonably practicable, safe and without risks to health

(b) arrangements for ensuring, so far as is reasonably practicable, the safety and absence of risks to health in connection with the use, handling, storage and transport of articles and substances

(c) the provision of information, instruction, training and supervision as is necessary to ensure, so far as is reasonably practicable, the health and safety at work of employees

(d) so far as is reasonably practicable as regards any place of work under the employer's control, the maintenance of it in a condition that is safe and without risks to health and the provision and maintenance of means of access to and egress from it that are safe and without such risks

(e) the provision and maintenance of a working environment for his employees that is, so far as is reasonably practicable, safe, without risks to health, and adequate as regards facilities and arrangements for their welfare at work.

There are further duties for employers in that they must also prepare and, as often as is necessary, revise a written statement of health and safety policy, and bring the statement and any subsequent revision to the notice of all employees. They must also consult appointed safety representatives with a view to making and maintaining arrangements to aid effective cooperation in promoting and developing measures to ensure health and safety at work.

HASAWA (1974, S7) also indicates the general duties of employees at work:

(a) To take reasonable care for the health and safety of himself and other persons who may be affected by his acts or omissions at work.

(b) As regards any duty or requirement imposed on his employer or any other person by or under the relevant statutory provisions, to cooperate with him so far as is necessary to enable that duty or requirement to be performed or complied with.

A further duty is placed on employees:

No person shall intentionally or recklessly interfere with or misuse anything provided in the interests of health safety or welfare in pursuance of any of the relevant statutory provisions. (HASAWA, S8)

Reproduced with permission of the controller of Her Majesty's Stationery Office.

### Discussion of Activity 12.2

Your list probably included some indication that employers were to take responsibility for having a safe workplace with safe equipment that would not injure anyone, and you also probably thought that employees too should take care not to harm anyone at work. There are no specific rules about lighting or temperature in the way that there are in the earlier acts. Instead the Act is trying to involve people and make everyone take some responsibility for his or her actions. This approach is therefore moving towards a human resource management approach, and health and safety are not just in the domain of the human resource specialist but is shared with others. Sometimes the human resource specialist does have some aspects of health and safety included in his or her job description, and he or she may, for example, be expected to chair the safety committee if there is one.

### Safety representatives

As we said earlier, there is a duty for employers to consult with and involve safety representatives in the workplace. In October 1978 the Safety Representatives and Safety Committees Regulations came into effect. These regulations form part of the Health and Safety at Work Act, and within a year over 100,000 safety representatives were in post. The regulations provide that any recognised trade union can appoint safety representatives, and they recommend that in general the people who are appointed should have worked for that employer for at least two years so that they have a reasonable range of experience from which to draw. In some trade unions the shop stewards take on the role of safety representative, while in others the safety representative is a separate post. The people to fill these positions are, however, selected by the trade union, not by the management. Organisations where there are no recognised trade unions can still appoint safety representatives, and they are normally elected by the workforce.

The safety representative's main function is to represent the employee in consultation with the employer on issues relating to health and safety in the workplace, and they can investigate hazards or potential hazards as well as carrying out inspections of the workplace. They are entitled to paid time off to perform their duties and for training to enable them to carry out their duties effectively, and they may also require some facilities such as the use of a telephone, a filing cabinet and a room to conduct interviews. If two or more safety representatives make a written request to management for a safety committee to be established, then the employer is legally obliged to do so.

The Management of Health and Safety at Work Regulations 1992 (MHSWR), discussed later, add to the Safety Representatives and Safety Committees Regulations 1977 and specify that every employer shall consult safety representatives in good time with regard to:

➤ the introduction of any measure at the workplace which may substantially affect health or safety of the workforce
➤ arrangements for appointing or nominating a 'competent person' who is able to assist the employer to carry out risk assessment exercises and help him or her in carrying out duties in relation to health and safety
➤ the health and safety information that the employer is supposed to provide to employees
➤ the planning and organisation of health and safety training
➤ the health and safety consequences of the introduction of new technology at work.

### Safety officer or safety adviser

None of the legislation actually specifies the need for a safety officer but, as the law has grown in complexity, many organisations have felt that it is necessary to appoint a person to specialise in this area of work. This is a management appointment and must not be confused with the trade union/employee appointed safety representative. Safety officers are sometimes appointed to advise senior management without being part of any other department and report directly to the Board, but in many organisations they form part of the human resource management department. Smaller organisations may not wish to appoint a full-time safety officer and may instead call on the expertise provided by independent consultants to act as safety advisers.

The Framework Directive (Article 7), which is discussed later, says that employers must designate 'a competent person' who has practical and theoretical knowledge of particular equipment and who is able to identify any problems that may occur with it. The provision of this directive is reflected in Regulation 6 of the Management of Health and Safety at Work Regulations 1992 and clearly refers to a management nominee, although not necessarily to the safety officer but to someone who because of his or her knowledge and experience of particular machinery, plant or equipment is able to identify problems or defects in it. That person needs to be able to carry out risk assessment for health and safety for employees and the public, and must monitor and review protective and preventive measures. A safety officer may fulfil this role but is not likely to be the only designated competent person, as she or he is unlikely to have the required level of knowledge or experience for all machinery.

It is important that anyone appointed as safety officer or safety adviser has the status and level of competence to provide authoritative advice to management and the workforce on aspects of health and safety.

### Safety committees

Safety committees have to be established, as we said earlier, if two or more safety representatives request the organisation to do so, but many organisations do not wait for this request, and it is good practice to set up a safety committee in any case. The main objective of a safety committee is to promote cooperation between employers and employees in instigating, developing and carrying out measures to ensure the health and safety at work of employees. They are likely to provide some or all of the following functions:

➤ study figures and trends for accidents and notifiable diseases
➤ examine safety audit reports
➤ consider reports and factual information provided by inspectors
➤ consider the reports of safety representatives
➤ assist in development of safety rules and safe systems of work
➤ monitor the effectiveness of safety training in the workplace
➤ monitor the effectiveness of the safety and health communication in the workplace
➤ encourage publicity for health and safety programmes in the workplace
➤ provide a link with the appropriate inspectorates.

### Membership of the health and safety committee

The membership of the committee should be agreed between management and the employees. The committee should normally include equal numbers of people from management and the workforce and should have representation from different areas of the workforce and different grades of management. People such as the organisation's doctor, nurse or company safety officer should also be invited to attend as ex officio members. It is a good idea for the person who chairs the committee to have sufficient status within the organisation that they can authorise money to be spent on necessary aspects of health and safety without having to refer all such decisions to higher authority. A senior member of the management team would fulfil this role well, although in many organisations the chair of the safety committee may also alternate between management and the workforce.

**PAUSE FOR THOUGHT 12.1**    *The phrase 'as far as is reasonably practicable' is used several times in HASAWA. What factors do you think should be considered in determining whether or not something is 'reasonably practicable'?*

This phrase means that circumstances, risks and cost need to be considered when an employer is endeavouring to make the workplace safe for employees. It would be very difficult to make anywhere completely safe and eliminate all accidents. Accidents are by definition something that you cannot predict; nevertheless, many situations do occur where it is possible to predict that someone could be injured if improvements are not made, and employers should try to anticipate the likelihood of these types of accident and take steps to prevent them from occurring. 'Reasonably practicable' means that a calculation must be made in which the risk is compared with the sacrifices, cost and level of effort needed to avert that risk. If there is a very slim chance that a comparatively minor accident might occur, but this chance could be eliminated by spending thousands of pounds on new equipment and also by disrupting the workforce, it might not be considered to be reasonably practicable to do so. If, however, the risk was of a serious injury or possibly death, then it would be reasonable to take every step and spend any amount of money to eliminate this risk. The term 'as far as is reasonably practicable' therefore means that the employer should do as much as they can to try to eliminate risks but that they need to review the balance between the risk and the amount of effort required to eliminate that risk.

### Control of Substances Hazardous to Health Regulations (COSHH) 1988

These regulations were made under the Health and Safety at Work Act 1974 and came into effect on 1 October 1989. This is another far-reaching piece of legislation comprising nineteen regulations and four approved codes of practice. COSHH is designed to protect anyone who works with substances that could be hazardous to health. The regulations apply to all workplaces and include all substances with the exception of asbestos, lead, materials that produce ionising radiations and substances underground, which all have their own separate legislation.

COSHH regulations require all employers to carry out an assessment of risks to their employees from substances that are identified in the workplace as being potentially hazardous to either their employees or others who might be affected. Any risks that are identified must then be controlled. While it would be easy to assume that these regulations would not have much effect on ordinary workplaces, this is not in fact the case, as many of the substances identified as potentially hazardous will be found in any workplace – e.g. fluid for photocopiers or cleaning products – so in reality all workplaces are affected. The main areas that employers should focus on are:

➤ assessing the risk of substances used and identifying the required precautions
➤ introducing appropriate measures to control or prevent the risk
➤ ensuring the correct use of the control measures, and that equipment is regularly maintained
➤ conducting health surveillance to monitor health of employees where there is a known identifiable risk
➤ informing and training employees about risks that may arise from their work, and informing them of the necessary precautions to take.

### The Framework Directive

The European Union Framework Directive has broad objectives which were implemented in EU member states by 31 December 1992. The main objectives of the Directive were to introduce measures to encourage improvements in safety and health of workers at work. In order to do this it contains general principles concerning the prevention of occupational risks, the protection of health and safety, the elimination of risk and accident factors, as well as informing, consultation and providing balanced participation in accordance with national laws.

The British response to the EU directive was made in the Management of Health and Safety at Work Regulations 1992, which were accompanied by an approved Code of Practice which came into effect on 1 January 1993. Five further sets of regulations were also implemented in Britain on 1 January 1993 and these have become known as the 'six-pack'. The 'six-pack' comprises:

➤ Management of Health and Safety at Work Regulations 1992
➤ Workplace (Health, Safety and Welfare) Regulations 1992
➤ Provision and Use of Work Equipment Regulations 1992
➤ Personal Protective Equipment at Work Regulations 1992
➤ Health and Safety (Display Screen Equipment) Regulations 1992
➤ Manual Handling Operations Regulations 1992.

### The Management of Health and Safety at Work Regulations 1992

This is the law in the UK that implements the Framework Directive. The HASAWA covers some parts of the directive but there are also new things that employers need to do, such as carrying out certain detailed procedures, assessing risks, implementing certain safety measures and communicating with staff on health and safety. The Act has itself been incorporated into law under the 1974 HASAWA. The key features of this regulation include the following.

Employers shall:

➤ carry out assessment of health and safety risks to both employees and the public (this may be done in writing or on computer)
➤ monitor and review protective and preventive measures
➤ appoint a competent person or persons to be responsible for protective and preventive measures
➤ establish emergency procedures
➤ give comprehensible and relevant information and training to employees (the training can be provided by a suitable training provider other than the employer)
➤ cooperate with any other employers who may share the same work site.

Employees shall:

➤ use equipment in the way in which they have been trained to use it
➤ report any dangerous situations or any problem areas that they spot in the arrangements that the employer has made for health and safety.

These regulations are intended for use in cases of criminal action against an employer, and may not be used in any civil cases as evidence of negligence.

**PAUSE FOR THOUGHT 12.2** *To what extent do you feel that the Management of Health and Safety at Work Regulations 1992 differ from the HASAWA 1974?*

These regulations are more forceful than HASAWA and specify that employers 'shall' do certain things, whereas HASAWA only expected employers to carry out its provisions 'so far as it is reasonably practicable' to do so. You have already seen in our discussion of the role of safety representatives and safety officers how the 1978 regulations have strengthened their roles.

The new regulations also mean that employers have a legal duty to predict what could go wrong, before it actually happens, and to take preventive action to avoid it happening. They must record the preventive action that they have taken. This is referred to as risk assessment and is the same principle as under COSHH, but it is now applied more widely. This will be discussed more fully later in the chapter.

The new regulations require employers to be proactive and actively manage activities aimed at protecting the health and safety of their employees. This is more in line than previous legislative measures with the human resource approach of being proactive and actively managing human resources.

### Workplace (Health, Safety and Welfare) Regulations 1992

This is intended to rationalise older pieces of legislation and provide clearer ruling as to exactly what facilities the employer should provide for the employee.

Employers shall:

➤ provide a good working environment with appropriate temperature, ventilation and level of lighting
➤ carry out maintenance and be responsible for keeping the workplace clean.

### Provision and Use of Work Equipment Regulations 1992

This law aims to bring together many older laws governing equipment used at work. Employers shall:

➤ consider when they purchase new equipment the working condition of the equipment and risks that it may pose to employees
➤ ensure the provision of appropriate levels of lighting and warnings about the safe use of the equipment
➤ ensure that the equipment is suitable for the use to which it will be put
➤ provide adequate information and training
➤ provide adequate protection from any potentially dangerous parts of the equipment or machinery.

### Personal Protective Equipment at Work Regulations 1992

These regulations replace part of more than 20 old pieces of legislation which were concerned with provision of protective equipment for employees. They aim to ensure suitable provision of protective equipment such as head protection, high visibility clothing or safety harnesses.
Employers shall:

➤ ensure that equipment used is suitable for the job to be done
➤ adequately maintain, clean and replace equipment as necessary
➤ store it safely when it is not in use
➤ ensure correct use of the equipment
➤ inform and train employees in the correct use of the equipment.

### Health and Safety (Display Screen Equipment) Regulations 1992

This law implements the EU's Visual Display Unit Directive and specifies minimum levels of health and safety for people, who spend a large part of their time at work working in front of computer screens. It is primarily aimed at the prevention of damage to their upper limbs, and to prevent eye strain, fatigue and stress.
Employers shall:

➤ assess the risks and reduce any that are found
➤ ensure that work stations meet at least the minimum requirements
➤ ensure that the work is planned to include breaks and changes of activity
➤ arrange for employees to have their eyes tested regularly at time limits designated by the optician appointed by the employer and provide spectacles if necessary
➤ provide appropriate training for users of visual display units.

### Manual Handling Operations Regulations 1992

This aims to reduce the levels of injury and ill-health associated with manually handling of loads at work.
Employers shall:

- ensure, as far as is practicable, that employees don't need to use risky techniques when handling loads
- assess whether any risks are inherent in the manual handling that has to be done
- take necessary steps to reduce risks by introducing mechanical help, ensuring loads are lighter and assessing the capabilities of the individual
- ensure the provision of information to all employees
- if employees sometimes work on another employer's premises, liaise closely with the other employer.

This legislation is far-reaching in its scope although its effects will vary from one organisation to another, depending on the nature of the work undertaken. Some practical effects of the legislation are worth considering further here.

### Reporting of Diseases and Dangerous Occurrences Regulations (RIDDOR) 1995

RIDDOR 1995 came into effect on 1 April 1996 and requires employers to report certain work related accidents, diseases and dangerous occurrences to the enforcing authorities so that they can identify risks and investigate serious accidents. The following briefly describes some of the circumstances in which reporting should occur:

- The death or major injury of an employee, or of a self-employed person working in the organisation, or of a member of the public must all be reported to the enforcing authorities immediately and this must be followed within ten days by a completed accident report. Reportable major injuries include fractures, amputation, dislocation, loss of sight.
- If an employee or self-employed person working on your premises suffers an accident or injury which requires that person to be absent from work for at least three days, then a completed accident form must be sent to the enforcing authorities.
- Some work-related diseases, such as occupational dermatitis, skin cancer or occupational asthma have also to be reported on a disease report form to the enforcing authority as do infections such as hepatitis, tetanus or tuberculosis.
- There may be instances where something occurs which does not actually result in a reportable injury but which could have done. For example, the collapse of a lift, or an explosion in a closed vessel are likely to constitute a dangerous occurrence, even if no one is injured. Any dangerous occurrence has to be reported immediately by telephone to the enforcing authorities. An accident report form should also be completed within ten days of the dangerous occurrence. (Details of where to find more information are given at the end of the chapter under Further study.)

The enforcing authority will be the environmental health department of the local authority if the type of the business is an office, retail or wholesale, warehousing, hotel or catering, sports or leisure, a residential home or place of worship. Accidents or dangerous occurrences which happen in any other type of business will need to be reported to the area office of the Health and Safety Executive.

### *Safety policy statement*

You will remember that under HASAWA one of the duties of an employer is to provide a safety policy statement to show each person's responsibilities and the arrangements they have made to carry out the policy. The safety policy applies to all organisations that employ more than five employees. This is supposed to be a document that can be used to show in a practical way how the arrangements for health and safety are to be carried out in the workplace, and it should be designed to have a genuine effect on health and safety working practices. This means that it should be clearly written and should be easily available to any employee, and a copy should preferably be given to each employee. It does not mean that it is a secret document, as some companies in our experience seem to think, kept locked in a filing cabinet well away from the gaze of employees. In order to encourage awareness of health and safety and produce an effective safety policy document, it is also advisable that a range of people should be involved in its design.

The six-pack regulations do not alter the requirement for a safety policy but they do specify some extra features for which the employer is required to keep a written record. As a result of this many employers are including or attaching these to the safety policy document.

A safety policy should incorporate the following features and is normally written with three main sections:

➤ a statement of management intent
➤ the organisation of health and safety
➤ arrangements made for implementing the policy.

#### A statement of management intent

The safety policy should indicate the approach to health and safety that the organisation is planning to take, and should include some general reference to the responsibilities of directors, line managers and employees and a statement about the importance of health and safety to the organisation. This section should also link to the organisation's mission statement if it has one, and show how health and safety will contribute to the organisation's overall aims or objectives.

#### Organisation

The safety policy should show management's approach to health and safety and who is actually responsible for specific tasks. The safety policy is basically concerned with people, their duties and their accountability. It should include a management chart showing the chain of command in respect of health and safety, with a clear statement that the ultimate responsibility for health and safety rests with the Board or chief executive or equivalent. The safety policy document should carry at the end the signature of the person with the ultimate responsibility for health and safety at work. There should be a clearly defined role for the safety adviser, if such a position exists, and clear explanation of his/her relationship to senior management and line management. This part of the document should also indicate the role of those appointed as 'competent persons' to assist the employer in implementing the safety policy as required under the Management of Health and Safety Regulations 1992. The role and functions of the organisation's safety committee and the safety representatives should also be specified, as should the responsibilities of individual employees, which now include a duty to report hazards or any shortfall in the employer's preventive measures.

### Arrangements

This section should establish systems and procedures and the practical arrangements for their implementation. It should also show the system for monitoring safety and for publishing results. The section of the safety policy covering arrangements should be a practical section that is regularly reviewed and updated. The arrangements should include:

- those for effective planning, organisation, control, monitoring and review of preventive and protective health measures
- the procedures for dealing with emergencies
- how information will be provided
- what instruction and training will be provided for people at all levels in the organisation
- a commitment to consultation and a positive form of worker involvement with health and safety representatives
- a commitment for the board to consider periodic health and safety reports
- a commitment that health and safety will be considered in relation to the purchase of any new materials or equipment
- a requirement for all sections or departments to add their own local safety policy statement as a supplement to the organisation's overall safety policy statement
- the findings of risk assessments, although this is likely, for all but the smallest organisations, to form a supplement to the policy document.

Remember that people need to be aware of their responsibilities as, if something goes wrong and a serious accident occurs, the Factory Inspectorate will want to know who was responsible. The inspectors would carry out a full investigation and would also want to examine the safety policy document. If a supervisor did not know that he or she was responsible for checking that a protective guard was in place, then the employer would have to be able to prove that he or she had informed the supervisor of his or her responsibilities and had also trained him or her adequately in the fulfilment of these responsibilities. Many tasks will of course be delegated to different levels of management and employees do, as we have seen, have some responsibility for their own actions. Senior management cannot, however, abdicate their ultimate responsibility for overall safety within the organisation, and must try to ensure the health and safety of their employees and others affected by their employees' actions. Those who carry the ultimate responsibility for this, such as the Board of Directors, could face prosecution and possibly a large fine or even a spell in prison for individual directors if their organisation is found to be at fault. Similarly, others with specific responsibilities such as safety officers, human resource managers, line managers or training officers could be charged and convicted of an offence.

Read the following case study and carry out Activity 12.3. The case study will be used later in the chapter as the basis for activities 12.4 and 12.5.

## Case study
••••••••••••••

The Sheffley Company employs nearly 330 employees and specialises in the production of steel castings. The organisation has a Director, Mr Jones, whose great-grandfather founded the business. There is a new Production Manager, Mr Tandy; an Import and Export Manager, Ms Jeffries; and an Administration Manager, Mrs Groves. Mr Tandy has eight line managers reporting to him, who have a total of 280 employees working for them. Mrs Groves has a Payroll Manager, a Canteen Manager and a Personnel Officer reporting to her and Ms Jeffries runs the Purchasing, Goods Inward and Goods Outward Departments, and the Warehouse and Export Sections.

The work involved in the production of steel castings is hazardous and the company has not had a good record with regard to health and safety. It is not only in the production areas that there have been problems – the offices also have suffered rather a large number of accidents which have required employees to have more than three days off work to recover.

The new Production Manager decides that something must be done about the record for safety, and in the weekly meeting with the production supervisors he informs them that from next week any employee who does not wear the protective equipment provided will be dismissed. The safety equipment comprises safety boots, safety goggles and overalls.

During the lead-up to the introduction of the safety equipment, notices are put up to explain the disciplinary penalty for non-compliance with the regulation, but information about the use and location of some of the equipment is not provided. Neither the safety representatives nor the safety committee have the opportunity to inspect the new protective equipment or to advise employees on its suitability.

The employees prove to be reluctant to wear the protective goggles which, they complain, pinch their skin and impair their vision. The Production Manager realises that the enforcement of safety is going to be problematic, and at the next week's meeting informs the supervisors that they do not have to be too rigid in their enforcement of the rules.

Two serious accidents occur just a month later in the production area and a further serious accident occurs in the offices. In the first incident molten metal splashes on to the foot of an employee, causing serious burns. In a separate accident a few days later an employee slips, splashing molten metal close to his eyes. Luckily his sight is saved, but he suffers severe burns and scarring. The accident record in the offices is also unsatisfactory, and one employee is injured when chemicals used in the photocopier spill on her leg causing a severe itchy rash to develop. Other employees in the wages office complain of back-aches and head-aches which they say are caused by poor lighting, uncomfortable chairs and badly adjusted screens on their visual display units.

ACTIVITY **12.3**
· · · · · · · · · · · · · ·

Design a safety policy statement for the Sheffley Company. Remember that this should be a practical document that can be used by people in the organisation. Use the three sections and main headings that we have given earlier (see p. 309).

## Risk assessment
· · · · · · · · · · · · · · · · · · · ·

The idea of assessing and controlling risks was introduced to Britain with the Control of Substances Hazardous to Health Regulations 1988, when employers had to assess the risk of harm to people from certain substances being used at work. This was developed further in the 'six-pack' regulations in 1992. The 1992 Code of Practice for the Management of Health and Safety at Work made it a legal duty for employers to assess and record health and safety risks, and to appoint a 'competent person', i.e. a person who has been suitably trained and who is allowed adequate time and facilities to perform this role should assist in this and other safety tasks.

Every organisation has to carry out its own risk assessment, and strategies for this should be devised by management after consultation with all interested groups in the workforce. However, there are normally three key stages in the process of assessing and controlling risks:

➤ identify potential sources of harm
➤ assess the likelihood or risk that each of these hazards will cause harm
➤ design, implement and monitor measures to eliminate or lessen this risk.

One way in which organisations carry out risk assessment is to rate each hazard against three scales – likelihood, severity and extent of harm – using a points system to assess these. To get some idea of how this might work in practice, try the following Activity.

ACTIVITY **12.4**
· · · · · · · · · · · · · ·

Think of the three accidents that occurred in the Sheffley Company case study. The organisation should obviously have carried out a risk assessment before these accidents occurred and should, as the first stage in the risk assessment process, have already identified these three situations as being potentially hazardous. The second stage is to assess the likelihood or risk that each of the situations will cause harm. Using the scale given in Table 12.1, assess the potential risks in these three situations and see which, according to your assessment, has the highest score and hence the most potential risk of causing harm:

1   the risk of injury from transporting molten metal
2   the risk of injury from employees slipping or falling in the production area
3   the risk of injury from handling or transporting chemicals used in the photocopier.

### *Discussion of Activity 12.4*

This is a very easy way of completing the second stage of risk assessment but is perhaps a little too simplistic. Activity 12.5. will ask you to focus on its problems.

*table 12.1*

**Risk assessment
(Activity 12.4)**

| | Risk 1 | Risk 2 | Risk 3 |
|---|---|---|---|
| **Likelihood of Harm**<br>Certain 4 pts<br>Probable 3 pts<br>Possible 2 pts<br>Slight 1 pt | | | |
| **Severity of harm**<br>Major 4 pts<br>Serious 3 pts<br>Minor 2 pts<br>Slight 1 pt | | | |
| **Extent of harm**<br>V. extensive 4 pts<br>Extensive 3 pts<br>Limited 2 pts<br>V. limited 1 pt | | | |

Total score risk 1 _____
Total score risk 2 _____
Total score risk 3 _____

ACTIVITY **12.5**

What problems can you identify with this method of assessing risks?

### Discussion of Activity 12.5

In Table 12.1, all three categories are rated in the same way. It is likely that an organisation would need to develop its own weighted scales, with clear descriptions of what is meant by each category, and that normally the severity rating should be weighted more heavily than the other two categories. After all, any risk of death should be treated very seriously and given a high rating even if there is a very slim chance of this actually ever happening.

Other factors may also need to be taken into account, such as the vulnerability of particular employees or whether the risk exists only in particular circumstances. However, an exercise such as this will provide the opportunity for systematically assessing risks and may help to indicate a priority for action.

Assessing the risk is not the end, as something must then be done to control or minimise the risk. This is the third stage in the process of assessing risk.

### Control measures

The Code of Practice for the Management of Health and Safety at Work 1992 suggests a hierarchy of control measures in order to eliminate or minimise the risk. These are the measures in the suggested order of priority:

1  substitute safer equipment or materials
2  tackle risk at source by improving design features, e.g. use remote control mechanisms, or protective barriers or guard machines

3   replan work procedures, e.g. minimise weights to be lifted or introduce mechanical lifting devices

4   use protective clothing.

The substitution of safer equipment or materials is considered to be the first priority here, even though other alternatives may be possible. This is because a safe system will not need constant monitoring, whereas using protective clothing or replanning work systems is likely to involve frequent checks and constant supervision, and so is less certain in its effectiveness.

ACTIVITY **12.6**

Look once again at Activity 12.4 and the three situations where you assessed the risks. Make a list of the control measures that might be considered for each of these risks. Whatever the method chosen to eliminate or minimise risk, it will still be necessary to monitor the effectiveness of this method as accidents may still happen. The employer would not have a good case if he knew of the hazard's existence, took some steps to try to eliminate it, but then forgot to carry out maintenance to keep the safety equipment in good order.

## Health

So far, we have focused primarily on the legalistic approaches to safety. It is important for employers not only to try to prevent accidents and ill-health as encouraged by the legislation but also to be proactive and take measures to promote improvements in safety and encourage developments to ensure good health.

**DID YOU KNOW?**

*It is estimated that absenteeism costs Britain between £4 billion and £5 billion each year, and this wipes out between 2% and 5% of the profit of an average business (Sheppard, 1995).*

The high cost of absenteeism seems to be a strong financial reason for taking measures to promote and improve health. Many employers have provided health screening services and membership of private health insurance schemes for their managers, and some are extending this provision to the workforce as a whole. Increasingly, organisations are actively trying to promote a healthier life style among their employees. Among the measures that have been tried are:

➤   help for smokers to quit, with support/self-help groups and psychologists giving advice and support

➤   a healthy diet, with a wider choice of health foods on the menu at work

➤   membership of a health club or purchase of multi-gym exercise equipment for employees to use to get fitter

➤   stress management programmes

➤   policies and education programmes on HIV/Aids

➤   policies and education on substance abuse.

In organisations where these programmes have been made available to all the workforce on a long-term basis, there have been benefits to employees' health, with weight reduction and improvements in blood cholesterol and blood pressure levels, and also improvements in absenteeism rates. It is claimed that the cost of the introduction of this type of programme is more than offset by the savings from lower rates of absenteeism.

However, some work-related illnesses seem to be increasing. It was predicted by Dr Julian Peto in *The Lancet* (Shepherd, 1995) that asthma and asbestos-related cancer will cause up to 3000 male deaths a year by 2020 in the UK. This is more than three times the current death rate for men and women. The TUC and National Asthma Campaign showed that nearly 500,000 people are affected by asthma because of their work. This is ten times more than previous statistics have indicated, so there is still plenty that employers need to do to tackle this cause of ill-health at work.

The HSE tries to draw attention to the need for employers to pay attention to the health of their workforce. It launched a campaign in May 1995, due to last for three years, called 'Good Health is Good Business', to try to highlight the fact that managing workplace health risks can provide benefits such as reduced sickness costs, lower labour turnover and lower recruitment costs. The HSE also stresses that there are other benefits to managing workplace health risks, such as a feeling that the company cares, which is likely to result in improvements in morale and productivity.

Failure to take steps to reduce risks in the workplace is likely in the future to lead to higher insurance payments for organisations as insurance companies start to link premiums to the way that they manage risks of accidents and ill-health.

## The HRM approach to health and safety

We said at the beginning of this chapter that it is not enough for employers just to be concerned about preventing accidents in order to comply with legislation, although that in itself is a good start. The human resource management approach has tended to emphasise the need for individuality, flexibility and adaptability, although it is true that one cannot be flexible about whether or not to implement laws. Clearly employers have to act within the law or face prosecution. We have shown in this chapter that there has been a change of approach within the law, from mere compliance with minimum legal requirements in the legislation prior to HASAWA, to the encouragement of increased involvement of all and compliance with legal requirements 'so far as it is reasonably practicable' under HASAWA, to placing the duty on managers that they must introduce management systems, implement these systems and monitor the effectiveness of them as expressed in the 'six-pack'.

Although the newer legislation is more forceful and hence more prescriptive, in some respects it is more in tune with the human resource management approach, since there is an emphasis on the need for managers to manage, on the development of strategies, procedures and systems for improving health and safety, as well as on a need for monitoring the implementation of these systems. This approach to health and safety should link with the overall business objectives of maximising efficiency and effectiveness by improving morale and reducing costs, and also allows for some scope for individuality and flexibility in how this is to be achieved. It is the approach to health and safety that we would advocate, and it is a very different approach to the purely legalistic one of just being concerned with not breaking the law. The HRM approach to health and safety involves the following features.

➤ The need to create a culture in which health and safety are seen to be important to the organisation. The safety policy statement will contribute to this if it is effectively written, known about and acted upon. The legal requirements must be complied with and risk assessments carried out, as well as gathering information about health and safety and carrying out a cost–benefit analysis. If there is to be a culture of health and safety awareness, there also need to be campaigns and publicity, and involvement of top management, individuals and teams. There need to be regular communications and discussion of health and safety and the contribution that improvements will make to the organisation's overall effectiveness, so that all members of the organisation realise that health and safety are important to the way it operates.

➤ Commitment from the top to the achievement of progressively higher standards as expressed in the mission statement and safety policy. Top management must not only sign the policy documents but also set a good example in relation to health and safety, and emphasise that it is an area of importance to them and to the future of the organisation by showing their interest and by setting up new systems and monitoring the effectiveness of these systems.

➤ Commitment throughout the organisation, with all parties clear about their own responsibilities for health and safety, the targets they have to meet, and the contribution these make to the organisation's objectives. This should be considered as an aspect of performance management, as individuals and teams would be encouraged to take responsibility for their own actions and to agree and work towards targets when making improvements.

➤ Managers to demonstrate by their example their commitment to the importance of a safer and healthier work environment. They should also find ways to motivate everyone to make a contribution to health and safety improvements. Prizes and awards to individuals and teams can have an important effect.

➤ Policies and procedures designed to take account of the importance of a safer and healthier environment. There should also be effective systems to monitor their effectiveness.

➤ Policies to be backed by adequate resources for equipment and training. Provision of good health and safety costs money but the cost of not providing these can be higher, as any cost–benefit analysis is likely to prove.

➤ The setting of realistic and attainable targets for everyone in the organisation.

➤ Encouragement of all to take responsibility for their own actions and involvement of all in health and safety.

**REVIEW QUESTIONS**

1  Interview people (friends, family or work colleagues from a range of organisations) about their own responsibilities in relation to health and safety and then about their perceptions of other people's roles in their particular organisation. Try to establish how the roles relating to health and safety differ for managers, other employees, human resource managers, safety

officers, safety representatives and someone designated to be a 'competent person'. Are these roles the same in different types of organisation? How do they compare with what we said earlier in the chapter about these roles?

2 Obtain a copy of the safety policy for either your college or your workplace.
   (a) Use this to identify the roles of various people in the organisation in relation to health and safety.
   (b) Use the safety policy to assess whether health and safety are linked to the organisation's strategic objectives.

3 Design a checklist for carrying out a safety inspection in the workplace. Use your checklist to actually carry out an inspection of a designated area either at work or in your college. Write a report about your findings for the safety officer.

4 Write a short report in which you assess the impact of one piece of health and safety legislation on an organisation of your choice.

5 Prepare arguments and then debate the following statements in two teams. Try to persuade the members of the other team to your point of view.

TEAM A: There is much too much legislation regarding health and safety at work and this is unnecessary as it is in the employers' interests to look after their employees. Legislation merely hinders employers in their ability to run their businesses effectively.

TEAM B: Legislation is necessary to control employers who would otherwise ignore health and safety issues at the expense of their employees' health, safety and welfare.

**SELF-CHECK QUESTIONS**

Answer the following multiple choice and short answer questions. The correct responses are given on page 429 for you to check your understanding of this chapter.

1 Which of the following was the first piece of legislation designed to protect everyone at work, and also to protect others who were not at work, such as customers or passers-by?
   (a) The Factories Act 1961
   (b) The Offices Shops and Railways Premises Act 1963
   (c) The Fire Precautions Act 1971
   (d) The Health and Safety at Work Act 1974
   (e) The Control of Substances Hazardous to Health Regulations 1988.

2 Which of the following pieces of legislation established the Health and Safety Commission?
   (a) The Factories Act 1961
   (b) The Offices Shops and Railways Premises Act 1963
   (c) The Fire Precautions Act 1971
   (d) The Health and Safety at Work Act 1974
   (e) The Control of Substances Hazardous to Health Regulations 1988.

3 An improvement notice is issued when
   (a) something is found to be so dangerous that the factory inspectorate feels it necessary to stop work immediately
   (b) improvements are required by the factory inspectorate but the employer can decide when these should take place

(*c*) improvements are required by the factory inspectorate within a specified period to bring the equipment or process up to the required standard

(*d*) the required improvement has been made by the employer

(*e*) improvements are required by the safety committee to be made within a specified period.

4  The term 'so far as it is reasonably practicable to do so' means

(*a*) that employers must do everything in their power to make the workplace safe

(*b*) that employers may weigh up the costs of a safety improvement as against the risks when deciding whether to make the improvement

(*c*) that employers must assess the risks of substances used and identify the required precautions to be taken

(*d*) that employers have a legal duty to predict what may go wrong before it happens

(*e*) that employers should be proactive and actively manage health and safety issues.

5  The Management of Health and Safety at Work Regulations contain the following legal requirement:

(*a*) that employers must do the best that they can to make the workplace safe

(*b*) that employers may weigh up the costs of a safety improvement against the risks when deciding whether to make a safety improvement

(*c*) that employers must assess the risks of any substances used by employees and identify the required precautions to be taken

(*d*) that employers should carry out an assessment of health and safety risks to both employees and the public

(*e*) that employers should carry out an assessment of health and safety risks for their employees only.

6  The term the 'six-pack' refers to the following six pieces of legislation:

(*a*) The Factories Act 1961, The Offices Shops and Railways Premises Act 1963, The Fire Precautions Act 1971, The Health and Safety at Work Act 1974, The Control of Substances Hazardous to Health Regulations 1988, Manual Handling Operations Regulations 1992

(*b*) The Factories Act 1961, The Offices Shops and Railways Premises Act 1963, The Fire Precautions Act 1971, The Health and Safety at Work Act 1974, The Control of Substances Hazardous to Health Regulations 1988, The Management of Health and Safety at Work Regulations 1992

(*c*) The Factories Act 1961, The Health and Safety at Work Act 1974, The Control of Substances Hazardous to Health Regulations 1988, The Management of Health and Safety at Work Regulations 1992, Workplace (Health, Safety and Welfare) Regulations 1992, Provision and Use of Work Equipment Regulations 1992.

(*d*) Management of Health and Safety at Work Regulations 1992, Workplace (Health, Safety and Welfare) Regulations 1992, Provision and Use of Work Equipment Regulations 1992, Personal Protective Equipment at Work Regulations 1992, Health and Safety (Display Screen Equipment) Regulations 1992, Manual Handling Operations Regulations 1992.

(*e*) **The Health and Safety at Work Act 1974, The Control of Substances Hazardous to Health Regulations 1988, Management of Health and Safety at Work Regulations 1992, Workplace (Health, Safety and Welfare) Regulations 1992, Provision and Use of Work Equipment Regulations 1992, Personal Protective Equipment at Work Regulations 1992.**

**Refer back to the case study in this chapter (pp. 310–311)and answer the following questions. Suggested answers for these are included in the tutor's pack.**

7   **Describe what the role of the safety committee should have been within the Sheffley Company.**

8   **Imagine that you are a consultant brought in to advise about health and safety at the Sheffley Company. Write a report to the Director in which you outline the improvements that should be made in health and safety at Sheffley, and recommend how these improvements should be introduced.**

## References

HMSO. *The Health and Safety at Work Act* 1974, chapter 37, S2, S7, S8.

*Health and Safety Commission Annual Report 1993/94*. HSE Books, 1994, 3, 62, 98, 108, 129.

Health and Safety Executive. HSC announces new procedures when inspectors issue improvement notices. HSE Press Release: C10:96, 5 February 1996.

Health and Safety Executive. *Be Safe: Save Money. The Costs of Accidents: A Guide for Small Firms*. HSE Books, 1995, 4.

Health and Safety Executive. *Health and Safety Commission Annual Report Summary 1996/7*. HSE, November 1997 (on website at http://www.open.gov.uk/hse/ssb.pdf)

Health and Safety Executive. *Safety Statistics Bulletin 1996/7*. HSE, July 1997 (on website at http://www.open.gov.uk/hse/ssb.pdf)

Peto, Julian in the *Lancet*, quoted in Shepherd, Guy, Sick Notes. *Personnel Today*, 18 July 1995.

Shepherd, Guy. Sick Notes. *Personnel Today*, 18 July 1995.

## Further study

### Books

HSE publications exist on a wide range of topics, from general books to detailed explanations of specific legislation. The following are some of its publications that we have found particularly useful.

Health and Safety Executive. *The Safety Representatives and Safety Committee Regulations*. HMSO, 1988.

Health and Safety Executive. *Management of Health and Safety at Work Regulations 1992*. HMSO, 1992.

Health and Safety Executive. *Personal Protective Equipment at Work: Guidance on Personal Protective Equipment Regulations*. HMSO, 1992.

Health and Safety Executive. *COSHH: a Brief Guide for employers – the Requirements of the Control of Substances Hazardous to Health (COSHH) Regulations 1988. HMSO, 1988.*

Health and Safety Executive. *Workplace Health Safety and Welfare, Approved Code of Practice for Workplace (Health, Safety and Welfare) Regulations 1992.* HMSO, 1992.

Health and Safety Executive. *Management of Health and Safety at Work: Approved Code of Practice.* HMSO, 1992

Health and Safety Executive. *Work Equipment: Guidance on the Provision and Use of Work Equipment Regulations 1992.* HMSO, 1992.

Health and Safety Executive. *Five Steps to Risk Assessment: A Step by Step Guide to a Safer and Healthier Workplace.* HSE, 1997. (This is a leaflet which is intended to help employers and the self employed to assess risks in the workplace and it has a clear, easy to follow step by step approach to risk assessment.)

Health and Safety Executive. *Essentials of Health and Safety at Work.* HSE Books, 1994. (An excellent introduction, aimed at employers, with practical advice, checklists and action plans.)

Health and Safety Executive. *Display Screen Equipment Work: Guidance on the Health and Safety (Display Screen Equipment) Regulations 1992.* HMSO, 1992.

Health and Safety Executive. *Manual Handling – Guidance on Regulations 1992.* HMSO, 1992.

The Health and Safety Executive. *Be Safe – Save Money.* HSE, 1995. (A leaflet outlining the advantages and consequently the savings that employers can make by investing in health and safety.)

The Health and Safety Executive. *Enforcement Policy Statement.* MISC 030, HSE, 1996. (This leaflet gives practical guidance about the alterations to the procedures which affect the way in which improvement notices are issued.)

The Health and Safety Executive. *Five Steps to Successful Health and Safety Management.* HSE, 1992. (This provides basic guidance on the steps to take for managing health and safety.)

The Health and Safety Executive. *RIDDOR: Everyone's Guide to RIDDOR 1995.* HSE, 1996. (This gives an outline of the main areas of RIDDOR 1995 including the types of major injuries, dangerous occurrences and diseases which are notifiable under RIDDOR 1995.)

The Health and Safety Executive. *Writing a Safety Policy Statement: Advice to Employers*, HSC6. HSE, 1997. (A useful leaflet taking an employer through the main stages in writing a health and safety policy statement.)

The Health and Safety Executive. *Your Rights When Health and Safety Inspectors Take Action*, MISC 033. HSE, 1996. (This leaflet gives practical guidance about the alterations to the procedures which affect the way in which improvement notices are issued.)

Howells, Richard and Barrett, Brenda. The Health and Safety at Work Act 1974 – a Guide for Managers IPM, 1982. (A clear guide to HASAWA.)

Stranks, Jeremy. *Management Systems for Safety*. Pitman Publishing, 1994. (An excellent clear account of the steps organisations should take to change their approach to health and safety, with particular reference to recent legislation.)

Stranks, Jeremy. *A Manager's Guide to Health and Safety at Work*. 5th edition, Kogan Page,1997. (Clear guidance for managers and others who are interested in health and safety.)

### Articles

Fowler, Alan. How to produce a health and safety policy. *Personnel Management Plus*, January 1994. (An excellent short article which gives practical advice on how to produce a safety policy statement.)

Fowler, Alan. How to make the workplace safer. *People Management*, 26 January 1995. (An excellent introduction to the topic of risk assessment.)

Health and safety – six danger zones. *Personnel Today*, 8 December 1992. (An excellent short summary of the 'six pack' regulations.)

Sheppard, Guy. Sick notes. Special report on health and safety. *Personnel Today*, 18 July 1995. (Provides an up-to-date account of the costs of occupational ill-health.)

### Internet

The Health and Safety Commission          **http://www.open.gov.uk/hse**

# CHAPTER 13

# Partnership and employee involvement

Chapter 1 established that the HRM approach to managing employees, especially the part of it known as soft HRM, entails developing strategies and using techniques that result in employees giving their best efforts for the success of the organisation and reaching their full potential. This approach to management recognises that the contribution of the human resource is critical to the creation of a competitive advantage. Subsequent chapters have examined specific functions that can be performed in such a way as to acquire such employees (HR planning, recruitment and selection), retain them (payment systems), and develop them (performance management, training). The willingness of employees to contribute their best efforts, however, can be affected pervasively by the way they are treated on a day-to-day basis, by their relationships with managers and by the attitude they perceive management in general to have towards them. This is a matter of organisational culture which develops in part from the philosophical stance of senior managers and the owners of enterprises as to the role they expect employees throughout the organisation to play in the life of the organisation.

This chapter examines the basic stances that managers can adopt towards the workforce and the likely reaction of employees. We look in particular at the philosophy of partnership and at the techniques of employee involvement which are believed to enhance the willingness and ability of employees to contribute to the achievement of their organisation's goals.

**PAUSE FOR THOUGHT 13.1** *Given that the aim of human resource management is to use the potential of employees, how would you expect this to be achieved in terms of general management attitude towards employees and their place in the decision-making process?*

In keeping with basic concepts of motivation theory, you have probably stated that employees are more likely to produce greater effort if they have a sense of responsibility and a feeling of achievement from their work. According to Frederick Herzberg *et al.* (1959) and later work by Richard Hackman and Greg

Oldham (1980), one of the ways to achieve this is by job enrichment. One method of enriching jobs is to shift responsibility for making some decisions from supervisors to more junior employees. This is known as a vertical job loading factor, designed to improve motivation. Employee empowerment became a business buzzword in the 1990s, and this too involves devolving the responsibility for decision-making through all levels in the organisation.

The fact that we can talk about the *devolution* of decision-making implies that it lay elsewhere before it was devolved. Traditionally owners and managers have regarded the right to make decisions as being theirs, an attitude reflected in the ideas of Frederick Winslow Taylor (1911). In Taylor's concept of management science, managers were to plan and control the work and give orders, while other employees were meant simply to carry out these orders. Taylor's ideas were underpinned by a view that workmen (at that time Taylor's work was primarily involved with men rather than men and women together in the workplace) were motivated only by money and the possibility of gaining financial incentives for producing more work.

Later theories of motivation, such as those of Herzberg, moved away from this concept of money being the only motivating factor for employees, but in spite of a growing acceptance of the fact that people look for responsibility, achievement and a sense of autonomy at work, the debate over the managerial prerogative to make decisions has continued. The ability or willingness of managers to share their decision-making powers with employees at a lower level in the organisation's hierarchical structure will be very much influenced by those managers' general attitude towards management–workforce relationships. The two major philosophical stances have been described as unitarism and pluralism, and latterly the focus of debate on employee relations has shifted to the concept of partnership.

## The unitary and pluralist perspectives

The type of relationship that will develop between employer (as represented by managers) and employee, and the techniques that are utilised to regulate this relationship, are influenced by the beliefs of the employer. You will see that a unitary stance is likely to result in a workplace culture that is different from what you would expect to find in an organisation headed by pluralists. These concepts were developed in the work of Alan Fox (1974).

### The unitary perspective

Unitarists believe that all members of an organisation have the same interests, that they will all accept the organisation's goals and direct all their efforts towards the achievement of these goals. This implies that there is no conflict in such organisations; if conflict were to arise, it would be attributed to some misunderstanding of what the goals are or to deliberate trouble-making on the part of some individual. The unitarist stance also implies that the person or persons leading the organisation have decided what the goals are, and there is an expectation that everyone who joins the organisation will internalise those goals. Unitarist organisations, therefore, depend on strong leadership from the top and are likely to purposefully recruit like-minded members. The signature of this philosophy is the belief that there is a common goal towards whose achievement everyone is directing his or her efforts.

### The pluralist perspective

Pluralists, on the other hand, believe that in any organisation a range of interests are likely to be represented among the members. One example of this is that employees are likely to be interested in increasing the pay they receive for a unit of work, whereas managers and owners will be concerned to increase profits. This is a clear example of differing objectives or a plurality of interests in the workplace. The existence of different interests means that conflicts are likely to arise as the various parties pursue their interests, and pluralists accept that this is natural and needs to be managed. These conflicts should be managed in such a way that they do not disrupt the running of the organisation, or even so that they potentially contribute to its success.

**PAUSE FOR THOUGHT 13.2** *Considering what you have just read about the unitary and pluralist approaches to employee relations, which would you consider to be more likely to accept unionisation of the workforce and which more likely to resist it? Give reasons for your choice.*

Unitary employers are more likely to resist unionisation; pluralist employers are likely to accept unionisation more readily. Unionisation implies the existence of different sets of interests and the will to set up mechanisms for resolving these differences. Pluralists accept the existence of these differences and the need to work towards their resolution, whereas unitarists expect everyone to have the same goals. According to unitarists there should be no conflict, and therefore no need to have mechanisms for representing differing points of view and resolving conflict. Pluralists recognise from the outset that differing interests in the workplace will have an impact on the achievement of organisational goals, and therefore need to be incorporated into the decision-making process. This is an important point to bear in mind when you read about the methods employers can adopt for involving employees in decisions.

## Partnership, participation and employee involvement
••••••••••••••••••••••••••••••••••••••••••••••••••••••••••

As well as the effects that involvement in decision-making has on employee motivation as discussed earlier, there is also a broader philosophical debate about the role of owners, managers and employees as players in the industrial relations scene. Are owners the only participants in industry with the right to make decisions? Are the providers of capital the only ones with a vested interest in the success of an enterprise? The concept of stakeholders suggests that the success of a company does not affect only those who have a financial stake in it, but that a range of people have a direct interest in what a company does.

Everyone who is affected in any way by the actions and decisions of an enterprise is a stakeholder, including:

➤ employees, who depend on their organisation for their livelihood and for the pleasantness or otherwise of their work life
➤ customers, who have their own requirements of the organisation and who expect companies to take their concerns into consideration
➤ suppliers, who depend for their own livelihood on the success of client organisations
➤ the community, which depends on companies to protect the environment.

This raises again the question of managerial prerogative in deciding what should happen in the workplace versus the right or the desire of employees to have their interests represented. Arguments for maximising employees' input include their democratic right to have a say in any decisions that will affect them directly, their vested interest in the success of the organisation, and, on another level, the fact that it makes sense to use the expertise that is available throughout the organisation.

The above discussion touches on major political and ethical questions to which there are no easy answers, and certainly no one answer that everyone will accept. In the discussion of the role that employees should play in an enterprise there is often perceived to be a tension between economic and social imperatives (McGlynn, 1995). Improvements in employee consultation, especially if they are legislated and therefore compulsory, are frequently seen as essentially social measures that impose unnecessary costs on businesses. But it is congruent with HRM thinking to see these improvements as measures leading to economic success; that is, you can attain a competitive edge by maximising the contribution of your employees, and the contribution of employees is greater the more they are consulted on, and therefore involved in, what is happening in the organisation. These arguments lead us into a discussion of the concept of partnership and the Labour Government's support for it.

## Partnership
●●●●●●●●●●●●●●●

Coupar and Stevens (1998) make some interesting comments about the long-established pedigree of partnership, but the partnership concept in modern times emerged more clearly as part of the employee relations agenda in 1997, and the terminology appeared with increasing frequency throughout 1998, although an IPA paper on the benefits of partnership had already appeared earlier, in 1992. A clear link can be seen between a strategic goal of innovation and partnership as a method of engaging the full commitment of employees (Allen 1998), and the Labour Government elected in 1997 firmly espouses the idea of partnership (*Fairness at Work 1998*, Chapters 1 and 2), presenting it as one of the 'three pillars' which support its 'strategy for achieving competitiveness' (s1.3). So obviously, partnership is now well and truly on the employee relations agenda for the foreseeable future.

As with HRM, partnership is an evolving concept and several commentators have observed that there is as yet no accepted definition of what partnership is and what it encompasses (Beardwell, 1998; Marchington, 1998). As the Government points out in its *Fairness at Work* paper, businesses should be free to adopt a contingency approach and develop whatever programmes suit their particular circumstances. It may be, then, that the search for an authoritative definition of partnership is not a productive exercise.

We have gathered a number of descriptions of partnership from several publications, and present them here followed by a comment on the similarities that emerge.

ACAS (1997a, p. 13)
employers and employees working together jointly to solve problems

Beardwell (1998, p. 36)
key components might include high degrees of communication, personal development, employment security and an emphasis on ethical people management

Allen (1998, p. 41, describing the partnership deal agreed between Tesco and Usdaw)
individual representation; consultation and communication; values; and understanding and promoting the business

Monks (1998, p. 176)
➤ employment security and new working practices
➤ giving employees a voice in how the company is run
➤ fair financial rewards
➤ investment in training

Coupar and Stevens (1998, p. 157)
1  a commitment to working together to make a business more successful
2  understanding the employee security conundrum and trying to do something about it
3  building relationships at the workplace which maximise employee influence through total communication and a robust and effective employee voice.

Common themes that emerge among these definitions are the importance of security, the common aim of business success, and the concept of employee voice.

Of these three components, the one which is probably the most contentious is job security, implying, as it seems to, that employees are promised their jobs will be safe no matter what happens. On the other hand, as John Monks points out: 'Security in exchange for positive work flexibility is at the heart of the partnership approach' (1998, p. 176). Monks goes on to cite a number of companies, for example Rover and Scottish Power, that have committed themselves to avoiding compulsory redundancies wherever possible.

The combination of a 'common aim of business success' and the concept of employee voice' is interesting, given our previous discussion of unitarism and pluralism. Working in partnership calls for the recognition of a mutually desirable goal (business success), but seems to imply at the same time that employees may have different opinions from management and that therefore some mechanism is needed to facilitate 'employee voice'. We shall return to this point after the discussion of participation and involvement.

Some further interesting points to note about partnership before investigating ways in which it can be achieved are as follows:

➤ Partnership can be achieved in both a unionised and non-unionised environment. There is nothing to stop a non-unionised company from making arrangements with its employees to consult with elected representatives on a wide range of issues. On the other hand, the Government obviously feels that if the majority of employees in an organisation wish to be represented by a union, employers should not be obstructive. The new legislation on union recognition proposed in the *Fairness at Work* paper would ease the path to unionisation somewhat (where it is desired), and is currently the subject of much debate.

➤ In support of partnership development, the Government proposes to fund the training of managers and employee representatives in developing the skills necessary to initiate and participate in these activities.

➤ The Government also intends, in its periodic review of ACAS, to examine ways in which the service can expand the good work it already does in this area of endeavour.

There is a definitive link between partnership and employee participation which can be the channel for employee voice, and between partnership and employee involvement initiatives in that these can represent the way to achieve partnership. Coupar and Stevens (1998, p. 157) state that 'the IPA [Involvement and Participation Association] sees partnership as a unique combination of employee involvement processes which has the potential to maximise the benefits to the company and to employees in the process of change'. They also comment (1998, p. 151) on the previously mentioned phenomenon, that 'companies typically use a very wide range of differing activities to develop the mix needed to gain staff commitment and achieve success in the marketplace'. The IPD (1997, p. 8) also sees employer and trade union commitment to partnership as 'supported by mechanisms for communication and involvement'. We shall now review the concept of worker participation and a variety of employee involvement practices that have been identified in various companies.

### Participation and involvement

The word 'participation' is often used as an umbrella term for all forms of worker participation and employee involvement, and sometimes participation and involvement are used interchangeably. Cascio (1991), for instance, uses the term 'worker participation' when referring to practices that we shall designate as employee involvement, as does Bennett (1994). Even the IPM/IPA code (1990) claims to cover both, but in fact talks mainly about involvement. The mechanisms for encouraging employees to participate in decisions do, however, differ in their intent and effect, so we shall distinguish between participation and involvement.

Farnham and Pimlott (1995) define the terms worker participation and employee involvement as different aspects of the relationship between authority and decision-making in organisations. They describe these concepts as follows:

➤ Worker participation 'aims at changing the basic authority structures of enterprises ... by legislating for employee representation on company boards.' 'The law gives rights to employees or places restrictions on managerial power and authority.'

➤ Employee involvement aims 'to get the support and commitment of all employees in an organisation to managerial objectives and goals, thereby reinforcing a sense of common purpose between management and employees.' 'Employers and management are prepared to share decisions with or devolve them to employees or their representatives.' (Farnham and Pimlott, 1995, p. 83)

A further definition of involvement, which will help to give some clarity, comes from the IPM/IPA code (1990, p. 11) which states that it is:

> ... a range of processes designed to engage the support, understanding, optimum contribution of all employees in an organization and their commitment to its objectives.

**PAUSE FOR THOUGHT 13.3** *How would you distinguish between the concepts of participation and involvement?*

The definition of worker participation refers specifically to a relationship regulated by legal statute, and there is an element of protecting employees' rights in the face of resistance from management. The concept of involvement, in contrast, is defined as a management desire to inculcate organisational values in employees. The major differences, then, relate to a tension between a reliance on regulation (participation) versus a flexible and voluntary approach (involvement), and between management's initiating action (involvement) or being constrained (participation).

You should now be able to connect these definitions of participation and involvement with the previous discussion of the unitary and pluralist approaches to employee relations. Since the attitudes and philosophy of owners determine their relationships with their employees and the framework they will choose to adopt, it can be stated that each type of employer is more likely to favour either participation or involvement.

**PAUSE FOR THOUGHT 13.4** *Consider the definitions of employee involvement and employee participation. Which one is a unitary employer likely to adopt? Which one is a pluralist employer likely to adopt?*

The wording of the definitions of involvement may have given you a clue. Since this entails everyone accepting the common aim of the organisation, albeit then being involved in deciding how to achieve this aim, employee involvement corresponds to the unitary viewpoint. Employee participation recognises that groups within an organisation will have different points of view, and allows for input on those differences to decisions before the major decisions are made at board level. In accepting the validity of the existence of differing interests, employee participation is pluralist in nature.

The concept of partnership, however, allows for the development of both participation and involvement. This is exemplified by the Government's urging businesses to voluntarily develop a range of techniques to empower employees and by the signing of the Social Chapter, which includes the adoption of the Directive on European Works Councils (EWC). The EWCs entail setting up legislated participative mechanisms as will be described more fully in the next section. However, the Government does not intend to legislate at this time for national works councils, preferring employees, probably, though not exclusively, through union representation, to develop mutually agreed partnership with their employers, i.e. on a voluntary, not a legislated basis. We have noted that partnership means that there is a common goal for employers and employees alike to recognise and pursue, but the notion of employee voice suggests that employees may at times differ with employers and may wish to be represented by a trade union. With partnership, then, there is the possibility of a blend of some aspects of unitarism with some aspects of pluralism: we can have the pursuit of the unitarist common goal within a pluralist framework.

### *Worker participation*

Participative structures have been a subject of debate for many years among the member states of the European Union, and a number of proposed directives have failed to be adopted. These include the Vredeling directive and the fifth company law directive, which each contained broad proposals on consultation and information. On 22 September 1994 a directive of more limited scope was adopted, and this is the European Council Directive on the establishment of a European Works Council or other procedure in Community-scale undertakings or Community-scale groups of undertakings for the purposes of informing and consulting employees. The main background details of the directive and features of the works councils are described in the following paragraphs, and a fuller outline of events that preceded the adoption of the directive and of the development of European thought on employee consultation and information can be found in Gold and Hall (1994) and Mill (1991).

The key issues in the directive are that employees should be properly informed and consulted about major issues that will have an impact on them. The directive refers to transnational undertakings where decisions could be made in one country that would affect employees in another country. In such circumstances, it seemed essential to most member states in the European Union that proper mechanisms should be in place in order to ensure that employees in the different countries of a transnational operation receive equal treatment with regard to information and consultation. This is the objective of the works council directive.

When the Maastricht Treaty on European Union was ratified in 1993, the UK government opted out of the agreements on social policy, but the Protocol on Social Policy and Agreement on Social Policy, which are annexed to the treaty, allowed the other member states to adopt social policy measures without having to consult or gain agreement from the UK. This was the background against which the Directive on European Works Councils has been developed.

Approximately 100 UK-owned undertakings were affected by the directive because they have establishments in other member states that meet the threshold requirements. They were obliged to adhere to the directive for employees located in other member states, but this obligation did not extend to employees located in the UK. That is, they did not have to establish works councils in relevant UK establishments, but they could do so if they chose to. Two UK-owned multinationals that quickly decided to establish works councils in their undertakings in the UK were BP Europe and United Biscuits (see *Industrial Relations Review and Report*, December 1994, for more details).

The date set for the implementation of the directive was 22 September 1996. If companies established a transnational agreement on information and consultation covering the whole workforce before this date, the directive would not apply; i.e. companies that made an agreement by then would not be constrained by the terms of the directive. This is, in fact, what companies such as BP Europe and United Biscuits opted to do.

By the end of 1997, this scenario had changed, when the Labour Government ended the UK's opt-out from the Social Chapter by signing the Treaty of Amsterdam. This means that the Directive on European Works Councils now applies fully to relevant companies in the UK. The Directive is to be implemented by December 1999.

The essential characteristics of the directive and the prescribed process for developing and implementing a European Works Council are listed below.

### Characteristics

➤ The threshold at which employers come under the terms of the directive is that they have at least 1000 employees within the member states and at least 150 employees in each of any two member states.
➤ The terms of the directive come into effect either when management initiates action or when a written request is made by at least 100 employees or their representatives in at least two undertakings in at least two member states.

### Process

➤ Management and labour meet each other in order to establish a procedure for consultation about the issue of a European Works Council.
➤ There are four possible outcomes of this consultation process:
  – the parties establish a European Works Council (EWC)
  – if they decide against an EWC, they may establish an alternative procedure for information and consultation on transnational issues
  – the parties agree not to have a specific procedure relating to transnational issues
  – the parties fail to reach agreement.
➤ The directive establishes a framework for handling confidential information.
➤ If the parties fail to reach agreement, there are minimum standards that will be applied: an EWC will be established and will meet management once a year, or more often if necessary, to be informed and consulted on any matters that will significantly affect the employees. Matters that the

EWC will consider include the structure of the undertaking, its financial situation and the future development of the business. These issues set down in the minimum standards are a good indicator of the kinds of issues the ministers from the member states felt employees should be consulted on.

### Employee involvement

Our focus in the rest of this chapter is on employee involvement, as this is more closely related to the HRM approach, is more reflective of current arrangements in UK undertakings, and also reflects the current government's preference for voluntary rather than legislated measures. Whereas worker participation mechanisms are usually laid out in legal terms, employee involvement programmes represent a much more flexible approach, and the techniques used often focus narrowly on decisions related to how the individual's job should be performed.

The only legal obligation related specifically to employee involvement initiatives is contained in the Companies Act 1985, which enjoins employers of 250 or more employees to declare which measures they have taken, and report on developments over the past year in their annual report, particularly with regard to provision of information, regular consultation, and financial involvement schemes. You can see an example of this in the ACAS annual reports which always include a section on the actions ACAS has taken to develop the involvement of its own employees.

#### Employee involvement techniques

Make a list of at least three techniques that could be used to promote the involvement of employees in decisions relating directly to their work or in general to make employees feel more that they are an equal partner in the workplace. As you read through the next section you can check your list against the mechanisms that are discussed here.

The Employment Department (1994) used six categories, each with a range of initiatives, to describe employee involvement. These are summarised in Table 13.1 and discussed in more detail below. The Employment Department's categorisation is not an all-inclusive definition, i.e. you do not have to be involved in all the listed activities at the same time to say you are practising employee involvement.

Research conducted by Marchington *et al.* (1993) revealed that a variety of measures are taken up by companies at different times. It also seemed that individual managers adopted their preferred measures, which might well be dropped when they moved on. This is an unfortunate aspect of the voluntary and flexible nature of involvement arrangements. As you will see in the discussion of the initiatives, a longer term commitment on the part of managers is needed if the techniques are to work to best effect. Formal partnership deals agreed between managers and employees may introduce an element of continuity into this scenario.

*Sharing information*
➤ team briefing
➤ employer and employee publications
➤ company videos
➤ electronic news systems.

table *13.1*

**Employee involvement categories and areas for action**

| Sharing information | Team briefing<br>Employer and employee publications<br>Company videos<br>Electronic news systems |
|---|---|
| Consultation | Staff suggestion schemes<br>Staff attitude surveys<br>Works committees<br>Health and safety committees |
| Financial participation | Profit-related pay<br>Employee share schemes |
| Commitment to quality | Continuous improvement<br>Team work<br>Total quality management<br>Quality circles<br>Self-managed project groups<br>Employee award schemes |
| Developing the individual | Performance management<br>Staff appraisal schemes<br>Employee development programmes<br>Investors in people<br>A qualified workforce |
| Beyond the workplace | The community<br>The environment |

Keeping people informed is often described as one of the cornerstones of employee involvement, and in fact provides the foundation on which many of the individual techniques can be built. Without information it is impossible for people to develop and contribute their own ideas. The will to share information is an essential component of involvement, and the list above gives an indication of some of the vehicles that can be used to get information to employees: face-to-face in small, regular meetings (team briefing), materials that could use the written word, graphics or electronic systems such as e-mail (company and staff newsletters, notices, posters), and video film. Careful consideration should be given to choosing the form of communication most appropriate to the type of message.

In their survey of employee involvement in 25 organisations, Marchington *et al.* (1993) found briefing sessions and company newspapers to be among the techniques used by the largest number of employers, with 19 of the 25 companies indicating that they use them.

*Consultation*
➤ staff suggestion schemes
➤ staff attitude surveys
➤ works committees
➤ health and safety committees.

Along with sharing information, consultation is a key concept in developing good employee relations, and much of the ongoing debate about the development of mechanisms to improve the employer–employee relationship centres on the employee's right to 'information and consultation'. Of the information-sharing techniques we have discussed in the preceding section, briefing sessions allow for some immediate feedback from employees, but most of the other vehicles encourage only one-way communication. Remember that effective communication requires feedback, which suggests that consultation has to go hand-in-hand with information. The consultation mechanisms named in this section essentially provide a route for employees to feed ideas back to their employers. These vehicles only represent true consultation, however, if there is an honest willingness to consider the ideas proffered and to incorporate reasonable suggestions into the decision-making process.

Most staff suggestion schemes are linked with a reward for successful suggestions, especially those where a cost saving for the organisation or other improvements in productivity can be identified. The reward does not, however, have to be financial for people to feel encouraged to contribute their ideas. Often people wish merely to see their expertise recognised, gaining a sense of achievement from this, and they need only to be encouraged by the introduction of a recognised scheme. The reward for successful suggestions could be linked to information vehicles from the first category, i.e. a mention in the company or staff newsletter.

Staff attitude surveys will be dealt with later in this chapter when we look at ways of developing and monitoring the success of employee involvement initiatives. You will find information about health and safety committees in Chapter 12.

Works committees to promote information and consultation involve meetings of management and employee representatives who may be elected directly or nominated through the trade unions. Their terms of reference can be tailored to the requirements of individual companies, and may vary widely from one company to another. In their work with companies, ACAS very often establish joint working committees to solve a variety of problems. These works committees are not to be confused with the works councils in countries such as Germany which are established within the legislative framework in place for participative structures.

**DID YOU KNOW?**
In 1994 Rover's employees made 30,000 suggestions, which resulted in savings of £8.5 million for the company. (Employment Gazette, July 1995, p. 271.)

*Financial participation*
➤ profit-sharing schemes
➤ employee share schemes.

A number of schemes, often with tax relief on savings approved by the Inland Revenue, exist to provide employees with financial participation in their companies. These include group or individual bonuses (which *are* subject to income tax) linked to the company's profit performance, and ownership of shares.

Again, various schemes exist in relation to share ownership. In some schemes, known as employee share ownership plans or ESOPs, shares are bought by a trust for employees, usually at no direct cost to them, and are later distributed to them; other schemes give employees the opportunity to buy shares directly. A variety of arrangements exist regarding the percentage of shares that employees can hold, what happens to the shares when an employee leaves the company, and, very importantly, whether the shares are voting or non-voting shares. If ownership of the shares gives employees a voice at shareholders' meetings, this is essentially a form of employee participation as it has been defined in this chapter.

*Commitment to quality*
- continuous improvement
- team work
- total quality management
- quality circles
- self-managed project groups
- employee award schemes.

The human resource management approach and modern ideas about employee motivation go hand-in-hand with an emphasis on the social aspects of work. Human beings on the whole work better in groups, they respond to the stimulation of feedback on their achievements, and there are synergies in terms of improved ideas and methods of working to be gained from having people work in teams rather than as isolated individuals. All these factors are reflected in the techniques listed above.

The benefits to be gained from the formation of teams and self-managed groups ties in with the work done by Trist and Murray at the Tavistock Institute (1993). You may have encountered their concept of socio-technical systems in your course on organisational behaviour. Basically this theory says that organisations must pay attention to the social systems in the workplace as well as the technical systems when designing jobs.

Total quality management emphasises the responsibility of each individual for ensuring the quality of his or her work and de-emphasises the role of supervision or inspection. This puts responsibility firmly with each individual employee. If this is combined with employee award schemes, it heightens an individual's awareness of the contribution he or she can make to the company and of the extent to which this is valued. The term 'quality circles' is linked with an approach adopted by Japanese companies, but the method stems from the work and thinking of an American, Dr W. Edward Deming. Essentially quality circles involve having a group of people, usually from one work area, meet away from the shop floor to discuss improvements that could be made in the work systems. The group analyses data and sets up proposals which are presented to senior managers who consider the new ideas and report back to the quality circle, either accepting the proposal or explaining why it is rejected. Since this requires a greater level of analytical skill than the employees may need for their jobs, quality circles often have a facilitator who provides assistance in the presentational aspects but does not contribute ideas as far as content is concerned.

Continuous improvement is an umbrella term for any programme that focuses on identifying and solving problems or exploring opportunities to improve the company's performance. These programmes often focus on an improved response to customer requirements or a reduced rate of errors which can be targeted by a combination of initiatives such as team work, quality management and problem-solving groups.

Marchington *et al.* (1993) also found total quality management/customer care programmes to be among the most frequently identified employee involvement arrangements: these practices were present in 19 of the 25 companies they surveyed.

*Developing the individual*
➤ performance management
➤ staff appraisal schemes
➤ employee development programmes
➤ investors in people
➤ a qualified workforce.

All the employee involvement techniques that we have discussed contribute to the development of employees: better communication means that people are well-informed; encouragement to share ideas through consultation equates with encouragement to develop ideas rather than accept the status quo; financial participation increases awareness and knowledge of the economic performance of the company. Employee development extends the boundaries of knowledge, interest and understanding and enables each employee to feel more involved and more able to participate in decisions. Chapters 7 and 8 explore in detail all the practices listed above related to developing people and the contribution that they make to the organisation.

*Beyond the workplace*
➤ the community
➤ the environment.

The Employment Department (1994) proposed that attempts to make employees feel more committed should not be limited to activities at work. We have stated in other contexts, for instance with regard to human resource planning, that employers need to be aware of the community within which they operate, and this can mean the global community as well as the local community. A number of employers have empowered their staff to become involved in community initiatives such as working with schools or with disabled persons. This has the effect of increasing the loyalty of employees and strengthening the company's public image.

A similar argument is extended to environmental issues. If employers show concern for the environment and enlist employees in methods of protecting the environment, this is likely to gain loyalty and make employees proud to be associated with the organisation.

**The purpose of employee involvement**
We have discussed the rights of employees to be involved in making decisions that will affect them and touched on the motivational aspects of this, presenting these as reasons for pursuing a programme of employee involvement.

Another component that we should consider, however, is the economic imperative that must inform managerial decisions. The decision to increase employee involvement is, after all, initially a management decision, especially if we use the term to refer to voluntary activities rather than those that have been legislated. An important concept in terms of the expected motivational outcomes of employee involvement is employee commitment. The direct effect of involvement in the organisation is expected to be an increase in the individual employee's commitment to the workplace or the job, which will be reflected in increased productivity, lower labour turnover and reduced absenteeism. This constitutes the economic argument for encouraging employee involvement initiatives, and the ACAS Annual Report (1997a, p. 14) mentions research by Dr Mari Sako which offers some evidence that improvements in business performance are in fact an outcome of employee involvement.

The human resource management approach is intent on maximising the contribution of employees as a critical success factor, and increasing employee commitment through involvement is seen as a way to do this. There may, however, be some problems with the contention that involvement arrangements result in increased commitment. Commitment is an attitude, and the connection between attitudes and behaviour is not a straightforward one. Behaviour depends on a variety of influencing factors, including values and beliefs and what each individual sees as motivating factors, so attitudes are not always reflected in behaviour. For instance, if a person has a positive emotional reaction to a management innovation, we could say that that person may feel greater commitment to the job or the organisation. If, however, that person is influenced by co-workers who are not like-minded, and the person values his or her relationship with those co-workers, then the positive attitude may not be reflected in subsequent behaviour. In fact, the person may attempt to rationalise the positive feelings away. Employee involvement could therefore engender a positive attitude in some people and not in others, and even where it does result in positive attitudes it is only one feature of the workplace, and other influences could result in this positive attitude's not being reflected in the behaviour managers are hoping for. You will find a fuller explanation of these concepts in Cascio (1991).

This discussion of attitudes and behaviour is included just to sound a cautionary note that increases in commitment and productivity are not a foregone conclusion. In general, however, the introduction of employee involvement initiatives is welcomed by the workforce and results in a positive response. Some reactions will depend on the culture and relations that have traditionally existed either in a company or in a particular industry. If employees do not trust management, they will greet management initiatives with scepticism. If employers wish to encourage change in these circumstances, they will have to build trust, which can only be achieved in the long term. Companies should choose arrangements that best suit their individual situation, which is one of the reasons for the government's preference not to impose schemes, but rather to depend on encouraging employers to develop programmes voluntarily.

**Implications of employee involvement for management**

It is obvious from what we have said above that the introduction of employee involvement has implications for organisational culture and the managerial role. In its booklet *Effective Organisations: The People Factor*, ACAS (1997b) recommends an approach it calls 'quality of work life' (QWL), which is very similar to employee involvement. It describes the essential message of the booklet to be that:

> ... improved levels of organisational effectiveness and hence competitive edge can be achieved by further developing the contribution of people in organisations. This requires the development of more rewarding, satisfying, effective jobs and work environments both rooted in the active encouragement of involvement at all organisational levels. (ACAS 1997b, p. 6)

The booklet goes on to contrast QWL values, culture and job design with control values, culture and job design. Essentially the QWL approach equates with a programme of the initiatives we have described as employee involvement, whereas control implies that managers adopt a Theory X approach (which you will remember from Chapter 10), retain decision-making powers, and use Taylor's approach to job design. We should emphasise, however, that the ACAS view of QWL would entail a *programme* of involvement initiatives and not the pick-and-mix approach that Marchington *et al.* (1993) felt they sometimes encountered. The development of QWL requires commitment and a long-term perspective, and ACAS is prepared to assist employers in developing these systems as part of its mandate to improve industrial relations.

The empowerment of employees also calls for new skills on the part of both managers and employees. Managers who have been used to a control style may need training in the techniques of participative management, and employees may need confidence-building sessions and training in decision-making. A move away from a control culture and close supervision can also have an impact on organisational structures, and the traditional tall hierarchies with many reporting levels give way to the more modern, flatter structures towards which many organisations are moving.

ACTIVITY **13.1**
..................

You are the Head of Personnel at the headquarters of a national chain of supermarkets. The stores have always operated with a very hierarchical structure and a set of rigid rules. Major decisions about the business are made centrally by a board of senior executives, and only information that is deemed necessary is passed down the line to the next level of staff. The normal chain of command consists of a regional manager, a store manager, department managers and unit supervisors. Personnel at each level deal only with the level above them. Shop assistants expect explicit instructions from their supervisors, and will refer all matters to a supervisor if a question arises on which they have not been briefed. The extent of each person's authority is strictly defined, e.g. shop assistants cannot deal with returned items; unit supervisors are responsible for deciding when displays will change, what to display, and for maintaining the general tidiness of their area. All employees know their role and their limits, and managers and supervisors do not ask for opinions from their subordinates. This is accepted by all staff members, and everyone who has been with the company for any length of time is used to the way things are done.

A new chief executive has recently joined the company, and she is not pleased with the current way of running things. She asks you to investigate ways of changing the culture to improve the contribution from every employee, and to prepare a confidential report for her.

1 Draw up a list of the changes that could be made and how these changes would be implemented.
2 List the benefits to be gained if you try to implement your suggested changes, and the problems that may be encountered.

### Developing, implementing and evaluating an employee involvement programme

The IPM/IPA code (1990) provides an action plan for implementing involvement practices, and ACAS (1997b) provides a very useful generic model for implementing change which can be adapted and applied directly to involvement arrangements. An extended model adapted from the ACAS booklet is shown below.

*Stage 1*
Arrange initial meetings between management and employee representatives (elected by the workforce or designated by recognised trade unions) to explore ways of improving the current situation through employee involvement initiatives.

*Stage 2*
Reach agreement on the approach to be used, using a third party facilitator such as ACAS if necessary. Ensure that issues of communication to the workforce are included in the details agreed at this stage.

*Stage 3*
Set up a joint steering committee to develop a plan covering the selection, development, introduction and coordination of the employee involvement practices.

*Stage 4*
Through the steering committee, extend the planning stage to involve individuals and work groups to analyse problems and deal with particular issues.

*Stage 5*
Develop alternative solutions and approaches; evaluate feasibility; select the optimum solution.

*Stage 6*
Implement the practices, and provide any necessary preparation and training.

*Stage 7*
Evaluate the success of the new arrangements, and review the arrangements.

In stages 3–5 of the model there will inevitably be much emphasis on choosing which initiatives to pursue. There is no set model of employee involvement, so various combinations of techniques will be found in different organisations. Stage 5 of the model will probably be concerned with problems of the acceptability of various packages of practices and employee attitudes towards them, particularly if the past culture means that there is a fair amount of scepticism on the part of the workforce towards new measures.

**PAUSE FOR THOUGHT 13.5** *What factors will affect the choice of employee involvement initiatives in any particular organisation?*

Some of the factors that ought to be included when choosing the appropriate practices are:

➤ the preferences of the owners and managers
➤ the preferences of employees ascertained through consultation
➤ the past and desired culture of the organisation
➤ the suitability of certain measures to the type of organisation – non-profit organisations, for instance, would have to devise alternatives to share ownership schemes.

Whatever choices are made, there should be wholehearted acceptance and commitment on the part of all involved, but particularly on the part of management, to making the new practices work. ACAS (1997b) stresses that there has to be a long-term commitment; change will not happen overnight and a period of consultation, training and adjustment will be necessary.

Stage 2 mentions the possibility of involving a third party to help develop plans and solve problems. ACAS has a continuing mandate to work towards the improvement of industrial relations, and its officers have broad experience in helping organisations to promote employee involvement initiatives.

As you have seen, communication is both an employee involvement practice and a crucial component of the development, implementation and review stages. If you remember the communication model we discussed in Chapter 11 (p. 275–277), you will recall the important role that feedback plays in effective communication. One way of getting feedback is to use employee attitude or opinion surveys. This is especially appropriate to evaluate the effectiveness of employee involvement practices, since what employers are looking for are more productive attitudes, and surveys of this nature have themselves been identified as an involvement practice. They are appropriate both for identifying which kinds of initiatives employees would like to have and for monitoring the success of those initiatives once implemented. The survey should ask for employee opinions about what is most important and what should be done first, i.e. it should result in a prioritised list of what concerns employees.

ACTIVITY **13.2**

Examine the change model for developing, implementing and evaluating employee involvement initiatives. Review the communication model described in Chapter 11. Consider the issues addressed in the communication model as you review each step in the change model, and comment on what the communication model should alert you to when considered alongside the steps to be taken in the change model.

A further factor to be considered in implementing change of any kind is the training needed if managers and employees are to develop new roles and relationships. A range of additional skills might be required for some involvement practices, e.g. facilitators of and participants in quality circles need skills in the analysis and presentation of data, as already mentioned; team leaders need skills in eliciting input from people who are not used to sharing their views and who may therefore initially be hesitant to do so.

## Conclusion

We have discussed a range of management approaches to the workforce, and the implications that different philosophies have for the ways in which and the extent to which employees might be encouraged to participate in the decisions made in the workplace. The development of employee involvement initiatives and partnership deals is likely to be found in companies that espouse the tenets of human resource management. Through the use of involvement and partnership practices, these companies will attempt to maximise their employees' contribution to the achievement of organisational goals while also benefiting the employees themselves directly.

**REVIEW QUESTIONS**

Brief answers to these review questions are provided on page 429

1 Describe the two main philosophical approaches underlying management–employee relations, and comment on the likelihood of each of these espousing worker participation or employee involvement initiatives.

2 Explain the connection between employee involvement and employee commitment.

3 Describe the history of initiatives to improve employee consultation and information in the European Union.

4 Name the major components of partnership, and comment on its aims.

**SELF-CHECK QUESTIONS**

Answer the following multiple choice and short answer questions. The answers are provided on page 429 for you to check your understanding of this chapter.

1 Which of the following statements best describes the unitary perspective?

 (*a*) Managers expect all employees to espouse the organisation's goals. There are occasional conflicts of interest which managers settle by negotiation.

 (*b*) Managers espouse the organisation's goals and recognise that employees are likely to have their own set of interests. Differences in interests are regulated by negotiated agreements.

 (*c*) Managers expect all employees to espouse the organisation's goals. There are no conflicts of interest.

2 Participation and involvement are both ways of involving employees in the decisions made in the workplace. Match each term with the correct statement below.

 (*a*) _____ means that employees have input into decisions that affect their own jobs.

 (*b*) _____ means that employees have input through representatives to decisions made at a strategic level.

3 Participation is the method that you are most likely to find in unitarist organisations. (TRUE or FALSE?)

4 What is the threshold number of employees at which the European Directive on Works Councils obliges a community-scale company to establish a works council?

5 Which of the following statements are NOT true?

   (*a*) The Labour Government actively promotes partnership deals in the workplace.

   (*b*) Partnership deals can only be made when the workforce is not unionised.

   (*c*) Partnership deals can be made in both unionised and non-unionised companies.

   (*d*) Partnership deals can only be made in a unionised environment.

6 Which of the following was not named specifically by the Employment Department as a technique for promoting employee involvement?

   (*a*) quality circles

   (*b*) peer appraisal

   (*c*) team briefing

   (*d*) profit-related pay.

7 Managers can confidently expect that employee commitment to work will be a direct result of employee involvement initiatives and will lead to improved motivation and productivity. (TRUE or FALSE?)

8 What does the acronym ESOP stand for?

9 Which techniques did the Employment Department identify as being part of sharing information?

10 Which of the following has NOT specifically been identified as a standard component of partnership agreements.

   (*a*) improvements in job security

   (*b*) fair wages for employees

   (*c*) consultation on matters affecting employees

   (*d*) provision of flexible benefits.

## References

Advisory, Conciliation and Arbitration Service. *Annual Report*. ACAS, 1997a.

Advisory, Conciliation and Arbitration Service. *Effective Organisations: The People Factor*. ACAS, 1997b.

Allen, Michael. All-inclusive. *People Management*, 11 June 1998, 36–42.

Beardwell, Ian. Voices on. *People Management*, 28 May 1998, 32–36.

Bennett, Roger. *Employee Relations*. Pitman, 1994.

Cascio, Wayne F. *Applied Psychology in Personnel Management*. 4th edition, Prentice Hall, 1991.

Coupar, Willy and Stevens, Brian. Towards a new model of industrial partnership: Beyond the 'HRM versus industrial relations' argument. In: Sparrow, Paul and Marchington, Mick (eds). *Human Resource Management: The New Agenda*. Financial Times Pitman Publishing, 1998.

Department of Employment. *The Competitive Edge: Employee Involvement in Britain*. Employment Department, 1994.

*Fairness at Work*. Government White Paper, May 1998. (The paper can be viewed on the Internet at http://www.dti.gov.uk/IR/fairness/fore.htm)

Farnham, David and Pimlott, John. *Understanding Industrial Relations*. 5th edition, Cassell, 1995.

Fox, Alan. *Beyond Contract: Work Power and Trust Relations*. Faber & Faber, 1974.

Gold, Michael and Hall, Mark. Statutory European Works Councils: The final countdown? *Industrial Relations Journal*, Vol. 5, No. 3, September 1994, 177–186.

Hackman, J. Richard and Oldham, Greg R. *Work Redesign*. Addison-Wesley, 1980.

Herzberg, F., Mausner, B. and Snyderman, B. *The Motivation to Work*. John Wiley & Sons, 1959.

Institute of Personnel and Development. *Employee Relations into the 21st Century: An IPD Position Paper*. IPD, 1997.

Institute of Personnel Management and Involvement and Participation Association. *Employee Involvement and Participation in the United Kingdom: The IPA/IPM Code*. IPM and IPA, 1990.

Marchington, Mick. Partnership in context: towards a European model? In: Sparrow, Paul and Marchington, Mick (eds). *Human Resource Management: The New Agenda*. Financial Times Pitman Publishing, 1998.

Marchington, M., Wilkinson, A. and Ackers, P. Waving or drowning in participation? *Personnel Management*, March 1993, 46–50.

McGlynn, Clare. European Works Councils: towards industrial democracy? *Industrial Law Journal*, Vol. 24 No. 1, March 1995, 78–84.

Mill, Cherry. The long road to employee involvement. *Personnel Management*, February 1991, 26–27.

Monks, John. Trade unions, enterprise and the future. In: Sparrow, Paul and Marchington, Mick (eds). *Human Resource Management: The New Agenda*. Financial Times Pitman Publishing, 1998.

Taylor, Frederick Winslow. *The Principles of Scientific Management*. Harper, 1911.

Trist, E. and Murray, H. (eds). *The Social Engagement of Social Science: A Tavistock Anthology*. Vol. II: The Socio-Technical Perspective. University of Pennsylvania Press, 1993.

## Further study
················

### *Books*

Advisory, Conciliation and Arbitration Service. *Employee Communications and Consultation*. ACAS, 1997.

Bennett, Roger. *Employee Relations*. Pitman, 1994. (Part of the M+E Handbook series, this book provides a concise introduction to a wide range of employee relations issues. Chapter 6 deals with employee participation.)

Guest, David and Peccei, Riccardo. *The Partnership Company: Benchmarks for the Future*. Involvement and Participation Association, 1998. (The report summarises the results of research into companies that use the partnership approach.)

Involvement and Participation Association. *Towards Industrial Partnership: A New Approach to Relationships at Work*. IPA, 1993.

Institute of Personnel Management. *Quality: People Management Matters*. IPM, 1993. (Reviews the techniques used to achieve quality and provides several case studies of UK companies.)

Sparrow, Paul and Marchington, Mick (eds). *Human Resource Management: The New Agenda*. Financial Times Pitman Publishing, 1998. (Part 2 of this book. 'Developing partnership and employee voice', contains six excellent chapters giving different perspectives on partnership.)

### *Articles*

Arkin, Anat. Personnel management in Germany: At work in the powerhouse of Europe. *Personnel Management*, February 1992, 32–35. (Includes a brief review of the structures for employee participation in German companies. First in a series about personnel management in the EC member states apart from the UK.)

First British European Works Councils established. *Industrial Relations Review and Report*, No. 574, December 1994, 4–7. (A description of the EWCs set up by BP Oil Europe and United Biscuits, involving UK employees even before the directive was adopted by the UK.)

Fowler, Alan. How to manage cultural change. *Personnel Management Plus*, November 1993, 25–26.

Fowler, Alan. How to manage suggestion schemes. *Personnel Management Plus*, July 1994, 28–29.

Fowler, Alan. How to plan and use attitude surveys. *Personnel Management Plus*, June 1993, 25–26. (The 'How to . . .' articles provide some helpful practical advice on activities that might be included in starting up an employee involvement programme.)

Hilton, Phil. The key to staff commitment. *Personnel Management Plus*, June 1993, 18–19. (Examines the relationship between involvement and commitment.)

McGlynn, Clare. European Works Councils: towards industrial democracy? *Industrial Law Journal*, Vol. 24 No. 1, March 1995, 78–84. (An explanatory note outlining the background to the European Works Council Directive and the position of companies in Britain. This issue of the journal is a special issue entitled 'Towards 1996: A Review of European Labour Law'.)

McNeish, Keith. How to implement share schemes. *People Management*, 24 July 1997, 38–40.

O'Reilly, Noel. Question Time. *Personnel Today*, 6 December 1994, 22–23. (Describes how companies are using opinion surveys to involve employees and manage change.)

Pendleton, A., McDonald, J., Robinson, A. and Wilson, N. The impact of employee share ownership plans on employee participation and industrial democracy. *Human Resource Management Journal*, Vol. 5 No. 4, Summer 1995, 44–60. (For anyone who wishes to investigate financial participation in more detail.)

Pickard, Jane. The real meaning of empowerment. *Personnel Management*, November 1993, 28–33. (An examination of empowerment techniques and the resultant feelings of involvement, with examples from three British companies.)

We're in this together: profit-sharing schemes. *IRS Employment Review*, March 1998. (Report of a survey of the financial participation schemes in 40 organisations.)

### *Audio-visual*

Executive Business Club. *Valuing People, Part Two: Motivation*. EBC, 1992. (Video.) (The initial ten minutes of this video are of particular interest on the topic of involvement. Pete Wickens, then Director of Personnel and Information Systems at Nissan, gives his views on involvement at Nissan. The rest of the video provides an interesting background discussion of motivation in the workplace.)

BBC2. *Working All Hours*. A Money Programme Special. BBC News and Current Affairs, 1995. (Two programmes transmitted in September 1995 about the effects of job insecurity on employee motivation. The first programme contains a segment on employee involvement at Rover.)

# CHAPTER 14

# Discipline and grievance

## Objectives:

*By the end of this chapter you will be able to:*

➤ understand the meaning of the terms 'discipline' and 'grievance'

➤ understand the role of human resource managers and line managers in discipline and grievance handling

➤ explain the importance of the ACAS *Code of Disciplinary Practice and Procedures in Employment* and the ACAS advisory handbook

➤ describe the main stages in a disciplinary procedure and in a grievance procedure

➤ write appropriate letters for a disciplinary procedure

➤ design a simple disciplinary and grievance procedure.

In any organisation, however good the management and however highly motivated the workforce, there will be occasions when problems or difficulties occur between management and employees. In order that employees are able to work to their optimum performance and that these problems do not turn into even bigger issues, suitable ways of dealing with them need to be devised before they occur. If the problem has arisen from something that management has done, this may result in the employee concerned having a grievance. If, however, it is a problem arising from the behaviour or attitude of an employee, then disciplinary action may be called for.

Human resource managers are concerned to get the best out of people, and although the human resource approach tends towards a dislike of rules and procedures, in favour of a more individualised approach, there are times when this is not possible because of the need to comply with legislation or Codes of Practice. This is the case where discipline and grievance are concerned. While discipline and grievances are individual issues, it would be unfair to treat each case in a totally different way, and to do so might result in a claim for unfair dismissal against the organisation, or dissatisfaction among the workforce. Human resource managers need to consider these issues and design suitable procedures in order to enhance both the performance management process within the organisation and to enable employees to contribute fully to the strategic objectives of the organisation.

## Discipline: an introduction

The *Shorter Oxford English Dictionary* defines discipline in the following ways: 'To subject to discipline; in earlier use, to educate or train; later, to bring under control.' The term 'discipline', as we can see from this definition, can be used in various ways. It can refer to self-discipline, where an individual as a result of practice and training works in a ordered, self-controlled way, or is trained by others to work in a certain way, or it can be used to refer to the need to discipline someone by pointing out to them the error of their ways or by punishing them for mistakes that they have made. Human resource managers are concerned to motivate people to ensure they reach their maximum potential, and the adoption of a punitive approach is unlikely to facilitate much motivation.

Students dealing with case studies about disciplinary situations often tend to respond initially by enjoying the power to punish and often want to dismiss the alleged offenders. Sometimes new, inexperienced managers may adopt the same approach. In reality this approach is likely to prove counter-productive, as valuable staff who have been costly to recruit and train would be lost, and the motivation of everyone concerned would be low. Handling a disciplinary situation in an unfair way may result in the employee being dismissed, but this might also result in a case for unfair dismissal being brought against the organisation. This could be expensive if the company lost, and in any case would be expensive in terms of:

➤ the time needed to prepare for the tribunal
➤ the time lost
➤ disruption caused as witnesses are called
➤ the bad publicity for the organisation itself
➤ the poor employee relations likely to ensue because of unfair handling of a disciplinary situation.

In order to try to minimise these problems and to encourage employers to handle disciplinary offences in a fair and reasonable manner, ACAS published a code of practice in 1977 and ten years later an advisory handbook, Discipline at Work. A discussion of these will help to clarify what is meant by discipline and what are the correct procedures.

### *The ACAS code of practice concerning disciplinary procedures*

Since the Employment Protection Act 1975, the Advisory Conciliation and Arbitration Service (ACAS) has had the right to publish codes of practice, and in 1977 it published *Code of Practice 1: Disciplinary Practice and Procedures in Employment*. This aims to help all who may be concerned with this topic by providing practical advice about handling disciplinary procedures. A code of practice has an interesting status in law. An employer cannot have an unfair dismissal case brought against it in an Industrial Tribunal just because it has not carried out a procedure as stated in the code of practice, but it would ignore the code of practice at its peril, as failure to comply with it is likely to be used as part of the evidence against it in an unfair dismissal case.

In the code, ACAS clearly states that although disciplinary rules are likely to be mainly designed by management, other groups such as trade unions, line managers and employees should also have a part to play in formulating them. ACAS emphasises the fact that the main reason for having disciplinary rules is to promote fairness and set standards of conduct, and to provide a fair method of dealing with alleged offences. If the rules have merely been designed by management without the involvement of other interested parties, employees may be more cynical about management's motives and individuals may feel that when they are disciplined it is because of victimisation, or because their supervisor dislikes them. In order for the disciplinary procedure to be credible to employees, it is clearly in management's interests to involve them in its design. Good employers will certainly appreciate this need.

Other employers, however, may merely be motivated in their provision of a disciplinary procedure by the need to comply with the legislation. The Employment Rights Act 1996 requires employers who employ 20 or more employees to provide them with a copy of their disciplinary procedure within two months of the commencement of their employment.

These factors should prove sufficient to motivate the employer to provide a disciplinary procedure but, if not, in the last resort some employers may be motivated by the fact that they may need evidence that they have acted fairly and followed a fair procedure in the event of an alleged unfair dismissal claim before an industrial tribunal. For whatever reason, it is obviously important to adopt a clear disciplinary procedure so that both the employer and the employees know what standards of conduct are expected and what may happen if these standards are not achieved.

### The essential features of a disciplinary procedure

The ACAS Code of Practice (1977) lists the following as essential features of a disciplinary procedure.

'Disciplinary procedures should:

➤ be in writing
➤ specify to whom they apply
➤ provide for matters to be dealt with quickly
➤ indicate the disciplinary actions which may be taken
➤ specify the levels of management which have the authority to take the various forms of disciplinary action, ensuring that immediate superiors do not normally have the power to dismiss without reference to senior management
➤ provide for individuals to be informed of the complaints against them, and to be given the opportunity to state their case before decisions are reached
➤ give individuals the right to be accompanied by a trade union representative or fellow employee of their choice
➤ ensure that, except for cases of gross misconduct, no employees are dismissed for a first breach of discipline
➤ ensure that disciplinary action is not taken until the case has been carefully investigated
➤ ensure that individuals are given an explanation for any penalty imposed
➤ provide a right of appeal and specify the procedure to be followed.' (ACAS Code of Practice, Paragraph 10.)

It may seem obvious that rules should be in writing and should specify to whom they apply, and that disciplinary issues should be dealt with quickly. If they are not written down people will remember the rules differently, and varying approaches to discipline will occur. Employees may be uncertain as to what they can and can't do, and supervisors and managers may adopt different approaches to discipline between different departments, with some supervisors unsure of what action they have the power to take.

In some cases it may be legitimate to have different rules for different departments. A catering department is likely to have rules about hygiene that are not likely to be as relevant to a transport department. So the rules should specify to whom they apply.

It is necessary to indicate what disciplinary actions may be taken so that there is a level of consistency and employees know what misdemeanours are regarded as serious by management. In order to be fair, the employee should know of the case against them and have an opportunity to state their case and, if they want, have a trade union official or a friend accompany them.

Employees can make genuine mistakes, and it is extremely expensive to recruit and train staff. On these grounds alone it pays to be fair to employees and to avoid dismissing them wherever possible. In order to give employees a fair chance it is important not to dismiss anyone for a first breach of discipline, unless it is a case of gross misconduct. This ensures that the individual has a chance to learn from his or her mistake.

Management may also occasionally make mistakes, and the employee may not have committed a disciplinary offence at all. To prevent someone being disciplined for something they did not do, it is important to ensure that no disciplinary action is taken before a full investigation into the alleged offence has been carried out.

If employees are to learn from their mistakes, then they need to be very clear about what they did wrong, how to do it right, and also to have a clear explanation of any penalties imposed. It is still possible that in spite of all these precautions occasionally management may make a mistake in disciplining a person. In order to remedy this and to ensure that people don't feel that they are being disciplined just because their supervisor doesn't like them, it is important to have an appeal procedure that is made known to them.

### Discipline at work: the ACAS advisory handbook

In 1987 ACAS produced a handbook intended to complement the code of practice and to provide more detailed practical guidance. This does not have the same legal status as the code of practice, which has been reprinted and is contained within the handbook, but gives advice based on developments in case law since the original code of practice was produced and gives several examples of good practice for both large and small employers. It shows a recognition of the fact that there is an increasing degree of complexity in disciplinary cases, and provides advice on specific situations such as cases arising from poor performance and from absences.

The handbook also makes clear that, as well as the 11 features listed in the code of practice, a disciplinary procedure should possess the following characteristics.

➤ It should apply to everyone, regardless of their length of employment. This would ensure that new employees, who may not have the length of service to bring an unfair dismissal claim, are also treated fairly.
➤ It should be non-discriminatory and apply to everyone regardless of their sex, marital status or race.

> ➤ If there is an investigatory period during which the employee is suspended from work, the disciplinary procedure should ensure that this period of suspension is with pay and that there is clear guidance as to how the pay should be calculated.
>
> ➤ If in rare circumstances suspension without pay is used as a punishment, this should be clearly specified in the person's contract.
>
> ➤ The procedure should ensure that, if there are disputes about the facts of the case, no disciplinary penalty should be imposed until there has been a full investigation which has concluded that the balance of probability was that the employee in question has committed the offence.

### Discipline at Work: the ACAS self-help guide to producing discipline and grievance procedures

In 1997 ACAS produced this self-help guide designed to complement the handbook and give practical help for those involved in the design and operation of both discipline and grievance procedures. The guide helps by giving examples of both formal disciplinary and grievance procedures but also emphasises the importance of the informal process in both discipline and grievance handling.

The ACAS code of practice, advisory handbook and self-help guide all add a great deal to our understanding of disciplinary procedures, and help to ensure that the organisations which follow them have procedures that are fair and just and are likely to contribute to the organisation's achieving its aim of getting the optimum performance from its human resources.

### Grievance: an introduction
••••••••••••••••••••••••••••••••

The *Shorter Oxford English Dictionary* defines grievance as: 'The infliction of wrong or hardship on a person; injury, oppression; a cause or source of injury.' When referring to grievances it is useful to follow the approach of Pigors and Myers (1977) and identify the strength of the feeling about the behaviour or attitude of management that has resulted in injury, and how this is then expressed. Pigors and Myers distinguish between dissatisfaction, complaint and grievance.

> Dissatisfaction: anything that disturbs an employee, whether or not he expresses his unrest in words.
> Complaint: a spoken or written dissatisfaction, brought to the attention of the supervisor and/or shop steward.
> Grievance: a complaint which has been formally presented to a management representative or to a union official. (Pigors and Myers, 1977, p. 229.)

We shall use the term 'grievance' in this way as a form of dissatisfaction about which the employee feels sufficiently strongly that he or she formally raises the issue with his or her management representative or shop steward.

There are no codes of practice or advisory handbooks concerning the handling of grievances which, as defined above, are complaints formally presented to a shop steward or to management. Grievances may arise for a multitude of reasons. An employee may become dissatisfied with his or her hours of work or working conditions, he or she may feel a supervisor shows unfair favouritism to others, or may feel dissatisfaction about pay or sexual harassment. Some grievances may appear trivial and others, such as alleged sexual harassment, may be very serious, but to the employee concerned they will all have been serious enough to raise formally.

Some grievances may become a collective issue, with negotiations between management and a trade union arising over an issue such as a collective grievance about pay or working conditions. This chapter will focus solely on grievance as an individual issue.

### Reasons for having a grievance procedure

Employees need to know how they can raise a grievance and seek redress for any grievance that they might have. They need to feel confident that their grievance will be treated in a fair way and that they will get to know the result of raising this grievance within a short period of time. It is also important to settle the grievance quickly, to prevent it becoming a larger grievance that involves more people and takes longer to resolve.

The Employment Rights Act 1996 provides a legal requirement for employers who have at least 20 employees to supply a copy of their grievance procedure to all employees, within two months of the start of their employment. This includes temporary employees if they are going to be employed for more than two months.

If there were no procedure for raising and resolving grievances, it would be likely that employees would grumble to colleagues, and not only their work but the work of the department would be liable to suffer as a result. Therefore the main aim of the grievance procedure is to settle disputes fairly and as near to the source of grievance as possible. If there were a grievance over an issue such as safety or harassment, failure to provide a mechanism to deal with the grievance could result in serious repercussions, with perhaps accidents or a sexual or racial harassment case occurring. A grievance procedure in effect provides a safety mechanism to prevent issues from getting out of control. It also ensures that management have a channel to hear about issues that may be worrying their staff.

### Discipline versus grievance

Disciplinary action is, as we have seen, normally initiated by management to express dissatisfaction with, and bring about changes in, employee behaviour; grievance, on the other hand, is normally initiated by employees for similar reasons, but in respect of management's, or perhaps co-workers', behaviour. There is a need for fairness and justice in both procedures although they are initiated by different parties. Because of this it is sometimes claimed that they are the opposites of each other, and should be viewed as complementary processes in industrial justice.

**PAUSE FOR THOUGHT 14.1**   *Consider what you have just learned about grievance and discipline. In what ways do you consider discipline and grievance to be opposites? Are there any facts which make you think that they are not truly opposites?*

As we have shown, discipline and grievance are both concerned with fairness and justice. They differ in that the people who initiate the action in each case differ. The management initiates disciplinary action against employees, and employees initiate grievances mainly against their supervisors and managers. In this way they may be considered to be opposite faces of industrial justice. However, this disregards the balance of power in these cases. To consider them to be true opposites would entail the assumption that when an employee initiates a grievance they have the same amount of power as management, which is clearly not the case. An employee who has a grievance will not be able to insist that action is taken against the person who has caused the grievance, and will have to rely on management's willingness to take action.

### *The role of the human resource manager*

Discipline and grievances are sensitive issues requiring skilful handling, and in many organisations they have traditionally been an area that has been left to human resource managers. This has been partly due to the fact that the human resource managers were likely to be trained in skilful handling of sensitive interpersonal issues, but also many managers and supervisors were often unwilling to tackle something that might result in their unpopularity and cause difficulties in maintaining a suitable relationship with someone they had to work with on a daily basis. This attitude has changed considerably in recent years, as more and more of the human resource function has been devolved to line management; line managers in many organisations are nowadays expected to handle any discipline or grievance situations that arise in their section, at least in the early stages. Human resource managers still have several important roles to play, however:

➤   in devising the procedures
➤   in providing specialist advice
➤   in ensuring that everyone is aware of the procedures and acts consistently
➤   in ensuring that line managers are suitably trained
➤   in monitoring the effectiveness of the procedures.

The ACAS Code of Practice recommends that grievance and disciplinary machinery should be kept separate, although some organisations do provide for an appeal against a disciplinary action being handled through the general grievance procedure. We have now discussed the nature of both grievance and disciplinary procedures, and at this point we shall follow the advice of ACAS and discuss each separately in more detail.

## Discipline
············

### *Disciplinary offences*

It would be impossible to itemise fully the range of behaviour that might result in disciplinary action being taken. Employers seem to regard the more common offences as being issues about absenteeism or timekeeping or poor performance at work. There may also be concern about a range of issues including failure to obey organisation rules, such as rules about health and safety, theft, sexism, racism, problems arising from fighting or threatening behaviour, and alcohol or drug abuse. Many employers divide offences into two categories depending on the seriousness with which they are viewed within that organisation. They list issues that they regard as disciplinary offences, and then itemise as gross misconduct further offences that they consider to be more serious. These offences may be handled in different ways, depending on the seriousness with which the organisation views them.

**PAUSE FOR THOUGHT 14.2** *Consider any organisation that you know reasonably well, perhaps one where you have worked yourself.*

1   *What disciplinary rules did the organisation have?*
2   *How were these disciplinary rules made known to you?*
3   *What were considered to be disciplinary offences?*
4   *Were there any offences that were regarded as particularly serious in this organisation and that constituted gross misconduct? List these.*
5   *Compare your list with the list made by someone who has experience in a different organisation. Can you find reasons for the differences and similarities?*

It is probable that there were disciplinary rules in most organisations and these were made known to you, either informally by your supervisor telling you about them or, more likely, by you being given or shown a copy of them as part of your induction to your new job. It is likely that in most organisations there will also be a list of offences that might constitute gross misconduct. When you compare your list with that of a friend who has worked in a different organisation, you will probably have listed many of the same offences as ones that constituted gross misconduct. Theft, dishonesty, verbal or physical abuse are likely to be regarded as serious in most organisations. It is also probable that there will then be some variation in your lists as to what else constitutes an offence, depending on the attitudes in that particular organisation and the nature of the work done there. If there is a serious concern about fire hazards, then smoking in an unauthorised place may constitute gross misconduct. This is often of concern in retail organisations, where there might be a danger to large numbers of staff and customers and where some goods sold may be easily flammable. Organisations involved in food preparation may be particularly concerned with hygiene, and may list offences concerning lack of personal hygiene as ones that could constitute gross misconduct.

**PAUSE FOR THOUGHT 14.3** *Tim Hancock has worked for your organisation for nearly a year. He has in general been a good employee, but you have noticed that recently he has started to arrive about 10 minutes late for work each morning. You are his supervisor. Describe the action you would take.*

The way in which you, as Tim's supervisor, choose to deal with this situation depends on a number of factors. First there is your own attitude to this issue, but there is also the attitude of the organisation to issues of poor timekeeping to consider. You may have personal views about this but you need to act in a way that is consistent with the organisation's views. Personally you may not feel too concerned about this issue as long as the work gets done, or you may take the view that it is a form of dishonesty when an employee steals time from an employer. In some organisations this may not be viewed as a problem at all. Employees may have the opportunity to create their own flexi-time system without management worrying unduly about this. However, the views of the organisation will be expressed in its disciplinary procedure, and it is likely that poor timekeeping will be an area of concern. If that is the case you, as Tim's manager, have to do something about Tim's lateness. It is not as yet a particularly serious offence, but it has the potential to become more serious if left unchecked. There may of course be a perfectly good reason why Tim has suddenly started to arrive slightly late for work. The first thing that needs to be done is for you to have a chat with Tim about it and try to find out the reason for this change in behaviour. This can be informal. It gives Tim the opportunity to explain, and also lets him know that you are aware of his lateness and are concerned about it. If he has a good reason then you will have to consider your reaction. If there is illness at home, this is likely to be a temporary situation, and you may reach an arrangement with Tim about his time of arrival for a limited period of time which can be reviewed at a later date. If the problem is related to a change in a public transport timetable, you may have to consider whether you can be flexible or not.

**PAUSE FOR THOUGHT 14.4** *Jasmine has worked for your organisation for nearly five years. Her work has always been good, but recently you have received many complaints from customers about the goods that they have ordered being late or not being received at all. You check through the records and find that all these delays can be traced back to orders that Jasmine has dealt with. You are Jasmine's manager. How will you deal with this situation?*

As Jasmine's manager you will have to take some action about her poor quality of work since it is causing problems to customers, and there have been complaints. However, you know that Jasmine has always been a good worker so you need to talk to her about the problem and try to find out what the cause is. Once again, you need to have an informal chat with her to find out the cause of the problem and then decide on the action to take. You may find that there is a perfectly good reason, such as a problem relating to home life, for the change in the standard of her work. If this is the case then a counselling interview is likely to be most appropriate. If, however, there doesn't appear to be a clear reason, an informal discussion which lets Jasmine know of your concerns and reaches agreement about expected improvements should suffice.

### *The informal disciplinary procedure*

In both these situations we have recommended that initially the supervisor should have an informal discussion with the employee concerned. This will give them a chance to state their case and enable you, as their manager, to do something to try to resolve the problem. This, in many cases, will be all that is needed. In many organisations disciplinary cases never get beyond this informal stage, and nothing more than an informal discussion is needed. Many organisations would regard this as a stage where, rather than disciplining an employee, a counselling approach would be more useful. ACAS uses the word 'counselling' in a slightly different sense from the way in which we have described it earlier in this book (Chapter 11): it recommends counselling rather than the disciplinary interview as a good way of resolving problems. ACAS says that counselling 'should take the form of a discussion with the objective of encouraging and helping the employee to improve.' (ACAS 1987). This differs from our definition of counselling, where the manager is concerned not to interfere or impose his or her own views or opinions on the employee. The ACAS use of the term implies rather more direction from the manager than true counselling. For this reason it is perhaps better to refer to this stage of discussion as an informal discussion and part of the informal disciplinary procedure. It may be that this informal discussion does involve the manager or supervisor in giving some direct advice about behaviour. The right word at the right time may do much to help deal with a breach of discipline, but it is not the same as counselling in the sense that we have used it previously. The *ACAS Self-help Guide to Producing Disciplinary and Grievance Procedures* (1997) emphasises the point that it is important that managers, supervisors and employees are all aware of the difference between an informal 'telling-off' or informal discussion and action which occurs as part of the formal disciplinary procedure.

It may be necessary to hold a true counselling interview if the individual's work is suffering as a result of personal problems. In this case the supervisor or manager should certainly not be telling individuals what to do, but should seek to help them to work through their problem and find their own solution appropriate for them. In either case, there is a need for an informal stage before getting into the disciplinary procedure proper. If the poor timekeeping or poor work is due to a problem outside work, then counselling is likely to be more appropriate than a disciplinary approach. However, sometimes this may not work and there may be a repeat of the offence or the work may not improve. In this circumstance it is likely that the manager will have to use the formal disciplinary procedure.

Organisations need to have clear disciplinary procedures to set standards for behaviour and in order to ensure fair treatment for those who are alleged to have broken the rules. We should distinguish here between the informal procedures, already discussed, and the formal disciplinary procedure. The most common stages in the formal procedure are given in the next section.

### *The formal disciplinary procedure*

This will be set out in writing and needs to fulfil the criteria already discussed as essential features of a disciplinary procedure. There should be several sections to the procedure itself. These will vary according to the size of the organisation, but are likely to include:

1   the purpose and scope of the procedure
2   the principles that underlie the procedure
3   the stages in the procedure itself
4   the nature of gross misconduct
5   the appeals procedure.

### The purpose of the procedure

The disciplinary procedure is likely first of all to explain why a disciplinary procedure is needed. It will probably indicate that the aim of the procedure is to help all employees to achieve high standards of conduct, attendance and job performance. It will also indicate what action should be taken if there is a breach of disciplinary rules, and refer to the need for fairness and consistency for all. It would also be useful to emphasise here the fact that the formal disciplinary procedure should only be started if discussions under the informal procedure have failed to bring about the requisite change in behaviour.

### The principles that underlie the procedure

This section is likely to include a list of several of the essential principles that ACAS gives for a disciplinary procedure. This may vary in detail according to the size and nature of the organisation concerned. For example, in a small organisation where a simple disciplinary procedure is required, it might say that

1   the procedure is to investigate fully the offence, and no action will be taken until this investigation has been completed
2   to ensure fairness the employee concerned will have an opportunity to state his or her case and be represented by a trade union representative or friend if so desired
3   the employee will have a right of appeal at any stage against disciplinary action that may be taken.

### The stages in the procedure

The disciplinary procedure normally includes the stages listed below. In some cases, where an offence is perhaps more serious, there should be a provision to bypass a stage and move to the next stage of the procedure. The most common stages in a disciplinary procedure are likely to be as follows:

1   oral warning
2   written warning
3   final written warning
4   dismissal.

*Stage 1 – Oral warning*

If there is no improvement after an informal talk, then the manager may need to invoke the organisation's disciplinary procedure. The first stage of this is normally to conduct a formal disciplinary interview and, if necessary, issue an oral warning. Care should be taken by managers not to start with an informal chat which turns into a oral warning. If a manager or supervisor is likely to issue an oral warning, then the employee concerned needs to be made aware that this could be the case and that they have a right, enshrined within the disciplinary procedure, to have a trade union representative or perhaps a friend to accompany them and speak for them, or at least act as a witness for them.

An oral warning should always be recorded so that there is a record of the date of the warning, the fact that it was an oral warning and the nature of the offence. This is a difference between the oral warning and the informal chat. The informal procedure might just be noted in the manager's diary to remind him or her about what happened, but it is not going to be quoted in evidence against the employee at a future date. The oral warning may have to be referred to at a later date, so even though it sounds like a contradiction in terms, an oral warning should be written down on the employee's record. To avoid a dispute, some organisations not only record the date and nature of the offence on the employee's record but also send the employee concerned a letter confirming the nature of the oral warning.

**PAUSE FOR THOUGHT 14.5** *Consider once again Pause for thought 14.3. If after the informal chat or chats there were still no improvement in Tim's timekeeping his manager would be likely to issue an oral warning.*

*Stage 2 – Written warning*

If the behaviour does not change after the first oral warning, then it may be necessary to hold a further disciplinary interview and if necessary to issue an official written warning. The disciplinary interview will be held so that the employee can state his/her case, and once again they will be invited to have a friend or their trade union representative present. This will be recorded and a letter will be sent to the employee concerned about the offence.

ACTIVITY **14.1**

Imagine that you are the manager of Tim Hancock and that Tim is still having problems with his timekeeping. He has been late five times this month already, and you issued him with an oral warning nearly three months ago. Prior to this you had several informal discussions with him about his timekeeping. He freely admits that he has a very active social life with lots of late nights, and just isn't very good at getting up in the mornings.

Write a written warning letter to Tim Hancock.

### Discussion of Activity 14.1

The letter that you write to Tim Hancock should state that it is a written warning and should indicate the nature of the disciplinary offence and the standard of behaviour that is required. You should also indicate the time-scale during which an improvement, is expected and the consequence of a failure to make the required improvement as well as stating that there is a right of appeal. An example is included, in Appendix 1 at the end of this chapter, for you to compare your letter with.

*Stage 3 – Final written warning*
If Tim Hancock still ignores the disciplinary interview and letter that you issued giving him a written warning, then the next stage is to conduct a further disciplinary interview which may result in the issue of a final written warning. Once again at the disciplinary interview he could be represented by his trade union representative and he will have an opportunity to state his case. If he does not have an acceptable reason for his poor timekeeping he will be clearly warned that he will receive a final written warning, and if there is no improvement then he will be dismissed. This letter will be kept on his file for a specified period of time and he will be advised of the appeals procedure. A sample letter is given in Appendix 2 at the end of this chapter.

*Discussion of letter of final written warning*
In this instance the warning has been issued by the human resource manager. As stated earlier, supervisors and managers increasingly take responsibility for disciplinary issues relating to their workforce. In some instances the human resource manager may be involved in the final stages of the procedure, but in others the manager may be responsible for issuing the final written warning after checking with the human resource manager that everything has been done correctly.

## The nature of gross misconduct

As we said earlier, organisations will have different ideas as to what constitutes gross misconduct. The employee should be given some indication of this also in the disciplinary procedure. It is impossible to design a list that covers all possibilities, but the organisation should list some of them. For example, the procedure may say that the following constitute gross misconduct and if any employee, after a full investigation, is found guilty of any of these offences he or she will be dismissed, even for a first offence:

➤ theft
➤ deliberate damage to company property
➤ fraud
➤ incapacity to work because of the influence of illegal drugs or alcohol
➤ physical assault
➤ sexual harassment
➤ racial harassment
➤ serious infringement of health and safety rules.

These are examples of offences that normally constitute gross misconduct, but it is not an exhaustive list and other serious offences may also constitute gross misconduct and merit dismissal.

It is also a good idea to state the company's position on criminal offences committed outside employment. There should be a statement in the disciplinary procedure indicating that a criminal offence which occurs outside of employment may be considered as gross misconduct and may result in dismissal. The word 'may' should be stressed here, as this is not an automatic reason for dismissal. The main considerations should be the nature of the offence and the type of work that the employee normally does, and whether the offence makes the employee unsuitable for his or her job.

In these cases, the employee concerned will normally be suspended from work on full pay, while a full investigation is being carried out.

### Appeals

The last section of the disciplinary procedure should indicate what the employee should do if he or she is not happy with the action taken against him or her. There should be a clear appeal procedure, with time limits for the submission of appeals stated.

### Suspension without pay

Before actually dismissing an employee, some organisations have an additional stage and use suspension without pay as a punishment. This needs to be clearly explained in the company's disciplinary procedure and in the employee's contract of employment if it is to be used, and it should be for no more than five working days. It is unlikely to be a particularly appropriate deterrent for an employee who tends to take time off work. It is clearly punitive in effect, so it is unlikely to be very motivating, but within some organisations it is seen as a last resort before dismissal is considered. It should also be clearly differentiated from suspension in order to investigate an alleged offence. In the latter case the suspension is to allow time for investigations to be carried out or to remove an employee from a difficult situation: there should be no stigma attached to it and it should be on full pay. When suspension is used in a punitive form it is without pay.

### The need for a record of warnings issued

Notice that in each of the letters sent to Tim Hancock, including, we hope, the written warning letter you wrote to him, it states that the warning will be recorded on Tim's file for a set period of time. The periods of time used in Tim Hancock's case were three months for each stage, but this will vary between organisations. It may perhaps be three months for a verbal or written warning and six months for a final written warning. Once that period of time has elapsed, if the employee has not committed the offence during the period of time, the letter and note of the offence should be removed from that person's record. If he or she later commits the same or a different breach of disciplinary procedure, then the procedure must be started again. So if the employee who has been given an oral warning for an offence concerning timekeeping then commits a different offence, for example, by carrying out poor quality work, the employer should not go to the next stage of the disciplinary procedure but should start with an informal talk and issue a separate oral warning if that proves necessary.

If the employer ignored the fact that the warning was out of date or was about a different type of disciplinary offence, then it could hardly expect to win its case if it eventually dismissed the employee and he or she later decided to go to an employment tribunal to claim unfair dismissal. Such actions would be regarded as procedurally incorrect.

If records of warnings are kept on an employee's file indefinitely, then this could prejudice the person reading the file at a later date against this employee. The employee may well have changed over the years and so an unfair impression of this person would be given. If there is a computerised record-keeping system for the personnel records, the employee will have the right, under the Data Protection Act 1984, to check his or her records to ensure that erroneous or out-of-date information is not being held and possibly used against them. If the personnel records are kept in a manual form new legislation will be in effect by October 1998. Refer to the section on Data Protection in Chapter 6 for more information. Many organisations would regard it as a matter of good practice to ensure that employees could see and check their records if required, and already have adequate systems in place.

### Groups that may pose particular problems

The ACAS Code of Practice also advises that certain instances may pose particular problems for employers in disciplinary matters. They list as particularly difficult cases:

- ➤ disciplinary offences that occur outside normal working hours
- ➤ offences that occur at times when the full disciplinary procedure is not available
- ➤ offences that involve trade union officials.

The case studies in Activity 14.2 and 14.3 serve to illustrate some of these areas of concern. How would you handle each of these cases?

**PAUSE FOR THOUGHT 14.6**  *Paul has worked for Shepley Computers for four years, and for the past six months has worked on the night shift. He has a blemish-free record and is a highly regarded member of the workforce. One hot night in summer he leaves work after signing in at nine o'clock and goes to the pub. He returns to work under the influence of alcohol, and his supervisor, who has noticed his absence, tells him that he is suspended and must go home immediately. Paul becomes abusive and threatens to punch his supervisor. He takes his supervisor by the shoulders and shakes him while all the time threatening to punch him. His supervisor tells him that he is dismissed and should collect all his money and documents at the end of the week.*

*Do you feel that Paul's supervisor acted correctly in this case? If not, how would you have handled this situation?*

Offences that occur when the human resources department is not available to give advice, as in this case, need particular attention. Supervisors and managers who work on the night shift are not likely to have the human resource manager to turn to for advice if a potential disciplinary situation suddenly occurs. They need to be very clear in their own minds exactly what powers are available to them, and to be extremely well trained. The supervisor initially acted well in suspending the employee. Suspension with pay is a useful technique when there needs to be an opportunity to calm the situation or when time is needed to complete an investigation into whether or not an offence has occurred. He then acted rather rashly in telling Paul that he had been dismissed. No-one should be dismissed unless a proper investigation has been carried out. Taking away someone's livelihood is a serious matter which could result in an employment tribunal case for unfair dismissal being brought against the organisation.

Even if being drunk at work or leaving work without permission is classed as gross misconduct, there still needs to be a full investigation, with an opportunity for Paul and the supervisor to state their cases and for union representation, before a disciplinary decision is reached.

**PAUSE FOR THOUGHT 14.7** *Jane has been employed by your organisation for 10 years. She works as the assistant manager in the wages office and has always been an excellent worker. You hear, on the grapevine, that she has been accused of stealing £100.00 from the funds of the local youth club, where she acts as treasurer.*
*Imagine that you are the manager of the wages office. What will you do when*

1 *you first hear the rumours*
2 *she is subsequently convicted but given a conditional discharge for this offence?*

This is perhaps one of the most difficult situations for a manager to deal with. If the offence had happened at work it would have been a clear case of theft from work and, after going through the disciplinary procedure, may have been considered gross misconduct with the possibility of dismissal. As it is, should the manager consider this to be a disciplinary issue or not?

Initially when you, the manager, hear of the alleged theft from youth club funds you will need to talk to Jane about this and find out her side of the case, just as you would in other situations. You then have three options.

1 You could do nothing, if you are satisfied with her explanation.
2 You might consider suspending her on full pay pending the result of the court case. This would remove her from the situation at work where there would be gossip and rumours, and would also ensure that if anything went missing from work she would not be automatically accused. In many ways this is an attractive option, but the manager would need to be aware that the company may be paying Jane for several months before her case is heard.
3 You could consider moving her to another section where she would not deal with cash handling, although of course many wages offices do not necessarily deal with money anyway. This would have the same advantages as in 2, but she would be earning her wages. She still might be accused, however, every time anything went missing. You may of course not have any other suitable post to which she could transfer, and depending on her contract you may need her agreement to the transfer.

If she is found guilty, then there are once again a variety of appropriate responses. The main guidance is given in the ACAS Code of Practice, which states that offences which occur away from the workplace should not be treated as automatic reasons for dismissal. It goes on to say that the most important factor will be whether the nature of the offence makes the employee unsuitable for their particular job.

In the case of Jane, it would be possible to say that since she was found guilty of theft, this would affect people's view of her in a position of trust and so she may be dismissed for gross misconduct. Most disciplinary procedures follow ACAS's guidelines and include a section which states that offences which occur outside work may constitute gross misconduct. Dismissal should not be automatic, however. Other options are available and it depends on the circumstances.

These two case studies, concerning potential disciplinary offences that occur away from the place of work outside normal working hours, help to illustrate some of the more difficult cases that may arise and show how useful it is to refer to the ACAS Code of Practice on Disciplinary Procedures for guidance in these areas.

Further guidance is provided by the ACAS (1987) *Handbook on Disciplinary Procedures*.

### Absence control

Absences are often another area of particular concern to employers. In many organisations an absence control procedure is used, and this may result in the disciplinary procedure being used less frequently. Absence control systems usually require the employee to telephone the supervisor on the first day of absence, and the supervisor will go through a checklist of points with him or her. If the supervisor is not available there will be a second or a third designated person with whom the absent person will have to speak. An interview will be held with the supervisor or other designated person when the absentee returns to work.

There will also be a system of visits for people who are absent on a long-term basis to ensure that the organisation stays up to date with their current situation and knows when to expect them to return to work. Supervisors and managers will be aware of the level of absenteeism in their sections and will encourage good attendance.

The aim of an absence control procedure is to minimise the need for the use of the disciplinary procedure, by creating a culture in which everyone is aware of the importance of good attendance and of their value to the organisation. The danger is that some employees may feel pressurised into returning to work before they are really fit, and this may prove to be counter-productive, resulting in their needing more time off later to recover fully.

### Disciplinary procedures and ill-health

If a person has a record of short-term absences without suitable explanations or adequate medical evidence, then they can be dealt with under the organisation's normal disciplinary procedure. There is usually a specified level of absence, e.g. 10 days in three months, after which more formal controls will be introduced, leading to counselling or disciplinary action as appropriate. If employees are away on a long-term absence due to a genuine illness then the situation needs to be dealt with in an entirely different way. You cannot warn someone that there must be an improvement in their attendance if you know that this is impossible because of the nature of their illness. Instead, regular contact needs to be maintained with such employees to establish the likelihood of their return, and medical evidence needs to be sought. A company doctor's advice may be needed. In the end it may be that the person is unable to return to work in the foreseeable future, and it may be necessary to consider whether there are any other suitable jobs that they may be able to undertake, or whether their employment needs to be terminated. Other factors such as whether they have exhausted the company sickness pay scheme, or the age of the person and whether they could take early retirement under the company pension scheme, will need to be considered here in order to find the best solution for both the employee and the organisation. There is also likely to be a need for employee counselling and advice, and this process, if handled with the sensitivity it deserves, is likely to be extremely lengthy.

### *Disciplinary interviews*

The actual disciplinary interview is similar in many ways to other forms of interview discussed in Chapter 4. The manager who is conducting the interview will need to prepare thoroughly, have the relevant information to hand and arrange for a quiet room with no disturbances and with an appropriate layout in which to hold the interview. The interview should be conducted in a systematic and fair way in order to ensure that all the relevant information is considered. The manager chairing the interview should explain clearly the purpose of the interview, who is present and why they are there, and the sequence of the interview. The manager should state the nature of the complaint against the employee and the facts that have been revealed by management's enquiries. The employee or his or her representative is given an opportunity to state their case and, if witnesses are called, an opportunity to question the witnesses. A calm atmosphere should be encouraged in which all parties can clearly express their point of view. After further discussion the manager should sum up and adjourn before reconvening to announce the decision.

If insufficient care is taken in the way the disciplinary interview is handled, it could develop into an acrimonious dispute which is not likely to prove at all motivating to anyone and which might result in a costly case of constructive dismissal or of unfair dismissal being brought by the employee. (Constructive dismissal and unfair dismissal are discussed fully in Chapter 15.)

### Handling styles for disciplinary interviews

Any form of interaction between manager and subordinate could be handled in a number of different ways. Consider the following case study and the alternative answers given. Indicate which you would prefer in dealing with this particular disciplinary situation.

ACTIVITY **14.2**

Sam has been working as a clerk in the accounts department for six years. He makes many errors with the figures, and his reports to his supervisor are often late and then have to be done again accurately. He seems to spend a great deal of time on the telephone chatting to friends.

Imagine that you are Sam's supervisor. What action will you take? Read the following statements and, assuming that you have the authority to take any of these actions, circle the number beside the statement which is closest to the way that you think you would be likely to behave.

You call Sam into your office and say you want to discuss his work. You say:

1  'Your work is inadequate and you spend too much time chatting on the telephone. Since your work is not good enough I have no alternative but to issue you with a formal warning. What do you feel has gone wrong?'

2  'Tell me how you are getting on in your job. You have been here six years. I'd like to hear your views and for you to try to identify any areas which you feel may be causing problems.'

3  Your work is not good enough and you spend too much time chatting on the telephone. Since your work is not satisfactory I have no alternative but to issue you with a formal warning immediately.'

4  'How do you feel that you are getting on in your job? Are there any parts of the job which you are concerned about? I've noticed that you don't always get your work done accurately on time. Why do you feel this is? You also seem to spend a great deal of time on the telephone. Why is this? (You consider his answers and then tell him that you will make a decision about his future in the organisation in the next couple of days.)

5  'Tell me how you are getting on in your job. Do you feel that there are any problem areas? I want to make sure that you are clear about your job and are happy. The company will also benefit as you are likely to be more efficient. I'd like to discuss any issues that might contribute to achieving both of these aims and then agree what action to take to make this possible.'

6  'Your work is inadequate and you spend too much time chatting on the telephone. Since your work is not good enough I have no alternative but to issue you with a formal warning immediately. I do not feel that you are suited to this type of work at all and unless you are able to make a big improvement in the near future it would be much better for you, in the long run, to find something that does suit your talents elsewhere.'

### Discussion of Activity 14.2

Wright and Taylor (1984) suggest that there are six ways of handling manager–subordinate interactions. They list these as tell, tell and sell, tell and listen, ask and tell, joint problem-solving, and ask and listen.

In the case above:

1  refers to a tell and listen style
2  is ask and listen
3  is tell
4  is ask and tell
5  is joint problem-solving
6  is tell and sell.

Clearly managers can use a variety of different styles to suit different occasions and circumstances. From what we have said so far it would seem that the most appropriate style for a manager to adopt would involve the employee and give him or her a chance to state his or her case. The joint problem-solving approach (response 5) or the ask and tell approach (response 4) would be fairly appropriate. This would be in line with ACAS's views about setting standards of conduct. If discipline is viewed in a more punitive way, then the manager is more likely to adopt a tell approach, such as response 3, or perhaps a tell and sell approach, such as response 6. These have advantages in that a clear, quick decision is made, and the tell approach may be useful as a last resort when other methods have failed. The tell and sell approach has a similar advantage of brevity and clarity, and aims to encourage cooperation by persuading the employee of the advantages of complying, or the disadvantages of non- compliance. However, in terms of trying to motivate the employee to change his or her behaviour, joint problem-solving, where the employee has clearly had a say, or ask and tell, where the employee has at least been consulted, are likely to prove more successful in the long term.

There is evidence that not all supervisors and managers do actually always adopt the most appropriate style to achieve the desired change in behaviour. Research by Caroline Hook *et al*. (1997) suggests that while the most serious disciplinary cases are often handled with an appropriate participative style, many other disciplinary cases which are perceived to be less serious in nature are often dealt with by managers and supervisors in a fairly autocratic manner. According to Derek Rollinson *et al*. (1997) the key factors which influence the handling style that the managers actually adopt appear to be the amount of inconvenience that the transgression causes to the manager personally and the length of service of the employee. This means that training is vitally important for all those involved in handling disciplinary cases to ensure that an appropriate style, likely to result in a change in behaviour, is always used by the supervisor or manager.

## Grievance

As we stated earlier, we use the term 'grievance' to refer to a complaint that has been formally presented to a management representative or shop steward. We earlier distinguished a grievance from a complaint. A complaint is a spoken or written dissatisfaction brought to the attention of the employer or the employee's trade union.

### *The informal grievance procedure*

The Labour Research Department (1995) conducted a survey of the grievance procedures of 85 organisations. They found that the majority of complaints are resolved in an informal way, making it unnecessary to raise them as a formal grievance. Informal grievance procedures seem to be just as important in organisations as informal disciplinary procedures. However, a small number of complaints will not be resolved informally, and for these it is necessary to have a grievance procedure.

We have already outlined the reasons for having a grievance procedure, and in the next section will consider the form that the grievance procedure should take and the main points to be considered when designing a grievance procedure, before considering the way in which the grievance interview should be handled.

### The formal grievance procedure

In order that both employees and managers are clear about how to handle grievances, a grievance procedure should be designed and issued to all employees. It is a good idea, once again, to involve various groups in the design of a procedure to suit a particular organisation.

A suitable format for the grievance procedure might be to use similar headings to those used in the design of a disciplinary procedure. Suitable headings could be:

1 the purpose and scope of the grievance procedure
2 the principles that underlie the procedure
3 the stages in the grievance procedure
4 exceptional circumstances
5 the appeals procedure.

#### The purpose and scope of the procedure

This section is likely to indicate which employees are covered by this particular procedure if there are slightly different procedures for different groups. It should also state that the aim of the procedure is to settle any grievances as near to the source of the grievance as possible. In order to minimise problems at work and ensure a happy and productive working environment, the procedure should be simple to use and rapid in operation.

#### The principles that underlie the procedure

This is likely to include some statements concerning the employer's views on fairness and justice and how these will be achieved, e.g:

➤ all employees have a right to raise a grievance that they may feel with their supervisor or manager without fear of recrimination against themselves
➤ grievances will be investigated within specified time limits and the person with the grievance will be notified of the outcome
➤ at each stage of the procedure they will have the right to be accompanied by a trade union representative or a friend
➤ if the employee is not satisfied with the outcome of raising their grievance they will have a right of appeal.

#### The stages in the grievance procedure

Although under the Employment Rights Act 1996 there is, as we said earlier, a requirement to provide all employees with a copy of the grievance procedure within two months of the start of their employment, this actually specifies only a one-stage process. The employee merely has to be informed of the person with whom a grievance should be raised. The Labour Research Department

(1995) found that 80% of the grievance procedures that they reviewed had between three and six stages after the informal stage. We do not feel that there is any advantage in having more levels in the procedure, even if there are more levels in the management hierarchy. We would suggest that three main levels, with a fourth level of appeal to a joint body or to independent arbitration, should prove adequate for most organisations. Outlined below are the possible main stages in the grievance procedure.

*Stage 1*
The employee should raise the grievance, either orally or in writing, with the immediate supervisor, who will reply within three days.

*Stage 2*
If it has not been resolved, the employee should request an interview with the manager, within one week, to discuss the grievance.

*Stage 3*
If it has not been resolved at stage 2, the employee should raise the grievance with the general manager or director.

*Stage 4*
Subject to the agreement of both parties, if the grievance is still not resolved, a Conciliation Officer from ACAS may be asked to become involved, or another acceptable outside or joint body might be asked to intervene.

*Time limits*
You will have noted that fairly strict time limits were specified in the section on stages in the procedure. If there is not a satisfactory response to the grievance within a specified time limit, then the employee should be able to raise the grievance with the supervisor's immediate management. There should be a clear time limit for each stage of the grievance procedure, as without this there is a danger that, although a manager or supervisor may have good intentions to deal with a grievance, it will nevertheless be overlooked.

*Representation*
The employee should have the right to be accompanied at each stage by his or her trade union representative or by a friend.

**Exceptional circumstances**
In exceptional circumstances it may not be practicable to raise the grievance with the immediate manager. This may be because the grievance is caused by the manager or because the manager will not be available, perhaps because of illness, to deal with the grievance with the urgency that it deserves. In those exceptional circumstances the grievance may be taken to the next level of supervision.

**Appeals**
A right of appeal should be specified for each stage, with time limits within which the appeal should be heard.

**PAUSE FOR THOUGHT 14.8** *Shazia, the shop steward, asks you for time off to make a complaint to the general manager about something in your department. You are the manager of that department: what will you do?*

Shazia, as the shop steward, is entitled to reasonable time off to carry out her trade union duties, so she is in order to request time off. However, as we said earlier, a grievance should be settled as near to the source of the problem as possible. You need to remind Shazia, who as a shop steward should certainly be aware of this, that if she has a grievance herself, or if she is acting on behalf of one of your department, then you are the person with whom the grievance should first be raised. You should point out that if you cannot deal with this satisfactorily within the specified time period then of course she may then raise the grievance, in line with the grievance procedure, with the general manager.

Although there is a need for grievances to be settled as near to the source of grievance as possible, this becomes difficult if the grievance is about the manager or supervisor concerned, so if the grievance is about you as the supervisor, Shazia may be unwilling to discuss it with you. Nevertheless, if it is about you, you will need to know about it sooner or later, so at least you should ascertain the nature of the grievance before allowing it to go further.

### Grievance interviews

Many of the features of a grievance interview are the same as for other types of interview. There is a need for a quiet, private room arranged to facilitate ease of communication. The employee or his or her representative is likely to do most of the talking, since they are raising the grievance. There may be a need to call witnesses, and after hearing all the evidence from both sides the manager may wish to adjourn before reaching a decision. The manager must ensure a fair hearing and that everyone concerned is aware of the purpose of the meeting, who is to be called as witnesses, the time limits within which a decision will be reached, and the way in which the decision will be announced to the employee concerned. If there is not a swift and fair resolution of grievances, the grievances may tend to build up and the work of the section is likely to suffer. At worst this could ultimately result in a high labour turnover or a high level of absenteeism, as people remove themselves from a situation where they feel unhappy, or it might escalate into an industrial dispute.

#### Handling styles for grievance interviews

The grievance interview can be a particularly difficult interview for the supervisor or manager to handle as he or she may feel threatened if it seems that an employee is challenging his or her authority by raising a grievance.

ACTIVITY **14.3**

James has been employed as a porter by your organisation for two months in the warehouse. He says that he has a grievance and is unhappy about the duties that he has been allocated. He says he always gets the most unpleasant and boring jobs to deal with.

What action will you take? Read the following statements and, assuming that you have the necessary authority to take the action, circle the number beside the statement closest to the way you think you would be likely to behave.

You ask James into the office to talk about the grievance. You:

1   Ask James to tell you why he is unhappy doing certain jobs. Which jobs does he regard as boring? Which jobs are unpleasant? You then think about what he has said and tell him of your decision.

2   Ask James to tell you about the job he is doing, what he doesn't like and why he feels that he has a grievance. You ask a lot of questions to try to establish what the problem is and listen thoughtfully to the answers.

3   Tell James that as a warehouse porter these are the jobs that he has been employed to do and he had better get on with them.

4   Tell James that as a warehouse porter he must get on with these jobs. Then ask him which jobs he feels particularly unhappy about and why and listen to his views.

5   Ask James to tell you about the work he is doing as a warehouse porter. Explain that the organisation needs productive workers and that you would like to find a way of making him happier in his job, but also making sure that the organisation gets all the work done in the most efficient way. Say that you would like to consider different approaches and try to establish what is most suitable for you both.

6   Tell James that as a warehouse porter he must get on with the jobs. Explain to him that although many of the jobs are boring and sometimes unpleasant they are nevertheless all vital to the running of the organisation, and it is essential that he completes them. As his expertise develops he is likely to get other jobs to do.

### Discussion of Activity 14.3

The work of Wright and Taylor (1984), which we referred to earlier, suggests that six different styles may be used in handling interpersonal relationships. In this case the responses are as follows:

1   is ask and tell
2   is ask and listen
3   is tell
4   is tell and listen
5   is joint problem-solving
6   is tell and sell.

Once again the types of approach that are likely to be most appropriate are the ones that involve the employee in finding the solution. Clearly response 5, the joint problem-solving approach, would be particularly useful here but in real life you would have more information, and other approaches might prove to be appropriate too.

The research by Caroline Hook *et al.* (1997) suggests that in general managers and supervisors do appear to use appropriate handling styles for grievances. The one exception appears to be when the grievance raised poses a direct challenge to the authority of the manager concerned, and in these cases there remains a tendency for some managers to adopt a more prescriptive and less appropriate handling style (Rollinson *et al.* 1997). Once again training for all who are likely to be involved in handling grievances is vital to ensure consistency and fairness.

## Conclusions
••••••••••••••

We have shown in this chapter the meaning and the importance of grievance and disciplinary procedures to the organisation. Both specialist human resource managers and line managers have an extremely important role to play in the design of procedures that are fair to all; it is also important that cases of grievance or discipline are dealt with in accordance with the organisation's procedures. Knowledge and understanding of the ACAS Code of Practice, Advisory Handbook and the ACAS self-help guide for producing discipline and grievance procedures are valuable aids to help ensure that fair procedures are designed and that disciplinary and grievance interviews are handled well. The need for clear documentation and letters has also been discussed, as has the importance of adopting an appropriate interview style. In the next chapter we examine the consequences of getting a disciplinary case wrong, and discuss unfair dismissal and redundancy.

The mind maps shown in Figures 14.1 and 14.2 summarise the key points covered in this chapter. When you have examined these, test your understanding of the chapter with the review questions and activities and the objective test that follows.

*figure 14.1*

**Mind map: discipline**

figure 14.2
**Mind map:
grievance**

Brief answers to review questions 4 and 5 are provided on page 430.

**REVIEW QUESTIONS**

1   Interview both a line manager and a personnel manager and try to establish what roles they play in relation to grievance and discipline handling in the workplace. How do your findings compare with what we have said in this chapter?

2   Obtain a copy of an organisation's discipline or grievance procedure and compare it to our suggested outline for these. Identify and comment on the similarities and differences.

3   Obtain a copy of the *ACAS Self-help Guide for Producing Discipline and Grievance Procedures* (1997). Use this, and our suggestions in this chapter, to rewrite or modify either of the procedures you used for question 2 if you find that this is necessary.

4   Describe a model disciplinary procedure and comment on the approach that managers should adopt towards employee discipline.

5   You have joined an organisation which has expanded recently and now has 100 employees. This organisation started as a small undertaking with only 18 employees and has never had a formal grievance procedure. Write a report for the general manager outlining why it is important to have a formal grievance procedure and suggesting what the procedure should contain.

**SELF-CHECK QUESTIONS**

Answer the following multiple choice questions. The answers are provided on page 430 for you to check your understanding of this chapter.

1   According to ACAS, disciplinary procedures should be designed to:
    (*a*) provide a fair way to gather evidence against the offender
    (*b*) ensure that someone is caught for the offence
    (*c*) promote fairness and set standards of conduct
    (*d*) point out the mistake that has been made
    (*e*) Provide fair methods of punishing the offender.

2   According to Pigors and Myers, a grievance is
    (*a*) anything that disturbs an employee
    (*b*) anything that disturbs an employee and is discussed with the manager
    (*c*) a spoken dissatisfaction brought to the attention of the manager
    (*d*) a complaint that has been formally presented to a management representative or shop steward
    (*e*) anything that disturbs an employee and is expressed in words.

3   Which of the following are listed as essential features of a disciplinary procedure in the ACAS Code of Practice?
    (*a*) Be in writing, provide for fair punishment, specify to whom the rules should apply
    (*b*) Be in writing, specify to whom the rules should apply, ensure that (except for cases of gross misconduct) no-one is dismissed for a first disciplinary offence
    (*c*) Provide for the matter to be dealt with quickly, provide for witnesses to give evidence, ensure that (except for cases of gross misconduct), no-one

is dismissed for a first disciplinary offence
  - (*d*) Be in writing, provide for a fair system of punishment, specify all the offences that constitute gross misconduct
  - (*e*) Provide for the matter to be dealt with quickly, specify all the offences that constitute gross misconduct, ensure that except for gross misconduct, no-one is dismissed for a first offence.
4 The ACAS Code of Practice on Discipline at Work:
  - (*a*) provides guidance, but failure to comply with its provisions may be used in evidence against an organisation in an unfair dismissal claim at an employment tribunal
  - (*b*) provides guidance, but failure to comply with its provisions cannot be used in evidence against an organisation at an unfair dismissal claim in an employment tribunal
  - (*c*) complements the ACAS handbook and gives examples of good practice for employers
  - (*d*) complements the ACAS handbook by providing examples of new developments in case law since the handbook was published
  - (*e*) provides a detailed list of laws within which employers should work.
5 Once the time limit for a written warning has elapsed:
  - (*a*) the warning should still be kept on the employee's personal record file
  - (*b*) the warning should be removed from the employee's personal record file and placed in a central file in which records of all disciplinary offences are kept
  - (*c*) the warning should be removed from the employee's personal record file only if the data are stored on computer
  - (*d*) the warning should be removed completely from the employee's personal record file
  - (*e*) the warning should be removed from the employee's personal record file after a further three months has elapsed.
6 According to ACAS, if a serious criminal offence occurs outside employment:
  - (*a*) this is automatically considered to be gross misconduct and dismissal is justifiable
  - (*b*) this is automatically considered to be gross misconduct and dismissal may be justifiable
  - (*c*) this should not be treated as an automatic reason for dismissal – the main consideration should be whether or not the offence makes the employee unsuitable for his or her type of work
  - (*d*) this should not be treated as an automatic reason for dismissal – the main consideration is whether you think that the employee is likely to commit the offence again
  - (*e*) this should not be treated as automatic reason for dismissal – the main consideration should be the length of service the employee has had with your organisation.
7 The recommended first stage in a grievance procedure is:
  - (*a*) to raise the grievance with the top management immediately
  - (*b*) to grumble to your colleagues about your grievance
  - (*c*) to raise the grievance with your supervisor's manager
  - (*d*) to raise the grievance with the area manager

(*e*)  to raise the grievance with your immediate supervisor.
8     The ACAS advisory handbook *Discipline at Work* was first published in:
    (*a*)  1975
    (*b*)  1977
    (*c*)  1985
    (*d*)  1987
    (*e*)  1993.
9     Nowadays the role of human resource managers in handling discipline and grievance situations is:
    (*a*)  always purely advisory
    (*b*)  non-existent, as line managers deal with these topics
    (*c*)  purely to check on line managers and ensure they handle things correctly.
    (*d*)  only to design the procedures themselves
    (*e*)  a mixture of things, including advice and guidance.
10    The initials ACAS stand for:
    (*a*)  Advisory, Counselling and Aid Service
    (*b*)  Aid, Counselling and Arbitration Service
    (*c*)  Aid, Conciliation and Arbitration Service
    (*d*)  Advice, Conciliation and Arbitration Service
    (*e*)  Advisory, Conciliation and Arbitration Service.

## References

Advisory, Conciliation and Arbitration Service. *Code of Practice 1: Disciplinary Practice and Procedures in Employment.* HMSO, 1977.

Bargaining. Report 149, Labour Research Department, April 1995.

*Discipline at Work – the ACAS Advisory Handbook.* ACAS, 1987.

Hook, C., Rollinson, D., Foot, M. and Handley, J. Supervisor and manager styles in handling discipline and grievance. Part one – comparing styles in handling discipline and grievance. *Personnel Review*, Vol. 25, No. 3, 1996, 20–34.

Pigors, P. and Myers, C. S. *Personnel Administration.* 8th edition, McGraw-Hill, 1977.

Rollinson, D., Hook, C., Foot, M. and Handley, J. Supervisor and manager styles in handling discipline and grievance. Part two – approaches to handling discipline and grievance. *Personnel Review*, Vol. 25, No. 4, 1996, 38–55.

Wright, P. and Taylor, D. S. *Improving Leadership Performance.* Prentice Hall International, 1984.

## Further study

Advisory, Conciliation and Arbitration Service. *Discipline at Work – the ACAS Advisory Handbook ACAS*, 1987. (A very useful, clear and easy-to-read book which provides valuable guidance about discipline at work.)

Advisory, Conciliation and Arbitration Service. *Producing Disciplinary and Grievance Procedures: Self-Help Guide.* ACAS, 1997. (Clear practical guidance is provided to help in designing both discipline and grievance procedures.)

James, P. and Lewis, D. *Discipline*. IPM, 1992. (A specialist book written purely about discipline. It is clearly written and gives a great deal of information, especially about the legal issues relating to disciplinary procedures.)

Rollinson, D. *Understanding Employee Relations: A Behavioural Approach.* Addison-Wesley, 1993, Chapter 6. (This chapter explores a theoretical perspective of discipline and grievance handling and suggests the potential role of both processes in the light of recent HRM approaches to employee relations.)

Torrington, D. and Hall, L. *Personnel Management: HRM in Action*. 3rd Edition, Prentice Hall, 1995, Chapters 30 and 31. (Up-to-date chapters relating to both discipline and grievance situations, with suggested procedures for interviews.)

### Articles

Fowler, A. How to handle disciplinary interviews. *Personnel Management Plus,* November 1990, 20–21. (A short article which gives clear information about disciplinary interviews.)

Fowler, A. How to handle employee grievances. *Personnel Management Plus*, October 1994, 24–25. (Another excellent short article in the 'How to' series.)

Hook, C., Rollinson, D., Foot, M. and Handley, J. Supervisor and manager styles in handling discipline and grievance. Part one – comparing styles in handling discipline and grievance. *Personnel Review*, Vol. 25, No. 3, 1996. (An article which provides more detail to some of the research findings mentioned in this chapter.)

Rollinson, D., Hook, C., Foot, M. and Handley, J. Supervisor and manager styles in handling discipline and grievance. Part two–approaches to handling discipline and grievance. *Personnel Review*, Vol. 25, No. 4, 1996. (An article which provides more detail to some of the research findings mentioned in this chapter.)

### Audio-visual

Open College, *Interviewing: An Open College Course*. Produced by Yorkshire Television for the Open College with Channel 4, 1988. (A series of six interviews, including one relating specifically to disciplinary and grievance interviews.)

Video Arts. *I'd Like a Word with You*. Video Arts, 1979. (A humorous look at the consequences that can occur from classic errors in handling discipline problems.)

### Internet

The Advisory, Conciliation and Arbitration Service (Another source of information for ACAS **http://www.acas.org.uk**

publications, some of which are published
in full on this site)

The Department of Trade and Industry      **http://www.dti.gov.uk**
(Many useful DTI publications, discussion
documents and some pieces of legislation
can be found on this site.)

The Government                            **http://www.open.gov.uk**
(Useful information site especially for the
text of legislations such as the Employment
Rights Act 1996.)

The TUC                                   **http://www.tuc.org.uk**
(This gives the TUC's views on many current
issues and new legislation.)

## Appendix 14.1
....................

*Example of written warning*
Date

Dear Mr Hancock,

WRITTEN WARNING

You attended a disciplinary interview on _____ in the presence of your trade union representative. At the disciplinary interview the decision was taken that you be given a written warning about your poor timekeeping. Prior to this you had already received an oral warning on _____ _____ , but there has been no improvement since that date.

You were warned that you had continued to have an unacceptable level of poor timekeeping and that unless there was an improvement in your timekeeping during the next three months, we should have no alternative but to enter the next stage of the company's formal disciplinary procedure and issue you with a final written warning. You were told that this written warning will stay on your personal file for the next three months.

You have the right of appeal against this decision by writing to _____ within _____ days of receiving this letter confirming your written warning.

Yours sincerely,

Philippa Jason
Manager Dept X

## Appendix 14.2

........................

*Example of a written warning*
Date
Dear Mr Hancock,

### FINAL WRITTEN WARNING

You attended a disciplinary interview on _____ in the presence of your manager and trade union official. At this disciplinary interview the decision was reached to issue you with this final written warning about your poor timekeeping. You had previously received an oral warning on _____ and a written warning on _____ . Since these warnings were issued there has been no improvement in your timekeeping. You are now being issued with a final written warning and if there is no improvement in your timekeeping during the next three months this will unfortunately result in your dismissal from our employment.

This warning will be kept on your record for three months. You have a right of appeal against this decision in writing to _____ within _____ days of receiving this warning.

Yours sincerely,

S Hussain
Human Resource Manager

# CHAPTER 15

# Dismissal, redundancy and outplacement

**Objectives:**
................

*By the end of this chapter you will be able to:*
➤ explain what is meant by the term 'fair dismissal'
➤ explain what is meant by 'redundancy'
➤ define the term 'outplacement'
➤ describe the services that an outplacement consultancy may provide.

In Chapter 14 we explained that there may be occasions when not everything in the relationship between employer and employee goes smoothly: the employee may be dissatisfied with the employer and raise a grievance, or the employer may have to use a disciplinary procedure against an employee who is proving to be unsatisfactory. Human resource managers want to get the best from the people they employ: people are, as we have shown, very expensive to recruit and train, and HRM specialists will not wish to waste these resources. However, there will be occasions when it becomes inevitable that the organisation will have to end the employment of one or more employees, and line managers as well as human resource specialists will need to know something about this process.

This chapter will examine ways in which employment may be ended fairly. We shall then consider one particular type of dismissal – redundancy – and examine ways in which the effects of redundancy may be lessened by the provision of an outplacement service.

The chapter presents general guidance only, and is intended to provide not a complete or authoritative guide to employment law, but rather an appreciation of general principles with which students of HRM should be familiar and which they may use to guide them in dealing with people who are dismissed from an organisation.

It is important for a number of reasons that any dismissal should be fair. The workforce will be better able to trust and work effectively for a management that operates fair procedures and the reputation of the organisation in general will also benefit from this.

Fairness is both a moral and a legal issue, and sometimes organisations that have tried very hard to be fair in their procedures and practices will still be found in the eyes of the law to have acted unfairly. This may be because individual managers or supervisors have made errors in the way they handled an issue, or failed to document their actions adequately, or because of some legal technicality. HRM practitioners, therefore, need to be aware of the importance of legislation and must endeavour to have systems, procedures and training in place so that everyone involved in the dismissal process acts in a fair way. They also need to know where to find detailed guidance, as they cannot know in minute detail every aspect of the law: there are many specialist texts that can help with this. Although the HRM practitioner needs to be sufficiently aware of legislation and the need for fair procedures to be able to deal with issues that arise on a day-to-day basis, it may be that faced with an unusual problem, he or she will also need the advice of the company solicitor.

Legislation changes constantly, which means that you should be aware of general principles with regard to dismissal but you should always be prepared to check for the most recent legislation and the most recent interpretation of it, and not just rely on notes that you made years earlier. Textbooks become out of date, and you should always look for the most recent edition to guide you, although even this may not be enough to take account of the latest changes in law. We have listed some useful sources of information at the end of the chapter.

People leave organisations for a host of reasons, and of course not all who leave are dismissed. Resignations and retirements do not normally cause any legal problems to the organisation, but employers need to take great care in the case of dismissals that they abide by the law, and ensure not only that they dismiss for a potentially fair reason, but that the way they handle the dismissal and the whole dismissal process is also fair.

## Dismissal

Dismissal is defined by law as occurring when:

- a fixed-term contract expires and is not renewed, or
- the employee leaves, with or without giving notice, in circumstances such that he or she is entitled to go without notice by reason of the employer's conduct (constructive dismissal), or
- an employee is not allowed to return to work after a period of maternity absence when the employee has the legal right to do so, or
- the employment is terminated by the employer with or without notice.

We shall consider each of these points in turn.

### Fixed-term contract

The first case sounds straightforward enough, and occurs when there is a fixed-term contract for a particular period of employment. If the contract is not renewed, this technically counts as a dismissal although it is normally expected by both the employer and the employee. In some cases employers insert a waiver clause into a fixed-term contract so that the employee waives or gives up any right they may have to claim unfair dismissal at an employment tribunal. At the time of writing there is an appeal against an Employment Appeal Tribunal decision being awaited and this may help to clarify the situation. The Fairness at Work White Paper 1998 also suggests that the use of waiver clauses should be reviewed.

### Constructive dismissal

The second definition given here is a little more complicated, and is known as constructive dismissal. It is often hard to prove that the dismissal was unfair, as the person has normally resigned and given some other reason for leaving. It is later, when he or she realises that the resignation was because of the employer's conduct, that he or she might decide to bring a case of constructive dismissal. For a case to succeed, the employer normally has to have done something so seriously wrong that the employee was justified in feeling that he or she could no longer work in that workplace, as the employer's action would be regarded as a significant breach of the employment contract. A possible example is an employer who bullied the employee so that his or her life was a total misery and the person felt obliged to leave.

### Failure to allow a return to work after maternity leave

Provided that she complies with certain qualifying conditions, an employee who has been absent due to maternity leave is entitled to return to her former job within a specific period. If she is not allowed to return by her employer she will be regarded as being dismissed, and may make a complaint to an employment tribunal.

### Termination

The fourth definition of dismissal is a straightforward statement that an employer may terminate the employment contract. It does not address the circumstances in which this may occur, but raises questions about what is considered to be fair and who has protection in cases of unfairness.

**PAUSE FOR THOUGHT 15.1** *We said earlier that dismissal should be for a potentially fair reason and that a fair dismissal procedure should also be followed. What do you consider to be potentially fair reasons for dismissal?*

### Fair reasons for dismissal

You have probably listed offences such as theft, poor attendance, assault, fraud, being under the influence of drugs or alcohol, sexual harassment or racial harassment, or perhaps a serious breach of a safety rule. If you refer back to Chapter 14, you will see that these are all examples of misconduct or of gross misconduct, although poor attendance, if it is due to ill-health, may be an example of lack of capability. There are three other potentially fair reasons for dismissal besides misconduct and lack of capability, and each of these covers a wide range of situations. For a dismissal to be fair, an employer must be able to prove it was for one of these five reasons:

➤ the employee's misconduct
➤ lack of capability or lack of qualification to do the job
➤ a statutory restriction placed on the employer or on the employee which prevents the employment from being continued
➤ some other substantial reason that could justify the dismissal
➤ redundancy.

### The need to act reasonably

Do you think that if an employee is guilty, for example, of misconduct or proves incapable of doing the job, this means that if the employer dismisses him or her it will automatically be fair? In Chapter 14 we said that it was important for an organisation to have a fair disciplinary procedure modelled on the ACAS Code of Practice. It is important, if an organisation is considering dismissing someone, that it not only has potentially fair grounds for dismissing them (i.e. it is dismissing them for one of the reasons listed earlier), but it also acts fairly in the way that it carries out this dismissal. The organisation needs to have a fair procedure for handling dismissals and should have followed its own procedure in a fair way. This is what we mean by the condition that the dismissal also has to be actually fair. An employer should strive to be fair but may still face a claim for unfair dismissal, as dismissed employees may have a different perception of whether their treatment was fair.

Employment tribunals examine cases from two points of view. One is whether employers have acted reasonably in treating the grounds as sufficient reason to justify dismissal. The other is that they must satisfy the tribunal that they acted reasonably in the dismissal procedure. If an employee brings a claim for unfair dismissal, the tribunal will have to make a judgement about what happened after considering evidence from both parties; consequently it is important for employers to follow their own procedure and have clear records and documentary evidence.

ACTIVITY **15.1**
. . . . . . . . . . . . . . . .

Susan has been employed by your organisation for three years as a clerical assistant. During the past year there have been many problems with poor attendance and timekeeping. Susan's manager has tried to establish whether there is a problem underlying this poor attendance and timekeeping, but has found no clear explanation. Susan has been counselled about this situation and has gone through the disciplinary procedure, and she has been issued in the presence of her trade union representative with an oral warning, a written warning and a final written warning. The final written warning was issued only three weeks ago, and yet since then Susan has already had one day absent from work and has been late twice. She has not provided any good explanation for this, but simply says that she overslept and then did not feel like coming to work.

Do you think that the employer has potentially fair reasons for dismissing Susan? Give reasons for your answer. Which category of dismissal would this fall into?

If the employer does decide to dismiss Susan, do you think that it is being fair in the way that it is handling this dismissal?

### Discussion of Activity 15.1

This case looks from the evidence given to be a potentially fair dismissal on the grounds of misconduct, as Susan does appear to have behaved badly and the employer does appear to have a valid reason for dismissal. In this case, the management appear to have a disciplinary procedure which they followed and seem, from the evidence given here, to have acted reasonably and fairly. A case such as this would probably not go to an employment tribunal, but there may be other circumstances not given here that might lead Susan to feel her dismissal was unfair and to pursue a tribunal case.

### Lack of capability or lack of qualification

Lack of capability could arise for several reasons. We discussed the problems of absenteeism in the last chapter, and clearly not all absenteeism would fall into the category of misconduct as Susan's behaviour did. Many absentees are genuinely ill but the organisation, as we said in Chapter 14, may reluctantly, having exhausted all its procedures, have to consider whether or not to dismiss. This needs to be handled in a totally different way, but such a dismissal would be on the grounds of the person not being capable of doing the job.

Particular attention, however, should be paid to the requirements of the Disability Discrimination Act (1995) before making any decision to dismiss on ill-health grounds. If many of the absences are directly attributable to a disability the employer may have to discount these from their calculations when considering whether or not the employee's attendance record is satisfactory. This was the case in *Cox* v *the Post Office* (IT/1301162/97) where it was decided that the Post Office should have discounted Cox's absences due to asthma, since this is classed as a disability, from the figures for his attendance which they had used to justify his dismissal.

It is also important to note that if the illness itself leads to a disability the employer should first try to establish whether reasonable adjustments could be made to enable them to keep their job, before considering dismissal. According to Gill Sage (1998), an employment law specialist, 'No decision to terminate an employee's contract on the grounds of ill-health or to subject someone to any other detriment should now be taken solely on the basis of absence from the workplace (Sage, 1998, 24).

Some people may prove to be incapable of doing the job required because they lack the required level of skill or ability. This could be a reflection on the organisation's selection techniques or training, but if training and opportunities to improve have been given, it may be necessary to dismiss the person if he or she still proves to be incapable.

Lack of qualification is another potentially fair reason for dismissal. Although good selection procedures should mean that people who do not have the desired qualifications are not employed, there are many well-publicised examples of people who have lied about their qualifications and who have worked for an organisation for a number of years before being found out and dismissed. There have even been cases of doctors who have practised for many years without people realising that they did not have any medical qualification. In a case such as this there would be a potentially fair reason for dismissal.

### A legal reason

This is a rarer reason for dismissal, which deals with the situation where the employer would be breaking the law if it continued to employ that person. Possible examples of this would be employing a person who did not have a work permit, or employing a person who was legally too young to work full-time in that particular work environment, or possibly employing a driver who had lost his or her licence and was disqualified from driving.

### Some other substantial reason

This category is to cover eventualities not listed already, where there is a genuinely fair reason for dismissal that does not fit neatly into any of the listed categories. One example of this is where the contract is only temporary and is not renewed. Legally the person has been dismissed. They have not been dismissed because of their misconduct or because of lack of capability or lack of qualification, or even because of some legal requirement, so this form of dismissal would fall into the category of some other substantial reason.

### Redundancy

Many employers dislike discussing redundancies and invent other names for this type of dismissal. They refer to it as 'downsizing' or 'delayering', or even as being 'forced to let someone go'. It is certainly a very unpleasant form of dismissal for all concerned, as the person involved is not normally being dismissed because of anything that he or she has done wrong but as a result of the organisation's need to streamline its operations or cut back in some areas because of an unforeseen crisis, or perhaps through poor human resource planning. Many organisations are striving to be increasingly flexible in their deployment of people and often employ temporary or agency staff, with the result that redundancy affects more and more people in an increasingly wide range of jobs as these organisations move from traditional employment patterns to new ones. The legal definition of redundancy, under the Employment Rights Act 1996, is that a person is dismissed in the following circumstances:

➤ where the employer has ceased, or intends to cease, to carry on the business for the purposes of which the employee was employed; or
➤ where the employer has ceased, or intends to cease, to carry on the business in the place where the employee was so employed; or
➤ where the requirements of the business for employees to carry out work of a particular kind have ceased or diminished or are expected to cease or diminish; or
➤ where the requirements of the business for employees to carry out work of a particular kind, in the place where they were so employed, have ceased or diminished or are expected to diminish.

For the purposes of statutory consultation, but not for individual employment rights, a broader definition has been given:

➤ redundancy is defined as any dismissal for any reason not related to the individual concerned or for a number of reasons all of which are not so related (Trade Union and Labour Relations (Consolidation) Act 1992, S195).

This last definition is wider than the other one, and makes the assumption that if the dismissal is not due to anything that the individual has done then it must be a redundancy situation. This then means that the appropriate consultation must begin.

We shall return to the topic of redundancy later in this chapter.

### Who can bring a case for unfair dismissal

It is obviously important that all dismissals should be fair, but the law provides the opportunity for only some employees (those who have sufficient length of service), to bring a case claiming unfair dismissal before an employment tribunal. There are also other circumstances, which will be discussed later, in which dismissal will be automatically unfair, and where this qualification period does not apply. If you remember our discussion of equal opportunities issues in Chapter 3, you will recall that there was no mention of a qualification period for cases of sex discrimination or racial discrimination. This is because many cases of discrimination occur before people are actually employed at all. However, for most cases of unfair dismissal to be brought before a tribunal, employees do have to have been employed for a certain length of time, although the actual length of employment required has varied over the years. This means that some unscrupulous employers may be tempted to treat people who do not have sufficient length of service with them in an unfair way, as they know that a case for unfair dismissal cannot be brought against them.

The length of service requirement was introduced because it was felt that new employees normally need to have an opportunity to settle into a job, and the employer also needs time to assess whether or not they are capable of doing that job. This is reasonable, but the actual length of that period of time is perhaps more contentious.

Prior to 1985 the length of service required for full-time employees to have worked before they were eligible to bring a case for unfair dismissal was one year, but this was increased in 1985 to two years. The government stated that the two-year period was necessary to encourage employers to recruit new staff, and maintained that if this period were removed or reduced many employers would not recruit as they would be frightened of making a mistake in their selection, and then finding that they had a costly and time-consuming case to fight at an employment tribunal if they did eventually dismiss the person. At that time employees who worked between eight and sixteen hours per week were not eligible to bring an unfair dismissal case until they had been in continuous employment for five years, and employees who worked fewer than eight hours per week could never earn this entitlement no matter how many years they worked for the employer. In 1994 a House of Lords judgement, based on European legislation, led to the scrapping of these differences in qualifying periods between part-time and full-time employees, so that since 6 February 1995

> **DID YOU KNOW?**
>
> In 1997, 42,771 individual conciliation cases concerning unfair dismissal were received by ACAS. Of these 19,284 were settled, 12,077 were withdrawn and 15,177 cases went to an employment tribunal. There was a decrease in the number of unfair dismissal cases received in 1997 but these still accounted for approximately the same percentage of ACAS's case load, 23% in 1997, as compared with 22% in the previous year. Of the 19,284 unfair dismissal cases which were settled only 259, just over 1% were settled by the re-employment of the applicant. (ACAS 1998.)

part-time employees have also been eligible to bring a claim for unfair dismissal or for redundancy rights once they have worked continuously for two years for an employer.

In 1995 the two-year rule was challenged. The Court of Appeal has considered a case brought by Camden Law Centre on behalf of two London women who were dismissed in 1991 by separate employers after 15 months' service. The court found that the fact that the law had been changed from one year's qualification period to two in 1985 conflicted with the European Equal Treatment Directive and indirectly discriminated against women. Evidence suggests that, because of other commitments, women in general are less likely than men to have been with the same employer for more than two years. According to Korn (1995)

> The statistical evidence showed that in 1985 – when the qualifying period was increased from one year to two years – proportionately fewer women than men could meet the qualifying requirement. The difference was about 5 per cent of the total female working population. This statistical variation was fairly constant between 1985 and 1991 when the dismissals took place. This difference was sufficiently significant to amount to differential treatment and in breach of the Equal Treatment Directive.

As a result of these cases public sector employees who have more than one but less than two years service may now be eligible for protection against unfair dismissal if they were dismissed between 1985 and 1991, but any employer or employee who thinks the ruling may apply to them should consult independent legal advice. The case went to appeal to the House of Lords which in March 1997 discharged the declaration but referred various questions relating to the discrimination to the European Court of Justice for a ruling. At the moment this means that in general, with the possible exception already mentioned, the two year qualifying period still applies.

There may, however, be changes made to the length of the qualifying period, even before the European Court of Justice reaches its final judgement. In the White Paper *Fairness at Work* (May 1998), the government proposes to establish new rights for employees. They say 'as the economy becomes more dynamic, leading to more frequent job changes, the Government is concerned that this period is too long and a better balance between competitiveness and fairness would be achieved if it were reduced' DTI (1998).

Consequently one of the key proposals in the White Paper is to reduce the period of employment necessary for employees to qualify for protection from unfair dismissal from two years continuous employment to one year.

ACTIVITY **15.2**

The above was the situation as we wrote this chapter. Check what the current situation is with regard to length of qualifying period for being eligible to bring a case of unfair dismissal before an employment tribunal.

### Automatically unfair reasons for dismissal

Some reasons for dismissal are likely to be automatically unfair, and in these cases an employment tribunal does not need to go through the process of establishing whether there was a fair reason for the dismissal before it assesses whether or not the employer acted reasonably. These include dismissal related discrimination on grounds of sex, race or disability but also includes:

➤ trade union related dismissals
➤ dismissal on maternity related grounds
➤ dismissal for taking, or proposing to take, some action on health and safety grounds
➤ dismissal for having sought in good faith to exercise a statutory employment right
➤ dismissal of a shop worker or betting worker for refusing, or proposing to refuse, to do shop work on Sundays
➤ reasons connected with the transfer of an undertaking from one employer to another employer – although this is an automatically unfair reason for dismissal, unlike the other automatically unfair reasons, there is a two year qualification period
➤ acting as a representative for consultation about redundancy or business transfer or presenting oneself as a candidate to be this type of representative
➤ performing or proposing to perform duties in connection with an employee's role as an employee occupational pension trustee.

In these automatically unfair reasons for dismissal the employment tribunal does not have to go through the two-stage process, firstly establishing that there was a fair reason for the dismissal, then investigating whether the employer acted reasonably. In these cases the employment tribunal has to find the dismissal fair or unfair just with regard to the reasonableness of the actions of the employer and the reason for the dismissal.

#### Trade union related dismissals

It is an automatically unfair reason for dismissal if the dismissal is for trade union membership or activities. This will apply whether the employee is dismissed because of expressing his or her intention to join a trade union or not to join a trade union, or for his or her actual membership or non-membership of a trade union. It also applies if someone is dismissed just because of their trade union activities, such as handing out leaflets or going to a trade union meeting.

#### Dismissal on maternity related grounds

The law relating to pregnancy is complex but it obviously does not make very good business sense to dismiss someone in whom an organisation has invested time and training, just because she is pregnant. This is another automatically unfair reason for dismissal. An unfair dismissal of this type could also prove to be potentially very expensive for an employer as many claims of this type are also brought under sex discrimination legislation and there is no upper limit set on the amount of compensation that the woman could claim.

### Dismissal on health and safety grounds

Once again the dismissal will be automatically unfair if the employer dismisses the employee or selects him or her for redundancy because he or she tried to bring health and safety issues to the attention of the employer. It would also be an automatically unfair dismissal if it was because the employee carried out or even just tried to carry out designated duties relating to health and safety or prevention of accidents at work, or because of his or her activities as a safety representative or on a safety committee.

### Dismissal for wishing to exercise a statutory right

The dismissal will be automatically unfair if it occurs as a result of the employee bringing proceedings against the employer or alleging that an employer has infringed a statutory employment right such as a right to a minimum period of notice or the right of a trade union official for paid time off to carry out duties.

### Dismissal of a shop worker for refusing to work on Sundays

Shop workers or betting office workers who are dismissed for refusal to work on a Sunday are also able to claim this as an automatically unfair reason for dismissal. When Sunday trading was introduced, some workers feared that they would be dismissed if they were unwilling to work on a Sunday so this is designed to afford them some protection.

### Dismissal relating to the transfer of an undertaking

When an undertaking or business is transferred from one employer to another, for example when someone buys an existing business, and an employee is dismissed as a result of this transfer, the dismissal will be automatically unfair unless the employer (either the vendor or purchaser) can prove that there are economic, technical or organisational reasons for the dismissal. However, although this is one of the automatically unfair reasons for dismissal, in this instance there is a qualifying period of two years' employment before someone could bring a claim.

### Dismissal of a person because of his or her actions as a representative of the workforce for consultation about redundancy or business transfer

Another automatically unfair reason for dismissal occurs if the employer dismisses a person who was acting on behalf of the workforce, or who is proposing to act as their representative in connection with negotiations about redundancy or business transfer. This is to prevent unscrupulous employers from effectively 'shooting the messenger' by dismissing unfairly those who try to help or act on behalf of the employees.

### Dismissal of a person because he or she is carrying out their role on an occupational pension scheme

It is also automatically unfair to dismiss employees because, in their role as an occupational pension trustee, they may have to perform certain duties such as to question their employer about payments, accounts or actions that have taken place. Once again, in the light of various alleged occupational pension scandals, such as the Maxwell case, which have occurred in recent years, one can see that it is necessary to afford protection to employees who may have to challenge unscrupulous employers with regard to occupational pensions.

### Wrongful dismissal

Wrongful dismissal is based on contract law and relates to instances when the employer has broken the contract. One of the most common examples of breach of contract is when the employee is dismissed without notice in circumstances where this is clearly not deserved because of any wrong doing on the part of the employee, or where the employee is dismissed but with the incorrect period of notice. Unlike claims of unfair dismissal, there is no qualifying length of service required for eligibility to bring a case of wrongful dismissal.

### Compensation for unfair dismissal

If a former employee wins his or her case for unfair dismissal at an employment tribunal the compensation awarded may take several forms.

### Reinstatement

In this case the employment tribunal says that the employer must give the former employee their old job back on exactly the same terms and conditions as before and pay compensation for any loss of wages while not employed. Failure on the part of the employer to comply with this order is likely to result in additional financial awards, known as an Additional or Special Award, being made to the employee.

### Re-engagement

This means that the employment tribunal states that the employer must re-employ their former employee but it may be in a different job or on different terms and conditions of employment. For instance it may not be possible to give them back their old job as the vacancy may already have been filled by a new employee.

### Compensation

This means financial compensation and is divided into the basic award and the compensatory award. The basic award is calculated in the same way as the statutory redundancy payment which is discussed later in this chapter. It is calculated by taking into account the age, number of years in that employer's service and amount of the average weekly wage. At the moment the weekly wage included in the calculation is subject to a weekly maximum of £220.00 per week. The DTI publishes an easy table for calculating these figures.

In some circumstances there may be deductions taken from the amount awarded by the employment tribunal. For example, if the employment tribunal feels that the employee partially contributed to his or her own dismissal or if the employer offered to reinstate the employee and he or she refused unreasonably.

A compensatory award may also be made and this is to take account of factors such as loss of earnings, loss of pension rights or loss of benefits, such as company car or house. At the time of writing there are limits on both the amount that can be paid as part of the basic award and for the compensatory award, but in the White Paper *Fairness at Work*, the government has indicated that it would like to abandon these upper limits. There are already unlimited awards made, as mentioned earlier, in cases of dismissal related to sex, race or disability discrimination. An additional award may also be made if the dismissal was for trade unionism.

## Redundancy
••••••••••••••

We discussed earlier the fact that redundancy can be a potentially fair reason for dismissal. However, great care must be taken in the selection of those who are to be made redundant, and a large number of employment tribunal cases are brought each year where employees feel that they have been unfairly selected for redundancy.

### Steps to preclude the need for redundancies

Any organisation should choose first to take various steps to try to preclude or minimise the need for redundancies. Good human resource planning should help to minimise this need, but however effective the human resource planning there may still be a need for redundancies because of other problems, such as the unexpected loss of a large order or the failure of the business of a large debtor. However, it is good practice to consider other steps before actually making people redundant, and if this is done it may be possible to minimise or preclude the need for any redundancies at all. A calm objective review of the situation is called for, and a consideration of all possible alternatives, as it would be foolish to contemplate making good employees redundant if a simpler solution were feasible. These steps should include:

➤ asking for voluntary redundancies
➤ terminating the use of non-employees who are self-employed, or staff employed by agencies
➤ giving people the option of early retirement packages
➤ stopping recruitment
➤ stopping overtime
➤ starting short-time working
➤ ensuring that all employees over the organisation's normal retirement age actually retire
➤ giving employees the option of part-time work or job-shares
➤ use of retraining
➤ using natural wastage over a period of time instead of making employees redundant
➤ consultation with various groups in order to get suggestions to minimise the need for redundancy.

### Selection for redundancy

If these preventive measures fail or are not likely to achieve the desired reduction in staffing level, the employer needs to decide how to select and implement the redundancies. Ideally there should be an agreed redundancy procedure which has been negotiated with representatives of the workforce long before there was any threat of redundancy, and which provides clear guidelines and criteria for the employer to follow in the selection process. However, any such procedure needs to be checked regularly to ensure that it is up to date.

### Consultation

If there is an agreed procedure, then it should be followed. If no such procedure exists, the employer should reflect and weigh up the options instead of reaching a hasty decision and, most importantly, should consult with the workforce and trade unions, giving all those concerned an opportunity to state their case. Secrecy in redundancy normally results in worse problems, with rumours being rife and employees imagining the situation is worse than it actually is. Morale is always likely to be low when there is a threat of any redundancy, but rumour and uncertainty are likely to make it much worse. Under the Trade Union and Labour Relations (Consolidation) Act 1992 there is a duty to consult collectively when between 20 and 99 employees are likely to be made redundant at one establishment within a period of 30 days. For these numbers the consultation would need to start at least 30 days before the first planned redundancy. If more than 100 employees are likely to be made redundant, at one place of work within a 90 day period, this consultation must begin at least 90 days before the first of the redundancies. ACAS recommend that consultation should start as soon as possible. Until recently there was a legal duty to consult with any recognised trade union, even if only one person was being considered for redundancy, and to give the union information about the numbers likely to be involved and the proposed method of selection for redundancy, although not necessarily the actual names of those to be made redundant. It will always be good practice for human resource practitioners to involve the workforce and to consult with their representatives, and recent changes in law further encourage this process, although these changes also affect who should be consulted.

In 1994 the European Court of Justice ruled that employers must consult either a recognised trade union or an elected representative of employees affected by collective redundancies or business transfer of ownership. The Collective Redundancies and Transfer of Undertakings (Protection of Employment) Regulations 1995, came into force on 26 October 1995 and is the government's response to the European ruling. Employers now have a duty to consult with 'appropriate representatives' when 20 or more employees are to be made redundant. Prior to this legislation it was necessary to consult with a recognised trade union when 10 or more employees were to be made redundant. Employers now have a choice as to whom they consult and can either consult with non-union elected representatives of the workforce, or with the trade union, and this choice applies even if there is a recognition agreement with the trade union. If there is no recognised trade union then the employer must consult with employees' elected representatives. Failure to consult in sufficient time with the appropriate employees' representatives can also lead to a protective award being made by an employment tribunal. This means that the employees would still receive their normal wages for the protected period, and could do so for as long as 90 days if the failure to consult related to possible redundancies for more than 100 employees.

There is still an obligation to consult with individuals and to notify redundancies to the DTI; this information should be given on form HR1, and it should include details of the trade unions recognised by the employer as representing the employees who are likely to be affected, and also the date that the consultation process with those trade unions began. Failure to provide this information may result in a fine of up to £5000.

### Selection criteria for redundancy

Employers need to choose criteria for selection carefully. They can use 'last in first out', sometimes referred to as LIFO, or other criteria such as level of competence or attendance record.

ACTIVITY **15.3**

Read the following case study and answer the questions that follow.

The Spartan Insurance Company has decided that it is overstaffed and that it must cut back on its office staff. The departmental manager for administration recommends that the post room and print room, which between them employ seven staff, should be amalgamated into one section. This will eliminate the need for three members of staff.

The post room is run by Mr Arshad Mohammed, who is aged 34, is extremely efficient and has been with the organisation for three years. There are three other members of staff in this section – Mrs Sarah Sergeant, Ms Sandra Smythe and Mr Terry Gibbs. Mrs Sarah Sergeant, a widow aged 55, has worked for Spartan Insurance for 20 years. She has always been an extremely reliable employee, but since the death of her husband 18 months ago, she has suffered greatly from ill-health and has had a series of illnesses linked to depression.

Ms Sandra Smythe is a fairly recent recruit to the organisation. She is aged 25 and has been employed for six months. She has settled into the job well and is very efficient in everything she has to do, but is the first to admit that she still has a great deal to learn.

The most junior member of staff in this section is Terry Gibbs. He is only 20 and joined Spartan Insurance Company straight from school. He has been employed by the company for two years and seemed to have a few problems making the transition from school to work: Mr Mohammed has spoken to him once or twice about his attitude to work. More recently Mr Mohammed has had to warn him about his timekeeping, and he received a verbal warning and a written warning about this. The written warning is still current and does not expire for a further month, but Terry has taken this warning extremely seriously and there has been a noticeable improvement in both his attitude and his timekeeping.

The print room has three staff – Mr George Brownlow, Mrs Rashida Ali and Ms Sally Wilson. Mr Brownlow, aged 44, is the supervisor of this section but in reality he does not actually perform any supervisory duties. Neither is he qualified to service any of the machines. He spends most of his time grumbling about the company and telling the other staff to get on with their work. He has been employed by the organisation for ten years and it is generally thought that he was moved to his present job where he would be out of everyone's way, because of his generally uncooperative nature. It is believed that this situation was allowed to develop because he was a close personal friend of a former branch manager. This manager has long since left the organisation but Mr Brownlow is always clever enough not to do anything to warrant dismissal, and has not even received any warnings about his work. He is also a prominent local councillor and spends quite a bit of time attending council meetings.

Luckily for Mr Brownlow there are two very efficient employees who cover for his inefficiency and who do most of the work. Mrs Ali is 35 and has worked for Spartan Insurance for four years. She knows almost everything that there is to know about the machines and in effect runs the section. Sally Wilson is also extremely efficient; she is seventeen years old and has been employed for a year, having started last summer straight from school.

1   What criteria would you propose for selection for redundancy here?
2   Which employees would you select for redundancy?
3   Who would be selected for redundancy if you agreed to use the LIFO method?
4   Who would be selected for redundancy if you chose criteria based on poor attendance or level of competence?

### Discussion of Activity 15.3

You might have chosen criteria based on length of employment or factors such as level of competence or attendance and timekeeping.

If you chose to use LIFO then you would make the following people redundant: Ms Sandra Smythe (employed for 6 months), Mr Terry Gibbs (employed for 2 years) and Ms Sally Wilson (employed for 1 year).

If you chose criteria such as timekeeping and level of efficiency you are likely to have proposed the selection of Mr Brownlow, Mr Terry Gibbs and Mrs Sergeant.

The implications and importance of selection criteria are discussed below with further reference to this case study.

#### The importance of which selection criteria are used

You can see from Activity 15.3 that the criteria chosen when proposing the selection of people to be made redundant will make a big difference to who is actually selected. LIFO is often preferred by trade unions and it seems an objective method of selection, with those who have the shortest length of employment with the organisation being chosen for redundancy. This method also has the advantage of being easy to use and understand as well as being less costly in terms of redundancy pay. It may, however, as in this case, mean that those who are selected for redundancy are those who, although they have the shortest length of service, may be keen, enthusiastic employees who will have much to offer the organisation in the future. This might result in a stagnating, ageing work force who lack the skills and versatility required for future business success.

Employers often choose to use other criteria so that they can retain such employees while making redundant others who may not have given such good service, even though they have been employed for a much longer period of time. Caution also has to be exercised in this case to ensure that the criteria chosen are objective and fair. Just saying that someone has, for example, 'a poor attitude to work' is not likely to prove adequate grounds for selection for redundancy, as this is rather vague and subjective. More objective criteria need to be used, and the ability to do this depends on whether the organisation has effective records of employee capability and competence. You would need to break job performance down into several areas such as level of skill, knowledge, experience, flexibility, productivity, appraisal records. If you selected Mr Brownlow for redundancy, you would need to have clear evidence about levels of efficiency and output. If, on the other hand, you chose Terry Gibbs for redundancy because of his poor attendance record, you would have to ensure that there are clear records for absence and that the pattern of absenteeism does not appear high because of an uncharacteristic level of ill-health just prior to the redundancy period. Criteria such as disciplinary warnings also need careful checks to ensure that they are still 'live'.

Some criteria may also make the redundancies potentially unlawful if, for example, they apply disproportionately to one sex, one ethnic group, or to employees with disabilities. Whatever the selection criteria used, employers should take care to ensure that the criteria are neither directly nor indirectly discriminatory. Selection of part-time rather than full-time employees may, for instance, constitute indirect sex discrimination if the majority of part-time employees are women and the majority of full-time employees are men.

### *Rights of redundant employees*

#### Consultation with individual employees

Employers should consult with each individual employee who is to be affected by the redundancies, even if there has also been consultation with the unions or with employee representatives. This consultation should:

➤ explain why the redundancies are needed
➤ explain why the particular employee has been selected
➤ show any relevant documentation
➤ explain why no suitable alternative work is currently available
➤ explain any requirements during the notice period such as whether normal working or part-time working is required, whether payment will be made in lieu of notice, or what time off is allowed to seek alternative work or for training.

#### Suitable alternative employment

The employer should offer a suitable alternative job if there is one, rather than making the employee redundant. If the employee's job title is broad, there may be sufficient flexibility to make an offer easily. If this is not the case, the employer should not automatically assume that any alternative employment that involved less pay or status would necessarily be unsuitable to the employee; it should still be discussed. The employees should, however, be given sufficient information about any alternative job so that they can realistically reach a decision, and they should also be offered the chance of a trial period. This should be of four weeks' duration, and will give both the employer and the employee the chance to assess the job's suitability. It should start as the old contract finishes. If a longer trial period is required because of the need for retraining, this should be agreed in writing before the date of commencement of the trial period. If either party finds the new job to be unsuitable during this period then the redundancy situation will still apply, and the redundant employee will still be entitled to his or her redundancy pay.

If the offer of suitable alternative employment is refused by the employee, then the employer has the option of withholding redundancy pay. Any claim to an employment tribunal will have to assess the suitability of the offer and the reasonableness of the refusal.

### Right to time off for job searching or retraining

Employees who have worked for two years for the employer and are about to be made redundant have a statutory entitlement to a reasonable amount of time off from work to look for other jobs or to retrain in order to be able to improve their employment prospects. Any employee who is not allowed a reasonable amount of time off for these purposes can make a complaint to an employment tribunal

### Redundancy pay

Employers are expected to compensate any employee who has been made redundant and who has worked for them for at least two years in continuous employment, by paying them an amount of redundancy pay. The actual amount that the employee may be entitled to if they are redundant is calculated according to age, length of service and weekly pay. There is an upper earnings limit for the amount of weekly pay that may be included in this calculation, and this amount alters each year. Currently the limit on the weekly rate is £220. Redundancy pay is tax-free and does not affect the right to unemployment benefit. Furthermore, the amount that the employee receives is not affected even if she or he starts another job immediately. The calculation of redundancy is based on the actual age of the employee at the date of dismissal, and takes account of each year of service in the appropriate age band as follows:

➤ for each complete year of employment in which the employee was aged 18 or over but was below the age of 22, half a week's pay
➤ for each complete year of employment in which the employee was aged 22 or over but was below the age of 41, one week's pay
➤ for each complete year of employment in which the employee was aged 41 or over but was below the age of 65, one and a half weeks' pay.

ACTIVITY **15.4**

Consider once again the case study given in Activity 15.4 and the following information about the rates of pay of the individuals concerned. In order to simplify the calculation, imagine that each of the people concerned has worked for a whole number of years for the organisation.

Mr Brownlow: £300 per week
Mr Mohammed: £300 per week
Mrs Sergeant: £220´per week
Ms Smythe: £180 per week
Mr Gibbs: £130 per week
Mrs Ali: £210 per week
Ms Wilson: £120 per week

How much redundancy pay would each employee be entitled to?

### Discussion of Activity 15.4

Mr Brownlow has worked for the organisation for 10 years and is aged 44. He has worked for 3 complete years since age 41, so is entitled to $3 \times 1\frac{1}{2}$ weeks' pay = $4\frac{1}{2}$ weeks' pay. He has also worked for 7 years between ages 22 and 40, so is entitled to $7 \times 1$ weeks' pay = 7 weeks' pay.

Therefore Mr Brownlow would be entitled to $11\frac{1}{2}$ weeks' redundancy pay if he were selected for redundancy. His weekly earnings are above the maximum allowed in this calculation, so he would actually be entitled to $11\frac{1}{2} \times £220$ = £2,530.

Mr Mohammed has worked for the organisation for only 3 years and he is aged 34. He would therefore be entitled to $3 \times 1$ week's pay. Thus he would receive $3 \times £220.00 = £660.00$.

Mrs Sergeant has worked for the organisation for 20 years and is aged 55. She has worked 14 years since the age of 41 and would be entitled to $14 \times 1\frac{1}{2}$ week's pay = 21 weeks' pay. She worked for a further 6 years before she was 41 and would be entitled to $6 \times 1$ week's pay = 6 weeks' pay.

The total number of weeks of redundancy pay she is due is therefore 27. Her weekly wage is £220 which is the maximum entitlement. She would be entitled to $27 \times £220 = £5,940$.

Mr Gibbs is aged 20 and has worked for the organisation for two years. Since he is between the ages of 18 and 21 he will only be entitled to $2 \times \frac{1}{2}$ week's redundancy pay = 1 week's redundancy pay. His weekly wage is £130 and so he would be entitled only to £130 in redundancy pay.

Sally Wilson and Sandra Smythe would not be entitled to any redundancy pay as they have not worked for the required qualification period of two years, and Sally Wilson is also too young to be eligible for redundancy pay.

Tables are provided in the Department of Trade and Industry's (DTI) guide to redundancy payments which can be used so that this calculation does not have to be made in this way for every employee.

### More favourable redundancy schemes

You will have noticed that the statutory levels for redundancy pay are not very high, especially if the person concerned is young or has not been employed by that employer for very long. This seems to contradict the huge amounts of redundancy pay that some people are rumoured to receive. This is because some employers have decided to make a more generous provision than is required by law. They may do this in some of the following ways:

➤ calculating entitlements based on actual pay rather than applying the upper earnings limit
➤ reducing the length of qualifying period necessary to receive redundancy pay from two years to one

➤ adding amounts to the statutory scheme
➤ making a more generous calculation such as two or three weeks' pay for each year of service.

They may also be concerned to help their employees in other ways through this difficult period, and may provide an outplacement service.

## Outplacement

This is the international name given to the process that many employers use to assist redundant employees. Outplacement can be defined as the process whereby the employer actively helps the employee to come to terms with the redundancy and assists them in the process of finding a new job or developing a new career. It is a type of aftercare service for employees who are facing redundancy, though it is by no means standard practice for all employers to provide such a service. It has been defined by Alan Jones (1994) as 'the provision of support to candidates during the transitional phase between involuntary/voluntary job loss and resettlement'. This is a useful definition as, although much of outplacement is concerned with job search skills and the finding of a new job or career, there are other avenues to explore such as further training or part-time or voluntary work, or perhaps self-employment. This definition also states that support is provided to the candidate, and this makes it clear that the responsibility for the resettlement process still rests with the candidate himself or herself but that help and support will be given by the outplacement provider.

Traditionally employees who had been made redundant were left very much to fend for themselves, but large employers in particular have increasingly become concerned to provide an aftercare service for their former employees. Initially they concentrated on providing outplacement services just for senior managers as part of their redundancy package, but the provision of outplacement has spread and is now provided in many organisations to all staff who are made redundant. While outplacement is generally provided by or for employers, on occasions individuals whose organisation has not provided this facility may buy this provision for themselves, and a similar service is offered in many areas by the Department of Trade and Industry.

**PAUSE FOR THOUGHT 15.2** *What do you think are the main benefits to the employer of providing an outplacement service? Make a list before you read on.*

### The benefits of providing an outplacement service

Many human resource managers, when faced with making employees redundant, realise that it is important for the organisation to handle this difficult process as smoothly as possible, both for the sake of the individuals concerned and also for the morale of the remaining employees, and in order to maintain or even enhance the good reputation of the organisation. In particular, the benefits to the organisation are likely to include:

➤ improved morale for remaining employees
➤ key staff are more likely to remain with the organisation if they see that other employees are treated well even in a redundancy situation

> good public relations with the local community will be less likely to be affected by the redundancies if they have been handled well
> there may be fewer problems with objections from trade unions if a good outplacement service is provided.

Individuals vary in the effect that redundancy has on them. For a few people it may provide a welcome opportunity to change direction in their careers, while others who have worked for a long time for an organisation may find redundancy a very traumatic experience with which they need help.

The outplacement process normally consists of provision of the following services.

> Counselling about the feelings brought about by the redundancy itself. This may sometimes involve counselling the partner of the person who has been made redundant also.
> Counselling about career or other options.
> Provision of facilities for conducting a job search.
> Provision of facilities for writing letters of application or curriculam vitae.
> Help with writing curriculam vitae and applications for jobs.
> Psychological tests to assist in career choice.
> Opportunities for practising interview skills.
> Possible direct contact with prospective employers.
> There may be provision of facilities in which interviews can be conducted.

An outplacement service can be provided either 'in-house', by the human resource department, or by external consultants.

ACTIVITY **15.5**

List the advantages and the disadvantages of the provision of an in-house outplacement service and compare these with the advantages and disadvantages of external provision of an outplacement service.

**Provision of in-house outplacement service**

**Advantages**                                     **Disadvantages**

**Provision of external outplacement service**

**Advantages**                                     **Disadvantages**

### Discussion of Activity 15.5

Your list probably indicates that provision of an internal outplacement service is likely to be cheaper than using a consultancy. Since many redundancies occur as part of a cost-cutting exercise, employers will be loath to spend additional money and cost may be a major concern. However, an organisation may not have sufficient facilities or levels of expertise to provide the standard of service that is required. Not only that, but it may be difficult, or even impossible, for redundant employees who have recently been told of their redundancy by their line manager or by the human resource manager to be helped by counselling from the same manager or any other manager within the organisation. Even identifying managers or others with suitable expertise may be a problem.

On the other hand, there may also be problems in finding a suitable consultancy with a high degree of expertise in this area. Anyone can establish themselves in business as an outplacement consultant, and they do not necessarily have to have any qualifications. This has been a cause for concern in recent years, with some people being charged high fees for an inadequate service, which has resulted in the Institute of Personnel and Development's issuing a *Code for Career and Outplacement Consultants* (1991). This is a voluntary code of practice but gives some indication of the type of service and qualifications that an outplacement service should provide. It indicates that outplacement consultants should normally have qualifications in psychology, psychometric testing, careers guidance or personnel management, or have extensive experience in these areas. Ideally a firm of consultants would want people who had a range of qualifications in these areas. The IPD also make it clear that there should be a free initial meeting during which there is the opportunity to assess whether the consultancy provides the right sort of expertise to assist the person concerned.

### Conclusion

A discussion of dismissal and redundancy may seem a rather depressing topic but they are not inevitable stages if earlier advice for good human resource practices and procedures are followed.

We also intended the book to provide some practical opportunities via activities for those who are studying human resource management as part of their degree or HND course and an opportunity to consider and gain understanding of issues they may be concerned with, whether they pursue a career as a specialist in HRM or are concerned with HRM as part of their future managerial or supervisory role. If you have worked through the Activities you will have gained a much wider understanding of the subject, and we hope that you have also taken the opportunity to check your progress and understanding by completing the self-check exercises, and to follow up on our other suggested sources in areas that have a particular interest for you.

We have gone through the employment process in an almost chronological order, and examined the approaches of human resource practitioners to finding and selecting people by the use of human resource planning. We have also examined the employment relationship and how people should then be treated while they are working for the organisation, whether as employees or in some other capacity, how they should be trained and developed, and how they should be motivated and rewarded. We considered ways in which some problems may be prevented or, failing prevention, how they should be handled and we discussed this in relation to counselling and welfare, employee involvement, health and safety, and discipline and grievance handling. We have included dismissal and redundancy since it is likely that even with the best planning there will be occasional dismissals, as people operate from different standpoints and have different points of view, and will therefore not always act in the way in which the organisation hopes that they will act.

Dismissal and redundancy can be avoided to some extent by adopting good HRM techniques and programmes described in the rest of the text. Problems associated with redundancy and dismissal, both for employers and employees, will also be minimised by proper handling as described in this chapter.

Just like any other area of HRM, this area is also subject to change, so one needs to be constantly vigilant. A change under discussion at the time of writing that the reader may like to check is the reduction of the length of qualifying experience for many employment rights such as redundancy and unfair dismissal to one year.

All who are involved in the management of people, whether they call themselves HRM managers, personnel managers or line managers, must be aware of the need for strategic planning and clear links between everyone's work and the aims of the business even though most of you will not initially have the opportunity to operate at a strategic level.

All who are involved in human resource management also need to be aware of the law, and although this may be dealt with in more detail in other specialist modules in your course, we have felt it necessary to include brief summaries of relevant legislation in appropriate chapters for those of you who do not have the opportunity to study employment law modules. As you will have discovered by now, the law is always changing, and it is very important to ensure that you know how to find information about the current state of legislation.

**REVIEW QUESTIONS**

Brief answers to the review questions are provided on page 431.

**1** In June 1998, after rioting and damage was caused by football hooligans attending the World Cup matches in France, Tony Blair, the Prime Minister, urged employers to deal severely with those employees found guilty of football hooliganism. Many commentators interpreted this as meaning that such employees should be dismissed. What advice would you give to employers who found that one of their employees was guilty of football hooliganism?

**2** What are the likely effects of a change in the rules for eligibility for a claim of unfair dismissal, with the qualification period being reduced from two years to one year?

**3** Outline the circumstances that are considered to constitute fair dismissal and comment on the extent to which an organisation should be expected to avoid dismissing employees.

Answer the following multiple choice questions. The answers are provided on page 431 for you to check your understanding of this chapter.

1   Constructive dismissal is said to occur in which of the following circumstances?
    (*a*) The employer constructs a false case against the employee in order to dismiss him or her.
    (*b*) A fixed-term contract expires and is not renewed.
    (*c*) The employee leaves, with or without giving notice, in circumstances such that he or she is entitled to go without notice by reason of the employer's conduct.
    (*d*) The employment is terminated by the employer, with or without notice.
    (*e*) The employee is encouraged to take early retirement.

2   Which of the following is *not* a potentially fair reason for dismissal?
    (*a*) Misconduct.
    (*b*) Lack of capability.
    (*c*) Lack of a qualification.
    (*d*) A statutory restriction placed on the employer or on the employee
    (*e*) The employee does not have the relevant qualification period.

3   Which of the following is a good definition of outplacement?
    (*a*) The employee is placed temporarily in another organisation with a view to improving their job chances.
    (*b*) The employee is actively helped by the employer to come to terms with the redundancy and assisted in finding a new job or developing a new career.
    (*c*) A form of job share that is introduced to minimise the need for redundancies.
    (*d*) Another word for the redundancy process.
    (*e*) A service provided by consultants to employers to help them out when faced with redundancies.

4   Which of the following should *not* be one of the steps to take to minimise the need for redundancy?
    (*a*) Give people the option of early retirement packages.
    (*b*) Use natural wastage over a period of time instead of making employees redundant.
    (*c*) Dismiss all employees who do not have the necessary length of employment to bring a case for unfair dismissal.
    (*d*) Terminate the use of non-employees such as self-employed or agency staff.
    (*e*) Ask for voluntary redundancies.

5   An employer must disclose certain information to the trade unions before making people redundant. Which of the following is not one of the things that the employer must disclose at this stage?
    (*a*) The names of the people to be made redundant.
    (*b*) The reasons for the dismissals.
    (*c*) The proposed method of selection for redundancy.
    (*d*) The method of carrying out the redundancies.
    (*e*) The number and description of employees likely to be involved in redundancy.

## References

Advisory, Conciliation and Arbitration Service. *Annual Report 1997*, ACAS 1998.

DTI. Fairness at Work. Cm 3968, Department of Trade and Industry, May 1998, Chapter 3 (Web site at http://www.dti.gov.uk/IR/fairness/index.htm)

IPM. *Code for Career and Outplacement Consultants*. IPM, 1991.

Jones, Alan. *Delivering In-House Outplacement. A Practical Guide for Trainers, Managers and Personnel Specialists*. McGraw-Hill, 1994.

Korn, Anthony. Appeal court rules on unfair dismissal. *Personnel Today*, 29 August 1995.

Sage, Gill. Health warning, *People Management*, 16 April 1998.

## Further study

### Books

Advisory, Conciliation and Arbitrary Service Advisory Booklet. *Redundancy Handling*. ACAS, 1997. (An excellent clear guide to good practice.)

Croner's Employment Law Editorial Department. *Croner's Guide to Managing Fair Dismissal*. Croner Publications, 1993. (A clear step-by-step guide to assist employers to ensure any dismissal that they make is fair.)

Eggert, Max. *Outplacement – A Guide to Management and Delivery*. IPM, 1991.

We have found all the Department of Trade and Industry publications to be extremely useful. Those that are particularly relevant to this topic include the following.

PL 703, *Facing Redundancy? Time Off for Job Hunting or to Arrange Training.*

PL 707, (Rev 7), *Rights to Notice and Reasons for Dismissal.*

PL 712 (Rev 11), *Unfairly Dismissed?*

PL 714 (Rev 5), *Fair and Unfair Dismissal: a Guide for Employers.*

PL 808 (Rev 5), *Redundancy Payments.*

PL 833 (Rev 4), *Redundancy Consultation and Notification.*

Fowler, Alan. *Redundancy*. IPM, 1993. (An excellent detailed guide to good management practice in handling all aspects of redundancy.)

Jay, Linda and Patchett, Bob. *Croner's Guide to Managing Redundancy*. Croner Publications, 1995. (A clear summary of the law concerning redundancies, intended to help managers through the maze of legislation.)

Rubenstein, Michael and Frost, Yvonne. *Unfair Dismissal – a Guide to Relevant Case Law*. Eclipse Group, 1995.

Waud, Christopher. *The Daily Telegraph Employment Law 1994–5*. 10th edition, Kogan Page, 1994. (An excellent practical guide which covers most aspects of employment law and is designed for use by personnel managers, trade union officials, employers, employees and lawyers.)

### Articles

Crofts, Pauline. Outplacement: a way of never having to say you're sorry? *Personnel Management*, May 1992. (An excellent short article which explains the history of outplacement provision and the standards required.)

Fowler, Alan. How to manage redundancies. *PM Plus*, July 1990. (A clear short article which summarises good practice in relation to the handling of redundancies.)

*Income Data Services Briefs and Employment Law and Practice* are excellent sources of up-to-the-minute discussion of cases and changes in employment law. We also recommend for this purpose *Croner's Industrial Relations Briefing*.

### Other sources

ACAS telephone advice service. There are ACAS offices in most large towns and you should be able to find them in the telephone book. Alternatively, Department of Trade and Industry offices such as Job Centres should be able to give you their telephone number, which is also listed in DTI booklets.

### The internet

Law Rights – Employment Questions and Answers (This site provides fact sheets on a wide range of legal issues including employment law. It also has a series of questions and answers which may be useful for you in providing additional practice in answering questions relating to the legal issues raised both in this chapter and other areas of this book.)

**http://www.lawrights.co.uk/empq2.htm**

The Advisory, Conciliation and Arbitration Service (Another source of information for ACAS publications, some of which are published in full on this site.)

**http://www.acas.org.uk**

The Department of Trade and Industry (Many useful DTI publications, discussion documents and some pieces of legislation can be found on this site.)

**http://www.dti.gov.uk**

# CHAPTER 16

# The way forward

Throughout this text we have described current developments, particularly on a national or European basis, that have an impact on the practice of human resource management and life at work in general. We have also alluded to developments elsewhere in the world and occasionally taken a more historical perspective. The question that remains to be addressed in this final chapter is what does the future hold and how will this affect the HR practitioner?

One way of trying to forecast the future is to look at the past to identify trends and then predict how these are likely to continue in the years and decades ahead. We are living at a time in history when many minds seem to be more focused than usual on our place in it: the advent of a new millennium. Much effort is being devoted in many countries to finding a suitable way to celebrate such a supposedly momentous event (at least that provides a measure of employment), and the communications media will no doubt intensify their scrutiny of the history of the last century.

So what message does the out-going century hold for us in preparing us to meet the new millennium? The one major characteristic that most commentators seem to agree on is an acceleration in the rate of change to which we are exposed, a fact which makes predictions based on an analysis of past trends a seemingly futile exercise. There is a large body of literature on change and change management, and the term 'discontinuous change' has become established. No doubt you can think of different examples of change in the twentieth century which have affected or are likely to affect organisations and the role of the HR manager. We have chosen the following as examples which include some change which was momentous at the time and which could not have been foreseen a decade before, or even closer to, the event:

➤ Developments in information technology and communications are not only rapid but pervasive, affecting a multitude of people in a multitude of ways in both their personal and their working lives.

➤ Partly as a result of improved communication, the market for trade has become global, and a world view is necessary for adequate strategic thinking, particularly for large companies.

➤ The last two decades of the twentieth century witnessed the end of the isolation of Eastern European Communist countries. The Berlin Wall fell and the former East and West Germany merged into one country. In the 1990s, most of these countries, e.g. Russia and Hungary, are still struggling with their adaptation to their new *modus operandi*. Political and business observers will be interested to see what role emerges for these countries in the future.

> The development of market-driven economies in previously Communist countries in the Far East, such as China and Vietnam, means they are emerging both as opportunities for business and as competitors.

> In the late 1990s, the business world was taken aback by the collapse of a number of banks in Japan. Japanese workers were cited in the press as being totally crushed that their much vaunted job security was no longer there. The extent of the repercussions of these events for the rest of the world has yet to be measured.

You can no doubt add to this list of both gradual and unexpected events from the past decades and century. Balanced against the things that have changed, there are other important issues of concern related to business and humans in general, e.g. the intransigence of the massive scale of poverty and human misery on the Indian and African sub-continents, the threat of global warming.

Although it is important to react to global events, we must also plan for the future on a national and personal level. The adoption of the Euro, a unified European currency, in the EU has caused much debate in the late 1990s as a number of the member states get closer to adopting it. As citizens of Europe, we need to be aware of its impact. A unified currency is meant to simplify intra-European transactions. Is this what will actually happen? The currency also has a symbolic significance and is meant to lead to a strengthened feeling of European unity. Will this become an actuality in the first decade of the twenty-first century? In Chapter 13 we looked specifically at current developments in the field of employee relations. How will employee relations philosophy and climate evolve over the next few years in the UK and in the rest of the EU? Remember also that in Chapter 2 we pointed out that regional developments are very often of the most immediate importance for businesses and families in the decisions that they make.

How will all these changes affect the future role of HR managers? Will yet more of the role be devolved to line managers or will the HR role be outsourced or will a totally new role emerge? Will there be increasing mobility of labour between countries, or increased use of teleworking, or will organisations move their work from one country to another to take account of more favourable economic or political conditions, or will a completely new pattern of work develop? Maybe the lesson we must learn from this is to plan for the future and think strategically but to expect the unexpected and be flexible enough to deal with it.

On a personal level, one immediate consideration is what will you constructively do now with the knowledge and skills you have developed from studying this text? There are several possibilities:

> Many of you may already be at work, either in an HR capacity or in another field of endeavour, some will be about to find work or start a placement before returning for a final year of study. Whatever work situation you are in, you should find ample opportunity to apply and develop the ideas covered here on a practical basis. This calls for the use of the reflection and implementation stages of the learning cycle, which always leads on to further analysis and refinement of your knowledge and practical skills.

➤ You may at some stage decide to go on with further formal study in this field or you may simply be interested enough to continue reading out of personal interest. This book was written as an introduction to aspects of HRM, and every topic addressed here is worthy of study in greater depth. Our coverage fits with much of what the IPD calls core personnel and development, and there are generalist modules at a higher level, including Employee Development, Employee Resourcing and Employee Relations, each of which picks up and develops further the topics we have introduced. There are also many further specialist modules such as management development which deal in depth with topics we have touched on in this book.

Even when you have completed your formal education, it is necessary to go on learning to remain competitive in the world of work. One message that must have become clear while reading this book is that there is a constant need to remain up to date with changes and developments in law, political thinking, technology and practices. The concepts of continuous improvement and life-long learning imply that not only is there always room for each of us to do things better, but that we should always seek to learn new things. In recognition of this, many professional associations, including the IPD, require evidence of some sort of systematic Continuing Professional Development (CPD) from individuals who wish to maintain their professional membership. The IPD requests a record of CPD from members who wish to upgrade their membership, a record that should be both retrospective and project plans for the coming year.

In conclusion, we would like to reiterate our belief that we can look forward to a dynamic future, whatever the actual events. We cannot afford to be parochial in our thinking and must take a global approach to our planning while adopting a personal style of continuous improvement. Assuming that you have studied this text with a view to playing some active role in the business world, we hope we have succeeded in kindling your interest in some aspect of HRM which you can now proceed to develop.

## Further study

As well as studying HRM in more detail by undertaking generalist or specialist modules or by working towards NVQs, try to ensure that you develop a broader viewpoint so that you can consider HR issues within a national or international context. Read newspapers and journals such as *The Economist* on a regular basis. Watch informative TV programmes such as the national news broadcasts, the *Money Programme*, and special documentaries on life in other countries. Listen to the equivalent radio programmes broadcast on Radio 4. And, of course, use appropriate web sites.

# Answers to review and self-check questions

We have provided a skeleton guide to issues you might address in answering review questions. In an exam or for an assignment, you would be expected to develop the ideas more fully to show your understanding of the topic. You can also enhance your response by making references to further reading.

## Chapter 1 Introducing human resource management

### Answers to review questions

It is not possible to provide model answers to the review questions for Chapter 1 because you will all have arrived at very individual answers to the activities suggested.

### Answers to self-check questions

**1** (*c*), **2** (*c*), **3** (*b*), **4** (*d*), **5** (*a*)

## Chapter 2 Human resource strategy and planning

### Answers to review questions

1. ➤ The levels of strategy are corporate, business and functional.
   ➤ You might wish to review the generic strategies associated with the corporate level (growth; stability; retrenchment) and the business level (cost competitiveness; differentiation of products or services; focus on a niche in the market).
   ➤ In general, it is expected that business strategies will grow out of corporate strategies and functional strategies will grow out of business strategies. However, each level can provide useful information for the others. Human resource strategies will have a direct impact on all the other functional strategies, and conversely cannot be formulated without knowledge of what the other functional goals are.
2. ➤ Define job analysis as the process of documenting the tasks performed in a company and the skills required to perform these tasks.
   ➤ Describe how job analysis results in job descriptions, person specifications and competency profiles.

- ➤ Comment on the range of functions that are supported by these documents.
- ➤ Explain how job analysis contributes to these functions: e.g. up-to-date, standardised information.

3  ➤ Name the major stages and describe how each is carried out.
- ➤ Development of the corporate plan: issues and information to be considered.
- ➤ Estimate demand for human resources: techniques such as work study.
- ➤ Estimate supply of human resources: skills inventory; effects of labour turnover. Labour force issues.
- ➤ Formulate human resource action plans: describe the functional areas.
- ➤ Comment on the need for evaluation and feedback into the corporate objectives.

4  ➤ Comment on the decisions made throughout the human resource planning process: what the corporate objectives are to be; what skills are required to achieve these objectives; how the organisation decides whether it has these skills; what action is to be taken.
- ➤ Describe the sources of information for each of these areas: knowledge of product and market developments; managerial judgement; CPIS; statistical information about the labour force.

## Answers to self-check questions

**1** Growth; stability; retrenchment. **2** Cost leadership; differentation, focus. **3**(*b*); **4** Job title; reports to; responsible for; purpose of job; major duties. **5** Recruitment and selection; day-to-day performance management; long-term performance management/performance appraisal; identification of training needs; job evaluation. **6** Job modelling. **7** 50%. **8** 80%. **9** Problems with keeping new employees. **10** Estimate the supply of human resources.

## Chapter 3  Recruitment
......................

## Answers to review questions 1, 3 and 5

1  ➤ You should name and describe each relevant act: Sex Discrimination Act 1975; Race Relations Act 1976; Disability Discrimination Act 1995; Rehabilitation of Offenders Act 1974; Equal Pay Act 1970.
- ➤ Can you give a good description of the protection that each of these acts provides?
- ➤ Explain what is meant by direct discrimination, indirect discrimination, and victimisation.
- ➤ Discuss the need for equal opportunities policies, their integration into procedures, and the need for training and awareness throughout an organisation.
- ➤ You might also comment that some employers are looking to go beyond equality of opportunity by encouraging the active management of diversity in the workforce.

3 ➤ Explain how each section of these documents can help in designing a job advertisement.

➤ Comment on the need to give information of this kind so prospective applicants can engage in an informed process of self-selection.

5 ➤ Effects of an internal recruitment policy; the message that the employer rewards good performance.

➤ Adoption of and commitment to an equal opportunities policy.

➤ Treating people well and with respect in any telephone, written or personal contact.

### Answers to self-check questions

**1** (*c*); **2** (*b*); **3** (*a*); **4** The conviction is spent, so if you feel that John is otherwise qualified for the post, you have no good reason to reject him. He was entitled not to disclose his conviction since it was spent. **5** p. 63; **6** p. 64; **7** pp. 66/67; **8** No; **9** False. **10** pp. 67/68.

## Chapter 4  Selection: shortlisting and interviews

### Answers to review questions

1   The aim of selection is to 'choose the best person for the job'. Selectors gather and analyse information in an attempt to predict the performance of applicants in the job. This must be done as objectively as possible, by matching evidence of the knowledge, skills and personal qualities of applicants with the requirements outlined in the person specification. The selection process must also be fair, avoiding any unlawful discrimination in terms of sex, race and disability.

Methodical approaches include:

➤ having a selection policy and procedure which define the steps that will be followed in filling any vacancy

➤ using the person specification as a checklist when shortlisting applicants

➤ devising a set of standard questions to cover all the requirements on the person specification

➤ gathering a full set of information from all candidates and using this information to assess their suitability for the post.

Making sure that candidates can assess their own suitability for a post is also part of effective selection. Employers should therefore ensure that there is adequate opportunity for applicants to gather information about the company and the post during the selection process.

2   Validity and reliability are terms used in statistics to report on the results of tests. If a test consistently produces similar results when used at different times and administered by different people, then it would score high in reliability. Thus if an applicant was interviewed for a particular post by Mr Smith on Monday morning, and the same applicant was interviewed for the same post by Mr Jones on Friday afternoon, we would expect the same result if we thought that the interview was a reliable test. Research has, however, shown that interviews can be low in reliability.

Validity is an indicator of how well the test measures what it purports to measure. How well do interviews predict good performance on the job? Again, research has indicated that interviews can be low in validity. It must, however, be noted that a structured approach to interviewing can raise the level of both the reliability and the validity of employment interviews.

3   Employment interviews run a particular risk of being low in validity if they are approached in an unstructured fashion with the interviewers not properly prepared, and simply asking whatever they think is relevant in an impromptu manner. In these circumstances, interviewers are more likely to fall prey to perceptual errors than if they were conducting a structured interview.

Perceptual errors include the halo effect, the contrast effect, hiring in one's own image, and quite simply not gathering sufficient and relevant data.

These perceptual errors can be avoided simply by being aware of them and making a conscious effort to resist them. If a structured interview is conducted using a set of questions which is designed to elicit full information related to the person specification, and an attempt is made to assess all candidates objectively against these criteria, then the validity of the interview process should also increase.

4   The different types of questions that can be asked include open, closed, leading, probing, situational, and patterned behaviour description questions. Each kind of question will typically elicit a different sort of response from applicants, so interviewers should carefully design their questions to gain the specific information they are seeking.

Closed questions can be used to confirm information. However, the interview is an opportunity to gain as much information as possible, and open questions are more likely to encourage applicants to talk freely. Most questions used in an interview should therefore be open questions. Probing questions can also be used to clarify points or seek more in-depth information.

Leading questions, which indicate to the interviewee what the expected response is, are not useful.

Experienced interviewers can make good use of situational and patterned behaviour description questions. These require applicants to address their own behaviour in incidents which are typical of the post. Patterned behaviour description questions assume that applicants have previous related experience, whereas situational questions address what an applicant *would do* if faced with a particular situation in the future.

### *Answers to self-check questions*

**1** (*c*). **2** False. **3** (*b*). **4** (*d*). **5** (*d*). **6**(i) (c). **6**(ii) (*b*). **7** (*a*). **8** Patterned behaviour description. **9** Equal opportunities monitoring.

## Chapter 5  Selection: supplementing the interview

### *Answers to self-check questions*

**1** (*b*); **2** Validity. **3** No. **4** True. **5** (*c*). **6** (*b*). **7** False. **8** (*b*). **9** False. **10** (*b*).

## Chapter 6   The employment relationship

### Answers to review questions 1 and 3

1   It is not possible to forecast what you may discover when perusing recent articles or court cases because although some issues remain contentious for many years, there are always new issues arising too. However, you will probably notice that some new issues can be directly linked to new legislation which needs to be interpreted. The meaning of new employment legislation is often tested in Employment Tribunals and the appeal courts.

   Through doing this exercise, you will have further developed your competence in finding information. We hope you will also reflect on your learning. If you have done so, you may have realised a few implications including the following:

   ➤   new issues are constantly arising in the HRM field, and practitioners need to stay abreast of developments by engaging in activities similar the one you have just completed;

   ➤   you can adapt this activity to other issues too, such as unlawful discrimination, unfair dismissal, redundancy.

3   Annual leave; paternity leave: number of days/weeks allowed; may pay during paternity leave; may give more notice of termination of employment; maternity leave and pay provisions may be more generous than the statutory minimum.

### Answers to self-check questions

**1** (c); **2** Express terms are those that are addressed directly; implied terms are those that are not expressed directly but are taken as assumed. **3** Fidelity; obedience of lawful and reasonable orders; and working with due diligence and care. **4** Nine weeks. **5** One week. **6** Employment Rights Act. **7** Fourteen weeks but this is under review and may be increased to eighteen weeks. **8** False. **9** False. **10** Isolation of employees; difficulties with supervision.

## Chapter 7   Training and the learning process

### Answers to review questions

It is impossible once again to give answers to the review questions in Chapter 7 as your answers will be individual to you.

### Answers to self-check questions

**1** (a) This effect is known as a *conditioned response*. (b) The cat food is the *stimulus* for Caroline's cats to make an appearance. (c) *Association*. The cats have started to associate the sound of the kettle with the cat food being put out for it. (d) In time the sound of the kettle becomes the *Conditioned stimulus*, and the cats' response to it becomes the conditioned response. **2** (b). **3** (c). **4** (a). **5** (e). **6** (b). **7** (d).

## Chapter 8  Training and development programmes

### Answers to review questions

1   A possible source of information would be a recent issue of the the IRS Employee Development Bulletin. This is published monthly and is to be found within the IRS Employment Review which is published twice a month.

2   There is a huge amount of information on the Internet relating to these topics. Once you have chosen your topic and found information you will need to list all the key benefits from the introduction of that topic if you are to persuade a line manager about the topic. Consider the benefits to the organisation and the individual and particularly the potential benefits to the line manager, such as greater efficiency and higher productivity and an easier job with a more highly trained workforce.

3   If you interview someone from a large organisation you are likely to find that training and development is tied in very clearly with the strategic plan and objectives of the organisation and there are likely to be clear objectives set for the training and development department which clearly contribute to the overall objectives of the organisation. This is not the case in all organisations and some may still operate without making these links.

4   Answers should include comments on the cost involved in designing and running an induction programme, but should generally identify the benefits of easing a new employee into the workforce and how this is likely to result in a speedier route to full productivity, less labour turnover and fewer bad work habits being acquired. There should then be an outline of a suitable induction programme spread over some time.

5   Answers should define each concept and list the pros and cons of each: e.g. learning-by-doing in a realistic environment versus cost of errors and distractions. You should explain which technique you feel is the more successful overall.

### Answers to self-check questions

**1** No. **2** Yes. **3** No. **4** No. **5** No. **6** Yes. **7** No. **8** Yes. **9** No. **10** No.

## Chapter 9  Performance appraisal and performance management

### Answers to review questions

1   The main motivation theories that contribute to the philosophy of performance management are goal theory, reinforcement theory and expectancy theory. If you are not clear about these refer to an Organisational Behaviour textbook for more detail.

2   Discussion of the main elements that are likely to cause appraisal to be done badly: poor planning and communication; poor attitudes; conflict of objectives (e.g. reward or development); lack of managerial ability; lack of training of appraiser and appraisee. These can cause bad feeling and therefore the appraisal will not achieve the benefits that it should.

Contrast this with a discussion of the main elements likely to result in appraisal being done well and which subsequently results in an improvement in motivation and performance. Explain the uses of appraisal for development for the individual and how this could literally transform someone's life. Explain also the huge benefits that can be gained, for the organisation by the introduction of appraisal, e.g. by setting goals that tie in with the organisation's strategic objectives or by agreeing training provision that meets the needs of both the individual and the organisation. Feedback from the employees on goals is also important. Also explain how the introduction of appraisal can result in improved communication. You could also make the link between feedback and its role in motivational models. The fact that appraisal also focuses on the future and development towards it is also very important to both the individual and the organisation and ties in with the idea of strategic planning.

3   Outline how performance appraisal motivates employees and improves relations: provides better understanding on and agreement on goals; gives opportunities for praise/positive feedback; encourages agreement on training needs/use of appraisal for staff development; and results in improved communication. Performance appraisal should therefore help individuals and their team to contribute to the organisation's goals.
    You will achieve an even better answer by linking these factors with concepts from motivation theories (growth, achievement etc.)

Reasons for failure:
Lack of managerial skill and training. Explore typical managerial failures such as inability to give critical feedback. This could be in relation to lack of planning and preparation, poor interpersonal skills such as interview skills, poor communications skills, inability to build and develop teams and give feedback to individuals or team etc.. Also indicate that processes can be counterproductive, and comment on the need for managerial training and for commitment to the system.
    Address the use of appraisal systems for conflicting purposes: development and pay decisions may conflict and comment on the lack of employee involvement in the appraisal system.

4   Describe how performance appraisal systems are designed to provide feedback on past performance and how performance is measured in order to be able to do this; systems need to focus on future goals as well, and are used to identify training needs so that people can reach these goals; positive feedback is also given, and appraisal systems can be linked with pay awards (though this is problematic). Some comment on the link between goal setting and feedback and motivation should be made.

Link your answer to separate parts of the quote with a description of the performance appraisal system: systematic approach; formal mechanisms at stated intervals; use of evaluation and interviewer or evaluates performance, sets goals for the future and agrees how they will be met; opportunity to give positive feedback.
    The main benefits of performance appraisal are that people know where they stand and have opportunities to develop and be rewarded. There should

also be a sense of feeling valued since organisations provide this opportunity and invest time in them. There should therefore be a direct impact on their performance through goal setting. (This is also a motivational technique).

5   You should identify and describe three different approaches to performance appraisal e.g. individual appraisal done by supervisor/manager, peer appraisal or 360° appraisal.

The general benefits relate to improved performance, motivation, communication and relationships. The actual nature of these benefits will need to be discussed in relation to the particular approach used.

Other general benefits include the opportunity to focus on future developments and to achieve organisational goals.

You might also mention the pitfalls, such as problems if there is lack of clarity in the purpose of the appraisal, e.g. reward or development. You may also mention skills needed in giving feedback and discuss in relation to approaches used, e.g. in peer appraisal, would everyone have the required level of skills and not have personal vendettas to settle.

There is also, regardless of the approach chosen, a need to encourage ownership and participation.

### Answers to self-check questions

**1** (A) Judge, (B) Reward, (C) MBO (Management by Objectives), (D) Colleagues, (E) Subordinates, (F) Tell and sell, (G) Joint Problem Solving. **2** (*b*), **3** (*c*), **4** (*a*), **5** (*b*), **6** (*a*).

## Chapter 10  Payment systems

### Answers to review questions

1, 2 and 3 provide you with the opportunity to practice skills and seek relevant, up-to-date information for yourself and as such it is impossible to provide guideline answers here. The 'Pay and benefits bulletin', contained in the *IRS Employment Review*, is published twice a month and is an extremely useful source of articles and up-to-date information about pay and benefits in various sectors and organisations. This may be of help in getting the latest information on the Minimum Wage or rates paid to people on National Traineeships or New Deal. Publications such as *People Management or Personnel Today* may also prove useful, as should quality newspapers.

4   Your answer should define job evaluation as a method of deciding on the value of a job and address the need for a methodical approach. The points-rating method and its main benefits should then be outlined. Benefits of the points-rating approach to job evaluation include the fact that all jobs are rated using the same method and that these must be perceived to be fair. It is comparatively simple to use and understand and is analytical in nature.

428 HUMAN RESOURCE MANAGEMENT

The second part of the your answer should examine perceptions of fairness. Involvement of representatives of the workforce in the design and implementation of job evaluation is likely to improve employees perceptions of whether or not the system is fair. The points-rating method is an analytical approach to job evaluation and so does break each job into parts rather than analysing the whole job. This is generally regarded as being more objective and hence fairer than non-analytical schemes. It is also more likely that this system would be able to be justified in a tribunal if an equal pay/value claim was brought against the organisation. In order to be fair the Code of Practice on Equal Pay should also be followed.

5   Your answer will describe issues such as internal and external relativities and differentials. You will also include and take account of the issues raised by legislation such as the Equal Pay Act 1970 and the Equal Pay (Amendment) Regulations 1983. Systems of job evaluation which try to ensure that fair systems of pay are in place need to be discussed. Those based on analytical methods of job evaluation are likely to result in fairer systems and it will be easier to prove the fairness if necessary. Involvement of representatives of the workforce in the design and implementation of job evaluation is likely to improve employees perceptions of whether or not the system is fair.

Better answers will comment also on issues such as performance related pay and how this may affect perceptions of fairness. They should also refer to the Code of Practice on Equal Pay, published by the Equal Opportunities Commission (1997). There may be issues raised by the Consultation document Fairness at Work also, as this proposes to extend the same rights to everyone in the workplace, regardless of whether or not they are employed under a contract of employment.

6   Your answer should be in report form as if you are a consultant employed to advise this organisation. You need to describe various forms of both the analytical and non-analytical forms of job evaluation and outline the advantages and disadvantages of each. You should then decide on a scheme that you feel is most suitable for this organisation and make recommendations about its use. You are more likely to recommend an analytical form of job evaluation such as the points rating system. This would have benefits of being easy to justify but may be time consuming to introduce. However, since we are making recommendations for a fairly small organisation, cost is also likely be an issue here and this form of analytical job evaluation will probably be cheaper to install than any designed or provided by a firm of consultants. Better answers would also refer to the need for fairness in whatever scheme is introduced and the need to involve members of the workforce in decisions about which scheme should be chosen. Reference should also be made to the need to take into account legislation and also the guidance provided in the EOC Code of Practice on Equal Pay (1997).

## Answers to self-check questions

(a) No. (b) No. (c) No. (d) Yes. (e) Yes. (f) No. (g) No. (h) No. (i) Yes. (j) No.

## Chapter 11  Counselling and employee welfare

### Answers to self-check questions

**1** (*d*). **2** (*d*). **3** (*b*). **4** (*a*). **5** (*d*). **6** (*c*). **7** (*c*). **8** (*d*). **9** (*a*). **10** False.

## Chapter 12  Health and safety

### Answers to review questions

It is once again impossible to give ideal answers to the review questions here as your answers will depend on who you talk to or the organisation which you analyse.

### Answers to self-check questions

**1** (*d*). **2** (*d*). **3** (*c*). **4** (*b*). **5** (*d*). **6** (*d*).

## Chapter 13  Partnership and employee involvement

### Answers to review questions

1 ➤ Outline the concepts of unitarism and pluralism.
  ➤ Outline the concepts of participation and involvement; state how they differ from each other; identify each concept correctly as a unitary or pluralist idea.

2 ➤ Define employee involvement and give examples of individual techniques such as quality circles.
  ➤ Define commitment as an attitude; explain how this attitude might motivate towards more productive behaviour.
  ➤ Link the involvement initiatives you have described with motivation concepts; e.g. quality circles provide employees with feelings of responsibility and achievement because they see they can contribute their ideas.

3 ➤ You will have to read some of the References in order to gather more information for this question.

4 ➤ You should have identified elements such as job security, and information for employees and consultation with them to ensure an adequate channel for employee voice. Partnership recognises that employees are stakeholders in an organisation and have an interest in its success.
    The aim of partnership is to improve productivity and competitiveness by fully engaging the capabilities of employees.

### Answers to self-check questions

**1** (*c*). **2** (*a*) involvement, (*b*) participation. **3** False. **4** At least 1000 employees within the member states and at least 150 employees in each of any two member states. **5** (*b*) and (*d*). **6** (*b*). **7** False. **8** Employee Share Ownership Plan. **9** Team briefing; employer and employee publications; company videos; electronic news systems. **10** (*d*).

## Chapter 14 Discipline and grievance
••••••••••••••••••••••••••••••••••••••••••••••

### *Answers to review questions*

It is impossible to give model answers for questions 1–3 as these require you to conduct your own research, so you may all have slightly different findings.

4 You should give a straightforward description of a disciplinary procedure, based on ACAS guidelines, ensuring that you include all the main sections and emphasise the need for a full investigation prior to any disciplinary interview. It is also important to identify clearly the roles of those involved in the disciplinary process so that line managers and HR managers are sure of the extent of their authority. There should also be informal attempts to resolve the difficulties before the formal disciplinary process is started. Clear rules should form part of the procedure with an indication of what action is likely to result depending on the severity of the infringement.

Whatever action is taken should be swift, fair and consistent, but there must always be time for a full investigation. You should also emphasise the fact that the action decided should aim to bring about an improvement in behaviour and that the employee is clear about the acceptable level of behaviour expected of them. You should also ensure that there is a right of appeal and that warning letters are removed from the person's file when the warning has elapsed.

5 Your answer should be in the form of a report addressed to the general manager. When the organisation only employed 18 staff there was no legal requirement for them to have a grievance procedure, although it would still have been good practice to have had one. Now since there are 100 employees there is a legal requirement to produce a grievance procedure (The Employment Rights Act 1996).

You should explain not only the importance of the legal situation to the general manager, but also make clear that grievance procedures provide a useful way for employees to express their grievances, rather than becoming dissatisfied and expressing the grievance by poor quality work or by leaving the organisation altogether.

A model grievance procedure should be described in order to show what the grievance procedure should contain. This should be modelled on the ACAS Self-help Guide for Producing Discipline and Grievance Procedures (1997). Key features should include; an informal stage before the formal procedure is reached; grievances should be settled as near to the source of grievance as possible at the lowest level; a number of stages involving different people; time limits for responding at each stage and a right of appeal at each stage. There should also be a right to be accompanied by a friend or trade union official and for final appeals to be made to a specially constituted body or to ACAS.

### *Answers to self-check questions*

**1** (*c*). **2** (*d*). **3** (*b*). **4** (*a*). **5** (*d*). **6** (*c*). **7** (*e*). **8** (*d*). **9** (*e*). **10** (*e*).

## Chapter 15  Dismissal, redundancy and outplacement

### Answers to review questions

1    Remember that offences that occur outside of work are not automatic reasons to dismiss an employee. ACAS advise that what is important is the nature of the offence and whether it destroys the employer's confidence in that employee. According to *The Guardian* a CBI source described Mr Blair's comments as a legal minefield. Employers' organisations, civil servants and lawyers cautioned against the difficulties of sacking a worker for a conviction overseas, saying an employer would be open to legal challenge. The onus would be on proving that the company's reputation was being damaged.' Even dismissing someone because they are not able to do their job because they are in prison has been found by many organisations to not necessarily be a good enough reason for dismissal.

2    The Government hope that this will bring about increased flexibility in the work place and encourage employees to move jobs because they will no longer fear losing their protection rights concerning unfair dismissal.

They also hope that a shorter qualification period will encourage more employers to operate good employment practices and monitor the effectiveness of their employees more carefully than they have done in the past. It is also likely that the number of claims for unfair dismissal will increase, at least initially, as a result of this change.

3    You should outline the main grounds for dismissal as described in the Employment Rights Act 1996: incompetence, misconduct, redundancy, statutory bar, some other substantial reason. Better answers are likely to give examples of these types of potentially fair reasons for dismissal.

You should also explain that the process followed for dismissals is as important as the reason for the dismissal, and describe the need for a full investigation and hearing and the need to consider extenuating circumstances. Better answers are also likely to mention that some forms of dismissal are considered to be automatically unfair and for these there is only a one-stage process undertaken by the employment tribunals. You should outline some of the automatically unfair reasons for dismissal and indicate why these are designated as such.

You should express some considered opinion about the extent to which you feel that employers should try to avoid dismissals of employees. This is likely to include comment about managers taking early action to avoid the development of problems, the use of counselling skills by managers, the use of HRM planning to help avoid the need for redundancies; the training and development of employees if skills needs change; a proper recruitment and selection processes to help minimise numbers of dismissals. Following good HRM policies and procedures should help to minimise costs involved. Sometimes, however, it is still necessary to dismiss and then it must be for a fair reason and must be handled reasonably in accordance with the ACAS Disciplinary Code of Practice.

### Answers to self-check questions

**1** (*c*). **2** (*e*). **3** (*b*). **4** (*c*). **5** (*a*)

# Subject index

innovation 26–7
objectives 225, 246–8
stress 285–7

targeted recruitment 70
teleworking 159–60
termination of employment 160–2
  exit interviews 161–2
  notice 149
  retirement 162
tests of interest and motivation 110
theorist learning style 174, 176–8
Trade Union and Employment Rights
  Act 1993 148
Trade Union and Labour Relations
  (Consolidation) Act 1992 397, 404
training and development
  BS5750/ISO9000 218, 247
  definition 197–9
  employee development 197
  employment 209
  national targets for education and
    training 213–14
  new employees 201–5
  particular groups 200–5
  people, involved in 199
  recent developments 209–20
  strategic human resource
    development 199, 210, 212
  techniques 186–90, 193
training cycle
  assessing training needs 184–5,
    200–1, 206, 228
  carrying out 184, 191, 207
  designing 190–1
  evaluating 184, 191–2
  planning 184–91, 206
training organisations
  Employment National Training
    Organisation 211
  Industrial Training Boards (ITBs) 209
  industry lead bodies 202
  Investors in People 217–18
  learning organisation 217
  Management Charter Initiative
    (MCI) 216–17
  National Council for Vocational
    Qualifications (NCVQ) 209
  National Training Organisations
    (NTOs) 211–12
  Training and Enterprise Councils
    (TECs) 209, 217

training, types of
  continuing professional
    development 219–20
  external 185–6
  induction 202–5
  internal 185–6
  job instruction 206–9
  learning logs 219
  management 215–17
  mentor 218
  modern apprenticeships 214
  national traineeships 214–15
  national vocational qualifications
    (NVQs) 209–15
  New Deal 215
  youth training 209
transsexuals 58
Treaty of Amsterdam 1997 147, 152
Treaty on European Union 1992 (the
  Maastricht Treaty) 147

unitarism 10, 338–9, 343–4

validity of selection interviews 83, 92,
  106–7
variation of the terms of an
  employment contract 146

whole job ranking (job evaluation)
  264–6
work sample tests 112–15
work simulation 116
working conditions 155–60
  annual hours contracts 157
  fixed-term contracts 158–9
  flexible working 156–60
  job share 157–8
  part-time employment 158
  teleworking 159–60
working time 153–4
  annual leave 153–4
  derogations from the directive 154
  rest breaks 153
  working hours 153
Workplace (Health and Welfare)
  Regulations (1992) 321
works councils see European Works
  Councils
written statement of particulars of
  employment 148–9
written statement of reasons for
  dismissal 152

# Authors index